HISTORY AT WAR

Noble Frankland served in the RAF from 1941 to 1945, becoming a navigator in Bomber Command, and was awarded the DFC in 1944. He took the degrees of MA and DPhil from Trinity College, Oxford, in 1948 and 1951. After four years in the Air Historical Branch of the Air Ministry (1948–51), he became Official Military Historian to the Cabinet Office (1951–8) and co-author with Sir Charles Webster of the official history of the strategic air offensive, which was published in four volumes in 1961. He was Director of the Imperial War Museum from 1960 to 1982, and historical advisor to the Thames Television series, *The World at War*, from 1971 to 1974. He was created a CBE in 1977 and CB in 1982. His principal publications in addition to the official history (*The Strategic Air Offensive against Germany*), are *Nicholas II: Crown of Tragedy* (1960), *The Bombing Offensive against Germany: Outlines and Perspectives* (1965), *Bomber Offensive: the Devastation of Europe* (1970), *Prince Henry, Duke of Gloucester* (1980) and *Witness of a Century: the Life and Times of Prince Arthur, Duke of Connaught* (1993). He was general editor of *The Encyclopedia of 20th Century Warfare* (1989) and joint editor of *The Politics and Strategy of the Second World War* (8 vols, 1974–8).

D1471920

History at War

THE CAMPAIGNS OF AN HISTORIAN

by

NOBLE FRANKLAND

dlm

First published in 1998
by Giles de la Mare Publishers Limited
3 Queen Square, London WC1N 3AU

Typeset by Tom Knott
Printed in Great Britain by
Hillman Printers (Frome) Limited
All rights reserved

A CIP record of this book is available
from the British Library

ISBN 1–900357–10–0

Contents

List of Illustrations		vi
Illustration Acknowledgements		vi
Preface		vii
Introduction		1
1.	History in Sight	9
2.	Breaking into History	35
3.	History in Academe	60
4.	History in Whitehall	80
5.	History in the News	114
6.	History from the News	136
7.	History in the Gallery	160
8.	History on the Screen	179
9.	History on the Site	196
10.	History through Biography	210
	Conclusions and Comparisons	223
	Bibliography	231
	Source References	233
	Index	244

List of Illustrations

between pages 88 and 89

1. The author's Lancaster bomber crew, 1944.
2. Sir Charles Webster and the author's son, circa 1954.
3. Marshal of the Royal Air Force Sir Arthur Harris.
4. Marshal of the Royal Air Force Lord Portal, Admiral Sir Deric Holland-Martin and the author, 1968.
5. Marshal of the Royal Air Force Lord Tedder and Admiral of the Fleet Sir Algernon Willis, 1962.
6. The Prime Minister, Harold Macmillan, and the author, 1963.
7. The Minister for the Arts, Lord Eccles, Arnold Toynbee and the author, circa 1969.
8. The *War Exhibition* at the Imperial War Museum, 1980.
9. The Queen arriving at the preview of *The Life and Times of Lord Mountbatten* at the Imperial War Museum, 1968.
10. The reception after the preview of *The Life and Times of Lord Mountbatten.*
11. HMS *Belfast* passing through Tower Bridge, 15th October 1971.
12. Rear-Admiral Higham, the Minister for the Arts, Lord Donaldson, Sir Peter Masefield and the author in the engine room of HMS *Belfast*, 1978.
13. The author with HMS *Belfast* in dry dock at Tilbury, 1982.
14. The Imperial War Museum at Duxford Airfield.
15. Prince Henry Duke of Gloucester at the Imperial War Museum, 1966.
16. Prince Arthur Duke of Connaught from the portrait by de László

ILLUSTRATION ACKNOWLEDGEMENTS

Nos.3, 4, 5, 6, 8, 9, 10, 11, 12, 13, 14 and 15 are reproduced by permission of the Trustees of the Imperial War Museum. Nos.1, 2 and 7 are reproduced from photographs in the author's possession. No.16 is reproduced from the portrait of Prince Arthur by de László by permission of the Royal Society for the encouragement of Arts, Manufactures and Commerce.

Preface

I am grateful to my publisher for suggesting that this book about my experience of history and as an historian should be entitled *History at War*. It strikes me as particularly apposite for several reasons. First, a large proportion of my historical work has been devoted to the study of warfare or the tensions of international relations. In this respect, I am, of course, by no means singular, but I can claim that most of my work has been directed to questions which other historians had scarcely explored and which they have subsequently left largely untouched. Second, my activity as an historian has been accompanied by almost unending struggle. Sir Charles Webster and I had to fight a severe and prolonged campaign to secure the publication of our history of the strategic air offensive on our own terms as opposed to those of officialdom. Third, as Director of the Imperial War Museum, I was again confronted with a battle against officialdom, but this time the issues were different. In the struggle for the official history, the battle was to defeat a concerted attempt to emasculate our history so that it would fit the convenience of the mandarins in the 1950s and early 1960s. In the case of the Imperial War Museum, the mandarins were not trying to change what I wanted to do; they simply wanted to stop me doing it.

So war in the title of this book applies in different senses to two aspects of my work as an historian. It also applies directly to that part of my account which deals with my own experience as a witness of the making of history, for this was as a Bomber Command navigator in the Second World War. The circumstances of my life as an historian have indeed often been severe. If, however, some of my judgements of the people I have encountered seem harsh, others may appear too generous. I can only say that I have written as I have found.

I have to thank P. J. V. Elliott, Keeper of Research and Information Services in the Royal Air Force Museum, for giving me access to Sir Arthur Harris's papers at a time when they were not open for general inspection. Robert Crawford, the Director-General of the Imperial War Museum, kindly gave me access to the central files of the Museum, which were my working papers during the period of my own directorship from 1960 to 1982. Mrs Gill Smith, the Projects Officer on the Directing Staff of the Museum, was particularly helpful in tracing the material which was relevant to my themes. I must also thank Roderick Suddaby, the Keeper of the Department of Documents in the Museum, for his help and advice, especially with regard to some naval aspects of my work. Once again, I express my gratitude to the staff of the Oxford Public Library, whose efficiency, courtesy and patience are a model to admire. I am glad to mention that I have found the Public Record Office a much more agreeable place in which to work than it was a few years ago. I am grateful to my former tutor, Professor R.B. Wernham, for relating to me an episode in the saga of the selection of the official historians of the strategic air offensive of which no contemporary documentary record seems to have been made.

The deepest debts of gratitude which I owe are, however, due to my first wife, Diana, who died in 1981, and to my present wife Sarah. These debts are far more significant than the conventional ones which acknowledge merely patience, tolerance and so on: they are positive and crucial debts. Diana's linguistic skills enabled me, for example, to deal confidently with such material as the Speer archives when writing my thesis and also the official history. Though herself a student of modern languages, her intense interest in history and her skill in interpretation were of incalculable value to my work. Sarah, a student of history with important professional experience as a research assistant, has, in all my work since 1982, been a tower of intellectual strength and also, whenever documents seemed to have gone to ground in the many archives in which we have worked together, a regular ferret. In addition, she has provided all the systems needed to enable me to make constructive use of a computer. I must also thank her for reading and commenting on the whole of this book while it was in draft.

Finally, returning to my publisher, I am most grateful to him for his meticulous and patient editing of the typescript of this work. I alone am responsible for any surviving errors.

Noble Frankland,
Thames House,
Eynsham,
Oxford.
9th January 1998.

Introduction

My experience of history and as an historian has been more varied than I think is usual. The chances of life offered me glimpses of history in the making and, later, opportunities of discussing it with people who had been major protagonists in those events and related ones. In the conveying of history, I have had experience as an official military historian, as an ordinary historian and as a royal biographer. As Director of the Imperial War Museum, and arising from that position, I have been deeply involved in the presentation of history through exhibitions, which I have called 'history in the gallery'; with the production of it in television documentaries, which I have called 'history on the screen'; and with the preservation and organization of historic sites, or objects large enough to be regarded as sites, which I have called 'history on the site'.

These activities, which have occupied the bulk of my working life, have left a series of strong impressions on my mind and it is these impressions which have provoked me to write this book. I have written it not in the form of reminiscences, which, as a sole source, I distrust, but as history. In other words, I have assembled the available primary evidence and have used my recollections only where there is nothing better on offer. My object has been to re-discover what happened and to see what may be learned from it. In doing this, I have discovered many things, which at the time were concealed from me, and I have learned much which otherwise would have eluded me.

Many historians had written about the nature and use of history before I came to those aspects of the subject. Among the most interesting of them are R.G. Collingwood, G.R. Elton, Geoffrey Barraclough, E.H. Carr, Alan Bullock and John Vincent. But these historians have written theoretically or philosophically and they have confined themselves almost exclusively to the question of history written on the page. My construction is based upon practice. It is not confined to history on the page, and my conclusions are based simply on my own experience. I do not claim that my resulting beliefs are a lodestar; I assert only that they are the product of a hard and long school of varied and, for the most part, uncloistered experience.[1]

I have used the terms 'hard' and 'uncloistered' advisedly. I was fortunate to escape with my life from the glimpses of history being made that the Second World War afforded me, and I was also fortunate to emerge from writing my part of the official history of the war with a career ahead of me. In that career, I had to struggle for years with the powers that be to achieve a base from which I could seek worthwhile historical results. These trials have not been the lot of every historian; to me they have been crucial in forming and developing my view of history.

In particular, opposition to my ideas, which at times was a great threat to their realization, was a powerful stimulant. The most severe expression of this opposition came from the official mind in Whitehall, and I now think that it was fortunate for my morale and equanimity that I did not, at the time, know the full extent of it. From an examination of the Cabinet and Air files, recently made available in the Public Record Office, I now do. In later chapters, I will describe this saga in considerable detail, not only because it was so important in my own experience, but also because it sheds light on what powerful civil servants and service officers at the top of their professions made of history, and how they wanted to influence the writing of it. Such light is unlikely to be shed again. I find it hard to believe that much of what was said and written by these mandarins would have been said and written if there had been the knowledge that it would be open to public inspection during the lifetimes of at least some of the actors in the drama. The documents in question were released under the thirty-years rule between 1988 and 1996. When they were created there was a fifty-years rule. Had that continued to prevail, I would not have been able to see them until between 2008 and 2016, by which time I would have been between eighty-six and ninety-four years old.

Direct and powerful opposition of this kind, which was a real threat to my work as an official historian, is to be distinguished from the impediment of misunderstanding, which I think is the lot of all historians. At its most telling, this proceeds from people of ability and achievement who have been educated in unhistorical modes of thought. It is particularly evident in scientists and classicists, and I have found it very useful. The kind of argument it produces forces one to define one's terms and one's methods; occasionally one can convert the heathen. I will therefore cite a few examples of such things.

From 1948 until his death eleven years later, I had an extended dialogue with Sir Henry Tizard, the architect of the radar chain which saved the country in the Battle of Britain. He had an extraordinary range of talent and experience which carried him from an Oxford fellowship before the First World War to the office of Chief Scientific Advisor to the Government immediately after the Second. One of the reasons why he comprehended –

which the Germans did not – that the radar chain must have expertise on the ground and simplicity in the cockpit of the fighter, was that he himself, in the First World War, had been an experimental pilot. Though dedicated to science, he was also widely cultivated outside that subject, especially in the field of English literature. History, however, he regarded as largely nonsense. At our first meeting, he expressed his surprise that I should be wasting my time in the pursuit of it. None of the real truth got into the documents, he said. Scientific research would reveal the truth; historical research could not. This, as I began to convince Sir Henry Tizard, was a misconception, but as a judgement handed down by a great man to a young historian it was both stimulating and challenging.

Sir Burke (later Lord) Trend, who was Secretary of the Cabinet from 1963 to 1973, confronted me with a different kind of misconception which I failed to cure. Had I then known how he thought history should be distorted to suit the conventions of the official mind, I probably would not have tried. He believed that history offered exact solutions to such problems as the right or the wrong course of action, and that the sources of history could be divided into self-contained compartments. He asked me to provide him with a formula which would enable his staff to separate the strategic records of the Second World War from the operational, so that the former could be deposited in one institution and the latter in another. His idea was that strategy governed operations and that the two could therefore be separated as cause and effect. In theory, this might appear to be the case, but in practice of course it is not. The interaction of strategy and operations was not a one-way process. More often than not, indeed, strategy was the product of operational capacity, the art of the possible. In war, as Moltke observed, one must do what one can and not what one ought. Lord Trend was annoyed with me for raising difficulties of that sort. He was an excellent classical scholar and, as such, expected to find order and symmetry in history. As I was later to learn, he also thought that it should be tailored to suit the convenience and the politics of the time in which it was written.

A similar kind of misconception vitiated the basic plan for the official histories of the Second World War: a division was drawn between grand strategy and campaigns. This, Sir Charles Webster was later to remark, would cause the proposed five volumes of grand strategy to resemble a five-tier wedding cake without the inside. The general editor of the official military histories, Sir James Butler, ought to have known better. Though widely cultivated, he was more an historian than a classicist and he could never have asked 'classical' questions such as 'was Palmerstons's foreign policy beneficial or malignant?'; 'Was the Reform Bill a good or a bad thing?'; or 'Was the area-bombing offensive of the Second World War a success or a failure?'. The defect in his plan for the official military histories was surprising.[2]

In the 1950s I tutored a series of Royal Air Force officers, Flight Lieutenants and Squadron Leaders who were preparing to take the entrance examination for the Staff College. Virtually without exception they were convinced that the study of air history would provide them with solutions to Staff College exercises and that, in particular, by mastering a list of the principles of war they would become sound strategists. They did not think well of my insistence that, while history might offer guidance, it would not issue orders. The difficulty with these excellent, hard-working and dedicated men was that doctrine and not history was the goal of their endeavours.

In this context, doctrine is the enemy of history. After reading my thesis on the planning of the bomber offensive and its contribution to German defeat, Sir Ralph Cochrane, who was at the time Vice-Chief of the Air Staff, observed to me that I had failed to take proper account of fundamental Air Staff doctrines, such as, for example, that sustained bombing will drive the enemy onto the defensive and that Bomber Command had achieved this through its night offensive in the Second World War. This was part of the Trenchard doctrine, but it was not part of my thesis since the key to the collapse of German offensive air power in the west was its removal to the east, where the greater part of the German war effort was deployed after the invasion of Russia in 1941. Sir Ralph Cochrane, however, concluded our first conversation with an expression of faith: with a little instruction, he thought, I could yet be made into a sound historian. His faith, no doubt, was founded upon the 'instruction' the Air Staff had given to the air historians of the First World War, Sir Walter Raleigh and H.A Jones.[3]

The fact that Raleigh and Jones accepted, or at least reflected, Air Staff doctrines of the 1920s and early 1930s and made them the core of their study of the war in the air between 1914 and 1918 was not only in principle objectionable, but also in practice very damaging. The Air Staff's claims of what the Royal Air Force would achieve in the next war seemed to be given a seal of authenticity by the official history of what the Royal Flying Corps, the Royal Naval Air Service and the early Royal Air Force had seemingly achieved in the First. Though this approach did not captivate the Naval and Army Staffs, it certainly misled the Air Staff in the last three years of peace when serious planning for war with Germany was under way. Some of the strongest criticism of my work on the official history of the strategic air offensive in the Second World War came from Air Marshals, and their outrage was largely provoked by the failure of Webster and Frankland to follow in the steps of Raleigh and Jones.

Another form of misconception is often found in the minds of great men who have made significant contributions to the content of history, though not much perhaps to its understanding. Their misconception is that, having performed such great deeds, they alone can understand them. I have always had a sympathy with this attitude, for I have understood how irritating it is for great men to encounter lesser ones whose only qualification is that they are historians, and who presume to delve into their achievements, and place interpretations upon them that seldom accord with the views of the great man. It is an understandable point of view, but it is another historical misconception. People who achieve great things, especially perhaps in war, are usually single-minded, opinionated, ambitious, domineering and – as to the full circumstances of their achievements – blinkered. The three most memorable exponents of this attitude who crossed my path were Field-Marshal Montgomery, Lord Mountbatten and Sir Arthur Harris. I got to know Montgomery and Mountbatten quite well. Harris I never met, but I experienced his electric personality as an operational navigator in a Bomber Command squadron during the war, and after it I encountered, albeit at second hand, his thunderous disapproval of what I had written in the official history of the strategic air offensive.

Montgomery, Mountbatten and Harris all achieved things which substantially changed the course of history and, though they had entirely different backgrounds and characters, they were united in their zeal to ensure that the record placed upon their deeds the same estimate as they themselves thought was their due. They were also anxious that the darker aspects of their careers should be explained in the right senses. They all, indeed, had such darker aspects, as also do ordinary mortals. Montgomery had Arnhem, Mountbatten Dieppe and Harris Nuremberg. In their later years, I had much experience of their attitudes and aspirations and it is clear to me that they set their authorized biographers formidably difficult problems.

So far, I have summarized some historical misconceptions as revealed by the attitudes of individuals. In addition to these, or perhaps deriving from them, there are also group and national misconceptions, which, because they represent more than personal views and sometimes amount to public opinion, are far more powerful in democratic terms than the thoughts of mere individuals. Ex-service organizations have often struck me as being generators of singular examples of group misconception. At the Alamein Reunion, for example, when Montgomery was on the platform in the Albert Hall, there would not have been many votes for the view that the exploitation of the victory in the desert had possibly been too slow. In the Bomber Command Association, the view that the strategic air offensive achieved rather less than had been hoped, does not evoke much approbation. In such groups, criticism, or even analysis, tends to be regarded as disloyal and subversive. There is even the view, often very strongly held, that any criticism of the conduct of a campaign is disrespectful to the memory of those who died in it. No one writes with first-hand experience of what the dead feel, but from my own experience I can assert that I did not put my life on the line in Bomber

Command to sustain a myth. Though perhaps, if I had not been an aspirant historian, I might have done.

National misconceptions, which seem to arise from groups and then grow into stronger views with greater longevity, are truly formidable opponents to historical understanding. A striking example of such a phenomenon is Thornycroft's statue of Oliver Cromwell standing outside the Houses of Parliament in Westminster. Cromwell, who had told Parliament that the Lord had done with them and ordered the removal of the mace, which he called a bauble, was somehow seen by the Victorians as the upholder of parliamentary liberties. This, of course, did not reflect anything of the history of the Cromwellian period; it reflected a wave of liberal idealism in Victorian England that gave a rose-tinted view of the general who led the Parliamentary armies to victory over the royalists and then established a military dictatorship.

Such then are some of the misconceptions of history which have especially impressed me and have helped to form my own view of the realities and values of the subject. Among the many ways of perceiving the evolution of history, there are three that interest me more than others. The first is witnessing, or better still taking part in, its making. My experience of this has been small in the sense that I played a very small part in a great event, the Bomber Command campaign of the Second World War. Nevertheless, it has been sufficient to indicate to me the value of being a witness and also to warn me of its dangers. What the eye sees and what the heart feels by no means reflect what really happened, and yet the actual experience of history nourishes the mind and opens it more fully to the appreciation of other avenues of discovery.

The second way is to know history-makers and to be able to question them. In addition to Tizard, Montgomery and Mountbatten, to whom I have already referred, I have had significant discussions either orally or on paper, or in both ways, with many others who played major roles in the making of history. Despite the snares of this avenue, to which I have also already alluded, it does afford opportunities that are often unique. For example, I would never have understood how it came about that General Carl Spaatz virtually disregarded Eisenhower's bombing directive in the run-up to the invasion of Normandy in 1944, had I not known Spaatz and been able to examine the documentary evidence in the modified light of what he told me. Nor was this an unimportant thing to understand because Spaatz's apparently independent actions changed the balance of power in the air and led to allied air supremacy in a form which was more useful to Eisenhower than anything he had thought of.

The third way is to discover and study the primary deposits of history, which include archaeological and other remains, such as Egyptian tombs,

Roman villas and, more generally, the contents of museums; primary documentary, photographic and sound archives; and naturally the secondary
sources which are on offer in the works of other historians. My experience
of this way has been largely concerned with recent history, a good part of
which has been made in my own life-time, and I have preferred to work on
a scale which makes it possible to master rather than to sample the primary
sources concerned. Thus, I have written the greater part of the official history
of the strategic air offensive in the Second World War, and the biographies
of two princes of the nineteenth and twentieth centuries, for all of which I
had unrestricted access to the primary sources. As Director of the Imperial
War Museum for twenty-two years, I devoted much thought to the art of
demonstrating history through the study and display of artefacts ranging in
scale from an entire historic airfield, the former RAF station at Duxford in
Cambridgeshire, and an entire warship, HMS *Belfast*, to individual hand-
grenades, bullets and even postage stamps.

I have never been much interested in historical fashions such as those
which, for example, decree that the history of art or furniture is 'in' and that
the study of war is 'out', and that, therefore, the Victoria and Albert Museum
has a higher value than the Imperial War Museum. Such notions of importance come and go as do ideas of political correctness. In the long run they
are of little real importance. The scale on which history is studied does, however, raise important and difficult questions. Indeed, it raises what I conceive
to be the greatest problem of historiography.

Arnold Toynbee's *The Study of History*, though in its opening stages hailed
as a masterpiece, was later criticized, sometimes harshly, on the ground that
in its great sweeps of explanation and narrative it contained errors of detail.
The specialists, who worked on narrow and detailed aspects of history and
could never have even imagined the scope of Toynbee's vision, were not sorry
to find what they could demonstrate were mistakes. Much of this criticism
was petty and some of it, no doubt, was fathered by jealousy. Toynbee was
after all the most famous historian of his generation and his name is likely
to be remembered when those of most of his critics have been forgotten.
Nevertheless, there was a flaw in Toynbee's work. His scope was so great
that he could only arrive at his conclusions on the basis of what other more
specialized historians had written. He was the most industrious historian I
ever knew, but had he worked from primary sources he would surely not
have finished a third of one volume among all those he eventually completed.
What was wrong with his work was not that it contained errors, though of
course it did: the fault lay in the fact that his source material was of uneven
quality. His conclusions, therefore, arose from data which were not only of
unequal weight, but had disparate bearings upon the great man's thoughts.
It was as though a detective had relied solely on the reports of chief

constables, without himself having examined the scenes of crimes and cross-questioned the suspects and the witnesses. The chief constables too would have been of very various abilities.

Toynbee's uncle, Paget, had taken the opposite course. He spent virtually the whole of his life in the study of Dante and Horace Walpole. Probably in his day he knew more about them than everyone else put together. But was this not a little too narrow a field to enable us to say that Paget Toynbee's life was well spent?

In the art of history, my predilection is that it should be inspired by curiosity and by the wish to discover what happened, why it happened and what resulted from its having happened. Such work, however, to be authentic, must be based upon the most meticulous and exhaustive assembly and weighing up of primary evidence. This is a taxing business and anyone engaging in it will be familiar with a range of temptations to cut corners, to accept received ideas or even hearsay and to turn away from archival indexes, which sometimes seem hopelessly complicated. To be useful, it must be directed at subjects which can be seen to be either not understood or else misunderstood. Historians who repeat each other give the profession a bad name and they waste the world's timber resources and the time of their readers. To be realistic, the historian must recognize that the past can never be wholly rediscovered. The surviving evidence of what happened yesterday cannot match what actually happened. He not only has the task of interpreting his evidence and displaying it for his readers to judge, but he may also be permitted to inject his own flights of fancy about what lies beyond the evidence, although these too he must display to the reader for what they are.

CHAPTER ONE

History in Sight

I was first in the service of the Crown on 8th July 1941 when I was accepted for aircrew duties in the Royal Air Force. My rank was Aircraftman Second Class, which was the lowest on offer, and my trade was Aircrafthand Under-training Pilot. This, though rather long-winded, was not very grand and it did not even signify what I was eventually to do in the Air Force. I was in fact to become a Bomber Command navigator. Nevertheless, it was a decisive step in my life and in particular it was to provide me with my first experiences of the making of history. Eventually it was to enable me, from my own experience, to measure the gap between the impressions of an eye-witness and the conclusions of an historian with regard to the same events. For I was to fly on operations in the strategic air offensive against Germany and later also to become the official historian of it, as I have said. By the time I joined the Air Force, I had already been taking my first serious steps towards becoming an historian. In March 1941, I had won an open scholarship in history at Trinity College, Oxford, and I had started reading the subject under the tutorship of R.B. Wernham.

The Air Force authorities told me that, until I was required for full-time training, I was to be placed on what was called deferred, as opposed to active, service. They said that I should stay at Oxford, continue to follow the history school there for part of each week and, for the rest of it, start my air training in the University Air Squadron, which I had already joined. Having, therefore, had one term as a full-time undergraduate, I now spent two more as a part-time one and a part-time air cadet. By May 1942, when I was called for active service, I had completed roughly a third of the syllabus for a history degree and the whole of that for the initial training of an aircrew cadet.

At the time I thought of the these two activities as distinct, but I now see them as one moulding experience, for, in however small a way it may have been, I was simultaneously learning to be an historian and beginning to witness the making of history. This may seem an absurd claim since, as R.G. Collingwood rightly said, a student *in statu pupillari* is not an historian and an air cadet at the end of his initial training has witnessed little more than the problem of tackling subjects which may be – and in my case were – unfamiliar and difficult.[1]

Nevertheless, I make the claim. Learning about, for example, Castlereagh and Napoleon at the very time when Hitler was advancing into Russia, even if one had access only to the received views expressed in the textbooks of the day, seemed to me to link the past with the present and the future. Taking the first steps towards flying on operations in the Royal Air Force, at a time when it seemed that this was the sole remaining means by which Britain could make any offensive contribution to the war, invested the undertaking with an historical significance in my mind. Two further considerations enhanced these impressions.

During these days at Oxford I saw much of Arnold Toynbee, who was my father's cousin and who at that point was Director of Foreign Research in the Royal Institute of International Affairs and had his office in Balliol College. In March 1941 he told me that Hitler would attack Russia sooner or later with a view to gaining territory to be used as a bargaining counter in the eventual peace conference. Like Napoleon, Toynbee said, Hitler had superiority on land and had to use it. He said that Germany would attack Greece, but that we and the Greeks would hold them on a front, although not in such a favourable position as the Greeks had secured after repelling the Italian invasion. On another occasion, soon after Hess had landed in Scotland, he explained the incident to me as meaning that the Germans thought that the British government was carried on entirely by means of influence and wire-pulling on the part of the elite. Hess's plan, he said, was to gain the ear of a few influential men who would then easily overthrow what to him seemed to be the narrow Churchill clique. Such *aperçus* gave me the feeling of privileged access to the unrolling drama of history, for Toynbee had not only the prestige of being a famous historian but also the qualification of having been interviewed by Hitler before the war and even flown by the latter's personal pilot to Dachau, where he had been invited to question some of the inmates. He seemed to me to be both a sage and one in-the-know.[2]

The second consideration was that, despite my development as an airman being merely adolescent, I was already gaining a much closer contact with the sharp end of the Royal Air Force than was usually available to ordinary cadets at their Initial Training Wings. My Commanding Officer in the Oxford University Air Squadron was Wing Commander Peter Broad. The rather curious status of undergraduate-cadets gave much more intimate contact with such god-like figures than would otherwise have occurred. Broad, who looked heroic, had flown Hampdens on operations in Bomber Command and had won the DFC. He appeared to be not only a model to emulate but also a personal contact with the fighting war. Another more fleeting impression of the same thing was a young pilot officer who turned up in Hall one night at Trinity. He was H.M. Young, who had rowed for the college before the war and was now flying Hampdens on operations over Germany. He talked about the difficulties that had been encountered as well as the supposed successes. Later he was to achieve great distinction – as well as to lose his life – flying in Gibson's Squadron when the Möhne and Eder dams were breached in May 1943.

At Oxford, then, the study of the industrial revolution, the policy of Sir Robert Peel, the Napoleonic legend, the Eastern Question and so on mingled with learning how to diagnose and clear stoppages on the gas-operated Vickers machine-gun, practising the transmission of radio messages in morse code, grasping the basics of weather forecasting and even, on one occasion, taking the controls of a Tiger Moth and flying it over the Cowley works, which my instructor, Flying Officer Adams, told me were easy to pin-point owing to the camouflage in which they were painted. These halcyon days ended abruptly in May 1942 when I was called for active service. Though almost another two years were to pass before I took part in real war operations, I now embarked upon a course of education which I have subsequently realized was more testing and, therefore, more rewarding than any other I have received before or since. The brink of battle, too, is an interesting place.

The first step consisted in being graded as a pilot or an observer, which was the then way of describing a navigator, or a failure. As everyone wanted to be a pilot, everyone went on a course of about twelve hours flying in Tiger Moths. To be graded as a pilot, one had to make a solo flight within this time. I did not. Indeed, my instructor, Sergeant Kay, was, I think, rather afraid that I would kill him if I was left to land the machine myself, and myself if left to do it alone. It was a crushing disappointment, especially as one of my particular friends, John Pinsent, passed with flying colours in much less than the maximum time. He had not seemed to me to be a very likely candidate. He was a passionate classical scholar and spent the time – even when we were out at flying dispersal in our full flying-kit – reading Virgil and other such works. He later flew a successful tour of operations on Catalinas in Coastal Command and then came back to Oxford and got a first-class degree. But he told me that throughout the war he had only once been fired upon and that was by the friendly guns of Gibraltar. Meanwhile, I suffered the indignity of being graded as an observer. It was, however, one of the greatest strokes of good luck I have ever had, comparable, I have since thought, to another indignity which also proved to be a blessing in disguise. This was the disappointment of getting a second-class degree at Oxford after the war.

The trade of observer dated from the Royal Flying Corps in the First World War. Where there was room for a second man, an observer went along with the pilot. He did gunnery and, if there were any, he dropped the bombs and he looked over the side and tried to relate what he saw to a map. Thus, from the first, he was a rudimentary navigator, and that was what he remained more or less, until a surprisingly long time after the outbreak of the Second World War. When, in the course of 1940, Bomber Command was compelled by the prevailing conditions of air warfare to give up virtually all its plans for daylight bombing and seek the cover of darkness, it became apparent that one of the keys to success was going to be accurate long-range navigation, and that the basis of this would be dead reckoning.

By July 1942, when I arrived at No.1 Elementary Air Navigation School in Eastbourne, the old idea of an observer, though not yet the title, was dead and the new concept of a highly trained navigator had taken its place. The Eastbourne course was intensive and in nine weeks it covered the whole theory of air navigation with the exception of the use of radar, which was too secret to be communicated to cadets at this stage. There was no flying and we spent the greater part of every day at lectures and most of the long evenings working up our notes or reading the textbooks. Intellectually, especially in the case of astro-navigation, it was the stiffest work I have ever encountered and, as a training for the mind, it was, in my experience, second to none. It was curious that I and all the rest of my 'generation' of future navigators were lined up along the sea front in the hotels that had formerly brought Eastbourne its fame and its prosperity. They were now the first buildings the Germans saw when they made the short flight across the Channel to bomb and strafe the town, which they frequently did, though fortunately very ineffectively. They did demolish the Cavendish Hotel and thus kill a number of cadet navigators but they invariably missed the Grand Hotel, in which I was quartered. Another curious thing was that Air Commodore A.C. Critchley, the Air Officer Commanding 54 Group, to which we belonged, had become memorable in Eastbourne by asking what a sextant was.[3]

Among the extra-curricular duties at Eastbourne was taking one's turn on the roofs of the hotels from where one could give warning of approaching enemy aircraft and take pot shots at them with machine-guns. I once had such an opportunity and, for a fraction of a moment, thought I had shot down a FW 190. But as I turned to watch it crash, I saw shells being pumped into it by a Canadian manned Bofors anti-aircraft gun deployed immediately behind the front line of our hotels. It was rather a disappointment.

I was not on this duty on 19th August, but those who were counted more than a thousand of our aircraft heading out over the sea. This, as we later learned, was the air cover for the ill-fated Dieppe Raid. After the war I came personally to know how sensitive a matter it was to its commander, Lord Mountbatten.

Many of the aircraft we all saw on that 19th August were Mustangs, which were easily recognized by their ugly square-cut wing-tips. My memory of seeing these particular aircraft has been differentiated from everything else I saw that day by the subsequent development of this apparently rather poor machine into one of the most important aircraft in the history of military aviation. And, of all the strange birth pangs which tend to beset military aircraft, those of the Mustang seem to me to have been the strangest. When, in a later chapter, I come to describe the evolution of my understanding of the historical nature of the heart of air power, I shall return to the subject of the Mustang.[4]

At the beginning of September, those of our course who had survived the mid-term tests sat the final exams. I passed out second with an average of 82%. As I was by no means a natural at this kind of work, it reflected much credit on the instructors. Two of them were pilots, who had come into navigation instruction I know not how; the other two were observers of the pre-navigation age, one of whom only had flown on operations in Bomber Command. The members of this unlikely team, however, were thoroughly versed in the subjects they taught and all were brilliant teachers; I have never met their betters. I also owed a great debt to a fellow cadet who became a close friend. This was John Morris. He absorbed all the mathematical aspects of the course with consummate ease and had time to spare to drive them into my slower and duller brain. He had a delightful sense of humour. When about to join an operational bomber squadron, he wrote to tell me that the real test of a navigator was night bombing, but no doubt I was developing a theory of day bombing with Tiger Moths. Another side of his character was shown by the fact that when he flew on operations in Stirlings, he carried in his pocket a copy of Richard Hillary's *The Last Enemy*, which, he said, helped him with his job.[5]

The upshot of Eastbourne was that I was now qualified for posting to flying training at an Air Navigation School. Some of these were located in Canada, some in Scotland and some in South Africa. By the lottery of the business, I was sent to South Africa, and by another lottery it appeared that two troop-ships ahead of mine were sunk with the loss of a whole posting of cadet navigators. This meant that when we reached Durban we were transferred immediately to No.41 Air School at Collondale some six miles inland from East London in Cape Province, and forthwith started our flying training. Normally, cadets arriving in South Africa spent several months awaiting posting to flying school. Had this happened to me, I might well never have flown on operations in Bomber Command.[6]

The voyage to South Africa involved thirty-nine days on board the *Stirling*

Castle. For part of the journey we sailed in convoy with a naval escort, but at other times we sailed in the sole company of our sister, the *Athlone Castle*. From time to time there were hints of warfare. We could read the naval light morse-signals about the proximity of U-Boats and we could feel the thud of depth-charges; there was also the shattering racket of gunfire, though this, I think, was only for practice. The chief experience, however, was that of living like a sardine packed into a tin with nearly five thousand other people. Below decks, the ship had been stripped of most partitions leaving huge, long mess-decks on which we lived, much in the style of the eighteenth-century navy. At night, the whole central air space was filled with slung hammocks which all collided with one another at the slightest roll of the ship. I took to unrolling my hammock on the deck from where I could look vertically at these collisions and horizontally at a huge empty space. To my mind this was a form of luxury and I was glad that no one else seemed to favour the idea. My first feeling was of distaste for the other men: there were too many of them and they were too near. I thought a few days at sea would induce severe hatred. The opposite, however, proved to be the case, and by the time we disembarked at Durban I felt thoroughly well disposed to nearly everybody.

As is the way with things in wartime, we had followed a curious route and, after losing sight of the coast of Scotland, we were much surprised to find that our next landfall came up on the starboard and not, as we had expected, the port side. Instead of coming in at Freetown in Sierra Leone, we had in fact turned up at what proved to be Bahia in Brazil. We had to break our journey somewhere as we were running short of fuel and drinking water. While these deficiencies were remedied by an American oil-tanker and a single, rather small fire-engine built in London, several days elapsed. Viewed from the sea, Bahia looked unbelievably attractive. The tropical colours, to what had been an exclusively European eye, seemed exotic to a degree: small clean houses interspersed with numerous palm trees and punctuated by glorious white churches rose steeply from the sea front and gave an impression of paradise. At night, the scene was brilliantly illuminated and the churches leapt forth like jewels in a tiara. These were the first proper lights we had seen since 3rd September 1939, and we burst into the song 'when the lights of London shine again...'

Nor did Bahia shed its seductive impression when we went ashore. As we marched in strict formation up the rise of the town to a square at the summit, there were, it is true, some tight lips and hostile gestures, but these came from the German community. Everyone else, black and white, gave us a rapturous reception, jumping up and down, clapping and shouting 'Victoria'. We were the first British troops to be seen in Brazil after her entry into the war on our side. As we marched, there was a sudden torrential downpour, which then almost immediately rose from the ground as steam. I marched next to a particular friend, Derek Malim, who nearly trod on an enormous and brightly coloured spider; I heard him mutter under his breath, 'thank God I'm British'. We could not, alas, be entirely proud of that. Unaccountably, we were dismissed from the parade in the town square without any instructions. Some of the men drifted off into brothels and drinking dens and several of them came – or were brought – back on board in a shocking state of repair. These, however, were only six or seven out of a thousand in the expedition. Worse than this was that about a hundred of our soldiers, who were on the way to India, deserted and, so far as I know, were not heard of again. An Argentinian friend in our party told me that groups of bandits were operating to the south-west of Bahia. Perhaps our deserters knew this. My friend also told me that the population of Bahia, which had been 12,000 in 1919, was now 300,000. After all this, having never previously been beyond Brittany, I began to feel much more cosmopolitan.[7]

The training in South Africa was fully as intensive as that in Eastbourne and it was apparent that the authorities wished to get us back to England with navigators' brevets as soon as possible. We did all the theory again and sat examinations of much the same kind as those in Eastbourne; but this was really only to fill in the time between the flights on which we advanced from theory to practice – or at least practice of a sort. Our aircraft were elderly Ansons, for which the supply of spare parts seemed to have dried up. Repeated engine failures gave one some idea of what flying in the First World War must have been like. Most of the pilots were South African. Several of them seemed to be very bored by the work, and one, with whom I flew, repeatedly dropped off to sleep. To complete the course, about a hundred hours of flying were required, but, in order to speed things up, three pupil navigators went on each flight, so that there was only about thirty hours of dead-reckoning navigation for each of us. The second and third navigators did map reading, took astro-shots and, when the pilot lost interest, flew the aircraft. Only about a tenth of our flying time was done at night.[8]

In addition to our repeated engine failures and occasionally sleepy pilots, there were some other excitements. On Sunday 21st December 1942, we were given a day off and several of us repaired to the beach at East London for the enjoyable swimming which was to be had there. While we were lazing in the sun, the beach was suddenly invaded by special military police who shouted to us that an emergency had arisen and that we were to board a bus marked 'Recall' immediately. We did so and were driven back to our airfield at high speed. When we got there we saw that our Ansons were being 'bombed up' with real weapons and we were called at once to the briefing room. Here we were told that an enemy fleet had been spotted approaching South African shores and that we were going to attack it. Before we could take off, however, it emerged that the 'Japanese warships' were, in fact, a series of cloudlets, and life soon returned to normal. Years later, Admiral of the Fleet Sir Algernon Willis told me how, in March 1942, he was despatched with a force of four out-of-date R-class battleships to intercept the Japanese fleet, which was thought to be bound for an attack on Ceylon. This too proved to be a false rumour. Sir Algernon and I were able to agree how lucky both of us had been in that particular respect.[9]

Rumours of war did not entirely exhaust the possibilities for action, even while we were at this comparatively early stage of our flying training. Every now and again we were despatched to escort convoys rounding the Cape of Good Hope and search for German submarines, which were active in these waters. On one of these sorties, I flew as first navigator and, though we found no U-Boats, I was entitled to enter it in my log book as an operational flight. It was my first. Just over a year later, I was to carry out my second, which, as I had expected, was a very different matter.[10]

At last on 27th March 1943, having passed the exams and flown the required number of navigational hours, I formed up with those of my course who had also passed on the Wings Parade. After various drill evolutions, we were individually marched up to a South African Colonel, who clipped an observer's brevet onto each of our tunics. Four of the course, of whom I was one, were now to receive commissions, but we were told that we were to be dressed as sergeants until we reached England: there was insufficient accommodation for officers on board the troop ships. The brevet seemed a great prize and the commission a scarcely lesser one. Becoming an acting sergeant was a disappointment, if only because it meant another voyage under hard conditions similar to those on the *Stirling Castle*.

After a short stay at an Imperial Forces Transit Camp near Capetown, I sailed for home with thousands of others, including some nine hundred Italian prisoners of war, on board the P & O liner *Stratheden*. There were also some civilians on board. One was a girl who had escaped from Bangkok on the evening the Japanese arrived there. There were two other girls, who had escaped with scarcely less notice from Burma. The Italian prisoners of war were delightful men and well liked by all of us, who took turns standing guard over them. Their living quarters were even more crowded than ours, but they were given food which was markedly better than what we got. The most exciting thing about the voyage, however, was that we found ourselves in company with HMS *Warspite*, which I already knew was one of the most famous of all our battleships. She gave us a great sense of security; indeed, one day she opened fire on some unfortunate vessel on the horizon. Flames leapt from the mouths of the guns, then came the crash as of thunder which shook our ship to the keel, and finally columns of water were hurled into the air miles away on the horizon. Suddenly the air was full of bursting anti-aircraft shells and we heard the clatter of machine-gun fire. None of us knew what all this was about or what the result of it was, but I expect the Captain of *Warspite* did; he sent out a Walrus seaplane to have a look. We were glad to see it being craned back on board after it had returned and alighted near its mother ship. When I joined the Air Force, I had not expected to witness such a spectacle. It remains vividly in my memory.[11]

Our first port of call was Freetown. We approached on the evening of 28th April 1943 in line ahead, *Warspite* and a cruiser in the van, ourselves in the centre and the White Star liner *Britannic*, brimming, as we were, with troops, bringing up the rear. Our flanks were covered by destroyers, which, in their customary manner, tore hither and thither in busy haste. Evidently their manoeuvres were also productive, for we were told that they had destroyed a U-Boat. Their depth-charges threw terrifying columns of water into the air and once more *Stratheden* was shaken to her foundations. We had arrived in a port which the war had elevated to the first importance and as we came onto our mooring half a mile off the town, we saw some familiar sights including the *Stirling Castle* and the Armed Merchant Cruiser *Alcantara*, which had sailed with us on parts of our outward voyage. There were as yet no major docking facilities and we did not come alongside or disembark. A huge wharf was, however, under construction. Various striking figures came to and fro from shore to ship by launch, including the Flag Officer, West Africa. I watched a white man, of whom there were said to be only about a hundred in this the most unhealthy place imaginable, come up the side of *Stratheden* to supervise the taking ashore of four or five wooden cases; he had black sleek hair, a pallid face, and he wore a white suit. He seemed to me to have stepped straight out of the pages of Somerset Maugham. After that we waited only long enough to take on fuel before putting to sea again.[12]

After a few days, we entered the official danger-zone and were ordered to sleep in our clothes. Bits of news were broadcast in short bursts. We heard that thirty of our bombers had failed to return from an attack on Dortmund. That, it occurred to me, would account for an entire course of navigators, pilots, bomb-aimers, engineers, gunners and wireless-operators. Then a gale hit us and *Stratheden* was hurled about like a cork on a very high sea. We shipped water on 'A' deck seventy feet above the water-line and our engines constantly raced as the propellers rose into the air. We watched great columns of spray flying over *Britannic*'s bridge and *Warspite* seemed to be completely awash: as she plunged, all we could see was her superstructure giving her the look of a monstrous submarine. In the midst of this, we were ordered to action stations to repel enemy air attacks. None of our ships was hit. *Warspite* signalled us that she had picked up U-Boat transmissions. 'Use DF', her message ran. We knew, of course, that DF meant direction-finding radio; we had used it ourselves in our Ansons. A day or so later, *Warspite* signalled us again. This time we read 'Thank you for your close cooperation hope to see you soon'. She turned abruptly to starboard and, with her two escorting destroyers, disappeared into the distance. After the war, I learned from Admiral Willis that *Warspite* was bound for the Straits of Gibraltar and the Mediterranean where we were at last re-establishing naval dominance. He knew because, at that time, *Warspite* was responding to his orders. How amazing the war would have been if one could have known then what was happening.[13]

On 10th May 1943, I woke to see that we were steaming up the Clyde, and the next day I found myself at a Personnel Reception Centre in Harrogate. I was allowed to assume the commission which had been granted to me in South Africa and become, in effect, an Acting Pilot Officer on probation. It had always struck me as rather a silly rank, especially as I was a navigator – or at least I thought I was.

Before being posted into Bomber Command, as I had long wished to be, there were two further short steps in Training Command. The first consisted of twenty-odd hours flying in Tiger Moths from No.7 Elementary Flying Training School at Desford. This was all in daylight and it gave me the opportunity to improve my map-reading as we flew low enough to be under the cloud. It was not easy; the blast of air one encountered in an open cockpit made it difficult to orientate a map and the painful bombardment of hailstones was hardly an encouragement to look over the side. It was a further whiff of what flying in the First World War must have been like. It also gave one pause for thought as to how the likes of Sir Alan Cobham, Amelia Earhart and Amy Johnson had achieved their miracles of open-cockpit flying in machines similar to the Tiger Moth. Most of my time at Desford, however, was spent in being taught to fly the machine myself, and before the end of the course I became reasonably proficient at loop-the-looping, falling-leaf-spinning and so on. This was a bonus, which, for navigators, was unusual; it was also a potential advantage, for there was now a single pilot policy in Bomber Command, which meant that there was a marginal addition to the safety factor if members of a bomber crew other than the pilot knew something, if only very little, of his skills.[14]

At the end of July 1943, I was posted to No.3 Advanced Flying Unit at Bobbington as the second step. The proceedings here were exacting. The object was to acclimatize us to night-flying under European – that is blackout – conditions, and, though we flew in the familiar Anson aircraft, it was, as I would now describe it, a culture shock. My confidence in being a trained navigator evaporated into the dark night and I discovered that success depended upon an intimate understanding between the pilot, the navigator and the bomb-aimer. We made simulated attacks on such places as Stafford, Peterborough and elsewhere using, as a substitute for bombing, the taking of photographs of our aiming points. As we had usually not met one another until we boarded the aircraft, numerous misunderstandings took place. On one occasion we got dangerously lost on the run into and out of the 'target'. The bomb-aimer thought that I would be keeping track of our position; I thought he would be. We also did very taxing navigational exercises in simulators. One of the handicaps was that the clocks went at double speed. A thirty-second minute is a poisonous measure for a navigator. Under these conditions, I managed to bring my 'aircraft' back from a simulated attack on Kassel to within four miles of base. This was thought quite good, but I knew it was not good enough. Learning how to get round such difficulties was the object of the training at Bobbington. I was glad when it was over and my time in Training Command came to an end.[15]

Having got into Bomber Command, I stayed in it for operational training – which I now began – on operations, or in the end as an operational instructor, until the war was over. The unit I joined was No.11 Operational Training Unit, which was based at Westcott with a satellite at Oakley, both near Oxford. I arrived there at the end of August 1943. The ambience was strikingly different from anything I had experienced before or even been able to imagine. All the instructors were tour-expired. One of them, Squadron Leader (later Wing Commander) Fraser Barron, had completed a tour in the Path Finder Force and wore the ribbons of the DSO, the DFC and the DFM. The senior navigation instructor was Squadron Leader Scrivener, who also had the DSO and the DFC together with the enormous added prestige of having flown on one operation as Wing Commander Guy Gibson's navigator. The latter had recently been awarded the VC. The aircraft were Wellingtons mark 1c, which had been operational at the outset of the war. They were now long retired from Bomber Command's front line but they nonetheless looked much more threatening and challenging than any aircraft I had been near before. We were in the second line and were liable to be called upon to reinforce the front line if a major effort, such as the famous thousand-bomber attack on Cologne of May 1942, were again to be ordered.

The first step was to get 'crewed up', which I described at the time as 'going to be as big a headache as getting married'. We were left a fortnight in which to make a love match, after which marriages were arranged for those who had not done so. My crew was the product of the voluntary process. First, over a snooker table in the officer's mess, I met an Australian Flying Officer, who was a bomb-aimer. Instinctively we understood each other and we soon decided to fly together. He knew a New Zealand flight sergeant, who was a pilot. This man seemed to be a most unlikely candidate. He was immensely old, being twenty-seven or even twenty-eight, and most of his hair seemed to be on the sides of his head; he looked more like an orchestral conductor than a budding Bomber Command pilot. I had no hesitation in backing the bomber-aimer's judgement and the New Zealander accepted our proposal.

The three of us had, I believe, made the best decision of our war careers. We then recruited a Canadian sergeant rear-gunner and an English sergeant wireless-operator. That made up the crew of a Wellington and off we set.[16]

Initially, the flying was mostly for the purpose of teaching the pilot, Flight Sergeant Murray Milne, the differences between flying an Oxford and a Wellington. They were considerable, but though Murray was not, and never became, a polished pilot, he had a ready aptitude for managing adequately. Flying with him at night while he repeatedly took off and landed doing 'circuits and bumps', was not a comfortable ride. Nothing, however, got broken and our confidence as a crew began to accumulate, perhaps the more so because fatal crashes among the others on the unit were by no means uncommon. We did gunnery exercises, which gave our rear-gunner, Sergeant Duncan, the chance to test his marksmanship by firing at air-towed drogues. We flew by night to a bombing range at Warpsgrove and our bomb-aimer, Flying Officer Gordon Pyle, attacked marked targets from heights of up to 8,000 feet. On 8th October, we took off in daylight from Oakley and flew courses which took us from there to Cambridge, Lincoln, Thetford, Cambridge again and so home via Westcott. In my log-book this flight is entered as a 'Special Dual Navigation Trip' and it is marked with the symbol ※. It thus appears to have been among the most uneventful and easiest of my undertakings at OTU. In fact, it was my initiation into the use in the air of a device that was loosely, though not quite accurately, categorized as radar and known as 'Gee'. This was too secret to be mentioned except by symbols.[17]

'Gee' seemed to be miraculous and indeed was extremely ingenious. It depended upon the transmission of pulses from three ground stations, 'A', the master, and 'B' and 'C', the slaves, which were situated along a line of about two hundred miles in length. Each slave transmission was locked to one from the master and the differences in time between the reception in the aircraft of the 'A' and 'B' and the 'A' and 'C' signals were displayed on a cathode-ray tube on the navigator's table. From these readings the navigator could locate his aircraft on two position lines, which were known as 'Gee' co-ordinates. The point at which the two co-ordinates intersected showed the ground position of the aircraft. A competent navigator could complete this process in less than a minute.[18]

I knew at the time that knowledge of one's ground position at a given moment was useful, not so much for itself but as a means of obtaining a 'fix' for the purposes of dead-reckoning navigation, which was the means of knowing where one was going to be at selected times in the future. The accuracy of 'Gee' over Cambridge, Lincoln and so on was amazing. But, as I was later to learn, it rapidly diminished with range and once one crossed the Dutch coast it was rendered ineffective by German jamming and was sometimes misleading because the Germans also broadcast bogus signals.

I have entered briefly into these technical details of one aspect of navigation in Bomber Command, not because I have changed the course of this book, but because I discern in them some important historical lessons and warnings. First, there is the need to recognize the importance in historical research, not merely of persistence and alertness, but also of technical awareness. Without the latter, my 'Gee' flight would appear to have been of little interest for whatever purpose it was being used. In fact, it was among the most important of all the training flights I ever made and it is also an indication of how the interests of security imposed upon the instructors the need to leave the imparting of this secret information to such a late stage – dangerously late, some might think. Second, the very ingenuity of 'Gee', and of many other even more sophisticated radar devices about which I learnt later in the war, has misled many of those who subsequently came to understand the technical principles involved but had not themselves operated the equipments in the face of the German defences, or at the ranges of many of the targets. This has resulted in much of the historical appraisal of Bomber Command operations being fundamentally unsound. It has also led to some incongruous moral judgements on the Bomber Command offensive.

When the pilot had become reasonably proficient at the controls of the Wellington bomber and so laid the foundations of crew confidence, it was my turn to build on this by demonstrating that I could navigate the aircraft over long distances at night, bring it over a target and then back to base. Unfortunately, the aircraft in which we made these long night flights were not equipped with 'Gee' so there were no navigational aids beyond those I had had on the Ansons at Bobbington. There was the added difficulty that it was now November. On two of our four long night flights, we encountered severe icing conditions. De-icing equipment on the Wellington 1c was not very efficient and the aircraft, with its two Pegasus engines, lacked the performance to climb above the danger levels. This forced us to change our flight plans, which, navigationally, was a most unwelcome development. Nevertheless, from my point of view, these flights were reasonably successful. I was particularly glad to be able to hand the aircraft over to the bomb-aimer when he could see the marked range at Warpsgrove after flying over Northampton, Goole, Pickering and Filey to a point half way across the North Sea and then to the target by way of Wells, Peterborough, Northampton and Preston Capes. When we completed the course at Westcott, however, I had done no more than twenty-three hours and fifty minutes of night navigational flying. The rest of the crew, with one exception, were correspondingly inexperienced, and yet we were now fully qualified to fly bomber sorties against Germany. Indeed, had the need arisen, we might well have flown at least one already.[19]

The exceptional member of our crew was the wireless-operator. The Englishman, whom we had originally recruited, had fallen foul of the authorities for words spoken to them which they did not like. He was sent away for disciplinary training and we were allotted a new wireless-operator, Warrant Officer Bosson, another New Zealander. He was returning for a second tour of operations, having completed one of thirty sorties in 1943. He seemed to be disgruntled and fatalistic; I doubt if we would have chosen him of our own free will. In the air, however, he proved to be an entirely different man and he and I, who had so much related work to do, operated as though hand-in-glove. In addition, he was immensely experienced and highly efficient. We soon got over the loss of our own choice, although he had shown the hallmarks of efficiency and had impressed us as an excellent prospect. All the same, he did not know how to guard his tongue and he was an inveterate tease. Eventually, this was to be his undoing. After his disciplinary training, he returned to an OTU and got 'crewed up' again. He then had the misfortune to be killed by his rear-gunner, whom he had so exasperated that he picked up a sten gun and shot him dead.

Had there still been Wellingtons in the front line of Bomber Command, we would now have been posted to an operational squadron. As it was, not only Wellingtons, but also the four-engined Stirlings, had been relegated to lesser tasks. Lancasters, Halifaxes and Mosquitoes had become the order of the day, or rather the night. We were destined for a Lancaster squadron, and so our pilot had to make another jump, from two to four engines. This also meant the recruitment of two additional members of the crew, a flight-engineer and a mid-upper-air-gunner. To fill the first vacancy, we were allocated an Englishman, Sergeant Darby, and, for the second, Sergeant Sneddon, another Australian. In these, as in the case of Bosson, we were extremely fortunate. Despite their lack of flying experience owing to the speed at which gunners and flight-engineers could be trained, both these men proved to be first class. Indeed, I do not believe that there can have been a better gunner than Sneddon in all Bomber Command. He flew nearly all our sorties as rear-gunner, where he moved when we transferred Duncan to another crew and took on board an English mid-upper-gunner, Flight Sergeant Knott.

The seven of us now entered the final phase of operational training. We flew about fifty hours on Stirlings and Lancasters at a Heavy Conversion Unit and then at a Lancaster Finishing School. Despite some diabolical weather, everything went smoothly for us except on one occasion when, through a mistake in our cockpit drill, we overshot the runway at Syerston and narrowly escaped going over the edge and dropping into the River Trent.

As a crew we were now generally functioning efficiently: Murray Milne had got the measure of the Lancaster, our long-distance flights were completed without navigational errors and we dropped our bombs accurately on the bombing ranges. Obviously we would not survive if the pilot could not fly the aircraft successfully. Equally, we were sure to be shot down, we were constantly told, if we could not navigate with such accuracy as to be on track and on time so that we would be flying in the company of what we could not see, that is, the concentration of our bombers. It was also self-evident that if we could not hit the target, there was no point in going. Having satisfied our instructors that these points were registered and that we had mastered the necessary skills, we were posted on 26th March 1944 to an operational squadron, No. 50 at Skellingthorpe near Lincoln. This belonged to No. 5 (Bomber) Group, which was commanded by Air Vice-Marshal Ralph Cochrane.

At this time, what subsequently became known as the Battle of Berlin was coming to an end. In the course of it, Bomber Command had lost the equivalent of the whole of its front line, but through the vagaries of war 50 Squadron had suffered only light casualties. It was probably for this reason that the Squadron's morale seemed to be very high indeed. Another thing which may have explained this was that our squadron commander, Wing Commander Heward, was a stiff disciplinarian who demanded total dedication to the tasks in hand and the highest standards of efficiency. He was liable to drop on gunners and question them about airmanship, on pilots and test them on gunnery, on navigators about bomb aiming, and so on. To say that he produced a spirit of alertness in his crews would be to understate his achievement. I had not previously served under such a formidable and effective Commanding Officer. For further encouragement, we had a Group Commander who was regarded as a ruthless martinet and we all stood in awe of our Commander-in-Chief, whom we never saw, but called 'Butch' Harris.

All this was as well, for we now entered upon a period of intensive operations in which our squadron was repeatedly decimated. The good luck of the Battle of Berlin had come to an end and we came face to face with the probability that our lives were unlikely to last much longer. New crews arrived and disappeared within a week, sometimes within twenty-four hours, and most of the old crews disappeared too. In what seemed to be hardly any time at all, we became one of the most senior crews on the squadron. In rapid steps, Murray Milne was promoted from Flight Sergeant to Flight Lieutenant and, for a time, until a more experienced man could be posted in, I was the acting navigation leader. I was barely twenty-two years old. We were in dead men's shoes but we had got there the hard and also the lucky way.

Our first operation was against the railway yards at Tours. This, at least in theory, was not the most difficult or dangerous of targets, but our initiation was marred by the failure of our rear turret. Efforts to make it work failed and it led to us taking off late and so getting behind the main stream of the bombing attack. At Tours, we identified our target, bombed and photographed it and returned to base. When orders to delay the attack were given in the target area by the master bomber, we were still out of range of his radio telephone. Thus, we were the last aircraft to take off on this attack and the first to return. It was disquieting, but no complaint was raised against us and in reality there was no means by which we could have known of the master bomber's intentions. On the following night, that of 11th April 1944, we took part in an attack on Aachen. Navigationally, things did not go well. Though exactly on track, we passed through the target area ahead of time without picking up the aiming point. We had to fly back and try again. In such a manoeuvre, the risk of collision was great, but nothing happened and at the second attempt we bombed successfully and at the correct time. There was then a pause of a week, after which we flew to Paris and dropped fourteen one-thousand-pound bombs on the railway yards at Juvissy.

Two nights later, we again set course for Paris but in the neighbourhood of Reading a sudden whiff of white vapour shot out of our starboard inner-engine and disappeared astern. Our engine-coolant tank had burst and the glycol had gone. We promptly feathered the engine to avoid a fire and, having reset the remaining three engines, continued on course for Paris. As we crossed the coast near Eastbourne, the temperature gauge of the starboard outer-engine suddenly rose into the danger zone. Again to avoid a fire we promptly feathered that engine too. Murray Milne now opened up full power on the two port engines but we soon found that not only could we not continue our climb, but that we were unable to maintain the height we had gained. In an involuntary descent we turned for home, still bearing our huge bomb load. We headed for Skellingthorpe, where, knowing the runway, Murray thought he had a better chance of making a landing than on one he did not know. When we got there, we were told by flying control to proceed to the Wash and drop our bombs. As we were going to hit the ground long before we could get to the Wash, we asked and received immediate clearance for a landing. As we approached, we jettisoned our petrol, which unfortunately fell on the WAAF site. With all the power on one side, Murray could not entirely straighten his landing line and we came down in something of a sideways skid. The tyres smoked and then melted but the undercarriage held and we came to rest unharmed in a virtually intact aircraft. We heard later that no one had landed a Lancaster before with a full bomb load on board, on two engines on the same side.

Having turned back short of the target meant that we could not count the flight as an operation and, indeed, before we knew whether we would be congratulated or disciplined, we had to await the Commanding Officer's verdict. He, in fact, had scrambled aboard our Lancaster even before it came to a complete halt. He was there to satisfy himself that there was no way in which we could have reached the target. We were much relieved that he did so satisfy himself.

After another two nights and some first aid work on our Lancaster, we took off for our first major German target, Brunswick, and then, in each case after two-night intervals, we attacked Munich and Schweinfurt. These were eventful and, in my mind, memorable nights. Coming out of the target area at Brunswick, we were picked up by a Ju88 night-fighter, which made two determined attacks on us but then lost contact. The same thing happened on the way home from Munich, except that this time the enemy fighter was an Me110. The engagement lasted for more than forty minutes, during which our fate was in the hands of our rear-gunner, Sneddon. Each time the enemy closed to seven hundred yards, but neither before nor after, he told the pilot to corkscrew towards the fighter, thus complicating its deflection angle. So we dived and corkscrewed and climbed and corkscrewed now to port and then to starboard throughout these forty minutes. To our amazement, we at last lost the fighter. We knew we were seven very lucky men. But where we were, or how we could get home, we did not know.

This for the next few hours was my problem. The first step was to reinstate the gyro-compasses, which had toppled during our evasive manoeuvres, and the second was to draw a circle of uncertainty within which the aircraft was bound to be. The diameter of the circle was in this case about a hundred and fifty miles in extent. From this somewhat imprecise starting point, I gave the pilot courses for home. As the time came when we should have been approaching the French coast on the final northerly leg, it began to grow light but, instead of the coast we were greeted by the ominous sight of a vast expanse of agricultural land. I could but hope that at least this might be France. Eventually, as our petrol supply was falling to zero, we did cross the French coast and we made a dash for the nearest airfield, which was Tangmere, where we landed at our last gasp. We had been in the air for ten and a half hours.[20]

For its forty minutes of combat and the ensuing navigational problems, the night of Munich has ever remained in my mind, but there was another reason for this. During this night of 24th April 1944, I 'met' Leonard Cheshire for the first time. He was the master bomber and, flying low in a Mosquito, he marked the aiming point and then directed us throughout the attack. As we ran in on Cheshire's marking, his cool, collected and precise instructions came through our earphones with the kind of tone one might have expected from someone seated in a comfortable arm chair telephoning from a drawing-room. Bosson, whose remarks were normally restricted to the necessities of the business in hand, suddenly urged me to switch off my cockpit lights, draw my black-out curtains and look out. He said that if I lived to be a hundred I would never again see anything like this. I looked out and beheld what seemed to be all the Guy Fawkes nights which had ever taken place, rolled up into a minute. Tracer-fire from German fighters flew across the picture, flak poured up from the ground in great loops and bombs began to cascade down around the brilliant spot-fires which had been placed on top of Leonard Cheshire's original visually-aimed marker.

Later it came to light that this attack, which was mounted by 5 Group alone, had caused as much damage as would normally have been achieved by the whole front line of Bomber Command. Such was the degree of accuracy that Cheshire had injected into night-, so-called area-bombing. We did not have to wait for that news to realize the incredible skill of Cheshire's tactics and the almost superhuman courage that enabled him to carry them out. It came as no surprise to hear afterwards that he had been awarded the VC.

Schweinfurt was a different kind of agony. At Munich we had bombed three and a half minutes ahead of schedule and we had flown directly into and out of the target area. At Schweinfurt we bombed twenty minutes behind schedule and spent an uncomfortably long time orbiting the target area while the master bomber tried to identify and mark the aiming point. This provided a golden opportunity for the German night-fighters and we counted dozens of our aircraft going down in flames. At last we were told to bomb, but the marking was scattered and we knew that the attack had not been a success. We also knew, before we left the target area, that Bomber Command had suffered very heavy casualties. Industrial haze and the weather had frustrated our tactics that night and when we got home, after a flight of more than nine hours, we and our surviving comrades were distinctly gloomy. One of our flight commanders, Squadron Leader Chadwick, noticing no doubt our depressed morale, asked us how we would feel if we had been resident in Schweinfurt and had seen a target marking red-spot fire falling into our back garden. This cheered us all up no end.[21]

And so, most surprisingly, with a number of variations on these themes, life went on. Schweinfurt was my sixth operational sortie; by the morning of 3rd June, I had completed eighteen. Then at half past two in the morning of 6th June 1944, we took off to attack a target at St Pierre du Mont just beyond the Normandy coast. Crossing the English coast between Bournemouth and Portland, we fused our eleven one-thousand-pound and four five-hundred-pound bombs and switched off our navigation lights. At eight minutes to five and as it grew light, I calculated that we were over the target, but at twelve thousand feet we were above cloud, so down we went. At eight thousand feet we broke cloud and there was the target. We bombed at five o'clock precisely and set course for home. As we re-crossed the Channel, we noticed that it was stiff with shipping of all shapes and sizes flying a forest of barrage balloons. It was an astonishing sight, but having seen it, I do not remember that we thought much more about it. We landed at Skellingthorpe at fourteen minutes past seven after what we thought was the most uneventful operation we had ever carried out. We were, however, rather surprised to be called out for another operation on the evening of the same day. At the briefing for it, we were given the positions of our own and the American troops ashore in Normandy. It was then and then only that I realized that what we had seen in the morning had been the opening of the Second Front, the invasion of Normandy. Since that, I have taken with a pinch of salt the assertion, 'I know, I was there'.[22]

On my twenty-second birthday, I set out on my twenty-sixth sortie. As an experienced crew, we were now asked from time to time to take a new pilot with us as what was called the 'second dickie'. This was to give him a little familiarization before setting forth with his own crew. The target was a V1 flying bomb installation at St Leu D'Esserent near Paris. Earlier this might have appeared to be a reasonably easy trip but, for some time past, the French air had been swarming with German night-fighters whose principal habitat in the past had largely been the German air. On this occasion, we had unpleasant brushes from which we were lucky to escape, but escape we did, although not with the prize we had sought. The objective that night was the destruction of a small target by the most precise means possible. As always over France, Belgium or Holland, we took the utmost pains to avoid killing people around the target as far as we could. We failed to damage the target to the desired extent and so, three nights later, on the night of 7th July, we were sent back to the same target, where, for the first time, we had the job of backing up the master bomber's initial marking. Over the target everything went well for us but as we were crossing the French coast on our homeward flight, we were suddenly jumped on by a German fighter, our first news of which was a stream of bullets plunging into our starboard wing. These set fire to the petrol inside it and a ghastly sheet of flame was blasted back from the leading edge over the surface of the wing and thence away behind us. We were not only in dire peril. We were also extremely conspicuous.

We were flying at sixteen thousand feet. Murray immediately put our Lancaster into a steep dive in the hope of throwing off the fighter and blowing out the fire. At a thousand feet, he had to level off; the fire continued to burn vigorously and the fighter had followed us down. It now flew repeatedly round us just outside the seven hundred yard range of our .303 guns, but for some reason it did not fire again. Perhaps its guns had jammed, perhaps its ammunition had run out, or perhaps the pilot thought we were already done for. Murray now transferred most, but not all, of the petrol from the starboard tank. He said that it was better to feed the fire than to offer it a tank full of petrol vapour; a fire was not as bad as an explosion. I calculated a course for the nearest friendly airfield, which was Ford, and for the longest ten minutes in my life we headed for it. As we did so, the fire continued to burn in the manner of a blow lamp and the wing began to twist; its aerodynamics were changed and our airspeed began to drop. As we approached Ford, it had fallen alarmingly near to stalling speed. We were warned that there was a crashed Mosquito on the runway but, not feeling disposed to hang around, we landed on the grass beside it. The moment the aircraft came to a stop, we all piled out and ran for our lives. As we did so, we passed the fire-fighters going in the opposite direction. At that moment, they were braver than we were.

After breakfast and a short sleep, we went out to see our aircraft. The twisted starboard wing had a broad streak of white across it and, through that part of the surface, it was easy to push one's fist. How it was that the wing had stayed on the aircraft, I could not then understand; nor have I been able to since. It had been the most awful experience of my life and I think the rest of the crew felt the same, although we did not talk much about it. I now knew the real meaning of the word 'petrified' and I knew that fear was to be perceived more by smell than by the other senses. None of us felt inclined to look over another Lancaster which had a decapitated gunner in the rear turret.

Our 'second dickie' of the first St Leu D'Esserent trip was sent to pick us up and at three thirty that afternoon we took off as passengers in his Lancaster. At twenty past four we were back at Skellingthorpe ready to resume our tour of operations. Further mishaps awaited us.[23]

For our thirtieth sortie we were briefed to attack a precise target at Revigny in Belgium and for this trip we again took a 'second dickie'. He was Flight Lieutenant Jimmy Flint, who had won the DFM and the George Medal on an earlier tour of operations. He seemed rather to lack confidence in us and was dressed up as a Breton fisherman, which would not perhaps have been very helpful in Belgium. His expectations, however, were not entirely without foundation. On the way out, we were repeatedly attacked by German nightfighters, both our gun turrets were knocked out, our wireless transmitter was smashed and, when we ran up on the target, we found that our bombsite had been put out of order too. If we had been over a German target, we would have dropped our bombs as accurately as possible on guess work, but over Belgium we could not do that. Feeling utterly frustrated, we turned for home, thinking that this would not count as a sortie. As, however, we brought back a photograph of the aiming point, we were told that it did.

At about this time we had been issued with special sun-glasses and, during our final operations, we flew two sorties in daylight. The first was very easy.

The Army had asked for the heavy bombardment of German positions in the region of Caen, which Montgomery's army was about to attack. We flew in a huge gaggle of over a thousand Lancasters and Halifaxes, attacked on a north/south axis, turned starboard and then flew directly home. The business was over in less than four hours and we spent only a few minutes over enemy-held territory. This, as we later heard, was the opening shot in a military operation which became famous under its codename of *Goodwood*. There was some controversy at the time as to how useful our efforts had been, but although six of our bombers were shot down, we were in no doubt that, on this occasion, our task was an easy one in comparison with that of our men on the ground.[24]

Our other daylight sortie was more exciting. The target was a factory at St Cyr in the outskirts of Paris which we were to approach along the line of the Seine. The formation was to be led by Wing Commander Doubleday, an Australian, who commanded one of the squadrons at our neighbouring aerodrome at Waddington. He was to be supported by two wingmen, one of whom was us. After about an hour of manoeuvring, we had got our mass of bombers into something like a formation, but as our pilots had little or no experience of this kind of flying, we knew that our American friends in the Eighth Air Force would not have thought much of it. Doing the best we could, we set course for the target while over Reading. As we reached the south coast, we were supposed to rendez-vous with a covering force of Spitfires, but this failed to materialize and we pressed on without that comfort. Presently, following the course of the Seine, we could see Rouen ahead and as we came over it, a dense barrage of flak came up. Wing Commander Doubleday, who like so many of his countrymen was not short on humour, threw back the canopy of his Lancaster and gave us the motorist's stop sign with his arm. We passed through the barrage unscathed, as did – so far as I could see – the whole of the formation behind. Some of the Lancasters, however, most unwisely began to weave as, in such circumstances at night, we all usually did. Since we were now in such close company, this produced an alarming risk of collision, and one of our comrades lost his nerve and moved out onto the flank of the formation where he was promptly picked off by predicted flak. His rear turret was knocked off and made a separate descent to its final crash. The remainder of the aircraft went into a spin, now clockwise, now anti-clockwise, and down it went releasing on their parachutes two of the crew on the way. I took my eyes off it just before it hit the ground.

The next excitement was the appearance ahead and well above us of a German fighter. It dived and charged straight at us. For the first and the last time on our tour of operations, Gordon Pyle opened fire from the front turret and seconds later nearly everyone else did from their rear and mid-upper turrets. As this fighter tore past close to us – so close that its iron cross and swastika markings were clearly and unpleasantly visible – the scene suggested to me a page in a schoolboy's war-picture book. I could not see what happened to the fighter, but I rather doubt if it survived. As we came to the target, we were struck by flak, but our new Lancaster seemed to absorb the damage without undue complaint. Finally, having failed to regather the formation, we all made our way home individually, taking advantage of a merciful dispensation of thick cloud. When we got back we saw on the black board in the de-briefing room that we were reported missing. Some-one must have misread the identification letters on the side of a crashing Lancaster.

There was at this time little respite from operations and within twenty-four hours of our return from Paris, we were being briefed again. This time the target was the railway installations at Givors near Lyons. As the time for take-off approached a violent thunderstorm broke out. We sat in our aircraft watching the control-tower fully expecting to see a red Verey fired which would have told us that the operation had been cancelled. It was not and so we took off. We flew four hundred miles through the most extensive and intensive thunderstorm I have ever seen. Sparks flew between the points of my dividers; the air was terribly rough and at times dangerously so. When we got to the target, we found that very few of our comrades had turned up. We later learned that most of them had abandoned the sortie and gone home. Unusually, no one had been criticized for having done so. We had great difficulty in seeing our aiming point and so did the master bomber. We orbited the general target area for twenty-three minutes and then, at last, having come down to seven thousand feet, we saw what we had come for and delivered our eight one-thousand and three five-hundred-pound bombs.

Three years after the war I motored across France and one day found myself in Givors. The railway area was still a scene of complete devastation; the bombing had evidently been highly accurate, but alas one load had under-shot and levelled a house. I hoped it had not been our load. Before leaving, I set up the town sign 'Givors', which had been blown out of the ground and was lying forlorn by the roadside. The people there, as at all the other French 'targets' I visited, were full of friendship for, and admiration of, Bomber Command. This was heroic of them and a rich reward for the risks we had taken in trying to avoid killing French people. On one occasion, indeed, when returning across France after attacking a target in Germany, we found that one of our fused bombs had got jammed in the bomb doors with its nose protruding into the slip-stream. My inclination was to get rid of it before its propeller-driven plunger cap unwound and dropped off. Gordon Pyle re-minded me that we were over France. He hung on to the bomb until we were over the Channel.

The Givors operation was my thirty-fourth and it proved to be my last. Our crew now joined the lucky minority of those which survived a tour of operations in Bomber Command. Murray Milne, Gordon Pyle and I were awarded the DFC. Dick Darby, Sneddon, Knott and Short, the wireless operator, were awarded the DFM. Thus every member of our crew was decorated, which in my experience was most unusual. The only regret we had was that Bosson, who had left us after twenty-five sorties because he was on a second tour, was not included in this hand-out. This was an injustice, but it was not one that troubled Bosson very much; he was now more concerned with the prospect of returning to farming in New Zealand.

I have since realized that bomber crews operated in many different ways. Our method was, perhaps, unusual. Murray Milne, the pilot, was the captain of the aircraft, but he operated as such only when matters of pilotage were the issue. When we were under attack, the gunners became the captains, and when we were in the target area the bomb-aimer was the captain. When we were not under attack, not taking off or landing, and not in the target area, I was the captain. This was an unspoken system which we evolved spontaneously, and it produced in our crew the nearest possible approximation to a single brain aided by seven pairs of hands. Other crews, of which I had knowledge, operated in a variety of different ways, ranging from those with autocratic pilots who interpreted their position as captain of the aircraft in a full and literal sense, to those who practised the opposite of this system, and went even further than that. The autocratic pilot, whether or not he was the senior in rank, held his crew in a strictly disciplined position of subordination. He motivated them, he gave them orders and, though he might sometimes take advice from them, he took all the decisions. Many who flew successful tours of operations used this system, and it was the method which the authorities expected in what, generally speaking, was a pilots' air force.

The other extreme can be illustrated by a case, which in itself was no doubt extreme, and of which I had knowledge. This was an all-Australian crew, whose pilot, on one of their early trips, decided that the state of the aircraft was so bad and the conditions prevailing so adverse that he would abandon the sortie. He asked the navigator to give him a course for home. The navigator, supported by the rest of the crew, refused to do so. To resolve this deadlock, one of the crew knocked the pilot out and he was then removed to the casualty bed and strapped down. Flying the aircraft as best they could, this crew proceeded to the target, bombed it and returned to base. They then released the pilot and ordered him to land the aircraft, which none of them could have done. They told the pilot that if he promised never to turn back again, unless they all agreed to that course, they would say nothing about the incident. The pilot gave them that undertaking. They flew a very successful tour of operations; the pilot was awarded the DFC and the rest of the crew received no recognition, nor of course in so far as the authorities were concerned, was there any reason why they should have done.

The Givors sortie was not only the end of my tour of operations, but, though I had no idea of this, it also proved to be the end of my war. From 50 Squadron, I was posted back to my OTU at Westcott and Oakley as a staff navigator, that is, as an instructor. It involved lecturing on operational techniques and examining the navigation logs and charts of pupil navigators; it also involved a certain amount of flying, usually with pupil navigators who appeared to be making mistakes which did not show on their logs and charts. This comparatively easy life, which appeared at the time to be but an interval between one tour of operations and another – probably against Japan – turned out, however, to be the end of my career in the Air Force. As soon as the Japanese surrender took place, I was granted a Class B release on the grounds of my scholarship at Oxford. Instead of going to the Far East, I shed my Flight Lieutenant's uniform, for that was what I had by then become, and went back to Trinity to resume the Oxford history school. All the history I was to make myself, had now been made. My future connection with the subject was to be academic.

I have recounted some of the experiences I had while serving in the Royal Air Force during the war, not to suggest that my part was of any great historical importance, but because it was a contribution to a great historical event. The strategic air offensive against Germany is uniquely interesting historically, as is the partly contemporary and partly subsequent offensive against Japan, in that it had no significant predecessor and is unlikely to have any successor. It is certainly important historically because of the results it achieved, the results it failed to achieve and the casualties it involved both among the German population and the Bomber Command aircrews. In the First World War, 38,925 British Army officers were killed in action, and in the Second World War, 38,205 Bomber Command aircrews, not all of whom were officers, were also killed in action. More than 7,000 more were killed during training or otherwise while not actually on operations against the enemy. I was part of this historic event.

It has become a truism that the Battle of the Somme, for example, was not just Robertson and Haig; it was also Captain Jones, Sergeant Campbell and Private Atkins. The strategic air offensive against Germany was not just Churchill, Portal and Harris; it was also Flight Lieutenant Milne, Flying Officer Pyle, Sergeant Sneddon and Flying Officer Frankland. Moreover, as I kept a diary at the time and have preserved several of my navigator's logs and charts, my flying log-book and many of the letters which I wrote to my parents, I have various means of checking my memory, which I have now understood would often have been distinctly inaccurate without them. Thus my account is primary evidence of how one crew in Bomber Command operated and, in greater detail, it reveals something of my part in that under-taking. What then are the historically interesting main points that emerge?

First, it will have been noticed how little I have said about the targets to which I directed my crew. This is because at the time I knew little about them. In those days, a target to me was a latitude and a longitude and a precise time of the night, or occasionally the day. Naturally, I knew the difference between an area-attack on a great German city and a precise blow at an installation in France, Belgium or Holland, but I made no moral distinction between them. A German target was generally a more arduous undertaking than a French one, if only because it usually involved a longer flight and more intensive flak barrages. A French target, on the other hand, could be fully as dangerous as a German one in terms of the main threat, that is, the German night-fighters. In addition, the care which had to be taken to restrict French casualties to an absolute minimum, did involve greater risks in the target area, such as flying lower and staying longer, as I have said. I did not see these as moral differences. They seemed only to be distinctions between what was obviously due to the Germans, on the one hand, and the French, on the other. Nor, half a century later, do I see this issue differently. In other words, there seemed – and there still seems – to me to be no moral ground on which the Germans should have been, or could expect to have been, treated in the same way as the French.

The area-bombing offensive against German cities originated in the inability of Bomber Command at that time to hit anything smaller. Its aim was the dislocation of the industrial, economic and military foundations that lay beneath the German war effort. The fact that it involved the killing of German civilians, including women and children, has to be considered in the context of the German war effort and the need for Britain to find some means of diminishing it. This issue is similar to that involved in the naval blockade of Germany and Austria in the First World War, which, incidentally, involved the starvation of civilians to much the same extent as area-bombing was later to involve killing them. If the choice was between allowing Hitler's war effort to develop unhindered towards a Nazi victory and undertaking the area-bombing offensive, the moral issue seems clear. As this was the choice after the fall of France in 1940 and the subsequent expulsion of the British army from the continent, the moral issue does appear to be uncomplicated.

The argument that area-bombing was immoral because later historical analysis, much of it my own, showed that it was less effective than had been hoped and that it absorbed a greater part of the Bomber Command effort than was strategically desirable after the means of making more precise attacks became available, carries no real conviction. Decisions about what to do in war can only be based upon the evidence available at the time and upon a consensus of those chiefly responsible. Among the latter, it is true, there were severe differences of opinion, especially with regard to the question of whether or not at least part of the effort devoted to the general area-attack on German cities should be diverted to more selective targets, such as, for example, oil plants, which – when the conditions were right – Bomber Command had the operational capacity to destroy in the later stages of the war. This, however, was not a moral dissension; it was a dispute about what would be most effective in speeding up the defeat of Nazi Germany and it was dependent on how the intelligence coming to hand was construed. To claim that one side or the other was morally right or wrong in the dispute is beside the point.

Looking back upon my part in the bombing offensive, and in particular the area-attacks on German cities in which I took part, I have no doubt that, in the light of what was then known and what was possible, there is no need for regret. As the subsequent historian of the campaign, I take a somewhat different view. That, however, arises from historical judgements of strategy and tactics and it is not a matter of morals.

The second historical point I make as a result of my war experience is about the unreliability of my memory and therefore probably of everyone else's. In writing my account in this chapter, I have constantly been surprised to find how different things were according to my records by comparison with what I remembered. I remembered being attacked by a German fighter as we were running out of the target area in Munich. In fact the attack came considerably later when we were at least 150 miles on the homeward journey from Munich. I remembered making an emergency landing at Tangmere after the St Leu D'Esserent raid. The record shows that we landed at Ford. In a conversation with my rear-gunner, Keith Sneddon, in January 1995, he remembered that we got lost on the way home from Schweinfurt. Actually we did on our return from Munich, but when I told him this I do not think he believed me. And so on. While it is well recognized that memoirs are un-reliable because of the prejudice of the authors, it is perhaps not so well understood that they are also liable to be highly inaccurate factually, even when prejudice is not involved.

Finally, I learnt from my war experience that the evidence of the eye-witness is unreliable, not only because it is inaccurate as to fact, but also because it is ignorant. It is not merely a question of the fog of war which often causes even the top commanders to have little or no idea of what is really happening; it is that the scale of things is too large and too terrible to be taken in.

These may seem to be elementary lessons, but for me they were a beginning.

CHAPTER TWO

Breaking into History

I returned to Oxford in October 1945 to complete my history degree, but between then and taking Schools, my final examinations, in November 1947 I did not spend much time thinking about the lessons of history I had learnt from my experiences during the war. I returned to conventional themes and became especially interested in diplomatic history in the eighteenth and nineteenth centuries. Among the books I read, Sir Charles Webster's two-volume study of Castlereagh's foreign policy impressed me as much as any. I thought that some day I might attempt a similar work on Carteret. The launching-pad for such a project seemed to be a fellowship at one of the Oxford colleges. J.R.H. Weaver, the President of my college, expected me to get a first-class degree; and so did Bert Goodwin, then a fellow of Jesus, who had tutored me in foreign history. As I was later to learn, my mediaeval tutor, Michael Maclagan, thought that I might have got a first had not the war interrupted my work and left me exhausted. These were charitable views, which I think were not shared by my principal tutor, R.B. Wernham. He expected me to be better at research than at writing essays for Schools and, at least as far as the latter point was concerned, he proved to be right.

Though I have since been surprised by the number of people who have landed fellowships on the basis of second-class degrees, some even going on to distinguished professorships, at the time I believed my second had ruled out an academic career. How could someone who did not wish to be a schoolmaster and who could not hope to be a don, become an historian? My wife and I who, after our sixteen wartime 'homes', had now settled in a house of our own near Oxford, spent a very gloomy Christmas and New Year as 1947 turned into 1948.

Suddenly an unexpected prospect arose. A vacancy for a narrator in the Air Historical Branch of the Air Ministry was advertised. Though I had never thought of being a military historian and despite advice that it would be foolish to take a job which was temporary, carried no pension and had little chance of developing into anything like a career, I applied. Towards the end of February, I was summoned to London to be interviewed. I reported at

Cornwall House, near Waterloo Bridge and had an inconsequential talk with some little grey men. They sent me on to King Charles Street, where I was received in his splendid office by the Librarian of the Air Ministry, who was also the Head of the Air Historical Branch. This was J.C. Nerney, who was a striking looking and powerfully built man. Everything was quite informal; indeed, during the interview, Chester Wilmot, then at the height of his fame, breezed in and talked about a broadcast he was to make on the anniversary of the foundation of the Royal Air Force on 1st April. I caught a glimpse of a new world and was deeply impressed. I was also delighted to find that Mr Nerney seemed to assume that I would be appointed. He spent most of the time talking about what I would be doing and hardly enquired as to my ability to do it.[1]

A somewhat agonizing five or six weeks then elapsed before one of the little grey men felt emboldened to declare that he was directed to offer me, subject to a probationary period of six months, a temporary non-pensionable appointment, subject to termination by one month's notice, and so on, and so on, as a narrator in the Air Historical Branch. I had got into the business of official military history.[2]

In the next twelve years or so, during which I pursued this career, I had ample opportunity, through the process of trial and error, to work up the techniques of research and writing that are required to deal with original documents in enormous quantities and harmonize the results. The eventual outcome was that I wrote a narrative of the evolution of Bomber Command in the last year of peace; a thesis on the planning of the bomber offensive and its contribution to German defeat in the Second World War, which gained for me the degree of DPhil at Oxford; and finally, as a joint author with Sir Charles Webster, the official history of the strategic air offensive against Germany in the Second World War, which was published in four volumes in 1961. Concurrently, I learnt much about the world of official history and, in particular, about the battles for survival which were imposed upon those who inhabited it and held to the principles of historical integrity. It was not, however, until 1994 and 1996, when I examined the voluminous files of the Cabinet Office and the Air Ministry, by then open for inspection in the Public Record Office, that I was able to see the whole picture. It proved to be a kaleidoscope of clashes between strength and weakness, decision and indecision, firmness and pliability, expediency and principle. There were battles between departments of state, and there were fierce and threatening attacks from some of the great figures of the Second World War.

It had long been foreseen that the most 'difficult' subjects in the scheme of the official military histories would be the war against Japan, because so much of it was so disastrous, and the strategic air offensive against Germany, because so much of it was so controversial. Of the two, the strategic air offensive gave substantially the more trouble. This was the campaign with which I – and after he joined the fray in 1950 – Sir Charles Webster, were concerned and it was we who were in the thickest of the gruelling battles.

When I joined the Air Historical Branch in 1948, such things were only on an uncertain and distant horizon. The principal task of the Branch was the production of factual narratives dealing with the various aspects of the war effort of the Royal Air Force. These had been started while the war was still in progress and, in those days, the narrators were mostly scholars of high academic standing who were for the time being serving as officers in the RAF. Among these was my tutor, R.B. Wernham. By the time I arrived these academics had been demobilized and had returned to their colleges. Their successors were for the most part a good deal less distinguished as scholars. Nevertheless, work on the narratives was proceeding apace. It was not intended that they should ever be published. They were designed to be the material on which the Cabinet Office official historians could draw for the air aspects of their work. There was a smaller but somewhat similar organization in the Admiralty, and a still smaller one in the War Office which for some reason, was administered by the Cabinet Office. Among these organizations, the Air Historical Branch, despite the loss of its best scholars, was pre-eminent. This was because J.C. Nerney was far and away the most imposing of the heads of the branches.

Before he was demobilized, R.B. Wernham had completed the greater part of the first volume of the bomber narratives, which he had entitled *The Pre-War Evolution of Bomber Command*. This elegantly written and impeccably scholarly study had in fact carried most aspects of the story up to 1938. The rest remained to be narrated, and there were a few loose ends to be tied. By one of those strokes of fortune which change one's life, this task was allotted to me. I was thus able to slide into original historical research with a masterly prelude in front of me written by my own former tutor.

I decided that I could not simply continue and complete Wernham's narrative. He had been carrying forward a large number of complex issues, some of which he had advanced further than others. Nerney left me a free hand and I used it to write, not a continuation of Wernham's narrative, but a supplement to it, which I entitled *The Last Year of Peace*. By the autumn of 1948 I had virtually written myself out of a job. Other narrators were beavering away on bomber narratives covering the war. The fact that much of this effort was devoted to the trees and very little to the wood did not mean that there was a place for me in the aftermath of *The Last Year of Peace*. The only hopeful thing was that Nerney seemed to be pleased with the quality of my work and he tended to send for me when the Air Staff asked awkward historical questions such as, why was Dresden bombed? Neither they nor he always liked my answers, but Nerney did show a surprisingly high degree of confidence in me as an historian.[3]

This gave me the confidence to suggest to him that I should undertake something beyond the scope of the standard factual narratives. I proposed that I should attempt an historical analysis of the intelligence upon which the bomber offensive had been based and that negotiations should be opened with Oxford to enable me to submit the result for the degree of DPhil.

As far as Nerney was concerned, my idea fell upon fertile ground. Following an initiative in October 1944, he had been investigating the possibility of associating the Air Historical Branch with Oxford and Cambridge in the hope of gaining academic authentication of the work done by his narrators and perhaps having some of it accepted as theses for doctorates in the Universities. In that quest, he was better placed than any of his colleagues in the Service Historical Branches, for only in his were professional historians employed. Indeed, at that time, Nerney had three established historians of high standing on his staff: namely, Squadron Leaders G.N. Clark, a fellow of Trinity College, Cambridge, R.B. Wernham, a fellow of Trinity College, Oxford, and A. Goodwin, a fellow of Jesus College, Oxford. He despatched Wernham to Oxford to make enquiries and, though some difficulties came to the surface such as how the secrecy of the material could be protected, the response was favourable. Thereafter, the impetus of the idea had got bogged down in a mire of bureaucratic nit-picking and by July 1945, in the absence of any work suitable to be considered as a thesis, the plan had ground to a halt.[4]

Nerney was very ambitious for the future of the Air Historical Branch and I was extremely worried about my immediate prospects as an historian. There was thus a coincidence of purpose between us and Nerney readily approved my proposal to write a narrative which would in fact be a thesis. He swept aside bureaucratic difficulties like the problem of secret documents finding their way to Oxford and indeed that of me, a civil servant, spending time in Oxford to meet the University's residence requirements. He immediately acceded to my request for his authority to show the work I had already done in the Air Historical Branch to Wernham and Goodwin so that they could speak with knowledge of it to the History Faculty in Oxford.[5]

This they duly did and the heavy guns represented by Professor Keith Feiling and Professor E.L. Woodward were fired in my favour. On 31st January 1949, armed with all the necessary Air Ministry approvals, I was formally admitted by the Secretary of Faculties at Oxford as a Probationer-Student for the degree of Bachelor of Letters. Six months later I was admitted as an Advanced Student and was on my way to the degree of Doctor of Philosophy.[6]

I now had the task of writing the thesis. Nerney's initial reactions to my plans were that they were too broad. He wanted the work to be 'absolutely clean cut to intelligence' and he feared that if I went into the question of the effects of the bomber offensive, I would be led into some 'very involved channels'. These, however, were exactly the channels into which I wished to be drawn and I had no illusions about the complexity of what I was proposing. I already knew enough to realize that there was no grammar of the subject of strategic bombing and hardly a vocabulary either, such as existed to guide naval and military historians. It was with these unknown or ill-defined questions that I wished to grapple. It was, therefore, very fortunate for me that Nerney suddenly executed a change of course which as a former navigator I put at 180 degrees. He now urged me to enlarge my scope so that I would in effect deal with virtually the whole subject of the bomber offensive except the actual bomber sorties, which he presumably thought would be adequately covered in the bomber narratives of the war years. Accordingly, I produced a revised synopsis of a much more ambitious thesis, which I entitled *The Planning of the Bombing Offensive in the Second World War and its Contribution to German Collapse*. In other words, the subject had developed into a study of the policies which lay behind the offensive and the extent to which they succeeded or failed.[7]

A thesis is not the same thing as a history, but Nerney made it clear to me that he thought that my thesis could become the foundation of the official history of the strategic air offensive, for which the Cabinet Office Chief Military Historian, Professor J.R.M. Butler, was – and for some time had been – seeking an author. Nerney told me that Butler had conceived the idea, put into his head I have little doubt by Nerney, that I should be appointed to be that author provided Wernham, as an historian of proven standing, would collaborate in some manner with me. After all, I was twenty-seven and had not yet published anything.[8]

Butler had already made two attempts to attract Wernham into his team of official historians and twice Wernham had declined. In November 1947 he had told Butler that he had had about as much of air history as he could bear, and that he had neither the time nor the inclination to resume it. In February 1949 Butler nevertheless returned to the charge. He told Wernham that he had failed to find a suitable author for the volumes to be written on the strategic air offensive. He observed that this was a very important and controversial subject. The author would have to deal with points on which Britain and America, the RAF and the other Services, and Fighter and Bomber Commands, had been at variance. The subject therefore had to be approached from an independent standpoint by, if one could be found, a trained historian. If such an historian also understood the RAF background, that would be an immense advantage. Would Wernham reconsider? No, he would not, was the answer.[9]

And so Nerney and Butler came to what proved to be the last card in their bid to recruit Wernham. 'The other day,' Butler wrote to Wernham on 19th May 1949, 'Nerney brought Frankland to talk, and I learnt that he was working under your supervision on a PhD thesis concerned with the Bombing Offensive.' He went on to suggest that Wernham and I might write the volumes as joint authors, the inference being that Wernham would lend his authority and that I would do the lion's share of the work. At least, Butler said, this would greatly reduce the amount of work Wernham would have had to do if he had been the sole author. Butler said he would call on Wernham in Oxford on Saturday 28th May. No one seems to have deposited a record of what happened at this meeting but, looking back after the lapse of nearly forty-six years, Wernham felt that he had a 'reasonably clear memory' of it. He was surprised and annoyed by Butler's persistence and said as much 'very bitterly indeed'. The meeting was over almost before it had begun.[10]

To me, Wernham's decision was a severe disappointment: it seemed to foreclose my chances of writing the official history of the strategic air offensive. In the event, however, it did not, and, as disappointments often are, it proved to be another stroke of fortune for me. Wernham, as he obviously himself appreciated, was far more suited to the pure academic life of Oxford, where he later became the Professor of Modern History, than to the rough and tumble of the official history of the strategic air offensive. Sir Charles Webster, though much less versed in the subject than Wernham – which incidentally was to lead to my having much greater scope – was altogether a more appropriate choice. But this was a development which was still some distance away in the future. Even at the time of Wernham's final refusal, however, the problem of finding an author for this controversial subject already had a considerable history of its own. To understand the position in which Webster and I were presently to find ourselves, it is now necessary to examine this history.

From the outset of the war there was the intention that an official history should be written. The War Cabinet set up a sub-committee known as the Committee for the Control of Official Histories, and it was for the consideration of this body that a paper was presented on 8th October 1941. With regard to military histories, it indicated that the plan should be to write about the war from an inter-service point of view, and that the scheme should be divided into two parts, one consisting of 'key' volumes dealing with the strategy of the war, and the other dealing with campaigns in all theatres covering the activities of the three services. Thus, the plan for the histories of the First World War, which dealt with matters under service divisions, was rejected. In this last respect, the paper represented a step forward but in another it took one backward. The distinction between strategy and campaigns was an historically unworkable one, if only because campaigns dictate strategy at least as much as strategy does campaigns. The Committee for the Control of Official Histories, though, was not likely to have much constructive thought to offer on such matters. It consisted of top civil servants whose idea of history is usually confined to the need for it not to cause controversy, or to reveal who did what. Nothing much happened beyond the Chairman, R.A. Butler, who was President of the Board of Education, throwing out the idea in September 1943 that his cousin, J.R.M. Butler, might be used in connection with the military histories, especially as he was at the time doing a rather dreary job in MI5. This idea at least did eventually bear some fruit, as we already know.[11]

The kick-start for the official military histories did not come from R.A. Butler or his Committee but from an unexpected quarter and a thoroughly unhistorical one at that, namely the great Air Force personage, Lord Trenchard. Returning from a tour of the Middle East in November 1942, Trenchard was moved to suggest the immediate appointment of an official air historian, who would then be able 'to imbibe by personal contact with the Air Force and its Commanders something of the spirit of the RAF'. He reproached himself for not having caused this to be done in the First War and hoped that, by correcting that mistake, a 'dry as dust' textbook which nobody but the Germans would want to read, could be avoided. Trenchard had just read Arthur Bryant's book on Charles II: he liked it and thought Bryant would be an excellent choice for the job.[12]

Lord Trenchard, to use his own phrase of an earlier date, was 'not good at writing. I cannot,' he added, 'set out my ideas in nice order.' These had usually been conveyed by word of mouth and transcribed by others. In this case, it fell to C.G. Caines, a Principal Assistant Secretary in the Air Ministry and Nerney's immediate boss, to discharge the role. Reporting to Sir Edward Bridges, the Secretary of the Cabinet and the principal member of the Committee for the Control of Official Histories, Caines said that there might be some confusion in Trenchard's mind as to the character of history and the aims the Committee had. All the same, he advised, it might be as well to take some forward steps in good time. This introduced Mr (later Sir) Norman Brook to the scene. Brook, at the time, was Deputy Secretary (Civil) of the War Cabinet, and it was to him that Bridges now turned for advice. Brook thought that the first step should be the selection of a chief historian under whose direction the various volumes could then be written by service officers. There was no need to trouble Bryant. Bridges agreed.[13]

General Sir Ronald Adam, the Adjutant General of the Forces, a man of refined taste and much enlightenment, was now consulted. He thought that General Wavell might agree to be the chief historian. This was, perhaps, a rather over-optimisitic idea, but Wavell had been removed from his

command in the Middle East and relegated to India by Churchill, and he was
also regarded as a particularly scholarly kind of soldier. A story used to
circulate that when Wavell was a school boy at Winchester and his father,
Major-General A.G. Wavell, told his housemaster that he intended his boy
to enter the Army, the housemaster assured him that there was no need for
that as young Wavell was really quite intelligent. Though Wavell did not
reject Adam's suggestion, he was unwilling to commit himself. In the outcome, he became Viceroy of India instead, and died in 1950.[14]

In Wavell's wake, the civil service converted Trenchard's initiative into a
slow rumble, but the direction was on the whole forward. Some preliminary
narratives began to be written and lists of candidates for the position of chief
military historian, as well as of possible authors for the histories, came under
consideration. In July 1946, G.N. Clarke declined an invitation from Sir
Edward Bridges to be chief historian. Meanwhile, a Treasury official, A.J.D.
Winnifrith, suddenly recalled R.A. Butler's idea of some years earlier that his
cousin, J.R.M. Butler, might be of some use. Within virtually no time at all,
the latter was offered and accepted the post of Chief Military Historian. By
October 1946, he had taken up the cudgels.[15]

J.R.M. Butler was a fellow of Trinity College, Cambridge; his father had
been Master of the College; and he was later to be its Vice-Master. His cousin,
R.A. Butler, after narrowly failing to become Prime Minister, was at present
the Master of Trinity. His brother, Nevile, was shortly to become the British
Ambassador to Brazil. In the following year, Butler himself was to be
appointed Regius Professor of Modern History in the University of
Cambridge. In 1920, when the future King George VI and his younger
brother, the future Duke of Gloucester, went up to Cambridge briefly as
undergraduates at Trinity, Butler was one of those selected to teach them.
He had written some notable books, including especially *The Passing of the
Great Reform Bill*. He was well connected, distinguished, able and safe. He
was also modest, refined and patient. He was not the sort of man to whom
it was easy to say anything unpleasant, unless one was Sir Charles Webster,
who could say more or less anything to more or less anybody.[16]

With the Chief Historian in place, it was now possible to map out a plan
for the official histories, appoint the authors and set the programme in
motion. There were, however, a number of difficulties, one of which was that
Butler initially showed himself to be substantially at sea as regards a sensible
overall plan. Had he not been so, how could he have proposed, as he did on
5th December 1946, that for a series which he knew was supposed to be
written from an inter-service point of view, there should be separate volumes
– one for Fighter Command including the Battle of Britain and another for
the Defence of the United Kingdom, or, to give a second instance, one volume
for naval operations in the Mediterranean, a second one for the Western

Desert and North Africa to Alamein, a third for North Africa from November 1942 to May 1943, and a fourth for the RAF in the Middle East? Nor would he have included, under the heading of campaigns, a volume entitled Bomber Command. He also displayed a marked degree of diffidence. As he was a civilian, he wondered how to ensure that the histories 'shall be in conformity with the best technical knowledge and opinion.' He wanted a Panel of service officers to be formed to advise him on the layout of the histories and on how proper connections could be maintained between the parts played by the three services. These officers, he thought, must possess the confidence of the official heads of their services; they would advise on the selection of authors and would read and comment on the drafts of the histories. It could be inferred from this that the official histories would be written to accord with the official views of the service departments and that, to a considerable extent, the divisions between them would be the divisions between the three services.[17]

Some amendment was made in January 1947 at a meeting summoned by Sir Edward Bridges when Butler met officials of the service departments. Among the changes agreed was that the volume on Bomber Command should become one on the strategic air offensive, which was rather a different thing. A further and marked advance was made when Major-General Sir Ian Jacob, having unofficially appointed himself to Butler's Panel, re-wrote the plan of the histories in a far more appropriate style. The path to the appointment of authors was now open, but here again there was a difficulty, indeed an awkwardness.[18]

Air Chief Marshal Sir Douglas Evill had been looking forward to an interesting and reasonably lucrative second career on his retirement from the RAF, which was to be in 1947. In January of that year he was, or thought he was, offered the job of official RAF Historian by Sir John Slessor, who at the time was Air Member for Personnel, and who three years later was to become Chief of the Air Staff. Writing to Sir Edward Bridges in March 1947, Evill said that Slessor had told him that he would shortly be receiving a formal offer from the Cabinet Office. This caused some consternation and the more so when it transpired that it was not simply an indiscretion on the part of Sir John Slessor but the product of an official sounding made by the Air Ministry with the approval of Sir Edward Bridges. The situation was made worse by a meeting of the Chiefs of Staff Committee with Butler. The top men did not attend but the Air Force point of view was expressed by the Vice-Chief of the Air Staff, Sir William Dickson. Butler had explained that he had no experience of military matters and that he would therefore want a Panel of service experts to advise him. Dickson said that Evill would be their man for this purpose, but he added that Evill should also 'assume in addition the responsibility for concentrating on the preparation of the air subjects to be contributed to the joint history'. Doing this and being a member of Butler's Panel would, Dickson said, be a full-time job. According to the minute of this meeting, Butler not only accepted but welcomed Sir William Dickson's proposal.[19]

In the Cabinet Office, it was seen that things had rather gone off the rails. If the members of Butler's Panel were to be employed full-time and if, in addition to advising Butler, they were also to write portions of the official histories, they might well prove to be a hindrance rather than a help. Who would know whether they could write or not, or whether they had any of the qualifications 'of a good historian'? If, however, they were employed as was now envisaged, Butler would be 'virtually compelled to accept their work for publication'. There was also the consideration that substantial salaries would be involved, which would be beyond the means of the fund granted to the Cabinet Office for historical purposes. Perhaps Butler could be persuaded that the full-time employment of these senior officers was not a good idea. If he could, then the search for authors with the qualifications 'of a good historian' would have to continue. If he could not, at least the search for someone to write the history of the strategic air offensive would be over: Sir Douglas Evill would write it and presumably the history of everything else the RAF had done in the war. Butler had not been much of a success so far.[20]

The key man now – as he was to remain throughout my connection with official history – was Sir Norman Brook, who had by this time succeeded Sir Edward Bridges as Secretary of the Cabinet. He sent for Butler and told him that it was 'inadvisable' that the members of his Panel should write the histories. Their job should be to read and criticize drafts and advise Butler. Butler still thought that members of the Panel should do some writing, but he now seemed to think that this might be no more than an occasional chapter. He also withdrew from the position he had endorsed at the Chiefs of staff meeting and agreed with Brook that Evill could not be the author of the 'air portions' of the official history. All the same, he might make some 'written contribution'. To get over the difficulty of the offers made to Evill, Brook thought that he might be employed by the Cabinet Office half-time as a member of Butler's Panel and half-time by the Air Ministry to write monographs.[21]

This ploy was rejected out of hand by the Air Ministry in the person of C.G. Caines. Moreover, the latter launched a strong counter-attack. Caines told Brook that Evill wanted to play a part in writing the air history and that the idea had been put to him as long ago as 1944 by Sir Archibald Sinclair, who was then the Secretary of State for Air. Evill had come to think of this work as his first choice of job on his retirement. He was not interested in part-time work and in any case the Air Ministry had no place for him in the writing of monographs, nor did their narratives need editing. He should be employed full-time by the Cabinet Office to write the air history. Brook agreed, subject to Butler 'freely' deciding to appoint Evill as the first of his authors, and he said he would arrange a meeting between the two men.[22]

At this juncture, with the fate of the history of the strategic air offensive hanging in the balance, D.F. Hubback, who was the Secretary of the Committee for the Control of Official Histories, happened to meet a Mr Mackenzie at lunch. Mackenzie had been Evill's Personal Assistant while the latter was Head of the RAF Delegation in Washington during the war. So Hubback took the opportunity of asking whether Evill could write. Mackenzie said he was certainly literate, that he was a 'careful and meticulous writer whose style of writing was more suited to detailed staff study rather than a general history intended for the educated public'. Hubback passed this intelligence on to S.E.V. Luke, who was a senior member of Brook's staff, and whom the latter now despatched to Cambridge to talk Evill over with Butler.[23]

Whether it was because the academic setting of Trinity College contrasted so sharply with the military one of the Chiefs of Staff Committee and the official one of the Cabinet Office, or simply that he had begun to think, Butler had undergone a complete change of mind. He said that, though he would be happy to meet Evill, this would not be a basis on which he could decide whether or not Evill was a good historian. Taking the bit between his teeth, he declared that he hoped he would be given free scope in choosing his authors and that he did not want one 'foisted on him by the Air Ministry in this way'. He added that he thought the selected historian should be impartial and that it would be a mistake to employ someone who had been involved in the campaign. Luke thought that if the Air Ministry agreed to nominate another for membership of the Panel, then the Panel and Butler might agree to 'acquiesce' with the Air Ministry's view of Evill as the air historian. Butler rather curiously agreed to this, but he added that he had recently had a talk with Lord Tedder, the Chief of the Air Staff, who was later to become Chancellor of Cambridge University. Tedder had promised Butler that he would be willing to help if difficulties arose in connection with the official histories. Butler told Luke that this was a 'card which might be played if all else failed'. Clearly Butler did not mean Evill to be employed as the air historian, but the Air Ministry were not done yet.[24]

When Luke explained to Caines how matters now stood, Caines told him that the Air Ministry would not put forward an alternative name as their nominee on the Panel, nor would they withdraw their demand that Evill should also be employed full-time as the air historian. 'In despair', Luke said that Butler would talk the matter over with Lord Tedder, but Caines simply welcomed this and said that Tedder's view would coincide with his own.

Only to a very limited extent, however, did this prove to be the case. Butler and Tedder met on 7th May 1947. Butler explained the Evill situation. Tedder agreed that the Air Ministry's Panel member and the author of the air history should not be the same man and he did not press Evill's appointment as one of the historians. On the other hand, he thought that Evill was well suited to be the Air Ministry's representative on the Panel, which he combined with the rather difficult assertion that Evill would need to be employed full-time. Butler said that he thought that whoever wrote the air portions of the histories should not himself have been concerned with the war-time events, especially as they were so controversial. Tedder agreed, but said that Evill had not played a leading part and that he had as an outstanding characteristic 'independence of mind and honesty'. Butler's Tedder card had not quite done the trick, but he had won the game all the same. Evill now accepted appointment as the Air Ministry's representative on the Panel without the added one of being an official air historian. The other services made no difficulties: Vice-Admiral Sir Geoffrey Blake was appointed to represent the Admiralty, and General Sir Henry Pownall the War Office. Sir Ian Jacob's self-appointment was officially confirmed with the condition that he sat in a personal capacity.[25]

Butler now settled rather more firmly in the driving seat. In September, he told the Panel that, though they were the representatives of their respective service departments, with which they should maintain close liaison, they must advise him on the basis of their personal opinions, and that they must maintain an impartial and independent position. He felt that the authors should, if possible, be independent civilians of good academic standing rather than service specialists. If, for example, the volume on the strategic air offensive were to be written by an airman, it might be criticized as biased and, if by a soldier, as uninformed and biased from another angle. The door was thus slammed on Evill's prospects as an official historian and he shortly withdrew from the Panel to do a quite different kind of job. He was replaced on the Panel by Air Chief Marshal Sir Guy Garrod. The hunt for an author for the volume, or volumes, on the strategic air offensive was on – and this brings us back to the point at which Butler sought, as I have already described, to recruit Wernham and possibly me too. Evill I never met, but I have in my mind's eye absolutely clear pictures of Professor Butler, Lord Tedder and Sir Guy Garrod. Curiously, though I had many dealings with him over a number of years, I have no recollection of Sir Norman Brook, later Lord Normanbrook. Maybe this has something to do with the anonymity of civil servants.[26]

On 17th February 1949, Sir Guy Garrod who, as I have just mentioned, had succeeded Sir Douglas Evill on Butler's Panel, submitted to the Panel six names as possible authors of the volumes on the strategic air offensive. They were those of T.D. Weldon, a fellow of Magdalen College, Oxford, who had served on Harris's staff at High Wycombe during the war; Professor W.J.M. Mackenzie, a former fellow of Magdalen recently appointed to the Chair of Government in Manchester University; P. Johnson, who was also a former fellow of Magdalen and Lecturer in Natural Science, and who had just been appointed Director of Studies at the Royal Air Force College, Cranwell; W.W. Rostow, an American, who was about to take up the Pitt Chair of American History at Cambridge; Professor C.H.M. Waldock, the Chichele Professor of International Law at Oxford; and finally mine. Had I known at the time that I was in this distinguished company, I would have been flattered indeed. The Panel concluded that none of these candidates had the 'necessary qualifications and at the same time was likely to be able to give adequate time to the work'. In my case, as I certainly had the time, it must have been the lack of qualification which was the difficulty. This was fortunate for me, for though I would readily have accepted the appointment if it had been offered to me, I doubt, knowing as I now do the battles which lay ahead, whether I, as a sole and unknown author, would have survived, or rather whether my book would have done so. Butler did not, however, quite follow the Panel's advice; he wrote to Professor Waldock and invited him to undertake the work, which he said would be controversial and difficult and he thought Waldock would probably not want to do. In this, he was right. Waldock did not.[27]

Butler had always had F.H. Hinsley, a fellow of St John's College Cambridge, in mind as one of his historians, but he began to wonder if he might be suitable for the strategic air offensive. He consulted the Master of the College, E.A. Benians. Benians thought not, though he felt it necessary to explain that he did not think that Hinsley was unsuited to be an official historian, only that he would be unsuited to be that of the strategic air offensive. Though Hinsley did later write the official history of British intelligence in the Second World War and, incidentally, in time became the Master of St John's, Butler again had to look elsewhere for an historian of the strategic air offensive. He invited Frank Thistlethwaite to do the job. He was another fellow of St John's and, during his war-time service in the RAF, had been seconded for duty in the Cabinet Office. He said he was very tempted but was too deeply engaged with an Anglo-American social history.[28]

It was becoming increasingly clear that academic historians, or even academics of different disciplines, were not keen to write the history of the strategic air offensive. Other ideas came into play, but Air Marshal Sir Douglas Collyer did not wish to be considered, and T.C. James, who was a rising man in the Air Ministry, was rejected on the grounds that taking time off to write this history would damage his career. And so Butler was driven to his final assault on Wernham in conjunction with myself, the outcome of

which we already know. At the same time, indeed on the same day, he was
also stalking another horse. This was C.E. Carrington, of the Cambridge
University Press. Carrington had won the MC in the First World War and,
though this was irrelevant and not mentioned by Butler, he had written a
brilliant account of his experiences, *A Subaltern's War*, which he had published under the pen name of Charles Edmonds in 1929. In the Second World
War, Carrington had been the Army liaison officer at Bomber Command
Headquarters from 1941 to 1943. From then until 1944 he had been GSO
1 (General Staff Officer) in the Air Directorate of the War Office. He told
Butler that he was a friend of Air Marshal Saundby, who had been Deputy
Commander-in-Chief, under Harris, of Bomber Command. Carrington
thought that he would not be *persona grata* with the RAF but he considered
that he could write an objective history of the strategic air offensive. Butler
believed that he was not academically in the highest class, but he felt that he
could do the job, provided someone checked that he kept his 'proportion'
right. At least, among all those Butler had so far approached, Carrington
alone was not only willing but keen to undertake the 'difficult' subject.[29]

Sir Ian Jacob, who at this stage was Director of Overseas Services at the
BBC, in addition to being a member of Butler's Panel, knew George Barnes,
who was Head of the Third Programme. George Barnes knew Carrington
well. Jacob now told Butler that Barnes was sure that Carrington would write
a first-rate history but that he could not control the expression of his views
whenever anyone disagreed with them. Barnes thought that if Carrington's
history did not carry conviction among the airmen and if the latter did not
like it, there would be 'ructions'. Jacob thought that it would be better to
use Carrington for some other subject. This was enough to put Butler off,
which was ultimately to prove extremely ironical, but he evidently failed to
trouble Carrington with his decision. Four months later the latter wrote to
Butler that he supposed nothing had come of their discussion earlier in the
year, and that he would be glad if Butler would now return to him some
papers he had written and had lent to Butler in connection with his candidature for the authorship of the strategic air offensive volumes. This induced
Butler to tell him, by telephone or in conversation it seems, that he had not
been thought acceptable in 'air circles'. Carrington was very disappointed
and he hoped that his Bomber Command friends did not regard him as their
adversary, which, he asserted, he was not. As to the papers which Carrington
had lent to Butler, Butler was almost sure that he had put them through the
letter box at the main door of the Cambridge University Press in Trumping-
ton Street. He seems to have known the Press well because he thought they
might still be there.[30]

I think this may have been the case, for Charles Carrington was the only
candidate for the work I eventually did with Sir Charles Webster – apart from

James, who was later a Trustee of the Imperial War Museum – whom I ever met. When I did meet him some seven years after his brush with Butler, he showed me the papers in question. So, by one means or another, he had got them back. By that time Carrington was the Professor of Commonwealth Relations at Chatham House, where I was the Deputy Director of Studies and well advanced towards the completion of the official history of the strategic air offensive. We became life-long friends and I appreciated his old fashioned and at times slightly absurd attitude to affairs, which was perhaps exemplified by the amount of effort he devoted to the study of Rudyard Kipling. He could certainly write with sparkle and conviction and the fact that, as George Barnes had said, he was prone to anger when disagreements arose, was by no means necessarily a disqualification for writing the history of the strategic air offensive. All the same, I am convinced that he could not have done it and that Butler was right, if for the wrong reasons, to drop him. Carrington never mentioned to me that he had been in contention for the job and he wrote a generous review of the work that Sir Charles Webster and I produced.

If Butler had rejected Carrington because he thought he might cause 'ructions', he was in the end to find that he had jumped from the frying pan into the fire. If, on the other hand, he had turned away from him because he thought he was not academically in the first class, he next took a most extraordinary step. After a brief flirtation with the curious idea that Sir John Slessor, who was shortly to become Chief of Air Staff, might write the volumes, which, of course, he would not, Butler invited Hilary St George Saunders to do so. There were many good points about Saunders. He had done some interesting and distinguished things. He had won the MC in 1918. Afterwards he had served on the Secretariat of the League of Nations and, for a time, he had been Nansen's private secretary. He had written umpteen novels and, during the Second War, a number of morale-boosting publications on the Battle of Britain and other topics. He was now the Librarian of the House of Commons and was also employed by the Air Ministry to write the so-called popular history of the Royal Air Force in the Second World War, which he was doing in conjunction with Denis Richards, who, though subordinate, was a much better scholar. He was a charming and amusing conversationalist and wrote in a fluent if rather flowery style and did so at great speed. He was not unduly concerned with factual accuracy and had little or no idea of historical research.

And yet Butler's Panel had now decided that Saunders was the best man they could find to write the history of the strategic air offensive, which they all knew was a difficult and highly controversial subject. In October 1949, with the approval of Sir Norman Brook, Butler invited him to do so. Nor did Butler seem to be discouraged on being told by Saunders that his health was bad and that he would therefore be unable to give an answer until the following spring, or by the news that he was already committed to a biography of Trenchard. Nor were Butler or the Panel dismayed when Nerney told them that recruiting Saunders would involve paying specially high fees and allowing him royalties on the book, which none of the other authors received, and which the Stationery Office did not normally pay. Brook said he did not mind provided the Stationery Office did not. They did, but they were persuaded to allow it on the grounds of the special difficulty of getting an author for this subject and Saunders being the best possible one.[31]

At the beginning of 1950, Nerney was despatched to France, whither Saunders had withdrawn for the sake of his health, to negotiate on behalf of the Cabinet Office what, in comparison with the terms on which the other official historians worked, was an exceptionally generous contract. He returned with the news that Saunders accepted provisionally. He said he would make a definite decision in the spring when his state of health would be clearer, if the offer was then renewed. Nerney inferred that Saunders was not a good bet and A.B. Acheson, the Secretary of the Cabinet Office Historical Section, told Brook that it would be advisable to look for an alternative author.[32]

At the time, I had no idea that Saunders had been offered the chance to write the official history of the strategic air offensive and if I had been told that he was even being considered, I would not have believed it. I think that Nerney had his doubts too. At any rate, by March 1950 he began consulting me anxiously about the quality of Saunders's work on the popular history. My reports cannot have done much to improve Nerney's morale. Saunders's wish for blood and guts had, I pointed out, carried him far out of his depth. Meanwhile Butler, weathercock-wise, swung away from this playboy of a historian and back towards one of high academic standing: he offered G.N. Clark, who had now become the Provost of Oriel College, Oxford, the 'Wernham' formula, namely, that he should write the history in some form of collaboration with me. Clark replied that strategic bombing was among three subjects from which, in about a year's time, he would make the choice for his next book. He undertook to tell Butler if he could think of anyone else who might be harnessed with me for the purpose. I was told nothing of this and nothing came of it. Clark, who had been a war-time narrator in the Air Historical Branch and had turned down the subsequent offer of appointment as Chief Military Historian, now disappeared from this scene. So did Hilary St George Saunders.[33]

By this stage, I had virtually completed the writing of my thesis, *The Planning of the Bombing Offensive in the Second World War and its Contribution to German Collapse*. I thought then, and I still do, that I had in this work discovered the meaning of the subject, placed it in the context of general military history, measured its qualities and defects and assessed the contribution it had made to Germany's downfall, both directly and indirectly. Again I thought then, and I still do, that I had virtually created for myself a corner in the subject. More to the point, Nerney thought much the same. He congratulated me warmly and, though I had yet to submit my thesis at Oxford for its formal reward, he showed it to Butler and talked freely about it in the circles that influenced the selection of official historians. Nerney even had the idea of pre-empting the Cabinet Office official history of the subject by publishing a revised and extended version of it.[34]

Such was my position when in May 1950 an economic historian, Professor M. Postan, who was writing one of the official civil histories, had the bright idea that Butler might try to persuade Professor Sir Charles Webster to undertake the official history of the strategic air offensive. On 19th May, Butler wrote to Webster, whom he had known since they were under-graduates at Cambridge, and invited him to do so. Butler said that the subject was among the most difficult to write and that it was also very important from the point of view of the effect it would have on future policy. It was considered, he said, that this history should be written 'not only by someone possessed of the necessary judgement and experience in the weighing of evidence but by someone whose name carries authority. If there were anyone who combined these qualifications with first-hand experience of air-fighting, that would be ideal; but years of search have produced no such person...' The Panel thought that it was more important to have an 'historian of authority without air experience than an airman whose name would not carry weight as an historian'. He concluded with the observation that an 'important consideration is that the assistance on the technical side could probably be provided by a young ex-bomber-pilot (sic) who is now working in the Air Ministry for an Oxford DPhil on an aspect of this subject'. Webster replied promptly saying that he was about to attend a conference in Florence and would not be able to consider the matter fully until after his return. He wrote, however, that he was attracted by the idea and said that he would welcome contact with airmen and their machines. He presumed that some flying would be required of the historian. There was much to make him hesitate. 'When I write about diplomacy,' he said, 'I at least know something about it at first hand.' He feared that he might not be able to master the technical side and he also believed that an economist would be more fitted to judge the effects of the bombing on Germany.[35]

From Nerney, I immediately got wind of this invitation and of the initial response to it. I was greatly excited by the news; I had not met Sir Charles Webster but, as I have remarked earlier, I much admired his work. It had a degree of detail about it and a contact with the original sources which I had so often felt was lacking in the works of other historians. I knew that he knew nothing about bombing, but I felt that I did, and I foresaw that my understanding allied to his eminence would be the experience of a lifetime. In this expectation I was not to be disappointed, but had I known at the time that Butler had put me forward as no more than a technical advisor, I would not have been so pleased. If Nerney knew this, he did not tell me; he led me to believe that, if Webster accepted, I would be a joint author to set his aims at their lowest. And when it came to the test, he was as good as his word.

In the meantime, Butler wrote to Webster saying that the Panel had noted his hesitation but thought it was not fatal. Postan, he said, thought that an economic advisor would overcome the problem of assessing the effects of the bombing on Germany and Nerney believed that so much preparatory work had already been done that Webster would be able to complete his task within two years. Webster began to look closely at the possibilities and, on 6th July 1950, he met Garrod and Nerney at lunch to talk things over. 'What amazing vitality Webster has!' Garrod wrote to Butler. He made it clear that the Panel wanted him and Webster had undertaken to think it over. He said he had more to write than he had years in which to do it. Butler, who had had lunch with Webster the day before, hoped that the answer would be yes. The matter still hung in the balance.[36]

Then on 31st July came the break-through. After much thought, Webster had decided to accept Butler's invitation. He warned him that he might not be as successful as he expected, but he felt it was his duty to 'attempt the task'. He said he was as busy as he had ever been in his life. He was Professor of International History at the London School of Economics and one of his colleagues there, P.A. Reynolds, had recently left to take up a Chair at Aberystwyth, so that an extra load of work devolved upon him. He was President of the British Academy and he was beginning to receive the proofs of his latest book, *The Foreign Policy of Palmerston*, which like its earlier companion, *The Foreign Policy of Castlereagh*, was about to come out in two volumes. He would thus not be able to do much work on the strategic air offensive for about a year. This did not disturb the Panel. They decided to recommend that an official appointment should be given to Webster.[37]

Butler, who a few days earlier had re-equipped himself with the latest version of my thesis, now summoned me to his room in the Cabinet Office. My wife and I were staying with her mother in Eastbourne, but we were naturally more than delighted to drive up to London to keep the appointment. It was Saturday 12th August. Butler told me that Webster had accepted his invitation to write the history of the strategic air offensive and that it was proposed that I should cooperate with him in the venture. He then handed me over to the administrative head of the Historical Section, A.B. Acheson, and told me to talk about money. As, however, Butler, had not made clear what shape my cooperation would take, we could make only limited progress on this front. I noted at the time that Butler seemed to be 'an inherently pleasant man' and Acheson, 'though courteous enough', I judged to be 'exactly the reverse'. The next step, obviously, was for Webster to get a sight of me, and this was arranged for 17th August, when I was again summoned to Butler's room. My wife and I drove onto Horse Guards Parade in very good time for the meeting at 2.30. As in those days there was no difficulty in parking there, my wife would wait in the car while I had the interview. Meanwhile, we both waited. Presently we saw Acheson 'escorting an elderly man with baggy grey flannel trousers & an uncommonly large hat into the Ministry of Defence entrance'. This, as we at once surmised, was Sir Charles Webster. I followed him in and came to Butler's room. There was Butler, Sir Charles Webster and Acheson and before us, resting on a table, was a copy of my thesis. It seemed, however, that only Butler had read any of it and he had so far confined himself to the concluding pages and the bibliography. I was in no sense examined and all I noted was that the conversation was entertaining and, so far as I could judge, satisfactory. I came away with the conviction that I had 'got a job and a position of some eminence'. Its precise nature and the degree of its eminence were, however, still to be settled, and that remained the position for several months to come.[38]

One of the hazards that confronted me, as I well knew, was the attitude of A.B. Acheson, but it was not until forty-five years later that I discovered that this particular difficulty had a funny side. After I had left the meeting, Webster told Butler and Acheson that he would be glad to have my help with the book if the necessary arrangements could be made. He had not yet read my thesis so he could hardly have been expected to commit himself further at this stage. Acheson, however, was anxious to show that there would be no difficulties about the arrangements. He said that I was prepared, and 'indeed anxious', to be associated in the preparation of the book and that I would be quite content to be paid at the same rate as I was earning in the Air Historical Branch, which was on a scale of £700 to £900 per annum. Nerney took exception to this. He said that my future prospects as an academic historian would be much affected by the status I was afforded in the partnership with Webster. He hoped that Webster might be prepared to accept me from the outset as a co-author whose name would appear as such on the title page. Acheson 'demurred'. He said that I did not attach any importance to my status in relation to Webster nor did I expect my name to appear on the title page. Nerney then said that Mr Frankland had probably given no thought to such matters and that he had an 'unworldly' attitude to questions of status and remuneration. Notwithstanding, he felt an obligation to watch over my interests. I must confess that when in 1995, in the reading

room of the Public Record Office, I came across this record by Acheson of
the exchange I could not help bursting into laughter. The sad truth is that I
had a distinctly worldly attitude to matters of status and remuneration. I am
glad to know, all the same, that the outcome was eventually settled by a
decision of Webster's, which was taken on academic grounds. Meanwhile,
my future continued to hang in the balance.[39]

This delay, which was to continue until May 1951, was very taxing to my
nerves but, as in the case of other apparent misfortunes that befell me, it
proved only to be a well disguised blessing. During these months, I bombarded Webster with memoranda and spoken explanations of the discoveries
I had made about the meaning of air power in general and of the strategic
bombing offensive in particular. I also warned him of many of the shoals
which would obstruct our voyage as official historians, if that, in the end,
proved to be the passage which we took. Though I almost blush now to recall
and see the record of how I lectured and hectored the great man, who had
eight times my experience and more than twice my years, he took kindly to
the experience, which he not only tolerated, but actively encouraged, and we
soon got onto very close terms. He also read attentively the whole of what
was virtually the final draft of my thesis and told me that, bearing in mind
the difficulties of the subject, he considered it was the best thesis he had ever
read. I felt honoured by the prospect of working with this eminent man and
he obviously and openly felt increasingly dependent upon me to do the work.
But there was still uncertainty as to whether our already close and excellent
relationship would develop into a fruitful partnership.[40]

The doubt and the delay was caused by the shoals of which I had warned
Webster. These concerned the freedom or otherwise with which the official
military historians were to be allowed to write. Butler had acquiesced in a
number of restrictions and allowed doubts to arise about others, which
Webster and I felt were unacceptable. These included some crippling clauses,
such as, for example, that the published histories would not include any
references to unpublished sources and that quotations from Cabinet or
Cabinet Committee minutes, including those of the Chiefs of Staff, were
'deprecated'. After Webster and I had discussed these and other restrictions,
he wrote to Butler politely but firmly objecting to several of them. He
accepted, of course, that direct quotation which would compromise current
cyphers was out of the question, but he also stressed the importance of a
measure of direct quotation. He said that if the histories contained no
references to unpublished sources, they would 'fail to serve any very useful
purpose'. As to the rule that the anonymity of civil servants must be preserved, he remarked that he did not expect that it would often be necessary
to mention them but, when it was, he did not see why they should be afforded
a protection that was denied to commanders in the field. He was disconcerted

by the inference that in the event of there being differences of opinion about the histories between the historians and civil servants, the views of the latter would prevail. He concluded by observing that he had thought he was joining a team of historians and that he had not intended to place himself 'under official direction'.[41]

These and other matters were to be discussed at a meeting of official military historians on 19th January 1951. Webster had decided not to attend it as he was not sure, he told me, what use of his letter – of which he had sent me a copy – Butler would make, and thought he might decide to confer with a smaller group in the first instance. Though I was not yet an official military historian, I was invited to attend this meeting. I remember it vividly. I described it at the time in my diary and I have the official minutes. Butler opened the proceedings with the rather characteristic statement that he did not intend any decisions to be reached. He told the meeting that he had a letter from Webster and said that he would reveal its contents as the discussion went on. A good deal of time was spent on matters of little immediate importance, such as how the maps were to be drawn, what colour the bindings of the volumes would be and how place-names were to be spelt. At length, however, some of the 'Webster issues' came before the meeting. Butler said that Webster had stated in his letter that the disclosure of differences of opinion in the Chiefs of Staff Committee would often be unavoidable. Everyone seemed to agree. All the same, Butler concluded that each historian should tell his story in the way that seemed best to him, and that 'if it was represented on grounds of public policy, that adjustments in a text prepared on this basis were desirable before it could be published, that would be a matter for discussion with the official authorities'. Webster and I were certainly well aware of what that would mean. Butler then revealed what Webster had said about not giving references to unpublished sources. Butler seemed to agree with what he had said, but some of the other historians at the meeting did not. The official minutes did not record their reasons but I remember one of them leaning across to me and whispering 'I say Frankland, what *is* a footnote?' This was Air Vice-Marshal S.E. Toomer, who was working in Major-General I.S.O. Playfair's team on the official history of the war in the Middle East. My diary tells me that one of the objectors was Playfair and that he said that footnote references only distracted the reader. His real ground of objection, though, I learned from Toomer, was that large sections of his work had already been written without any record of the sources having been kept. Toomer did not relish the idea of trying to trace these. Acheson succeeded in confusing all the issues of substance, talking about the need for submissions to be made and rulings to be sought. I privately recorded that I was 'flabbergasted at the wavery and inconclusive figure cut by Butler'. I thought he had fallen into the hands of the officials, and I was disgusted. As I knew that Webster would resign unless the issues were resolved to his satisfaction rather than that of officialdom, I also realized that my future as an official historian was highly precarious.[42]

Butler now set about trying to mollify Webster. It was unfortunate, he admitted, that he had agreed with Sir Norman Brook and Professor Hancock, the Chief Official Civil Historian, that references to unpublished sources should be omitted; but he thought the matter could be reopened. I urged upon Webster the importance of a properly referenced history of the strategic air offensive in view of the extraordinary ignorance about it that prevailed, not least, I specially mentioned, in the mind of Air Chief Marshal Sir Guy Garrod. I said that I hoped Webster would not give up, but I agreed with his view that he would have to do so unless the existing Cabinet Office regulations were relaxed. At one stage it seemed virtually certain that he would resign. But he presently told me that he was not without hope and believed, indeed, that there was support for his point of view in high places, which meant Sir Norman Brook. I tried to encourage him by speculating about who would enjoy the responsibility for causing his resignation. Meanwhile, in a hopeful spirit, I was working hard on operational matters, the chief gap in my thesis. As to the future, I was not overwhelmed by confidence and, as it were, to split the risk, I had applied for and got the job of arranging the papers of the third Earl of Clarendon in the Bodleian Library, a job which I ran in tandem with part-time service in the Air Historical Branch – to which Nerney had kindly agreed. Webster took a great interest in my work on Clarendon and encouraged me with his robust optimism. He read aloud to me passages from the proofs of his work on Palmerston that related to Clarendon. He thought there was insufficient scope for a full-scale study of Clarendon, in which he was right; Sir Herbert Maxwell's *Life and Letters* had more or less exhausted the subject. But he thought there was scope for me in related fields, and the more clouded the future of the history of the strategic air offensive became, the more attractive the prospect seemed that I might return to my original idea of being a diplomatic historian of the Webster type. Thoughts of obtaining a fellowship, in which Webster strongly backed me, began to return, but unfortunately (or as I now think fortunately) Balliol, Jesus and Christ Church all concurred in not accepting me. There was also another anxiety which might well have nullified all these considerations and plans.[43]

This was the Korean war. In February 1951, I recorded in my diary that the situation was improving and that the Americans were gradually recovering the ground south of the 38th Parallel which the Chinese had earlier occupied. However, the British armed forces were making plans for the recall of reservists and I realized it was possible that I would shortly be moving from writing the history of bombing to once more taking an active part in carrying it out. Nor, having survived one war, did I rate my chances of surviving another very highly. Like the fellowships at Oxford, this too, even more fortunately, came to nothing and more agreeable prospects began to reopen.[44]

On 26th April 1951 I received the degree of DPhil from the Vice-Chancellor, the Very Reverend Dr John Lowe, Dean of Christ Church. As the final part of my examination for it, I had been vivaed by two examiners who were subject to the terms of the official secrets act, N.H. Gibbs, who was one of the official military historians, and A. Goodwin, who, as I have mentioned, had been a narrator in the Air Historical Branch during the war. The thesis was deposited in a secret section of the Bodleian, where it still is, despite the fact that a copy is available to the general public in the Public Record Office. Oxford in general, and the Bodleian in particular, is not always up to the minute in its activities. Meanwhile, something more important had happened. Butler, Webster and Hancock had lunched together on 22nd February. Hancock had explained his experiences as the Chief Civil Historian and he seems to have outlined the restrictions to which he had agreed. Butler had then told Webster that, in the case of his volumes, though not necessarily in that of others, Sir Norman Brook was prepared to make exceptions, including over making reference to confidential documents. There was also discussion of two of the other 'Webster issues', namely the quotation of official documents and the anonymity of civil servants. Butler said that Webster seemed to be 'relieved greatly' and it appeared that all would now be well. Butler thought that Webster should have a talk with Brook himself about all these matters, and he told Acheson to arrange such a meeting. Webster, hoping to have done this beforehand, delayed telling me the news of this promising development until 18th March, by which time it had become apparent that the meeting with Brook would be somewhat delayed owing to a Cabinet reshuffle and a visit by Webster to Rome. He said that Butler and Hancock were a 'bit peeved' by the feeling that his views might be a reflection upon theirs, or in other words that his strength exposed their weakness. But Webster soothed them with the assurance that his ideas were personal to himself. In this, he was a good deal more tactful than usual. He told me that he now knew that Brook was prepared to treat our book as a special case.[45]

The meeting between Brook and Webster took place on 20th April. Butler and Acheson were there too. No minutes appear to have been taken but three days later Webster prudently wrote to Brook setting out what he thought had been agreed. He accepted that the views of individual ministers expressed in Cabinet meetings could not be revealed, but summaries of them given, for example, by a Chief of Staff would not be liable to this ban. He recounted that Brook had accepted that we would be allowed to give references to the secret sources we would have used, and that these would be numerous. Brook had also agreed, he said, that civil servants could be named, as could service officers, whenever this was essential. Finally he made it clear that Brook had agreed that, while publication of the book might be delayed, for example, by the outbreak of another war, it could not be stopped because retired or serving officers disagreed with the conclusions reached. The work would qualify for publication if the editor, Butler, found the standard acceptable. Brook approved virtually all of this as a true record. He cavilled a little about naming civil servants and claimed that he had intended his permissive rule to apply only in exceptional cases. He said the ministerial rule would also apply to Cabinet Committees and he added that, though it had not been mentioned at the meeting, he was sure that Webster would, in this connection, understand the principle of collective responsibility in the Cabinet. Webster replied that he had thought Brook had gone a little further on the matter of civil servants than he now claimed, but he made no difficulty about this and he said that he of course took Cabinet meetings to include ministerial Cabinet Committees.[46]

The point about ministerial views expressed in Cabinet was not one with which we took issue. We knew that elected politicians say one thing in public and another in private. If they found that what they said in private was published, they would say in private only what they said in public. This would have rendered the proceedings of the Cabinet farcical and would in effect have changed the constitution. If Webster and I may in some respects have had radical views, we were not revolutionaries. Webster had won a significant diplomatic victory, which proved to be decisive for our book. Without the concessions he had extracted, we would not, on principle, have been able to write it, and without the assurance he had won about the qualification for its publication, I do not believe that it would have been published. During the whole of this procedure, he was more patient than I think I would have been; he was more conciliatory than I had expected him to be; and he naturally had infinitely more prestige than I possessed.

The first outcome was that the Webster and Frankland partnership was secured. Indeed, immediately after the meeting with Brook and before the agreement had been confirmed in writing, I received a formal offer from the Cabinet Office of an appointment as an assistant historian to work with Webster on the official history of the strategic air offensive. Knowing that the bulk of the work and thinking that would be involved was going to be borne by myself, I did not feel that this was appropriate; nor did I think that Webster would. While he liked occasionally to talk about 'my' book, he knew, and in truth acknowledged, that it was at the least going to be 'ours'. I had also, throughout these months, been encouraged by Nerney to believe that I was to be the joint and not the assistant author of the work. So with some trepidation, because I knew that he disliked me, I sought an interview with Acheson, in whose hands such matters seemed to rest. In my heart, I did not really believe I would be able to achieve much beyond perhaps getting Acheson to agree that I might have some time off to continue my work on the Clarendon papers in Oxford. In the event, however, the rather abrasive relations I enjoyed with Acheson provoked me into a bolder course. I told him that it was not right that I should be kept on the salary I had been earning as a narrator in the Air Ministry, even if I was only to be an assistant historian in the Cabinet Office. I told him further that I did not wish to be an assistant historian and that I expected an appointment as a full historian so that I could be the joint and not the assistant author of the projected book.[47]

Acheson was very annoyed. He began to pace up and down the room talking about the possibility of finding someone else more sensible to do the job. When I asked him who that might be, I saw that I had called his bluff. He then advised me to accept the inferior position for a time and hope for promotion later when Webster would have had an opportunity to assess my ability. I told him that Webster had already had such an opportunity. More or less telling me that I was a fool, Acheson then fell back on the last resort of saying that I would have to see Butler to settle the matter. I was not very keen to have the sort of slanging match I had had with Acheson with Butler because I saw Butler as too refined and genteel for such stuff. All the same, I did not see how I could extricate myself, and I came up to London the next day fully expecting Butler to send for me and tell me to accept Acheson's decisions. By 3 p.m. nothing had happened, but at that moment the telephone rang. To my surprise and relief a voice said, 'This is Charles Webster'. He had got his letter of confirmation from Brook and wanted to consult me about it. Would I come to tea with him? So off I set to Webster's flat at 4 St John's Lodge, Harley Road. I arrived to find that Webster had been lunching with Hugh Gaitskell who at the time was Chancellor of the Exchequer, Sir Hartley Shawcross, the President of the Board of Trade, and the President of Harvard. It all seemed very splendid, much more so than Acheson's office. Webster told me all about his exchanges with Brook, which I have already described, and I told him about mine with Acheson. He said he would deal with the matter and a few days later I heard from Nerney that he had written to Butler backing me as joint author. Shortly afterwards, I received a revised offer from the Cabinet Office. The salary was greatly increased and I was to be a full Cabinet Office official military historian. I accepted. The saga of the search for an author, or authors, for the official history of the strategic air offensive had now at last come to its conclusion and it had done so immensely to my advantage. My sponsor had been J.C. Nerney but my passport to Webster's favour, and so to the position I had now attained, had been my thesis.[48]

CHAPTER THREE

History in Academe

Almost the whole of the content and a good deal of the philosophy of my thesis has been subsumed into the official history of the strategic air offensive and some of it into other books and articles I have written. The thesis itself, however, has never been published. Nerney did at one time think of publishing it, but that was when the prospect of finding an author for the official history seemed distant and uncertain. Once Sir Charles Webster and I were linked in the writing of the official history, the thesis fell into the category of a preliminary study, or a sketch, for the main work. Yet it was the most important stage in the development of my concept of historiography, and it was certainly the most original piece of work I have ever done. It is therefore necessary for me now to give some account of its nature and philosophy. That will also serve to indicate how, in my experience, the formation of an idea of history that raises a work above the level of mere narrative, is partly a matter of systematic research, partly one of reflection, and partly one of chance and luck.

When I started working on the strategic air offensive there was scarcely any serious published literature on the subject. I thought indeed that the issues could only be revealed by original research in the vast unpublished documentation. Most of this was still classified as secret, but especially as far as the Air Ministry and Bomber Command files were concerned, it was relatively easy to use. This was the result of the excellent filing systems used in the Air Ministry and at Bomber Command and also the sensible archival procedures adopted in the Air Historical Branch. I was nevertheless confronted, in such circles of air history as existed, with a generally received view of the bomber offensive. It ran on these lines: Bomber Command was initially ineffective because it had been starved of money in the inter-war years and was too small to achieve successful results. As it gradually expanded, it gradually became more effective. The area-bombing offensive began to sap German industrial strength, it drove the Luftwaffe onto the defensive; and finally, after delays caused by diversions of effort in favour of Coastal Command and the Middle East, it grew large enough to strike decisive blows against the heart of Germany. The Americans frittered away much of their resources through the foolish policy of daylight bombing, which they adopted against British advice; but eventually, through the great increase in their numbers, they made a useful contribution to the efforts of the RAF Bomber Command. Thus the pre-war Air Staff doctrine that the aeroplane was not a defence against the aeroplane, and that the bomber would always get through, was proved to be right. And so was the doctrine that a sustained and mounting bomber offensive would drive the enemy air force onto the defensive and gradually reduce enemy power to a state of impotence, in the same way that a naval blockade had done in times past.

The key to this received idea was that the air was too large to defend and that the force which attacked in greater strength would certainly win in the end. Therefore, as the Air Staff had also predicted, air power had introduced a new dimension in warfare, something which, by comparison with what was possible for armies and navies, was of revolutionary significance. Navies had to win their battles against an opposing fleet before they could impose their blockades; armies had to defeat opposing armies before they could usefully occupy territory and dictate peace terms. Air forces, however, should not be diverted by battles; they should seek to evade them and proceed directly to their strategic target, which in this case was the German war economy. This, the conclusion ran, was what had happened.

The most important conclusion in my thesis was that the opposite was the case. My research had led me to understand that, far from being a revolutionary innovation, air power had been shown to have conformed with, and been confined by, the same general principles of war as those that governed the conduct of armies and of sea power. The naval analogy struck me as being the most immediate and direct. At Nerney's suggestion, I made a close study of Mahan's works. They showed that the effective exercise of sea power depended upon winning and maintaining command of the sea, and that the only way in which this could be achieved was by the destruction and neutralization of the opposing fleet. Thus, for example, a blockade could only be enforced if the enemy fleet had been rendered ineffective. Mahan demonstrated from the evidence of history that this law was immutable. Attempts to circumvent it by the seemingly attractive method known to the French as the *guerre de course* invariably failed.

My attention was concentrated upon the *guerre de course*. Confronted by Britain, which possessed a powerful battle fleet and was dependent for her very existence on imports, it had seemed almost common sense for the Spanish, the Dutch, and the French to avoid Britain's fleet and strike directly at her commerce. The commerce raiders could be dispersed over the oceans, which were surely too large to be defended by a fleet of twenty or so ships of the line. Thus, in the War of the Spanish Succession, feeling unable to challenge the British fleet, Louis XIV had withdrawn his main fleet from the oceans and reinforced his commerce-raiding cruisers on the more frequented seas. The French had believed that this policy served their cause advantageously; but the British, despite some serious losses at sea, had found that their general prosperity increased steadily throughout the struggle. The losses of merchant ships to the French cruisers were not only insufficient to disrupt the imports the island country needed to continue the war; they even failed to prevent the expansion of her general trade. In other words, the local effects represented by the sinking of merchant ships by French cruisers, though serious in themselves, did not add up to any significant national effect upon Britain. In the outcome, it was the French and not the British who were reduced to poverty.[1]

When it was the turn of the Germans to succeed the French in an attempt to starve out the British, the submarine had been invented and brought to operational effectiveness. This seemed to offer the *guerre de course* a much enhanced prospect of success. The German U-Boat appeared to be far superior to a French commerce-raiding cruiser as a means of evading the British fleet and striking directly at her commerce. In two world wars the Germans made the attempt. On both occasions it produced dire crises, but on both occasions it failed. The principle which Mahan had enunciated for wooden ships held good for the age of steel battleships, submarines and naval aircraft. Germany and Austria starved in 1918 as inexorably as the grass had grown in the streets of Amsterdam in 1652.[2]

I came to an awareness of these aspects of the works of Mahan after I had worked intensively on the files of the Air Ministry and Bomber Command and also on those of Albert Speer, the Nazi Minister of Armaments, and other German leaders. I was thunderstruck. If one left out the tactical details and stuck to the strategic principles, there were passages in Mahan about the French and Dutch navies that read as though they had been about Bomber Command in the Second World War. I believed that I had found the key to unlocking the significance of the complex mass of evidence about the bomber offensive and producing a framework within which it could sensibly be described. For me, it was the end of long-winded narrative and the beginning of interpretative explanation.

Bomber Command's aircraft now took on the guise of the Spanish, Dutch and French commerce-raiders of yesteryear and of the German U-Boats of both the world wars. Having no means of combating the German fighter force, they had turned away from daylight attack and had sought the cover of darkness as a means of evading it. They had then proceeded directly to their strategic aim, which was the destruction of the German war economy to a point at which it would be fatally compromised, so that Germany would either be driven to capitulation, or at least be rendered incapable of resisting a military occupation. Clearly this had not happened. Nor, when I came to the German industrial and propaganda archives, and notably the Speer documents, was it possible to detect any prospect of such a result until the winter of 1944 to 1945. By that time, however, the policy of evasion had given way to the American policy of mounting a vigorous attack upon the Luftwaffe in being, that is to say, of engaging and destroying it in the air. Only then did the true meaning of command of the air become clear; it proved to be very similar to the command of the sea that the Royal Navy had so often established, especially in the eighteenth and early nineteenth centuries. Mahan proved to be a more reliable prophet of air power than Giulio Douhet or Lord Trenchard; the American Generals, Arnold and Spaatz, who demanded long-range fighters and knew how to use them with deadly effect in combination with long-range bombers, proved to be better strategists and tacticians than the British Air Marshals Portal and Harris, who clung to the *guerre de course* almost to the bitter end.

Here I have done no more than outline the idea. In my thesis I elaborated and, I believe, proved it. The result was a direct challenge to the essence of the 'Trenchard Doctrine', to much of the strategy which had governed Bomber Command during the war and to substantial elements in the doctrine of the British Air Staff in the late 1940s and early 1950s. As Lord Trenchard was still very much alive and the Air Staff were still using him and his ideas as ammunition in their continuing struggle with the Army and the Navy, and as American achievements were not always the most popular message, my position as a narrator in the Air Ministry became rather fragile. But, though I was uneasy and rather doubtful about my future career, I was well content, for I thought I had distilled some truths from, and seen a pattern in, the very large quantities of documents I had studied. Research, I had discovered, was not as is so often thought a matter of looking up and checking things; it had been a veritable voyage of discovery and explanation.

I mentioned earlier that in arriving at such a position there were elements of systematic research, reflection, chance and luck. Research had enabled me to gauge what had happened and why it had done so. Reflection had guided me towards the idea of distinguishing in war between apparent local effects, such as the undoubted flooding caused by the breaching of the Möhne and Eder Dams in May 1943 or the catastrophic destruction in Hamburg following the firestorms of July and August 1943, and national effects which would be seen in the national ability or otherwise to continue to mount an efficient and growing war effort. Chance had drawn me towards Mahan when, apparently out of the blue, Nerney asked my wife if I had read his works, which at the time I had not. Luck was certainly in play when I had the opportunity of working on the Air Ministry and Bomber Command material before it was removed to the Public Record Office. In its original settings and in the way in which it was arranged in the Air Historical Branch, it was readily accessible and logically ordered. For reasons beyond my comprehension, it has been jumbled in the Public Record Office, where working on it is now arduous, frustrating and not infrequently impossible. Luck was also in the ascendant when a hall porter in Cadogan Gardens, where I had my office, asked me what was to be done with a collection of packing cases which had been left in a basement nearby by the Department of Scientific and Industrial Research. I went to look at them. They proved to contain the many hundreds of volumes of the Speer papers which had been captured at the end of the war in Hamburg and Flensburg.

My conclusions about the nature of the bombing offensive rested upon what I thought were its two most important aspects, that is, the policies that governed it and the results it achieved. I knew well that there was a third factor which heavily influenced both these elements. This was operational capacity. While, however, I tried to probe the question of policy and that of results deeply, I decided that I would only sketch the outlines of operational capacity. Historically speaking, I realized subsequently that this was a mistake. Operational capacity, or what could be done, was fully as important as strategic intent, or desired objectives. Operational capacity also largely determined the results obtained by bombing. Indeed, what could ultimately be done governed what was done. Nevertheless, if I had attempted all three elements in equal strength, I would have produced a work too long to meet the regulations governing theses at Oxford. Had I pruned the three elements to meet the length rules, I would have rendered the whole work superficial. I therefore do not regret the decision I made, especially as when I later came, with Sir Charles Webster, to develop the thesis into the official history, I was able to make a full study of operations. All the same, I would have been more impressed by those who examined my thesis and passed it for a DPhil if they had at least commented upon this historical imbalance. As it was, they confined themselves to my omission of one footnote and one or two points of punctuation.

The crux of warfare is the results that are achieved by its various strategies and operations. Moreover, true results are not only difficult to ascertain, they are also the criterion by which the conduct of battles, campaigns and wars must be judged. However brilliant a commander may be, however much courage, determination, skill, resourcefulness and doggedness he may show, his place in history – as opposed to romance – must be governed by the results he does achieve. In discussing what I discovered about the policies that governed Bomber Command and the results it achieved, I will for this reason begin with results.

On the question of results, unlike that of policy, there was a large volume of printed though largely unpublished material. The greater part of it was contained in the reports of the United States Strategic Bombing Survey (USSBS), among which I found some twenty volumes that were directly relevant. The Americans, indeed, had tackled the question on a characteristically massive scale and by 1947 they had produced more than two hundred volumes. The British, again characteristically, had followed on a much smaller scale by establishing a far more modest British Bombing Survey Unit (BBSU). From this organization, I found five volumes that were of direct relevance.[3]

These reports were produced by high-powered teams of economists, statisticians and other theoreticians who invaded Germany as soon as the war was over, interrogated surviving leaders, and notably Albert Speer, examined such records as could be found and looked over factories, railway systems and other installations. Their findings were regarded as authoritative but no one seemed to know what they were. The American teams frequently contradicted one another and much of their work was of such a detailed nature that it formed no basis for any meaningful general conclusions. The British team concentrated mainly upon the importance and success of the attack on transportation; one of its most influential members was Professor Zuckerman, who during the war as Tedder's advisor had been a chief advocate of transport bombing. Although there were some nuggets of useful information to be dug out of this mass of British and American material, the general result was in effect more of a field day for the advocates of various competing bombing policies than a judgement on what had been achieved by them.

The statistical methods employed struck me as being historically unreliable. Arguments based on statistical evidence derived from questionnaires and therefore on replies to questions that could be fed into the then fashionable Hollerith machines, were virtually certain to be unsound. It was difficult to frame a question broadly enough to cover the possibilities and yet narrowly enough for it to be classifiable in Hollerith terms. In many cases the person being questioned would give an unreliable answer because the question did not fit the response he wished to make, or because he had forgotten the facts. The resulting parameters were often on a very large scale and the built-in assumptions were sometimes highly doubtful. In such conclusions, I seemed to have some support. Hugh Trevor-Roper had been invited by the Air Ministry to write up the BBSU reports into a clear historical account. He wrote a brilliant opening chapter, and then two more which were obviously much less satisfactory. He then abandoned the attempt, wisely in my view. I advised Nerney that the BBSU was not a workable basis for an historical study, a point which at the time he seemed to accept. All the same, this failed to prevent him from thinking that Hilary Saunders might bring his rapid-fire style of popular writing to bear upon the problem with better results. It was one of Nerney's silliest ideas and it fell to me to point out to him that Saunders was quite incapable of extracting anything meaningful from the tangle. Where Trevor-Roper had prudently decided to withdraw, Saunders was scarcely likely to prevail, and he did not.[4]

Years later I found it interesting to read G.R. Elton's succinct expression of my own reservations about the use by historians of statistical methods. But his strictures applied chiefly to the period before 1800. If he had read my thesis, I wonder whether he might perhaps have added at least a hundred and fifty years to this epoch.[5]

I decided that the only useful and historical way of tackling the problem of assessing the results of the bombing offensive was to approach it from a general as opposed to a detailed point of view. In other words, I resolved to abandon the attempt to 'add up' the consequences of individual attacks and instead to search for national results, which at their simplest would express themselves in overall failures of supply such as, notably, those that occurred in the case of oil in the last winter of the war, or, more subtly, in changes of policy on the part of the German government that were attributable to bombing. There were also the general consequences of the effects of various bombing policies and expectations of them that became apparent in the making and changing of policies on the part of the British and American governments.

This, for a DPhil student, was a risky line; historians normally proceed from detail to generality. If they do not, they often come in for a severe basting. For an employee of the Air Ministry, it also had its hazards. Naturally, the British and American air forces wished to believe that their efforts had been highly successful, and their successors in the post-war era wished to cash in on the prestige the proof of such wishes would confer. A powerful aid to wishful thinking was the spectacular nature of bomber operations. Even I had seen things such as the attack on Munich in April 1944 that made it hard to believe this sort of thing would not soon bring an end to German resistance. How much more difficult was it to believe that the far more spectacular destruction of the Möhne and Eder Dams in May 1943 had virtually no effect on Germany's ability to wage war and to continue the development of an upwardly mounting war production? Yet those beliefs and myriads of allied beliefs were the very issues at which I was now to strike. My position was further weakened by the fact, which I have already explained, that I was not writing in any depth about operational matters. The great importance of the dams raid and of the Munich attack was operational. It was through these that new techniques were brought to fruition, and it was through them that Bomber Command developed into a vastly more efficient force. Such agreeable matters were only peripheral to my thesis.

The results of my research into the effects of the bombing offensive showed that, for most of the war, they were very disappointing, and this applied not only to the British Bomber Command but also to the United States strategic air forces. The British policy of area-bombing, to which the force was driven by the lack of operationally feasible alternatives, was an inherently inefficient method of attack, the most important effect of which was to convince the Americans that they must try something else. But their attempt to mount precision attacks against selected and supposedly vital target systems was no more successful and, in terms of the casualties involved for the bombers, even more expensive.

Theoretically, the cumulative effects of British area-bombing should have knocked Germany out of the war. Indeed, Speer told Hitler that six more attacks on the scale of the Battle of Hamburg in July and August 1943 would do so. In the aftermath of that catastrophe he realized, though, that he had been wrong. He understood little of air power, and he had not appreciated that in Hamburg, and at the time of the attacks, there were a number of factors that were specially favourable to Bomber Command, ranging from the special suitability of the water-studded target for identification on the screens of the radar navigational aid, H^2S, to the surprise effect on the German radar defences caused by dumping masses of metallized strips codenamed *Window*. He had not appreciated that six more attacks on the scale and concentration of that on Hamburg were beyond the capacity of Bomber Command. In this way he underestimated the scope for repair and reconstruction, even in a city that had suffered such a terrible degree of destruction as Hamburg had. The Air Staff and Sir Arthur Harris made much the same miscalculations. There was no doubt that Hamburg had suffered a frightful blow which at the time was bound to appear to be virtually lethal. The German records, which I examined in the course of my research, equally left no doubt that the national effect on the German war effort as a whole was virtually nil. German war production was not reduced. On the contrary, it was about to experience a dramatic increase. Germany continued to deploy most of her air power on the Russian front. What was worse was that this general conclusion applied not only to everything that had happened up to and including the Battle of Hamburg, but also to everything that was to happen after it, including the Battle of Berlin, until March 1944, when a dramatic change began to take effect. If the war had ended in March 1944 for reasons other than a collapse of German civil morale, the Bomber Command offensive would have had to be described as almost a complete failure.

What was, perhaps, worst of all was that Bomber Command's subsequent great successes did not stem from these relatively barren years, beyond the basic truth that they had brought the force into being and hardened it in battle. The change did not come about, as was so often claimed, from an accumulation of experience in the area-bombing offensive; it was created by two extraneous factors. The first was the insistent military demand that Bomber Command should be employed on a special campaign to prepare the way for the Anglo-American landings in Normandy. This involved something quite distinct from area-bombing. The second was the revolution in American air strategy which was brought about by the failure of their alternative to British area-bombing.

That the American plan did fail seemed to me to be beyond doubt. There were three principal factors. Selective precision-bombing against specific targets, such as aircraft factories or ball-bearing plants, depended for its success on the ability of the bombers to find and hit them, and to go on hitting them until they were put out of action, and then hitting them again if and when they were repaired. Second, the selected targets really had to be vital to the German war effort: it was little use knocking down a factory if what it produced could be made or obtained elsewhere. Third, to sustain the offensive to a significant extent meant that the bomber casualties must be restricted to what could be absorbed without having to introduce a new and inexperienced front line every few weeks. On all three counts, the United States Eighth Air Force under the command of General Eaker failed. Accurate bombing from high levels, which is where the Americans flew, was frequently impossible in European conditions. All too often cloud obscured the ground – much more often than it did over Texas. The hope that the heavily armed and armoured bombers with their splendid and skilled tight formation tactics would make the force self-defending, proved to be false. Whatever tactics they employed, there was no way in which heavy bombers could contend with determined attack from high-performance interceptor fighters. After the disastrous casualties suffered in the attack on Schweinfurt in October 1943, the plan blew up. Moreover, in this attack, one of the most gallant of the war, in which heavy damage was done to the supposedly indispensable ball-bearing plants, the resulting effects were most disappointing. The Germans were not as short of ball-bearings as the Americans and the British thought, nor indeed as Speer at first believed. The attack, like so many of Bomber Command's area attacks, was impressive in local terms. In national terms it was of little significance. So while Bomber Command persisted with the Battle of Berlin, the American heavy bombers withdrew from the main contest. The British thought that the best and only policy for the Americans was to abandon day-bombing and join the British night area-offensive. The Americans thought otherwise, which brings us to the issue of bombing policy, the other main prong of my thesis.

British bombing policy, I concluded, had been vitiated and for much of the war rendered largely ineffective by a number of fundamental errors of judgement. As already mentioned, the most important of these were, first, the gross overestimate of the effects of bombing as such. Second, there was a huge underestimate of the difficulties that would confront a bomber crew in finding and hitting a target. Third, there was a serious failure to appreciate the strength of the war economy and national morale of Hitler's Germany. Finally, in the closing stages of the war, when operational problems had been largely overcome and command of the air had been won, there was a failure to agree on a unified bombing policy both as between the British and the Americans, and as between the various elements in the British high command itself. Portal, the Chief of the Air Staff, believed that oil was the weakest link in the German war-machine and that, now that its plants were within the power of Bomber Command to destroy, concentration on those relatively few aiming points was the surest way of bringing the war to an end. The hindsight of history showed that in this particular Portal was right, although at the time it had seemed to the C-in-C, Harris, and the Deputy Supreme Commander, Tedder, that he was not.

Harris, with much justification from his unhappy experiences of the misleading appreciations of such institutions as the Ministry of Economic Warfare and the Political Warfare Executive, which tended to be dominated by men who were clever rather than sensible, had lost confidence in all the 'panaceas' they had offered. He had come to believe that the only reliable policy was that of general area-bombing aimed at nothing more selective than all the major German cities and towns. An industrial nation, he thought, could survive attacks on selected elements of its composition because it could find alternative sources of supply or use substitute components. It could not survive – it seemed to him – the general devastation of all its major cities. The hindsight of history showed him to have been wrong about this. He underestimated the extent to which machinery could survive under rubble and be recovered and put back to work; the extent to which, and the speed at which, damage could be repaired; and the extent to which the German workforce would carry on regardless, either as a result of the efficiency of the Nazi rule of terror or the loyalty of the population.

As a Commander-in-Chief, it was not for Harris to make policy; his job was to carry out what had been decided by the War Cabinet and Air Staff. But things were not as simple as that. He who decides what is operationally feasible develops a large influence on what operations are ordered. Also, Harris, the man who had raised Bomber Command from the doldrums to a force of formidable power, had by the time the controversy came to a head in the autumn of 1944 acquired a prestige with his crews and the public at large that made it difficult to combat his views, or in the last resort to remove him from his command. There was in addition the important consideration that, for much of the war, area-bombing had proved to be the only operational policy open to Bomber Command if it was to maintain any kind of offensive pressure on Germany. Moreover, Bomber Command had for years been the only element of the British armed forces capable of rendering any substantial kind of offensive pressure. By the time that the possibilities had been changed and enlarged, Bomber Command had already made a huge investment of blood and equipment in the area offensive. It seemed wrong that when it could be rendered yet more effective, it should be abandoned, just as, on the Western Front in the First World War, it had seemed wrong to Haig that, after all those costly pushes, one more effort should not be made. Warfare of that kind and in those circumstances develops a rationale of its own. Harris, although not responsible for the initiation of area-bombing, had a much stronger position in its maintenance than his theoretical powers suggested.

Tedder, whose power stemmed from his position as Eisenhower's Deputy and chief advisor on air matters, accepted neither Portal's nor Harris's views. He advocated a common denominator theory of attack, by which he meant a policy in which as many elements of air power as possible could join, and the results of which would be of the greatest common advantage to the various aspects of the attack being made upon Germany; upon her U-Boats; upon her military communications; and upon her industrial production. With the advice of Professor Zuckerman, he concluded that the only target system to meet all these criteria was transportation. Like the oil plan, though for different reasons, this was shown by hindsight to have been a sound, workable and effective plan.

Thus, in the last autumn, winter and spring of the war, there were for Bomber Command three competing policies: oil, area-bombing of cities, and transportation. Maximum concentration upon oil or transportation could probably, it seemed to me, have finished the war before the end of 1944. As it was, the dispersal of the effort between the three systems and the fact that area-bombing continued to absorb by far the greatest part of the effort, allowed the Germans to stagger on until their armies were defeated and captured and their territory occupied by the armies of the Grand Alliance. Even so, by April 1945, bombing alone had sealed the fate of Germany. But this was too late to stand as a clear-cut victory and all that the bombers could legitimately claim was that their efforts had greatly facilitated the success of the allied armies.

The key factor in my argument has yet to be explained. The strategic air offensive of the British and the Americans began to be decisively effective in national as opposed to local terms only from May 1944 onwards. The root cause of this extraordinary change was to be found in the American disaster at Schweinfurt in October 1943. That had demonstrated to the Americans that the German defensive fighter force was the barrier through which their strategic bombers could not effectively pass. The British had learnt the same lesson in 1939 but they had then decided that the solution was to be found in the use of the cover of darkness as a means of evading those fighter defences and had thus been drawn into a *guerre de course*. In October 1943, the Americans took a different decision: they resolved to confront and defeat the German fighter force. They had learnt that their bombers could not achieve this and they knew too that their fighters alone, even if they had the range, could not do it either. They grasped the essential truth that this battle could only be fought and won if the bombers were used to force the German fighters into action and the American fighters could be there to shoot them down.

It was not, perhaps, wholly surprising that the British thought this was nonsense. How could the Americans put fighters with the range of bombers into successful combat against German short-range interceptor fighters? The very fact that a fighter could go the necessary distance, it seemed to them, would place it at a fatal disadvantage *vis à vis* the short-range defending fighter. Nevertheless, through the greatest irony in the history of air warfare, the British had already virtually placed the instrument by which this seemingly basic law of short-range against long-range could be reversed, at the disposal of the Americans. At its inception, the Mustang was an American aircraft, but the Americans did not fancy it. In 1940, they allowed Sir Arthur Harris, who was then Head of the RAF Delegation in Washington, to order it for British service. In 1942, it went into action with the RAF in support of the Dieppe raid. Its performance proved to be poor and it faded into the background. In their search for a long-range fighter, the Americans then took another look at it. They replaced its American Allison engine with a British Rolls Royce Merlin and made some other modifications. The result was astonishing. 'In the middle of December' [1943], I wrote in my thesis, 'the famous Mustang long-range fighter made its appearance in Europe. This formidable machine scored immediate and spectacular successes. For the Luftwaffe it was the beginning of the end.'[6]

In subsequent years, while engaged on the official history of the strategic air offensive, I learnt a great deal more about the Mustang than I knew while writing my thesis. Even then, however, I already knew enough to identify its introduction to the air offensive against Germany as a decisive turning point in the air war, and as the key to the winning of the command of the air over Germany by the allies. I think that this theory has subsequently passed into more or less general recognition. But when I first adumbrated it, viewpoints were very different and I found it surprising that even the American official air historians seemed not to have grasped the idea. As for the British, Lord Portal told me after he had read my thesis that he could not remember how it was that Mustangs could develop such a long range, and he could only account for their success in terms of the superior quality of the British pilots.

He still believed that a long-range fighter could not compete with one of short-range. In my thesis, I had not entered into the technical details of how, by the use of disposable auxiliary petrol tanks, the Mustang gained the range of a bomber and retained the performance of an interceptor fighter. Maybe I should have done! I did not feel it my place to remind Lord Portal that the vast bulk of the Mustang long-range fighters were flown, not by British, but by American pilots.[7]

In expounding my theory of air superiority and command of the air, I could not use the terms undefined. There was at that stage no generally recognized understanding of what they meant. Indeed, there was hardly any agreed grammar of air warfare and even terms as basic as 'strategic' were open to all sorts of different definitions. As I proceeded, I therefore had to decide what I understood by all these words and explain. This was a very useful exercise and a good form of discipline, for it was through the task of working out these meanings that I came to understand the structure of the subject. Lord Trenchard thought that air superiority meant the side which had the heaviest bomber potential. Lord Tedder defined it as the state of affairs when an attacking force could carry out its operations without effective inter-ference from the defending force. I thought Tedder's view was nearer the truth than Trenchard's, but it still seemed short of the mark.[8]

It seemed to me that Tedder's view did not take account of the difference between local and perhaps temporary conditions on the one hand, and gen-erally prevailing conditions on the other. A *guerre de course* might from time to time and from place to place produce conditions in which there was no effective defending opposition. Such, for example, had been the case during the Battle of Hamburg in July and August 1943. However, because they arose from special as opposed to generally prevailing conditions, those situations did not, as I saw it, constitute air superiority. Their fruits were only local and temporary.

I postulated that air superiority was to be measured by the extent of the gap between strategic desirability and tactical feasibility. When the two were separated by the weather alone, a state of air supremacy, or command of the air, existed. As the extent to which they were separated by the enemy fighter force varied, so the degree of air superiority fluctuated. I demonstrated how in the course of 1944 increasing allied air superiority developed into air supremacy, and I showed how the coordinated use of long-range bombers and long-range fighters introduced a series of developments which brought this about.[9]

In the light of this interpretation of the meaning of air superiority, I was able to discern the phase when the strategic air offensive turned from being relatively ineffective to being decisively successful, and the reason for it. I described how, in the first half of 1944, the German war economy was still expanding and how this was happening despite big mobilizations of man power for the Wehrmacht and despite all the damage Bomber Command's area offensive had inflicted. I observed that when the allied armies went ashore in Normandy in June 1944, the aim declared at the Casablanca Conference of January 1943 had not been achieved: the strategic air offensive had not destroyed the German war economy, nor had it fatally weakened the morale of the German people. 'Air power,' I wrote, 'had shown itself to be a decisive force in the conduct of military and naval warfare, but as an independent conception it seemed bankrupt of success.' In July 1944, I added, German war production had reached its highest level. I then went on to describe how, six months later, Germany was in chaos and the total collapse of her ability to wage war was imminent. Her basic industries of coal, steel, gas and electric power, oil and transport were all faced with ruin. This was primarily the achievement of strategic bombing. I stated that after four and a half years of sustained endeavour without proportionate success, strategic bombing had at last vindicated itself as a third means of waging war. This then was the phase of change.[10]

I explained that the conduct of bombing in this final phase was different not only in degree, but in kind, from any earlier attacks. There were, I conceded, a number of factors which contributed to this: for example, the increased size of the bomber forces, the greater destructive power of the bombs and further development in technical aids to navigation and bomb-aiming. But the most important factor of all, I concluded, was the increasing state of air superiority which by the autumn of 1944 amounted virtually to air supremacy. Such was the operative reason for the change.[11]

In my thesis of course, I displayed detailed and substantial evidence to prove the case; here I have felt it necessary only to outline it. The principal conclusions were that for most of the war the British Air Staff and the Commander-in-Chief, Bomber Command, were barking up the wrong trees. In their increasingly different ways, they were both persisting in the attempt to reach their strategic objectives by the evasion of the German fighter defences; they were conducting a *guerre de course*. German doctrine proved to be even less effective; the Luftwaffe was never a balanced force and its increasing preoccupation with the tasks of direct support to the army in the field meant that, in the end, it was incapable of confronting enemy air power. In striking contrast, the Americans grasped the essential that the success of bombing, as of other expressions of air power, depended upon the attainment of air superiority through combat in the air. They themselves lacked the weight of bombing to exploit this to the full, but the British with their larger and much more destructive bombs were able to compensate for this inadequacy.

Despite the insistence of my thesis on the ultimate triumph of strategic bombing, much of what I had written made melancholy reading. It was not therefore surprising that its reception by some of the distinguished officers among whom it was circulated was less than enthusiastic. Lord Portal more or less dismissed the main points in his characteristically polite but Olympian manner, as I have mentioned. He said he had no objection to my having a go at the brass hats, which trivialized the arguments I had put forward. Subsequent developments showed that Lord Portal's composure was probably due to the fact that he knew that my thesis was a secret document which would not be published. Also, he seemed not to understand that I was going on to write the official history of the strategic air offensive, which would be published, and that what I had said in the thesis was not to be my last word. I recorded at the time that much of what Lord Portal said about the bombing offensive I could have disproved with chapter and verse, but that I did not judge it my place to do so.[12]

Sir Ralph Cochrane, who had been my Group Commander in the war and was now Vice-Chief of the Air Staff, sent for me and Nerney to attend on him in his palatial Air Ministry office. He told me that although I had made some good points, I had failed to grasp that air superiority had been won through Bomber Command driving the Luftwaffe onto the defensive, that I had underestimated the success of area-bombing, and so on. He said that, with due Air Ministry instruction, I could yet be made into a good historian. I had been much in awe of Sir Ralph during the war: he had the reputation of being a stiff disciplinarian. Though I had by now changed into civilian clothes, that seemed to be something Sir Ralph hardly noticed, and I still felt distinctly nervous in his presence. I find it pleasant to recall today that, in later years, when we were neighbours in Oxfordshire, he became a close and stimulating friend. I will also relate in another chapter how, at the height of the row about the official history, he afforded me strong support. Sir Ralph Cochrane, when still an aspirant for the post of Chief of the Air Staff, was a rather different person from what he became after he had failed to gain that position and taken up other activities in his retirement. But I venture to believe that, in the interval between my interview with him in the Air Ministry and my later contacts with him as a friend, he had come to appreciate some of the finer points of distinction between Air Staff doctrine and air history.

Lord Trenchard averred that he had no objection to criticisms but that, all the same, he would 'roll in' some of his own regarding the views I had expressed. Unfortunately, however, he did not do so. The former Deputy C-in-C, Bomber Command, Sir Robert Saundby, did not like my work and he wrote Nerney some letters about it charged with 'ill-tempered emotion'. Unlike Lord Portal, who was even-handed in his attitude to the three services, Saundby was pro-Air Force at the cost of being immoderately anti-Navy and

Army. Even so, I came greatly to appreciate his highly informed and articulate conversation, although I learnt to be cautious about his criticism and praise, which was the product of a two-faced attitude fostered by a fundamentally weak moral character.[13]

These preachers of Air Staff doctrine, like several other Air Marshals who read my thesis, were unlikely to take readily to the views expressed in it and they especially objected to the argument I had advanced suggesting that there was no special dispensation for air power that lifted it clear of the restricting principles governing the conduct of war on land and at sea. They too seemed to take refuge in the belief that I could be reformed or that, if I could not, these corrosive opinions could be substantially suppressed. Such entrenched positions were not reserved for Air Marshals. The longest and by far the most detailed critique of my thesis came, not from an Air Marshal, but from Solly Zuckerman, Professor of Anatomy in the University of Birmingham.

Zuckerman had been an advisor on the staff of the Combined Operations Command during the war and after it he had, in many respects, put Lord Mountbatten in his pocket. During the war, he had performed much the same function as a scientific advisor to Tedder when the latter was in command of the Middle East Air Forces and later Deputy Supreme Commander, Allied Expeditionary Force. Scientific advisors did not confine their advice to matters of science and, as I have already mentioned, Zuckerman was an advocate of transport bombing. In 1960, he was nominated as the next Chief Scientific Advisor to the Secretary of State for Defence. I happened to be lunching in the Athenaeum with Sir Henry Tizard on the day that this was announced and, seeing Zuckerman enter the Club, I asked Tizard whether he thought it was a good choice on the part of the Government. Tizard said that Zuckerman was clever enough, but that he was too much of a courtier to be a sound advisor.

Courtier or not, Zuckerman was deeply, even passionately, concerned about aspects of my thesis which he deemed were unduly critical of scientific and other kinds of advisors who had worked on the problems of air warfare. He wrote to Nerney saying that he had read my thesis 'very carefully' and 'with great interest'. He believed that it was an important and 'highly interesting' document but that in certain respects it could be improved 'to the possible greater benefit of our future air planners'. With the letter, he enclosed nine and a half pages of closely typed foolscap sheets by way of comment. I was given a photocopy of these.[14]

The comments began very politely. Zuckerman thought that my work 'in general' was an excellent effort, and he said that I was to be congratulated on a scholarly piece of work which would prove useful, not only to people interested in history, but also to those concerned with the 'exact method' in the determination of bombing policy. Nevertheless, he thought, it needed a 'modification of approach'. Four general observations followed. First, he considered that I had made an unjustified attack upon an empirical approach to the determination of bombing policy and though he and, as he put it, any other scientist would agree with me about the use of unreliable evidence, it was another thing to cast doubts on theoretical calculations, and he claimed that I had used my hindsight as the measure of what should have been fore-sight in the war. Second, he thought I had not fully understood the method by which scientific viewpoints were introduced to the study of bombing, notably by Lord Cherwell in his famous minute in which he forecast the effects which would be produced by area-bombing. Zuckerman had himself helped in the drafting of this minute. Third, he thought that my attack on the use of statistical methods for the assessment of bombing effect was wholly unjustified. Finally, he was unhappy about my choice of facts to support the conclusions I had reached at the end of the study.

There then followed his extensive list of detailed observations. He challenged my statement that bombing expectations had been based upon the assumption that attacks would be accurate to within three hundred yards of the aiming point until April 1941, when the expected error was increased to a thousand yards. He said that, early in 1942, he had used an expected error of a thousand yards when making calculations for Combined Operations Headquarters. He denied my claim that the Chiefs of Staff were misled by a miscalculation of the effects the available bombing strength would have. He said they were not misled but that, in so far as they came to the wrong conclusions, the fault lay not in miscalculation but in the lack of calculation. He said that I had used the term 'expert' very loosely and that, for example, I had referred to 'railway experts' as people who understood the running of railways. (I had indeed.) But he went on to say that the advice of these experts to the Air Staff that twenty tons of bombs would put a junction out of action was the equivalent to the Convocation of Bishops advising that the injection of 0.2 mm. of methylcyanide into goats would make them read books.

And so Zuckerman went on for several more pages, presuming that I was a professional historian but lamenting the fact that I was not a scientist and a statistician. I think Nerney was rather worried. Zuckerman was an important man and a few days passed before I heard that he wanted to know how I had reacted to his comments on my work and that he would make time to see me to discuss matters. I told Nerney that there was no point in this until after I had sent a paper to Zuckerman setting out my reactions. Only after he had read this would we have a useful basis for discussion. Within twenty-four hours, I sent my paper to Nerney and he duly sent it on to Zuckerman.[15]

First, I dealt with the suggestion that I had attacked the employment of

empirical methods in the formulation of bombing policy and that, in criticiz-
ing them, I had been guilty of expecting the contemporary advisors to have
had foresight equivalent to the historical hindsight available to me. I observed that it was not empirical methods which I had attacked but, on the
contrary, the lack of them. I stressed that in advising on an oil policy early
in the war, the experts had accepted glib assumptions about the accuracy of
bombing without either enquiry or experiment. But I pointed out too that I
had recognized the extent to which these people had been working in the
dark. All the same, I asserted that an historian had to make use of his hindsight in coming to his judgements. If he did not, I said, his work would be
meaningless. I had tried throughout, I claimed, to be fair to individuals and
had avoided blaming them for mistakes in relation to things they could not
have been expected to know. In other words, I was pointing out to Zuckerman that hindsight should not be withheld from the judgement of history
and that it should only be withheld from individuals if their work – even if
it was actually wrong – was right in so far as contemporary understanding
allowed. As to the accusation that I was not a scientific expert and therefore
did not understand the basis on which Lord Cherwell's famous minute was
based, I conceded the first point and dismissed the second. I pointed out that
I had explained the content of what Cherwell submitted to the Prime Minister
and the influence on bombing policy it had had. Though I did not express it
in words, the inference was that the fact that Zuckerman had made an early
draft of the minute was not the main historical point any more than that Sir
Henry Tizard had thought the whole argument was exaggerated. The point
lay in the words Cherwell had employed, for his was the most powerful, and
indeed at this stage the operative, influence. I left it to my detailed replies to
deal with the condemnation of my attack upon statistical methods in the
judgement of bombing effects, and also the suggestion that in establishing
my conclusions I had picked my facts specially.

In formulating these detailed responses, I became increasingly aware that
in much of Zuckerman's rhetoric there was some very muddled thinking and
blinkered understanding. For example, his dismissive comments on my
criticism of the assumption that even night-bombing would be accurate to
within three hundred yards until as late as April 1941, when the expectation
was increased to a thousand yards, were made to look silly by his own
statement that, in forming his advice early in 1942, he had used an assumption of accuracy to within a thousand yards. I replied that this was odd. It
did not bear upon the question of the earlier three-hundred-yard assumption
and I said that by early 1942 it was common knowledge that the error was
a matter of miles and not of yards.

On the question of railway experts, the Convocation of Bishops and the
goats, I wrote, 'as to the goats – this of course, apart from being very witty,

is quite apposite but let us suppose that the Convocation of Bishops did tender advice in the sense suggested by Professor Zuckerman. Let us also suppose that the Government accepted the advice and that a large proportion of industrial activity was harnessed to the production of methylcyanide, and a great number of Doctors, to the detriment of their ordinary patients, were directed to carry out the operation. Suppose also that the goats, objecting to this treatment, caused a high rate of fatal casualties to the doctors, and that a large number of school teachers were re-employed in other professions on the assumption that they could be replaced in the schools by goats, then surely the advice of the Convocation of Bishops would assume a greater historic significance than the advice of some sceptic who said all along that goats would never read. Naturally, I was flattering Professor Zuckerman because, from his own admission, I well knew that during the war he had been one of the bishops.

I have only touched on the thrust and counter-thrust between myself and Professor Zuckerman, but as I write more than forty-three years after the exchange, it still amazes me how such an eminent man of science could, in historical matters, be such a fool and how, historically, such a fool could subsequently have been elevated into such a high position in the counsels of the nation. As I think of this now, the imperative need for C.P. Snow's 'two cultures' to embrace each other is ever more apparent. Sir Charles Webster, with whom I was now fully in harness, took a less dramatic view. He told me that my thesis contained much irony which had got under Zuckerman's skin. One or two of Zuckerman's points, he thought, were valid but most of them were simply pique. He said that my reply was good and justified, 'especially about the goats'. Zuckerman, he said, had not got a leg to stand on. I doubt whether Zuckerman thought this, but whether he did or not, I heard no more about a meeting with him to discuss the issues and I had to wait another twenty years before I met this eminent man in person. By that time, I think he had forgotten our skirmish and, as I had not been delving into my records, I had probably done so too.[16]

The fact that Oxford accepted my thesis as worthy of a DPhil and the warm congratulations I received for it from such eminent and closely positioned academics as Sir Charles Webster and Professor Butler no doubt corroborated Nerney's conviction that I had done well and, Zuckerman, Portal and Saundby notwithstanding, he wrote me a most generous letter. He said that the outcome was a great personal satisfaction to him as well as being of inestimable value to the status of the Air Historical Branch. The future role of air history in the academic field had indeed, he wrote, been demonstrated. As I learnt years later from the study of documents in the Public Record Office, Nerney had been striving for several years to obtain academic recognition for the work of his narrators and I alone among them had realized some of his ambitions. It was he who had given me the opportunity; it was he who stood behind me when the great men of his world seemed to be against me. But, while I remember him with deep gratitude I cannot place him in my Valhalla. I now know, as I did not at the time, that when the crisis of the official history arose, his hand was turned against me. More surprising to me even than this was the extraordinary behaviour of one of my Oxford DPhil examiners, Professor Norman Gibbs, who had by then become Chichele Professor of the History of War in the University of Oxford. My account of these two disappointments belongs to later chapters.[17]

CHAPTER FOUR

History in Whitehall

Sir Charles Webster was a big man. Large and bulky in body, ugly in face, short-sighted, imprecise in movement and carelessly dressed, he was naturally clumsy. When – since he wished to have the experience – we went flying in a Bomber Command Washington aircraft, he stepped on and destroyed a gyro-compass. On another occasion, when we were watching a test match against South Africa at Lords, his foot dropped into our next door neighbour's luncheon basket and smashed a bottle of gin. So far from apologizing, he exclaimed that gin was a vulgar drink and took his leave. The victim made no complaint, but turning to me, said that he was afraid he had annoyed my father. This was typical. Though some people complained of Webster, few did so to his face. Capable of considerable geniality, he was also, when it suited him, willing to be extremely rude without any inhibition. He exploited his size and used geniality or rudeness indifferently in the pursuit of his objectives, which were to a large extent the development of his own power and success. Coming from what used to be called humble origins in Liverpool, he tended to despise those who had had better starts, such as, for example, the chief military historian, Professor Butler. Innocently thinking that it might be to my advantage, I let it slip that Arnold Toynbee was my cousin. Webster looked surprised, paused and then assured me that he would not hold it against me. He tended to be combative with and critical of other historians, especially those like G.P. Gooch or Harold Nicolson who ventured into his own field. He disliked snobs and snobbery and, although intensely patriotic and loyal to the crown, he thought that trooping the colour was a silly ceremony. He wished that modern soldiers in their tanks and other twentieth-century outfits could have paraded before the Sovereign on his official birthday.

Webster did not own his home and was a true floating voter in the sense that he examined the issues at each general election, especially those concerning foreign policy, and voted for what he thought was the best case. He left £40,000 when he died, a substantial sum in 1961, but all of this was the product of his earnings and the shrewd advice of a friend who was a financier.

On the whole he was respectful of authority and he usually looked up to great men such as Ministers, Commanders-in-Chief and the like. Unfortunately, he also thought he knew how to handle such people. He had seen no action in war and he appeared to admire and perhaps envy those who had. He had reached the rank of Major in the First World War, but he had never been anywhere near the front and liked to boast of the part he had played at Versailles in helping Smuts to draft clauses for the constitution of the League of Nations. He had done the same sort of thing at San Francisco for the United Nations in 1944 and was knighted for his pains. He told me that he had had to think seriously about accepting or refusing the KCMG when it was offered to him; he thought his grocer might charge him more. But he was prepared to laugh when I suggested that these anxieties might not have detained him for more than a few seconds.

Webster's wife was almost completely the opposite. Nora was petite, chic, very pretty, elegant and shy. Her graceful and athletic movements seemed almost strange in Webster's company. She was not an accomplished talker and I doubt if she ever engaged her husband in anything approaching serious discussion. They had no children but were obviously devoted to one another. I think Webster's books were not widely read. They were, however, much respected and, by the time I met him, he stood in the forefront of the academic world as Professor of International History in the London School of Economics and President of the British Academy. His scholarship was taken to be formidable. His personality obviously was so.

Such was the colleague with whom I embarked in 1951 on the venture of writing the official history of the strategic air offensive. Our partnership was to last ten years. Webster died in August 1961 after we had finished the four volumes of the book, after the battle for its publication had been fought and won and after the text had gone to press. I was left alone to face the flak which came up when our work appeared in print. Had Webster died a year earlier, I doubt if I would have had to do so, for I doubt if the book would have been published. Though I had written most of it and was therefore much better placed than Webster would have been to deal with the media-inflamed row that blew up when the book appeared, I do not believe that I could have won the battle for publication on my own. It was Webster's prestige and not my years of toil that denied the Prime Minister, Harold Macmillan, the chance of suppressing the book, which I think he would otherwise have taken. My description of these bizarre events must be left until I have first explained how the book was written. Suffice it to say here that, had I not experienced them personally, I would have found it hard to believe they took place, and that, had I not been able to read the extensive documentation on them now available in the Public Record Office and elsewhere, I would only have known a fraction of what really happened. Personal experience alone is neither a reliable nor a sufficient means of understanding history, but it does have the advantage of opening the eyes and sharpening perceptions.

Webster approached the subject of strategic bombing with vigour and enthusiasm. He thought we ought to be able to write the best official military history ever written. He immersed himself in the documentation and wanted to meet all the commanders who had been concerned in the campaign. He thought at first that he would write about the strategies of the offensive and that I would do the operations. He knew from the beginning that the technicalities of the latter were, and would remain, beyond his understanding. Although he listened attentively to my lectures on the difference between course and track, the distinction between bomb-aiming and navigation (which Professor Zuckerman had confused), the effects of opposition on accuracy, the inevitable inequality of the conditions of combat between heavy bombers and interceptor fighters, and so on and so on, these proved to be matters which he could not grasp. He also soon came to realize that the strategies, or policies, that Bomber Command pursued were so heavily influenced by the operational capacities available that it would be easier for one mind rather than two to write coherently about them. The question then was, which part would Webster write? It had become clear that his task would be to deal with the third component, the results of the offensive; and that was what I hoped he would decide to do. We would then have had a book with three principal components: strategy, operations and results. In my scheme, the issues of intelligence appreciations would have been woven into the examination of strategy; but Webster was not quite satisfied with the idea. He thought that intelligence and results should be linked in a single examination. I accepted this and we therefore planned to produce the history in a series of chronological sequences, within each of which there would be sections on strategy and operations, which I would write, and appreciations and results, which Webster would write. In addition, Webster would write an introductory chapter dealing with the origins and development of Bomber Command before the war. For this he had, as a foundation, the excellent narrative, *The Pre-War Evolution of Bomber Command*, which R.B. Wernham had written. We also agreed that we would exchange our drafts and confer over them until we were ready to accept joint responsibility for our finalized versions. Such residual matters outside the scope of our plan as we found to be of sufficient importance and relevance would be dealt with in appendices. We also decided that we would print key documents *in extenso* which had a bearing on our three elements.

Webster and I fully recognized from the outset that a defect of our scheme was that it would involve a rather greater volume of repetition than was theoretically desirable. This would arise from the fact that, for example, in discussing strategy, I would be bound to refer to some of the intelligence that

Webster would be dealing with in his chapters. There was also the general consideration that we would be going over the same time-span three times, even if it was from three different aspects. We concluded, however, that we had no viable alternative. The subject was too complex to be dealt with in a straight chronological manner; we had to introduce functional divisions and, in any case, it seemed to be the only sensible way in which we could accommodate our respective scholarly capacities. In my view, only if Webster and I had been one man, could 'we' have written a better book. I do thus concede that, theoretically, a better book could have been written. But I also claim that it is right to accept that ideal aims must sometimes give way to practical possibilities.

As a prelude, we did some flying, as I have mentioned. This was the product of Webster's enthusiastic attempt to gain personal experience of life in Bomber Command, which he thought would enable him the better to understand some of the technicalities of the subject on which we were embarking. I rather admired the pluck which led him onto this path, but my enthusiasm for the project did not match his. I advised him to have a medical exam before getting into a high-level bomber and I now have to admit that I hoped he would fail it. I knew that if he did not, I would be honour bound to accompany him in the air. Webster easily trumped my ace. He went to see the C-in-C, Bomber Command at his headquarters near High Wycombe. There he was examined by an RAF doctor who told him that his heart and blood pressure were in excellent order and that he need have no fear about going up in a bomber. There being no escape for me, we duly journeyed in one of the C-in-C's grand cars to RAF Station Marham. The Station Commander, Group Captain B.A. Casey, put us up in his comfortable house and there followed three extremely energetic days. We were attached to 90 Squadron which was equipped with Washingtons. This was the name conferred by Bomber Command on the B29s that had been obtained from the United States. The object of the Washingtons was to lift the aircrews out of the era of the Second World War and into that of the jet-propelled Canberra, which would shortly come into service. The Washington was a far cry from the Lancaster and indeed the B17, and its array of automated equipment, including remotely controlled unmanned gun-turrets, made it a poor guide to the conditions under which Bomber Command and the Eighth Air Force had operated in the war. We did some formation flying in practice for the forthcoming fly-past on Battle of Britain day, and we flew in separate aircraft across the North Sea to bomb targets in Heligoland. Webster's aircraft attacked from 20,000 feet and he noted that, of the four bombs dropped, only two hit the island. My aircraft came in at 18,000 feet and we also dropped four bombs. One failed to detonate but the others seemed to find their mark. It was very unwarlike. We attacked in perfect visibility and made our approach straight and level. It looked – and I think was – extremely easy. We then came down to 500 feet and made several runs across the island, machine-gunning it as we went. I was rather surprised to see a number of manned trawlers in the vicinity, including one which was alongside in the port. These were apparently collecting valuable salvage but I was told not to bother about them as they had no right to be on an official RAF bombing-range. It seemed a shame that I had to impress upon Webster, who was full of excitement, that there was little or nothing to be learnt about the war from these experiences.[1]

While we were at Marham, the C-in-C, Air Chief Marshal Sir Hugh Pugh Lloyd, came and lunched with us. There was tremendous talk about air superiority, bombing accuracy and so on. Lloyd was a forceful character with strongly delineated views, but his grasp of the historical issues involved in the strategic air offensive of the Second World War seemed to me to be virtually negligible. I think he detected that this was my opinion from the nature and tone of my contributions, which he tended to interrupt with observations such as 'there's a bunny on the lawn', or 'was that a chaffinch or a bullfinch?' I enjoyed meeting this colourful and impressive character but it was nervous work. Webster charged in with questions he had rehearsed with me beforehand. The difficulties arose when he had to deal, unrehearsed, with the ripostes: it was then that he ran out, not of steam, but of infor-mation. This was unfortunate, for as we proceeded from one great man to another in a scintillating series of interviews, Webster disseminated the belief in such circles that he, as the official historian of the strategic air offensive, had little grasp of the subject. The other downside of these meetings was that Webster tended too readily to fall for the lines of argument that these great men developed. He would suddenly depart from the principles with which I had bombarded him and, if only for a short time, believe silly things such as that heavy bombers were capable of defending themselves. I do not believe, however, that he ever accepted anything quite so absurd as the view Sir Hugh Lloyd expressed to me on another occasion about the Battle of Britain. He said that the defeat of Fighter Command would not have been an event of any great significance; it would merely have made the going for Bomber Command a bit harder. His contempt for Fighter Command was perhaps only exceeded by his outright dislike of the Navy. Sir Hugh Lloyd not only had little understanding of the history of the service in which he had so notably distinguished himself, he also conspicuously lacked any appreciation of any of the branches of any of the services apart from the one he com-manded. With only a few exceptions, however, amongst whom Sir John Slessor stood out, this proved to be the norm for Air Marshals.[2]

After a visit to Supreme Headquarters Allied Powers in Paris, where he was deeply impressed by General Eisenhower, both on account of what the general said to him and more so of his striking personality, Webster wrote to me saying that he could now take on the Air Marshals on what he called the 'strategic Air Force' because he reckoned that they knew less of the subject than he did. Although he recognized that the going might be tougher with the likes of Sir Ralph Cochrane, whom we were about to meet to talk over the contents of my thesis, he was in fact developing an over-confidence which was soon to have some very inconvenient consequences. Admittedly, I had stirred a few hornets from their nest by circulating my thesis to Sir Ralph Cochrane, Sir Robert Saundby and others of the 'Air Force' persuasion, including Lord Portal, but Webster was now to plant his foot on the centre of that nest as firmly as he had done on our fellow cricket-watcher's luncheon basket at Lords.[3]

Webster spent the last quarter of 1952 in America where he sought out American air generals, academics and anyone else who would talk to him about the strategic air offensive. On 18th November he was in New York and, hearing that Sir Arthur Harris also happened to be there, he telephoned the former C-in-C, Bomber Command. Harris immediately invited him to lunch at his private apartment, 45 East 62nd Street between Madison and Park. He was received by Lady Harris, whom he found charming and attractive. Sir Arthur arrived shortly afterwards. Both were 'most hospitable and cordial' and they gave him a delightful lunch which they themselves had prepared. Harris told Webster that it was difficult to get good food well prepared: Britain lacked the material and America the skill, except in a few very expensive restaurants. Webster found Harris's potted meat and salad delicious and Lady Harris's Melton Mowbray pie was 'something to remember'. While Lady Harris intervened only to provide for their creature comforts, Harris and Webster embarked on a discussion of the bomber offensive that lasted for two hours. 'No one with whom I have talked,' Webster noted in his diary, 'has been more frank or more willing to discuss the problems of my work which is indeed largely his command.' Webster believed that this was due, at least in part, to his having shown at the outset sympathy with Harris's problems and point of view. All the same, Webster did venture to voice some criticisms of Bomber Command and he told Harris of my work. Harris said that he would be glad to read and comment upon my thesis.[4]

That evening Webster wrote to me. He was cock-a-hoop. 'You will probably be surprised to learn,' he began, 'that I have lunched to day with Sir Arthur Harris and had 2 hours conversation with him about Bomber Command.' Much of what Harris said, Webster wrote, was the same as he had put in his book, but sometimes the emphasis was different. Naturally, Webster informed me, he had told Harris 'all about you and your dissertation'. Webster asked me to have it sent out to America, and he hoped that this could be done in time for Harris to read it before Webster left for home, so that he could hear what Harris had to say about it. I received this letter on 25th November and the next day asked Nerney for permission to send off my thesis as Webster had asked. Nerney told me that this was impossible, giving as his first reason that a secret document of this nature could not be sent out of the country and as his second and, as I thought at the time, more operative one that Harris would make a most unpleasant row if he saw it. A few hours later Nerney telephoned me and read out a letter Harris had written to Sir Ralph Cochrane. It began, 'Who the devil is Sir Charles Webster?' and went on to refer to the London School of Economics, where Webster had told him he had his chair, as an organization concerned with the destruction of the British Empire. He said that Webster had told him he was going to make use in the history of Lord Cherwell's personal minutes to the Prime Minister and that this had infuriated Cherwell. He understood that Cochrane had read the preliminary study for the history, meaning evidently my thesis, and that it had infuriated him too. The tone of the letter, I recorded at the time, was extremely hostile. I thought it was unwise to have stirred up bitterness at this time, when all we required was peace and quiet and the necessary years in which to write a good book, after which, I thought, the deluge would not matter. But Webster was in blissful ignorance of the fact that he had put the cat among the pigeons and, in some haste, I seized my pen to warn him.[5]

In bringing Webster back to earth in this abrupt way, I could not give chapter and verse, as what Nerney had told me he had said in confidence, but I left him in no doubt that he had misread Harris's reception of him in New York and that, even if it might seem 'childish and absurd', Harris's conviction that the London School of Economics was dedicated to the destruction of the British Empire was a much more important consideration than any apparent courtesy which Harris might have shown to the Professor of International History in that institution. I told Webster that it might be unwise to show Harris my thesis or to disclose anything to him that might nourish 'the somewhat curious & clearly preconceived ideas wh. he seems to have formed about our book'. Webster was quite taken aback. 'Your letter naturally startled me', he wrote. All he could say was that nothing could have been more 'cordial or sane' than the interview with Harris which he had described to me. He promised, all the same, to be mindful of what I had said when he saw Harris again.[6]

And he was. 'In view of Noble's letter,' he wrote in his diary, 'I had been rather nervous about this second interview, but,' he added, 'nothing could have been more pleasant.' It was mainly a social occasion 'as I wished him to get a proper feeling about me and not think I was a red because I was at the LSE'. Webster therefore led the conversation in this direction, and he thought that he and Harris were able to agree on most things, 'e.g. the Germans and the communists'. Harris, however, said that the latter should be outlawed as owing allegiance to a foreign power. When Webster instanced the Roman Catholics, Harris seemed to think there was little difference between them and the communists. Even on this, they did not seem to be far apart. 'My Protestant blood and upbringing,' Webster wrote, 'if they did not force agreement, at least caused many cells to respond.' Harris asked him to tell him more about Noble, which, Webster recorded, he did and hoped that Harris would look forward to meeting him some day. All this was so pleasant that Webster wrote to me saying he found it hard to believe what I had written to him. He said that he would reserve his final judgement until we met again, but that he now felt he had taken pains to make his philosophy of life clear to Harris, and he thought he had succeeded in doing so. By the time I received this letter, I knew that it represented no more than wishful thinking. Nerney had kept me informed about more letters arriving in London from Harris on the subject of Webster. I decided that the whole business was childish. I was sure that we would both resign before submitting to pressure and I comforted myself with the reflection that Harris was not on the Air Staff and that he did not have a reputation for impartiality. Would that it had been as simple as that.[7]

This much I knew at the time. It was not, I have subsequently learned, anything like the whole story, nor was it enough to alert me sufficiently to the fire-power which was to be brought to bear upon our project, chiefly from an unholy alliance between Sir Arthur Harris and Lord Portal. Ironically, one of the principal issues on which they stood against us was a bitter dispute between themselves about bombing policy, which had taken place between November 1944 and January 1945. They did not want the public to know about it.

Webster and I, on the other hand, knew that this dispute was of prime importance in the history of the strategic air offensive. It arose from Portal's apprehension that, in the winter of 1944–5, Harris was devoting his main effort to a continuation of the area-bombing of German cities and that he was neglecting the target named as primary in his directive, namely, German oil production. In summary, Portal's belief was that area-bombing should continue only when the weather was unsuitable for attacks on oil plants. If enough effort was devoted to the latter, he believed that the war could be brought to an end very shortly. Harris believed that the intelligence concerning oil was the same sort of rubbish as that about ball-bearings had been. He thought that an intensification of area-bombing of cities was the only sure way in which Germany could be brought to her knees. After nearly three months of argument, a deadlock was reached and Harris suggested to Portal that if he was not satisfied with the way in which Harris was carrying out his directive, he should find another commander to take over Bomber Command. Portal ducked that issue and told Harris that he was to carry on as C-in-C and that they would have to wait until the war was over to see which of them had been right.[8]

When it was over, however, and the official historians sought to make a judgement as to who had been right and who wrong, Portal and Harris found themselves united in their determination that no such judgement should be made. They both demanded that quotation of their acrimonious correspondence of the winter of 1944 to 1945 should be omitted from the history. Though Webster and I were, at the time, only told parts of the story, we learned enough to realize that our book was under threat of emasculation or extinction. It would be emasculation if we accepted what Portal and Harris demanded and extinction if the Government failed to uphold the stand which, in the event, Webster and I were to make. The gulf between our view of official history and that of some of the principal figures in it became clear and the whole issue came to turn upon what the Prime Minister would ultimately decide. Since this issue concerned the basic nature and purpose of official history and since it also raised important questions about the scope of contemporary history, it is worth returning now to the meetings between Webster and Harris and tracing the episodes that developed afterwards and led to the Portal and Harris *démarches* when the book was ready to go the printers.

Not content with asking Cochrane who the devil Sir Charles Webster was, Harris asked the same question of Sir James Barnes, the Permanent Under Secretary of State at the Air Ministry, and Sir Maurice Dean, then the Second Secretary at the Board of Trade, but soon to succeed Barnes as PUS at the Air Ministry, in which he had spent a good deal of his career. Barnes told Harris that he could safely dismiss from his mind any idea that Webster was working against the interests of the Air Ministry. He wrote that Webster was one of the most distinguished British historians and that his credentials were 'unassailable'. He told him that Webster was being assisted by Dr N. Frankland, DFC, who had served in Bomber Command and, after the war, in the Air Historical Branch of the Air Ministry. He stated that the final version of the official history would not necessarily bear any resemblance to the thesis that Frankland had written in AHB and he explained that a draft of the official history would be circulated for comment to Sir Robert Saundby and others and that, together with the comments arising, it would then be studied by the Air Ministry. If the Air Ministry was then not satisfied that 'justice' had been done, an 'entirely new situation' would arise; but he did not want to speculate as to how this would be handled. He told Harris that he had recently discussed the situation with Saundby and that the latter thought it satisfactory for the present, on the understanding that if Webster

The author's Lancaster bomber crew, 50 Squadron, 1944. *Left to right*, Sgt Frank Knott, Sgt Dick Darby, Fl Sgt Keith Sneddon, F/O Noble Frankland, Fl Sgt 'Shortie' Short, F/O Gordon Pyle, Fl Lt Murray Milne

Sir Charles Webster and the author's son at Thames House, circa 1954

Marshal of the Royal Air
Force Sir Arthur Harris

At the opening of an exhibition
in the Imperial War Museum to
mark the fiftieth anniversary of
the foundation of the RAF,
1968. *Left to right*, Admiral Sir
Deric Holland-Martin, Marshal
of the Royal Air Force Lord
Portal, the author

At the opening of an exhibition in the IWM to mark the fiftieth anniversary of the foundation of the Royal Flying Corps, 1962. *Left to right*, Admiral of the Fleet Sir Algernon Willis, Marshal of the Royal Air Force Lord Tedder

At the opening of a special photographic exhibition in the IWM, 1963. The Prime Minister, Harold Macmillan, and the author

At the opening of an exhibition in London, *The Study of Toynbee*, circa 1969.
Left to right, the author, Arnold Toynbee, the Minister for the Arts, Lord Eccles

A section of *The War Exhibition* in the IWM, 1980

(*opposite above*) Arriving in the IWM for the preview of *The Life and Times of Lord Mountbatten*, 19th December 1968. *Left to right*, The Prince of Wales, Princess Anne, the author, Sir Deric Holland-Martin, the Queen, Lord Mountbatten

(*opposite below*) At the reception in the IWM after the preview of *The Life and Times of Lord Mountbatten*. *Left foreground*, the Prince of Wales and Sir Peter Masefield. *Behind them, left to right*, Diana Frankland, Queen Anne-Marie of the Hellenes, the Prime Minister, Harold Wilson. *Centre foreground*, Princess Anne and Dr Christopher Roads. *To their right*, the Duke of Kent. *Extreme right*, Peter Morley

(*Above*) HMS *Belfast* passing through Tower Bridge to enter the Pool of London, 15th October 1971

(*Below*) In the engine room of HMS *Belfast*, 1978. *Left to right*, Rear-Admiral Higham, the Minister for the Arts, Lord Donaldson, Sir Peter Masefield, the author

The author with HMS *Belfast* in dry dock at Tilbury, 1982

An air day at the IWM at Duxford Airfield

Prince Henry Duke of Gloucester at the
IWM meeting members of the staff, 1966.
Left to right, Miss R.E.B. Coombs,
J.E. Sutters, J.F. Golding, Peter Simkins,
W.P. Mayes, Prince Henry, Lt Colonel Simon
Bland, the author, Sir Algernon Willis

Prince Arthur Duke of Connaught,
reproduced from the portrait painted
by de László

and Frankland went off the rails, which it should not be assumed they would do, then the Air Ministry would go into the matter at the highest level. Dean wrote in a rather different tone. He sent Harris extracts from Webster's *Who's Who* entry and said that he was writing about the 'strategic air war' as an official historian. He added that he was told that he had a colleague for this task, 'a man named Frankland who was I believe at Bomber Command during the war'. He passed on the news that the Cabinet Office would be grateful if Harris would help Webster and Frankland with their research.[9]

Harris seemed to be slightly mollified. He now told Cochrane that he found Webster an 'intelligent old fellow' but he was disquieted by the fact that he insisted on having Frankland as a joint author. The latter, he had been told, was a 'somewhat rabid individual' where the Air Force and, in particular, Bomber Command, were concerned. He declared that he would be prepared to read the drafts of the history but that he was beyond worrying about what Webster and Frankland, or anyone else, had to say about the bomber offensive. Within five days, his earlier feelings had begun to reassert themselves. Replying to Sir James Barnes, he said of Webster that he liked the old boy, but that he was a very unfortunate choice by, as he persisted in thinking, the Air Ministry. Webster had sent him an article he had published in the journal of the American Consular and Diplomatic Services. In this, Webster had observed that the war had not been won by bombing alone; that showed how prejudiced he was. Frankland had been promoted; he was now a 'disgruntled Navigator from Bomber Command', who had written a hostile thesis. This was serious because Webster had a great admiration for him.[10]

Without further effort on Webster's part or mine, things soon got a good deal worse. At the end of February 1953, Harris wrote to the Secretary of State for Air, Lord De L'Isle and Dudley. He was now 'seriously concerned' about the history of the bombing offensive. It was wrong, he said, that the writing of the official history should be placed in the hands of the 'Labour Government's selection', a London School of Economics professor, who had already expressed derogatory opinions of Bomber Command. He went on to complain that this professor was assisted by Dr Frankland, who had written a thesis to prove the futility of the bombing offensive. Yet Webster himself had told Harris that he so admired Frankland's work that he had insisted upon his name being joined with his own as the author of the projected history. If this was correct, he thought that De L'Isle and Dudley would agree that there should be 'some reconsideration' of the question of who was to write the official history. It was perhaps fortunate that neither Webster nor I got wind of this letter.[11]

Meanwhile, Lord Portal was following a much more patient and diplomatic line. At the end of January 1953, he wrote to Webster saying that about a year ago he had read my thesis, which he described as a 'very interest-

ing work'. He had intended to organize a meeting of those chiefly concerned
to discuss it but had not got round to it. He now sent Webster the notes he
had prepared for the meeting that never was. Compared to the reaction of
Sir Arthur Harris, whose judgement had not of course been impeded by
reading the work, Portal's comments were mild stuff. It was wrong, he
claimed, to suggest that the commanders at the outset of the Second World
War had misread the principles of war; they knew what they were. The Air
staff had always been aware of the importance of air superiority. Britain
could not have produced a long-range fighter to boost the American effort.
In other words, there was not much ground for criticism of anything.
Webster, having returned from the United States, replied immediately thank-
ing Portal for his letter and 'valuable enclosure'. He was able to boast that
he had spent many hours in the Pentagon and had had a long talk with
General Doolittle. General Spaatz had unfortunately been on the wrong side
of America, but Webster had met some members of his former staff. He had
had some talks with Sir Arthur Harris and everyone had been most kind.
Everywhere he had found 'great recognition' of the part Portal had played
in determining the strategy of the war. Webster, who already knew Portal,
as both of them were members of the Council of Chatham House, asked if
they could meet to discuss some of the strategic issues of the war. He hoped
that Portal would agree that Noble Frankland might also be present. He said
that I had modified some of the opinions expressed in my thesis and that I
was 'really a remarkably able young man who is also both modest and
candid'. In addition, he said, Frankland knew the papers much better than
he did. Webster was usually candid, not always modest, but in this case he
clearly realized the special importance of Lord Portal's position. He told me
that we would have to be 'tactful on this first occasion'. I did not find it hard
to observe this last instruction; I was much in awe of Lord Portal. The result
was the rather uninspiring meeting I described in Chapter 3.[12]

    In these ways, partly known and partly unknown to us at the time, the
two most important figures in the Bomber Command offensive against
Germany came into our picture. In the official history, we reproduced their
portraits as the frontispieces to the first two of our volumes. The third most
important figure, whose portrait we used for the frontispiece of our third
volume, was Lord Tedder. Webster entertained him and me to lunch in the
Athenaeum on 20th May 1954. Clearly, I did not think that anything of any
great importance was said, for I noted in my diary only that what passed
was recorded in Webster's diary and so it was, except that the amusing side
was left out. We got off to a bad start when Tedder asked for gin as his
appetizer. Webster could hardly believe that a Marshal of the Royal Air Force
could ask for anything so vulgar. Nor did matters improve when a characteristically unhelpful waiter dropped a heavily bound Athenaeum menu into

the poached eggs Tedder had ordered for his first course. Despite these set-backs, we had an agreeable if inconsequential discussion of the war. While, as I will presently show, our difficulties with Harris and Portal intensified, we never had any with Tedder. In our book there was much praise and scarcely a criticism of Tedder. Of Harris and Portal there was also much praise, but there was also some criticism.[13]

In the meantime, though Harris had taken up an entrenched position, Portal retained an open mind, sufficiently open at least to enable him to be good enough to sponsor me for a Rockefeller Fellowship in the United States. This gave me the opportunity to delve into the records of the Eighth Air Force in the Air University at Montgomery, Alabama, and in a disused torpedo factory at Alexandria over the Potomac from Washington. This golden opportunity had been created for me by Webster, but I doubt if I would have been given such free access to secret material at a time when McCarthyism was in full flow had it not been for Portal's sponsorship. This was great generosity *de haut en bas*.[14]

In addition to Webster and Portal, I was also sponsored for the Rockefeller Fellowship by Butler and Air Chief Marshal Sir Guy Garrod, who was the air member of Butler's Panel of advisors. This was powerful support only slightly marred by Acheson's inevitable objections. He sent for me and told me that the official history of the strategic air offensive was not intended to be a comprehensive account of what the Americans did and that their part should only be explained to the extent needed to make our part intelligible. He was, therefore, doubtful as to whether it would be proper to pay my Cabinet Office salary while I was in America, if I insisted on going there. My point of view was that it would be impossible to write an authoritative history of the British part in the offensive unless the resources of the book were reinforced by significant research in the records of the United States Strategic Air Forces in Europe. I did not, however, have to argue the point with Acheson; Webster clubbed him down with the assertion that the British and American efforts were 'inextricably interlocked' and that, if I was not given a Rockefeller grant, I would have to go at the public expense. Clearly Acheson did not wish to pursue that avenue and, having duly been appointed to a Rockefeller Fellowship, I sailed for America on board *Queen Mary* at the beginning of October 1953.[15]

The Rockefeller Fellowship was a prize indeed. The prestige of the organization opened doors to the offices of the great and the clever; it sent hoteliers scuttling for keys to good rooms in hotels; and, above all – though in some cases not without difficulty – it landed me in the still secret archives of the United States Army Air Forces. It also led to my appointment as a Visitor at the Institute for Advanced Study in Princeton. Another advantage was that Rockefeller Fellows were let out on a very loose rein. Scarcely any red tape was involved and one was encouraged to do whatever seemed to be interesting and profitable.

I divided the three months I was in the United States between the Research Studies Institute of the Air University at Maxwell Air Force Base near Montgomery, Alabama, the Library of Congress in Washington, the Federal Record Center at Alexandria nearby and the Institute for Advanced Study. The Research Studies Institute proved to be a larger version of the Air Historical Branch in London and it seemed to me that its historians were too much under the thumb of the Air Force, by whom they were employed. I became increasingly convinced that official history of academic soundness could not be written under the aegis of the service with which it was primarily concerned. I am bound to say, however, that there was one historian at Maxwell whose moral courage and independence of mind were such as to make his views of strategic bombing important and interesting. This was Martin R.R. Goldman. Unfortunately, he did not long remain in the field of air history. I worked overtime in the archives and was able to penetrate into many issues which, on the evidence of the British records alone, would have remained obscure. As Webster wrote to me while I was there, 'when you marry one archive to another, they breed and produce results which can be obtained from neither singly'.[16]

The next excitement was 'marrying' the archives in the Federal Record Center at Alexandria with those I had now seen at Maxwell. For a time they seemed in danger of divorce. Unlike those at Maxwell and the former Army Air Forces themselves, these archives had not been transferred to the control of the newly created independent United States Air Force; they were still under the control of the Army. My high level clearance to see secret material belonging to the Air Force did not, I was told, apply to material which still belonged to the Army. After some rather hectic hours in the Pentagon I was, however, given the necessary papers and allowed into the former torpedo factory across the Potomac where I found rich seams of primary material concerning the Eighth Air Force and, in particular, the development of the Mustang long-range fighter. Again, at the high tide of McCarthyism, I was afforded a far greater degree of freedom of access to American secret documents than any American historian was given to the British equivalent. There also emerged the curious fact that the American official air historians had not been allowed to see these crucially important air force archives which belonged to the Army because, at the time of their origin, the air force had been the army air force.[17]

While in Washington, I was befriended by Professor Marvin McFarland of the Library of Congress. During the war he had served on General Spaatz's staff and, since it, had largely retained the role of historical advisor to the general. He now introduced me to the man I had long conceived to be the greatest air commander to date. On 4th December 1953, McFarland and I repaired in drizzly London-style weather to the *Newsweek* building. We entered a luxurious outer office where a girl told us, yes the general was expecting us. In less than a minute more he appeared, smartly dressed in a blue lounge suit and wearing spectacles, an impressive figure with a trace of whitish moustache and a rugged face but no bombast at all. Here was the commander of the United States Strategic Air Forces in Europe and later of the force which dropped the atomic bombs on Japan. Would we talk here or would we go up to the Press Club for a drink? McFarland said we would go up, and up we went. As we did so, General Spaatz made a complimentary remark about Lord Trenchard from whom he had just heard. Apparently Trenchard was under attack in the House of Lords from Admiral of the Fleet Lord Cunningham. General Spaatz placed us and our drinks in a corner of the room, seating himself at the right angle with McFarland on his left and myself on his right. He then seemed to pause for me to open fire.

I led off by explaining what Webster and I were trying to do and saying that I was in America because I did not believe that the thing could be done on a purely national basis from either side. Spaatz still waited, so I went to the point. I said 'General, tell me your attitude on L/R fighter escort'. With alacrity and precision Spaatz now sprang into action, counting off his points on the fingers of his left hand. It had always been planned, he said, to have bombers and fighters in the Eighth Air Force and with the fighters envisaged, chiefly the P38 Lightnings, fighter support could have been afforded up to the Rhine River. What they had not known was whether or not the bombers would be able to operate beyond the range of the fighters. The Royal Air Force, he said, had wanted to use all their own fighters and all the American ones for the defence of the United Kingdom; they had not realized the importance of their offensive role. He thought it very presumptuous of the Americans to come in after the RAF had been at war for two years and preach new doctrines; but all the same, he said, he had been determined that the United States Army Air Forces should run their own affairs and try their own techniques. The official line of the RAF had been that night-bombing was the best policy, but, General Spaatz said, when he got away from the upper echelons and talked to the men on the squadrons he found that there were doubts about the efficacy of night-bombing. In so far as they had thought about the use of fighters in support of bomber operations, the British had made the mistake that had proved fatal to the Luftwaffe in the Battle of Britain. The British, like the Germans, thought that fighter support should be in the form of close escort. This meant that the fighters had to keep station with the bombers, which they could only do by weaving to keep their ground speed down to that of the bombers. This reduced their range. If in 1940 the Germans had applied their fighters offensively in general cover, Spaatz thought that they would have won the Battle of Britain. I asked General Spaatz if in the course of his mission to Britain in 1940 he had been led to change any of his basic concepts. No, he replied, he had arrived and left convinced of the necessity and the possibility of daylight bombing. That was because he believed that the key to victory lay in successful attack on the enemy air force by bombing it in its factories and on its airfields, and by engaging it in the air as it rose to parry the bombing attacks.[18]

I was immensely struck by what General Spaatz said. He was devoid of pettiness, there was no rancour in his criticisms of others and he never seemed anxious to score points. Above all, what he said he had thought and done fitted well with what the documents I had seen indicated. In all these respects, he was unique among the many air commanders, British and American, with whom I had the privilege of conversing. Yet, when one came to examine what it all amounted to, the conclusion had to be, not very much. After all, what Spaatz told me he had thought and done was much the same as, on the basis of my research, I thought he had thought and done. There was virtually no divergence of opinion between us and therefore little or no new historical knowledge for me to digest. The difference between us was that I had worked out the principles of successful air warfare from the study of the evidence after the event and, in particular, by comparing what General Spaatz had done with what others like Sir Arthur Harris had attempted and I had enjoyed all the advantages of hindsight. General Spaatz had worked the same thing out in advance of events through the genius of his foresight and he had then had the courage and dominance to propel it into action. On this last point perhaps, I did gain from my meeting with Spaatz one important historical insight, which I could not have got from the documents. He told me that the support which he had had from Arnold, the Commanding General of the United States Army Air Forces, was such that if anyone had contrived to remove Spaatz they would have had to remove Arnold as well. Whether this was true or not (and I have heard the view expressed that it was not) matters little. The point is that Spaatz thought it was and this, I hardly doubt, gave him the confidence to interpret in his own way, and even to ignore, directives from General Eisenhower with what proved to be impunity and enormous advantage to the allied conduct of the war.

There was a marked warmth in my contact with General Spaatz and as we talked there seemed to be a twinkle in his eye. According to Professor McFarland, who knew Spaatz very well, this was not common. In our case, I think it arose from the fact that we had approached the same problems, myself from the easy end and he from the difficult end, and had come to a common conclusion in the middle, which was mutually flattering. The only other great man of action with whom I had this experience was Sir Henry Tizard. Whenever I was in America in subsequent years, Spaatz always found time to see me. He introduced me to General Eaker, whom he had displaced in the war, and though no new historical insights arose, there were some entertaining incidents. In January 1965, I found myself in the Army and Navy Club in Washington. I was facing General Eaker, who had his back to the window, which was in my full view. General Spaatz sat at right angles to it. I presently noticed clouds of dense smoke billowing up past the window, but did not quite like to say anything. When flames joined the smoke my nerve broke and I told General Spaatz that I thought the club was on fire. Spaatz said that he had of course noticed that some time ago, but it was none of his business: General Eaker was the President of the Club, he said. At last Eaker turned to look and immediately ordered us and everyone else out of the building.

Some years later I was invited to address a huge concourse of military historians and service people at the United States Air Force Academy in Colorado. In the centre of the front row of the vast auditorium sat General Spaatz and General Eaker. I was introduced by an American Professor, who chose to emphasize the criticisms of Bomber Command and the Eighth Air Force that I had made by that time, or was thought to have made, in the official history. Before I could rise, General Eaker stood up and declared that he had had enough of college boys and would have preferred to hear about the bomber offensive from someone who had been there. He then turned on his heel and, accompanied by Spaatz, walked out of the hall. They passed the rostrum and Eaker looked daggers but Spaatz winked. As they disappeared, I took the stand and declared 'I *was* there'. A resounding yell of maybe 800 voices rose to the roof and this was followed by prolonged loud applause. No doubt it was not very illuminating historically, but it was the only truly dramatic success I have ever had on the stage, and off it I fear that General Eaker must have heard the tumult.

After the excitement of discovery in the archives at Alexandria and the stimulus of meeting General Spaatz in Washington, the leisurely academic pace of the Institute for Advanced Study and the cultivated society revolving round Princeton University nearby were an anti-climax. My sponsor there, Professor Edward Mead Earle, showed me the greatest kindness, but he was, alas, already a very sick man with but a short span to live. In his day, he had known everyone from General Arnold down, but now he had only a little to say. Professor Sir Llewelyn Woodward, who had been one of my champions in the struggle to persuade Oxford to accept my DPhil thesis as a legitimate piece of history, kindly stepped into the breach, but, wonderful conversationalist that he was, he was not very strong on air power. He complained that there were too many mathematicians in the Institute, whose head at the time was Oppenheimer: they and the scientists, Woodward found, were immature souls with whom one could not have an intelligent conversation except within their fields of specialized study. This was a perception ahead of time about the 'two cultures' which C.P. Snow was later to whip into a journalistic lather. Perhaps because we were both exiles with homes in Oxford, Woodward talked to me more openly than I had experienced before. Our exchanges increased my respect for him and my admiration of his attitude to the study of history. I was also much interested in meeting a galaxy of American academic talent. Among those with whom I had deep conversations were Professor Frank Craven, who was the joint editor of the official history of the United States Army Air Forces, Gordon Craig, who became more and more distinguished as the years went on, Professor Henry Guerlac, a historian of science, whose brilliance and originality I have always remembered, and others of scarcely less distinction. Finally, before sailing from New York, I had lunch with Arthur Schlesinger Jr, who talked about his forthcoming study of Roosevelt and seemed impressed by my ideas on the possibility of Anglo-American historical research. I also renewed my acquaintance with my long-standing friend, Professor John Fagg, who had written much of those parts of the American official history that had dealt with the bombing offensive.[19]

I returned to Britain rejoicing that the official history upon which Webster and I were engaged was under the control, not of the Air Ministry, but of the Cabinet Office. I was more than ever convinced that direct air force control of the American official air histories had ruined them and that the same system would have had the same result in our case as it had had in that of the official history of the war in the air in the First World War. I was also delighted with the research I had done, which the Rockefeller Fellowship had made possible. Considerable areas of understanding in Webster and Frankland would otherwise have been areas of, at best, no understanding or, at worst, misunderstanding. And though I found and still find the advantages less easy to quantify, the experience of meeting so many Americans of distinction from the fields of action and of academia was intellectually lubricating.

Webster had foreseen the advantages that would accrue to me from this visit to the United States, for which he himself was so largely responsible. When the whole question of my going was at issue and there seemed likely to be a shortfall in the funds required, he offered to give me the money he had brought back, surplus to requirement, from his own trip. He told me that it would have been difficult for him to return this money directly to those who had organized his visit and that, after discussing his conscience with Nora, she had proposed this solution. He said that this was a great relief to him. 'After all,' he continued, 'ours is a joint enterprise and funds for it should be devoted to the best of our ability to the general object. I felt that it would be of immense value to our book if you went to the United States and saw the historians and some of the records. Your visit would lose some of its value if you were not in a position to benefit fully from it.' There was, he said, no question of either of us being indebted to the other except in so far as 'we both rely and trust one another to do his best for the book. I am determined,' he wrote, 'that it shall be the best we can do but it depends far more on you than on me and everything I can do to give you an opportunity to be even better than you are now is to my advantage.' I immensely appreciated Webster's offer and the generous attitude that accompanied it, but I am glad to find that I declined it even before he had put it into writing. This was as well, as I too duly returned from the United States with surplus money: it was difficult to spend one's provision of dollars in the face of American hospitality, especially that which I received in Montgomery, Alabama.[20]

As the first draft of our work approached its conclusion, Webster and I began to show it to those who we thought might have useful criticisms to offer and who, under the regulations, we were allowed to consult. The work was to remain secret until cleared for publication by the Cabinet Office. In April 1956, for example, we received Sir Ian Jacob's comments on the chapter I had written dealing with the strategic role of Bomber Command in the combined Anglo-American offensive from the Casablanca Conference of January 1943 to February 1944, when the approach of *Overlord* became the issue. Jacob said that he had found the chapter 'extremely interesting', particularly because of the light it shed on the character and views of the main actors and on the contribution each made. He took issue with me over my view that the overall command exercised by Eisenhower and its extent were axiomatic and that to doubt the need for it was 'archaic'. Jacob said that he belonged to the 'archaic' school of thought. He found that the chapter was fair to all the individuals concerned except that he wondered if it was right to give the terms of a minute Churchill had written condemning the bombing of Dresden and then, under pressure from Portal, withdrawn. In my reply, I agreed to re-examine the terms in which I had described the decisions to give Eisenhower the powers which he received, but I made no response to his point about Churchill's withdrawn minute. This made it obvious that I had no intention of taking it out. Indeed, I had not and Webster gave me full support in keeping it in. A minute withdrawn may, and in this case did, say more about a process of thought than a revised one.[21]

Sir Ian Jacob, a member of Butler's Panel of advisors, was vastly experienced, shrewd, highly intelligent, observant, helpful and reasonable. Personally he stood outside the issues discussed in my chapter with one exception. This was Winston Churchill, the great war leader, still very much alive, who wished history in its every detail to come out his way. To this end, he had charged a number of those who had served him closely at one time or another to look after his interests in matters of this sort. Jacob was one of them, and that, Webster and I knew, was the reason why he had raised this point. It was a straw in the wind. Jacob, though, was far too much aware of the arguments an historian might advance, especially if he was Sir Charles Webster, to make a scene. He was content to leave it that Professor Butler might have to decide the matter. This left it firmly in our court. We would, I believe, have been in a much weaker position if we had made use of Churchill's private papers. Webster, however, had had the wisdom and foresight to forego this opportunity. At the time, I was dismayed by his decision, but I came to see that it was prudent. As he had predicted, we were able to discover all we wanted to know about Churchill and the bombing offensive from the Cabinet, Air Ministry and Bomber Command files, to which, without regulation by Churchill, we had full access.

Jacob's straw in the wind was no more than that, but the ease with which Webster and I – and the integrity of our book – had survived this trifling threat may perhaps have led us to a degree of over-confidence about the future of the work. Had we known the content of the advice given to Sir Norman Brook by the Deputy Secretary of the Cabinet, we would have been anxious and incensed. Burke Trend told Brook that, though he had not read the whole of Webster and Frankland's history, he had looked over a list of the 'more critical passages' compiled by Brook's assistant for the official histories, Sir Edward Hale. He had concluded that much of the book made 'very unhappy' reading and he thought that the Cabinet Office might have to 'insist' on some parts 'being toned down'. He warned Brook that he would have to satisfy himself that the use of Churchill's minutes was in accord with the undertakings Brook had given to Churchill, and he mentioned that Webster and Frankland had quoted a memorandum issued at the outset of the war in which it had been said that 750,000 hospital beds would be needed to deal with the initial air raid casualties. In the event, 6,000 were needed. Churchill, he said, had later given currency to a figure of 250,000. Trend assumed that Webster and Frankland should adopt Churchill's figure. The authors, he pointed out, had described Churchill's mistrust of American air plans and, though this might be relevant to their purpose, it might also damage Anglo-American relations. Trend thought that, subject to the views of the Foreign Office, the authors should be invited to 'delete this paragraph, or at least to tone it down substantially, on grounds of the public interest'. He also thought that the revelations about Sir Richard Peirse were 'not entirely in the public interest'. Though Hale had told him that, if one was Prime Minister, 'one's very thoughts are history', Trend doubted whether Churchill would agree to the publication of his first minute about Dresden, which he had later withdrawn.[22]

In other words, Trend thought that Webster and Frankland should be told to suppress such passages as he thought might cause awkwardness; that because Churchill had misquoted the figure given for hospital beds, they should do the same, and that they should drop quotations Churchill might not like. Trend was thus shown to be living in a closed civil service world of his own in which he seemed to assume that his advice would never be publicly known and equally that the excision of vital historical evidence from the official history would also never be discovered. Butler – albeit with Hale rather than Trend – firmly resisted all these ideas and most fortunately none of them were conveyed to Webster and Frankland in the extraordinary terms employed by Burke Trend.[23]

Meanwhile, we had got permission to circulate either the whole or parts of the completed first draft to a number of the surviving leading participants in our story. Among those whose comments we invited were Lord Portal, Sir Arthur Harris, Lord Tedder, Lord Thurso, Sir John Slessor, Sir Norman Bottomley, Sir Robert Saundby, Sir Henry Tizard, Sir Richard Peirse, Sir Edgar Ludlow-Hewitt and Lord Newall. Harris declined to read the draft saying that he was not prepared to take any unofficial part in the proceedings, in which he evidently thought he should have had an official part. Quite what that should have been he did not vouchsafe, but he assured us that the procedure adopted had increased his admiration for Mr Henry Ford. In this way, Sir Arthur Harris gave up the chance he had been offered to see what we had said while it was still in draft and of giving us his reactions, which we would naturally have considered most carefully. Thurso, who, as Sir Archibald Sinclair, had been Secretary of State for Air in the war, proved to be too ill to respond; and Lord Newall, who had been Chief of the Air Staff in the last years of peace and the first one of the war, said that he was too old to take it on and that Sir John Slessor would know what he would have thought.[24]

Slessor's comments were calm, collected and mostly to the effect that, while he would like some phrases such as 'grievous neglect' and words such as 'dilatory' and 'inertia' left out, he was substantially satisfied with the work and was also inclined to believe that Sir Edgar Ludlow-Hewitt, whose comments he had seen, had got unduly steamed up about what we had written. In connection with his own comments, Slessor told me that he thought the draft was good although it could be improved by 'certain nuances of wording'. He was surprised at my insistence on the pre-eminence of contemporary documentation over the recollections of the principal characters of the time. He had thought that one of the advantages of contemporary historical writing was the availability of the latter. Even so, he admitted that the memory of participants was not wholly reliable and was in fact sometimes 'damned *unreliable*'. Whatever I may have said to provoke this particular observation, it was very much in line with my own view. Apart from some useful technical corrections, which we adopted, Sir Henry Tizard made only one point of substance: he thought we had been too tolerant of the Air Staff's neglect of the problems of navigation in the inter-war period. I was surprised; I thought we had been quite severe. Sir Henry pointed out, however, that a bomber squadron might have been sent to India, where it could have discovered the difficulties by the opportunity India offered of long flights between towns over country that was without lights.[25]

So far so good, but best of all was the response from Lord Tedder. 'I have read through your book twice – quickly I admit, but right through', he told us. He thought it was 'masterly and courageous'. 'Frankly,' he wrote, 'I had not thought that anything so near the truth would ever be likely to go on record.' Powerful voices were soon to be raised in the attempt to prevent precisely that.[26]

Among these was that of Sir Richard Peirse, who had had the misfortune to have been the C-in-C of Bomber Command when it was at its nadir or, more precisely, when its nadir became apparent. He was also responsible for a particularly ill-managed attack on Berlin and other targets in November 1941, for which he was rebuked by Portal and shortly afterwards despatched to India. Webster and I could not gloss over these melancholy but important events and equally, I suppose, Peirse could not but be much disturbed by what we wrote. He came to see us and there were hints about a libel action. We did not take these seriously because we had chapter and verse for all we had written. On the other hand, we wanted as far as possible to avoid denigrating men who had borne such heavy responsibility, even if they had failed to meet the challenges they faced. We therefore decided to modify our language so that it sounded less harsh but still meant the same thing. For example, we changed 'persisted in asserting' to 'again stated' and 'nevertheless it was obvious' to 'nevertheless it seemed to the Air Staff', and 'Sir Richard Peirse was on his way to India' to 'a change in the command had been made'. Peirse evidently recognized that he would not succeed in getting us to change history and, after a second talk with us, wrote that he was grateful for the time, trouble and particularly the patience we had given to the consideration of his point of view. I fear that there was no love lost between Peirse and ourselves, but at least civilities had been restored and the integrity of the book had survived.[27]

Sir Robert Saundby's comments, though lengthy, were more measured and far less emotional than his outburst after reading my thesis. Indeed, several of the points he made concerned matters of fact which we found to be correct and gratefully accepted. He did, however, want us to explain that the short-comings of Bomber Command at the outset were largely caused by Treasury frugality before the war and the loss of territory in western Europe soon after it began. We had recognized that these were factors, but we could not accept that they were the operative ones. He also wanted us to withdraw the suggestion that the Battle of Berlin in the winter of 1943–4 was a reverse and to say that it was a draw. This also we could not do. On the face of it, though, Saundby's advice seemed to have been useful and our exchanges were entirely courteous. Even so, the appearance of things is not always the same as their substance. Saundby gave Harris the impression that we had largely if not completely ignored his criticisms. Nor, in the case of Lord Portal, did appearances correspond with realities. After having had the draft of our book in his hands for several months, he wrote to say that the time he had meant to spend reading it had been absorbed by more urgent matters and that, as he would not now be able to find the time, he was returning the work to us unread. This proved, however, to be far from the end of Portal's part in the drama.[28]

So, having now made consultations with these and many other service and civilian experts of various kinds, and having taken due account of what they had said, we now formally submitted the work to Butler and his Panel of advisors. Butler himself seemed entirely satisfied. After reading the first half of the book, he told us that he greatly admired its 'thoroughness and fairness'. Even before he had read the second half, he committed himself to the hope that the whole work would soon be published. Having then read it all, Butler said, rather optimistically as it turned out, that all who had read this history had 'greatly admired it' and that they had been impressed by the 'vast research involved' and the 'skilful marshalling of the facts'. Air Chief Marshal Sir Guy Garrod, who had many observations to make, some of which revealed the extent to which he had failed to grasp the meaning of air superiority, was scarcely less pleased. What was needed for this controversial subject, he thought, was an 'analytical, scholarly and judicial' examination which would carry the highest authority. Our volumes, he said, met those requirements with 'outstanding success'. Sir Ian Jacob's considered view of the whole work was that it was quite outstanding. He noted that there was a certain amount of repetition, but he did not object to this as, in his view, it helped the reader to follow what was a very complicated story. He wondered if the Panel ought to consider whether or not differences of opinion in the high command should be so 'ruthlessly exposed'. He thought that they should be and that the characters involved should be big enough not to mind. The most difficult part, he shrewdly diagnosed, was that which showed how Portal had found himself unable to secure his wishes from Harris. He thought, all the same, that the whole story gave a 'remarkable insight' into the conduct of operations and demonstrated how difficult it was to achieve a uniformity of view among strong-willed commanders. There was, he concluded, nothing discreditable about the arguments; they showed that each commander was trying to get the policy he thought most effective adopted. Vice-Admiral Sir Geoffrey Blake thought that the work was an 'outstanding addition' to the official histories of the war and that in future there would be little doubt regarding the 'magnificent contribution' of Bomber Command to the war. Lieutenant-General Sir Henry Pownall found the story 'extremely interesting', the more so because, although he knew several of the leading actors in it, he had had 'no inkling' of the clashes of policy and personality between them. We had thus comfortably cleared the penultimate hurdle in our progress towards the publication of our book.[29]

The last stage of our odyssey was the required consultation with a number of Departments of State. These were to be given the opportunity of recommending changes in the draft, but they were not to impose them except for 'overriding reasons of current public interest'. This was a good civil service phrase which could mean a little or a lot and, in the latter case, could lead to conflict with another of our instructions to the effect that the official historians were to be independent and were not expected to present official views; they were to write as far as possible to the critical standards of academic historians. The War Office made no difficulties. They said that they had no comments to make on our draft. The Commonwealth Relations Office was slightly less tolerant. They asked us to tone down our criticism of Canadian reluctance to join the original scheme for overseas aircrew training. Webster took a sledge hammer to this. 'We do not intend,' he replied, 'to take any notice of the comment.' The Commonwealth Relations Office, he pointed out, did not deny that what we had written was true; what they suggested we should write was untrue. We had taken great care throughout our book to do justice to the contribution to the strategic air offensive which had been made by the Commonwealth. Butler accordingly informed the Commonwealth Relations Office that Webster and Frankland were 'reluctant' to make the changes suggested. He hoped the suggestions would not be pressed. They were not; the issue, the CRO decided, was not important enough to press. The Foreign Office was better; it had no objection to the publication of the book in its present form. The Admiralty complained that we had described the Battle of the Atlantic as defensive when in fact it was offensive. Webster told Butler that the Admiralty was quite silly on this subject. He left it to Butler to explain to their Lordships that the Battle of the Atlantic, from the tactical point of view of the ships engaged, was offensive, but that, from the strategic point of view of what the Royal Navy aimed to achieve in the context of the war, it was defensive.[30]

Though Churchill's retainers were still waging sporadic warfare about our use of his war-time minutes, Webster was clearly winning the day and, apart from this diminishing opposition, all the obstacles in the way of the publication of our volumes had now been overcome with the single exception of the Air Ministry. Here, unknown to Webster and myself, powerful forces of the upper echelons were mobilizing for battle. The first tactic was delay. The Air Ministry was supposed to offer its observations within two months and the first decision taken was that this was not long enough. Nerney, who had now retired from his position as Head of the Air Historical Branch, but who for some reason still acted in that capacity with regard to our volumes, seems at once to have realized that this might be a mistaken policy. When conveying the draft volumes to his superiors, he sent in a minute in which he said that the Panel of Butler's advisors, which included the air representative, Air Marshal Garrod, and 'those of importance' in the Air Historical Branch, had already made their comments, which 'in the main' had now been incorporated in the draft. He added that the Panel had been unanimous in congratulating Sir Charles Webster and Dr N. Frankland on having produced a 'most scholarly, comprehensive and judicial History of a singularly complex and controversial subject'. He said that 'one must agree with this view' and he warned his superiors that the work was based on exhaustive research among primary documents at all levels and, so far as it was possible to judge, was 'accurate and authentic as to the facts'. Had the upper echelons of the Air Ministry been motivated by even a feeble appreciation of the value of historical objectivity, they would surely have heeded the warning of their own recently retired chief historian and trimmed their objections to sustainable points.[31]

A limited reaction of this character, however, proved to be well below the sights of the Permanent Under Secretary of State, Sir Maurice Dean. After talking the matter over with Nerney and Nerney's successor, L.A. Jackets, he decided that he would try to persuade Harris to reverse his decision not to read the draft and get him to do so. He also thought Sir Edward Ellington, who had been Chief of the Air Staff from 1933 until 1937, might be got to look at the draft. If Lord Thurso was too ill to read it, perhaps Roger Fulford might do so on his behalf. Finally, he decided that ways should be found of talking Portal out of his refusal to look at the draft. All this would take up a good deal of time and of course if Portal and Harris could be drawn into the argument, there were likely to be the sort of ructions for which Dean was obviously looking.[32]

The first result was that Nerney began to show signs of responding to instructions from on high. He offered his superiors some further advice; he thought it important that there should be a ruling about the use Webster and Frankland had made of demi-official and personal correspondence without the concurrence of those concerned. He remembered that Vice-Admiral Blake had raised this point at a meeting of the Panel and that Webster had replied that considered, as opposed to demi-official and personal, memoranda did not always accurately reflect men's thoughts. Webster had said that nothing had been included which was not necessary in making clear the relationship of leading personalities. He said that the draft had been circulated or offered to all the principal people concerned. Nerney thought that it was essential that Thurso, Portal and Harris, who had all declined the opportunity, should be asked to give their concurrence. Then Nerney recalled that there was the question of Churchill's withdrawn minute about Dresden. This he said had also been raised at the Panel meeting by Sir Henry Pownall. Webster had replied that the withdrawn minute was valuable evidence. Nerney thought that a ruling should be sought on this question as a matter of public policy. Clearly there was a valuable framework of obstruction here, but as the options were weighed in the Air Ministry, there appeared to be some hazards too. Webster had said that he had been told that all the official records would be made available for the history, subject only to the non-disclosure of individual views in the Cabinet and ministerial sub-committees of it. He had given the impression that the disclosure of personal letters was necessary to the historian's explanation of events and that he 'might take rather serious exception to their deletion'. It also had to be doubted that the letters in question really were private letters. Webster had maintained that they were not and that they were all contained in official files to which the historians had been granted access. There was, however, a difference between access and publication. If these letters were published, it might prejudice the Air Ministry's claim to Crown privilege and that might lead to wider difficulties.[33]

Almost as predictably as night follows day, the Air Ministry sought legal advice. The Treasury Solicitor was asked if the publication of these demi-official and personal letters would prejudice Crown privilege and, second, did the writers of the letters own the copyright in them? The answers were disappointing. No, the publication would not compromise Crown privilege and no, the copyright in these letters certainly did not belong to their authors but, the Assistant Treasury Solicitor wondered, what about libel? Encouraged by this advice, the Deputy Under Secretary of State, H.T. Smith, felt able to report to Sir Maurice Dean that there were four issues at stake. First, how far was Webster and Frankland's use of the letters fair to the officers concerned? Second, how did copyright affect the matter? Third, was Crown privilege at risk? Fourth, was libel involved? Mr Smith was not sure that the Treasury Solicitor's advice had been sound. Crown privilege, he said, according to a statement of the Lord Chancellor, was provided to secure candour of communication with and within the public service. Ministers had the duty to deny access to such communications, and what a minister would withhold from a Court, he should also surely withhold from the official history of the strategic air offensive. He thought the Secretary of State for Air should either object or at least seek the opinion of law officers. Webster's claim to have been given a free hand did not, in Mr Smith's view, cut much ice; he could not claim that he had been licensed to break the law. Libel, however, created an awkward prospect because, if there was an action, the Air Ministry would be in Queer Street on the matter of Crown privilege. Indeed, it was all getting quite complicated. But that also made it promising from the point of view of the Air Ministry. Sir Maurice Dean wrote a stalling letter to the Cabinet Office saying they would need a longer period for the consideration of the draft volumes, which were very important for the Air Force. He had, nevertheless, identified one 'separable' point which he hoped Sir Norman Brook might be ready to deal with in the interval: this was the proposal of the authors to print in the volume of appendices the full texts of the letters exchanged between Portal and Harris in the winter of 1944–5. Dean wanted these to be deleted.[34]

In the meantime, Sir Dermot Boyle, the Chief of the Air Staff, had been called up to persuade Portal to intervene, which he had earlier decided not to do. Nor, from the Air Ministry point of view, was the first part of his reply to Boyle very encouraging. He said he had managed to read only parts of the draft before deciding that his memories were too hazy to enable him to make serious comment. Also, he did not want to seem to influence the history for the purpose of 'covering up or minimizing' mistakes he might have made as CAS during the war. He explained that he had, therefore, decided to accept the history as the work of an able and honest historian which, he said, he believed Webster to be, without agreeing or disagreeing with the presentation or conclusions. This was no use to the Air Ministry at all; but the second part of Portal's letter was much more promising. Actually, it largely contradicted the dignified stance of the first part. In this second part, he was sorry to hear that the history had 'overdone' the controversy between himself and Harris, although he supposed 'some mention' of it was 'unavoidable'. He said he was in favour of playing down this episode as much as possible without giving a false picture. He went on to declare that he was convinced that nothing of what he wrote demi-officially in the course of duty and which the gutter press might work up into a sensational story of personal controversy between himself and any person living or dead should be published during his life-time. He wanted the right to insist that everything of this kind should be paraphrased. This was excellent grist for Sir Maurice Dean's mill. He sent a copy of it straight away to Sir Norman Brook.[35]

On 14th July 1959, Sir Norman Brook held a meeting, which was attended by Sir Maurice Dean, Sir Harold Kent, who was the Treasury Solicitor, Sir Edward Hale, who was Brook's assistant with regard to the official histories, and Sir James Butler. The subject of discussion was the Air Ministry agenda of obstruction as reinforced by Portal's new intervention. The questions of Crown privilege, candour in exchanges between public servants and so on were reviewed again, but in the end the debate reached an impasse. It might be argued, it was admitted, that by embarking upon a programme of official histories the Government had 'by implication' decided not to press the issue of Crown privilege. There was also the difficulty that if the correspondence between Portal and Harris was not published, the position would not in fact be improved because there was such a detailed description of the controversy, together with copious quotation from the letters, in the narrative portion of the volumes. Portal might well argue that this section of the narrative would also have to be removed. That led to another difficulty: Sir Charles Webster would not be easy to move and he might decide to abandon the book rather than see it mutilated. This too would cause controversy. It was decided that Webster should be told nothing of these developments until the final comments of the Air Ministry could be put to him.[36]

At last, on 14th August 1959, H.T. Smith sent the Air Ministry's completed comments on the draft of the history of the strategic air offensive. They reached Webster on 20th August, a day on which I was away. Webster wrote to me that they were 'much worse than you thought of in your most pessimistic moods'. They were, however, not bad enough to depress Webster. He told me that Butler was on our side, that Brook was determined not to give in and that only Hale was behaving like a 'frightened rabbit'. He said I should not worry too much. 'These machinations,' he declared, 'cannot prevail.' It now fell to me to frame our reply to the Air Ministry comments.[37]

It was not an easy task, for the comments were not designed to correct or improve the book. They were designed to destroy it. They suggested that virtually every quotation in it should be removed on the legal pretext that such quotations would jeopardize Crown privilege. They listed some forty-two quotations they objected to on the grounds of what they contained, and another 153 they objected to, not on those grounds but on account of their being quotations. As the Air Ministry understood it, Mr Smith explained, the law, as declared in the House of Lords, laid upon the Secretary of State the duty to protect from disclosure all documents, regardless of their contents, that fell in a particular class. As the lists of these disclosures which they now supplied to us made clear, the particular class of documents they had in mind was that of all the principal and primary sources upon which our history was chiefly founded. But even that was not all. The Air Ministry took strong exception to massive and key portions of our narrative. Though they were kind enough to say that, in the main, the book was factually accurate and was also an absorbing story to read, they, nevertheless, asked for innumerable alterations that would have made it much less factually accurate and probably a good deal less absorbing as well. There were eighteen pages of typed foolscap suggestions which, if acted upon, would have removed almost every criticism of anything connected with Bomber Command and the Air Staff and also, incidentally, any words of praise concerning the United States Eighth Air Force. And these suggestions ranged from the trivial to the fundamental. For example, 'quite inadequate' had an emotive tone; 'inadequate' would do. At the other end of the range, they wished us to deny that in February 1942 a policy of area-bombing had been adopted. Several of the comments bordered on the ludicrous. For example, they objected to our having pointed out the lessons in the techniques of night precision bombing that were learnt from the attacks on the Möhne and Eder dams on the grounds that these were more akin to torpedo than bombing attacks. In answering all these points, as we had to do, I found it difficult not merely to remain patient but to keep my temper.

Although he was also very angry, Webster was a past master at such situations and he kept me in good order. He knocked out my sentence, 'We would regard it as futile to produce a book purporting to be a serious study of this great campaign which suppressed every fact remotely reflecting upon the efficiency of anybody connected with the Air Staff or the Royal Air Force' and substituted, 'We recognize that the Air Ministry has a deep interest in the book and we have carefully considered all their comments. But...' We rejected totally the suggestion that our quotations should be removed, though elsewhere we changed a word here and another there to oblige the Air Ministry but not to alter our meaning. Webster also wrote to Butler reminding him that he had been persuaded to undertake the task of writing the history on the grounds of it being a very controversial subject which would arouse considerable emotion. He had been told that, for this reason, it could not be written by RAF officers and that it required an historian of some repute who could be trusted to be impartial and be capable of maintaining his standpoint in the event of pressure being exerted on him by the Air Ministry or other ministries or persons. He went on to remind Butler that he had made it clear that he could only take on the work if he was allowed to produce a fully documented history, and that when he was told that this was contrary to precedent in the case of official histories, he had said that he could not undertake the work. He and Butler, he continued, had then agreed that the matter should be referred for decision to Sir Norman Brook and this had been done. Complete agreement had been reached. The only restrictions which would be imposed on Webster were that he would not reveal the views of ministers expressed in the Cabinet, that he would name as few civil servants as possible, and that he would write nothing that would endanger security. Without this freedom and without the assurance that no Department of State would have the right to censor the book or insist upon the omission of evidence, neither he nor Frankland would have considered writing the book. Any attempt by the Air Ministry to reverse this situation would, Webster stated, lead him and Frankland to refuse to allow the publication of the book under their names. He ended by assuring Butler that we would carefully consider all criticisms of our work and make any changes we thought were justified. 'In no case, however, have we changed anything which we thought necessary to include in order that we might give an impartial and accurate account of events.' Thus, without shadow of doubt and with a voice of authority unique in the world of official history, Webster made our position clear. Without his voice mine would have been no more than a cry in the wilderness.[38]

Webster and I thought that, though we had been firm on matters of principle, we had been restrained in our reply to the Air Ministry's comments. Butler did not quite agree. He thought we had been unduly polemical and hoped we would tone down some of our sharper phrases. He wondered, for example, if we could not change 'it is difficult to take this comment seriously' to 'it may be observed'. He did not, however, give us the opportunity to follow this advice because he decided not to send us the note in which he had proffered it. A safer course of action was settled; it was decided not to show our reply to the Air Ministry. Its tone, Sir Norman Brook was advised, was such that it could not be shown in that quarter. Unbeknown to us Brook had already gone into action more or less on our side. After looking over the Air Ministry's comments, which had drawn our 'polemical' reply, he told Mr Smith that he doubted the wisdom of pursuing the argument about Crown privilege. He agreed that there was much more quotation in the book than was usual, but he thought that there was enough in other histories to have raised the issue of Crown privilege if it had really been applicable. In any case, if the Cabinet Office now stopped the book, Webster would seek outside support and the resulting controversy would be more damaging to Crown privilege than the quotations in the history.[39]

Dean capitulated on the question of Crown privilege. He told Brook that, even if the Air Ministry had been right about it in theory, it might be ill-advised in practice to pursue it in this particular case. This, however, proved to be not a retreat, but a re-grouping. Dean still insisted that the quotations at issue should be withdrawn from the book on the ground that the officers concerned had not expected them to be published in their own lifetimes and that, even if they were not objectionable, they should still be withdrawn because they revealed 'intimate exchanges of opinion' within the Air Staff. The letter was endorsed in the Cabinet Office to the effect that it was not to be shown to Webster and Frankland.[40]

Meanwhile, Dean was moving up one of his heaviest guns in support of this line of attack. Lord Portal had now been shown the Air Ministry's comments on the book. Although he said that he had not read it, apart from a few passages to which his attention had been directed, he found the comments 'fully justified'. He was 'astonished' at the inclusion of so much quotation, which he thought was contrary to public policy and also an invasion of private rights. If publication went ahead, the position would have to be considered 'most seriously' by the people concerned. Harris too had returned to the firing line. Publication of these quotations would, he told Dean, be so serious a breach of confidence that the authorities concerned would have no reason to be surprised by the action he would take. He reminded Dean that Webster had from the outset expressed 'thoroughly biased' anti-Bomber Command opinions and that he insisted on working with 'one Dr Franklands' who, he was told, had failed to complete a tour of duty as a navigator in Bomber Command. So far had Harris fallen victim to a conspiracy theory of the biased Webster and the disaffected 'Franklands' that he even believed that we had added documents to be published as a 'malicious riposte' to his refusal to read the draft of our book. No one thought it necessary to mark this letter as unsuitable for the eyes of Webster and Frankland, but had it been shown to them, the Air Ministry might have had another kind of libel action to consider. I had after all been awarded the DFC, on Harris's recommendation, for completing a tour of duty as a navigator in Bomber Command. Even Dean was slightly alarmed. He assured Harris that the Air Ministry would continue to do its best to get the quotations removed, but in the meantime he appealed to him not to shoot the pianist.[41]

Dean sent a copy of Portal's letter to Brook and reported the less outrageous portion of the one he had received from Harris. While he thus intensified his fire-power, however, Butler's resistance was stiffening. He produced a gentlemanly version of Webster and Frankland's reply to the Air Ministry's comments and sent it to Brook. His measured terms did not much affect the gist of what we had said and did nothing to detract from our refusal to substitute what we saw as untruth for truth. He told Brook that we were both 'responsible historians' and he did not think that we should be pressed further to alter judgements reached 'after careful consideration'. Brook now saw that the time had come to reach a final decision but, before doing so, he acceded to Dean's request that there should be a further meeting. He also sought and obtained two concessions from us. First, he put it to us orally as his own opinion that by printing the entire texts of the Portal/Harris correspondence of the winter of 1944–5 in our volume of appendices, in addition to giving a full description of the arguments together with copious quotation in the text, we were affording the issue an unnecessary overemphasis. After much consideration, Webster and I decided to accept this point. We did so with some regret, but we could not claim that the removal of this part of our appendices concealed any essential history. That was fully developed in the text. Second, we agreed to soften the passage in which we described how Portal had reacted to Harris's suggestion that if his interpretation of Portal's directive was unsatisfactory to him, he had better replace him as C-in-C, and how Portal had decided not to do so and to wait until after the war to see who was right. The passage, as amended, showed clearly that Portal had ducked the issue, which was the main historical point, but it also made greater allowance for the difficulty of any other course of action.[42]

Though he had not put these points to us in the context of Air Ministry objections, Brook was no doubt pleased to have some concessions to lay on the table at his meeting with Dean. If so, he must have been disappointed. Dean complained that the authors had not acted upon the points of substance in the Air Ministry's criticism of their work. They had done no more than meet a few points of detail. The book, he said, would, therefore, create an unfortunate impression and would be damaging to the Royal Air Force. Brook said that the histories were not intended to cover up what went wrong: part of their object was to enable future governments to learn from mistakes. Dean feared that the press would emphasize the 'uncomfortable' parts of the book and he now produced a new gambit. He told Brook that he thought his Secretary of State would want the whole matter referred to the Prime Minister. He then passed on to the expectation that Portal and Harris would both find the book defamatory. Brook said that the quotations were regarded by the historians as essential for the very reason that the matters were so controversial. Harris, he added, having written his own book, merited less consideration than Portal, who had refrained. In the upshot it was agreed that Brook would now authorize the despatch of the book to the printers. Dean would get legal advice as to which parts of it were defamatory and would let Brook know the answer. Brook would then submit the matter for decision to the Prime Minister. Brook did not trouble us with all these goings on; he simply told us that he had authorized the despatch of our book to the printers. We thought the battle was over; Webster, indeed, never knew that it was not and I only learnt the real position more than thirty years later. Even the 'frightened rabbit', Sir Edward Hale, thought he saw the end of the tunnel. He hoped that they were now 'pretty well through with this'. He did not think anything as troublesome would arise again.[43]

Sir Maurice Dean had other ideas, and he continued to beaver away at the question of libel and to complain of the authors' failure to adopt the modifications to the text which the Air Ministry wanted. Nevertheless, on 27th January 1960, his campaign began to collapse. Sir Harold Kent, the Treasury Solicitor, replied to the Air Ministry suggestions that the book might be defamatory to Portal, Harris and Peirse with the opinion that it was not. Rather oddly, the Cabinet Office decided not to pass on this news to the Air Ministry and, more oddly still, they did not feel it necessary to bother Brook with it. Now, however, the only remaining obstacle in the path of the publication of our book was the Prime Minister. Had Webster and I known this, we would probably have had some sleepless nights.[44]

The Prime Minister was now in South Africa, where he had gone to tell them out there that the wind had changed. Sir Norman Brook was with him. It was better to assume, it was decided in the Cabinet Office, that what Mr Macmillan was about to hear from Brook on the subject of Webster and Frankland would be his 'first introduction to an official history problem'. Notwithstanding their other problems, Brook, therefore, supplied Mr Macmillan with what, in retrospect, seems to be a surprisingly long memorandum. Brook began by saying he thought the Prime Minister should be made aware of the 'uneasiness' felt in the Air Ministry about the publication of the history of the strategic air offensive. The book, he explained, had been written by Sir Charles Webster and Dr A.N. Frankland. Sir Charles Webster was, 'as you know', an eminent historian who had retired in 1953 from the Stevenson Chair of International History at the London School of Economics. Dr Frankland had had a 'distinguished flying career in Bomber Command' and had won the DFC. Since the war he had become a professional historian and was now employed part-time as such at Chatham House. The editor of the series was Sir James Butler who, until 1954, had been Regius Professor of Modern History at Cambridge. The official histories were written under the condition that the authors were given full access to official documents and that they and the editor alone were 'responsible for the statements made and views expressed'.

Having thus sketched the background, Brook now came to the point. The story of the strategic air offensive was not 'an altogether happy one', he wrote. Only in the later stages of the war did it become a story of success, which was the reason why all four volumes of the history were to be published simultaneously. Bomber Command had entered the war with neither the training nor the equipment to make it effective, but it was not until the end of 1941 that photographic evidence had brought this to light. In 1942 performance had begun to improve with the advent of the Lancaster and the introduction of navigational aids. Even so, the German defences, and especially the German night-fighters, were not 'really mastered' until the Germans had been pushed back to their own frontiers. Moreover, the 'proper use' of strategic bombers remained a controversial question until the end of the war. The history 'necessarily' dealt with this controversy within the Air Staff between the advocates of area-bombing and those of precision-bombing. For all its heroism, it was rather a 'grim story' and, Brook warned Macmillan, 'its grimness is not mitigated by the way in which the authors of this history have presented it'.

The Air Ministry felt, he explained, that the book was in parts unsympathetic and critical. They thought there was undue emphasis on mistakes and controversies and that publication could damage the reputation of the RAF. The authors had considered the written comments of the Air

Ministry and had made a number of changes to details, mainly of fact. They had been unable to accept the Air Ministry's criticisms of substance.

Brook continued that, in his judgement, the fear that the reputation of the RAF might be damaged was not a ground for intervention. The official histories, he said, were not designed to be propaganda for the services but to be an attempt to 'assess and present the truth'. Anyway, there was nothing that could be done. The Air Ministry, he stated, had agreed that if the book was suppressed, suspicions would be aroused and controversy would ensue which would be more damaging to the RAF than the book would be. The authors could not be required to change judgements they had made after ten years of careful study. Historians of reputation would not put their names to a book unless they had been free to tell the story as they saw it and in their own way. Furthermore, he added, the Air Ministry's view was not shared by all who had read the book. Lord Tedder had praised it as 'masterly and courageous' and had said that he had not thought 'anything so near the truth would ever be likely to go on the record'. He had hoped that there was no danger of officialdom trying to censor the work.

Up to this point Sir Maurice Dean, had he been aware of what Brook was saying to the Prime Minister, would have been most displeased; but Brook now came to a point which showed that Dean's tactics had produced some results. Brook told Macmillan that he was concerned about the disclosure of the details of arguments between senior officers of the RAF and especially those between Lord Portal and Sir Arthur Harris about area-bombing. He had been particularly worried by the proposal of the authors to publish in their volume of appendices the whole of a long correspondence between them on this subject. He was now able to tell the Prime Minister that, at his request, the authors had agreed to withdraw this. A great many quotations from the correspondence, however, remained in the text of the history and the Air Ministry thought it undesirable that so much of the correspondence, which revealed disagreement between the Chief of the Air Staff and the C-in-C, should be published. The authors, he pointed out, had said that the controversial nature of their subject made much verbatim quotation necessary, if distortion was to be avoided. 'And,' said Brook, 'there is great force in their argument.'

Portal and Harris, Brook thought, might make 'unfavourable public comment' when the book was published. Both had declined to read the draft and give their comments as others had done, but Portal had 'glanced' at it and objected to publication in his lifetime of quotations from his letters and minutes. Harris was not in a strong position; he had published his own book and could scarcely now object to an official version of the same subject. Also, it seemed to Brook, his reputation was not likely to suffer from what was said of him in the official history, where 'he stands out as a great

Commander'. Portal's case was different. He had not written a book and had maintained a dignified silence about the war. Also, there was not as much said about him in the official history to offset the bits in it which showed him in a 'rather unfavourable light'.

Thus, Brook conceded, there was a possibility of public controversy if the book was published. But if an attempt was made to impose changes on Sir Charles Webster that he was unwilling to make, he would certainly protest publicly and this would arouse 'an even worse type of controversy'. Brook concluded that the right course was to publish the book and, in the event of criticism, to reply that the authors and the editor were responsible for it. In any case, Brook thought, there was the consolation that 'official histories do not normally attract much public interest'.[45]

The Prime Minister's ruling was that 'we obviously cannot prevent publication'. He was in doubt, however, as to the propriety of quoting Portal's minutes and letters and he wondered if Portal's point could not be met 'at least to some extent'. Brook told the Prime Minister that he had been unable to persuade the authors to reduce the amount of quotation from the Portal/Harris correspondence they had included in their main text. He said that they 'contend', as historians, that they must give a 'faithful picture of the arguments'. Brook said there was much force in their case and that he was sure he could get no more from the authors. He recognized that there might be some awkwardness when the book came out, but he believed it would be much more embarrassing to have to face suggestions that the authors had misrepresented, or distorted by paraphrase, the arguments that had taken place between Portal and Harris. The Prime Minister summarily gave in; 'All right HM 26/2' was the extent of his reply.[46]

Had Webster and I but known it, the battle for publication without mutilation was now really over. Though we had abandoned the inclusion of the full texts of the correspondence between Portal and Harris in the autumn and winter of 1944–5 and, though we had agreed to a number of minor changes of wording to make some of our sentences less harsh, we had not altered the sense of what we had intended to convey. As we saw it, the truth of the matter was in the book. This was not to save it from a storm of abuse when it was published. As far as I was concerned, the battle was to be resumed. For Webster, alas, it was over.

CHAPTER FIVE

History in the News

Sir Charles Webster died on 21st August 1961. The four volumes of our history, *The Strategic Air Offensive against Germany*, were published seven weeks later on 2nd October. Sir Norman Brook had expected that it would not 'attract much public interest'. Webster, who had no reason to expect that he would be ignored, had foreseen that it would attract a good deal of attention. Shortly before he died, he and I had dined with Donald MacLachlan, the editor of the recently founded *Sunday Telegraph*. MacLachlan showed a pronounced interest in our history and we knew that his journalistic antennae were sensitive and acute. Had we known what Brook had suggested to the Prime Minister about the forthcoming public reaction, we would have thought him wrong in his expectations. Even so, we were to be proved almost as wrong ourselves, for what we had expected was so far removed, both in scale and in character, from what happened, that we were virtually in the same boat as Brook. The results of the confrontation of our history and the press amazed me and I am sure Webster would not have been less surprised.[1]

Though they may attract some reviews outside the scholarly journals, substantial documented historical studies are not usually the subject of news 'stories' in the so-called quality press and, still less so, in the popular press and on television. *The Strategic Air Offensive against Germany* proved to be a striking exception to this generality. It was also to become clear to me that, in adopting the term 'story' for their news items, the media were exposing themselves to the interpretation that a story is something made up, or worse still, something a school boy is enjoined not to tell. A more charitable view might be that fitting a history of 1,600 pages, as ours was, into the columns of news 'stories' was a task no easier than getting a gallon into a pint bottle. However that may be, there is no doubt that the press loves controversy and the more it senses this is to hand, the less time it has to examine the substance of a 'story'. Excitement develops into hysteria, discussion gets shorter and the print in which it is conveyed gets larger. The account of how Webster and Frankland were received by the press is a significant example of the uneasy relationship that prevails between history and journalism, or between those who insist on qualifying their sentences and those who insist upon them being unqualified, or else between those who can only accept what they have found out and proved in the light of the available evidence, and those who accept what they discover on the spur of the moment or – perhaps more often – what they hear.

The opening shots were fired in the *Sunday Telegraph*. On 17th September 'Albany' reported that next month would see the publication of the official history of the British bomber offensive. The recent death of Sir Charles Webster, the report continued, meant that Dr Noble Frankland, who was said to be thirty-seven (I had now been thirty-seven for two years), 'would be left alone to face the inevitable controversy'. The following Sunday, the same paper produced a large headline, 'Did Bombing Break the Germans?', to introduce a lengthy article by Sefton Delmer. This did not deal with our book, but it discussed the divided opinions held in Germany as to the effectiveness of the bombing offensive and drew attention to the imminence of the official history which, it announced, would be reviewed the following Sunday by R.H.S. Crossman MP. When next Sunday came, it was reviewed, but, in addition to that, the front page of the paper carried a sensationalized story about the book. 'Row Breaks over Last-War Bombing', it proclaimed in banner headlines. 'Sir Arthur Harris's Retort to Charge of Costly Failure', it continued. 'Bias Denied by Historian'.[2]

Crossman's review, which was spread over five columns of the paper, did not employ the phrase 'costly failure', but it did conclude with the observation that the bombing offensive, which was designed as an alternative to Passchendaele, had had consequences which were very much the same. Also, it appeared under a large headline, 'Bombing Victory That Never Was', and an editorial statement: 'Britain's bombing offensive against Germany failed, says the official war history out tomorrow'. Maybe it was on these sources that the *Sunday Telegraph* reporter drew for his news story on the front page. In it, he stated that the official historians had summed up like this, 'The will of the German people was not broken... and the effect on war production was remarkably small'. Thus armed, Sir Arthur Harris retorted that if you want to get a controversial subject treated fairly, you do not appoint people to write about it who have already made up their minds. Their history, he was reported to have said, 'exaggerates our errors and decries our victories'. In the face of all this and a good deal more of the same sort, my reported response, 'We were not biased. We kept an open mind', looked rather feeble.

I should probably have said more, because we had nowhere stated that the bombing offensive was a 'costly failure', or that it had been for 'three-quarters of the war', as was added in the body of the article; nor had we summed up as the *Sunday Telegraph* reporter had claimed. Indeed, we had done so saying the opposite. In the last sentences of the final volume of our main text we had written that 'both cumulatively in largely indirect ways and eventually in a more immediate and direct manner, strategic bombing and, also in other roles strategic bombers, made a contribution to victory which was decisive'. The phrase 'costly failure' and its attribution to Webster and Frankland as their description of the result of the bombing offensive was either invented by the *Sunday Telegraph* reporter or carelessly picked off a page in our second volume, where we quoted one of Harris's letters to Portal in which Harris said that attempts to carry out low-level attacks with heavy bombers had almost invariably proved to be 'costly failures'.[3]

Whoever had coined the phrase 'costly failure' had been very successful in journalistic terms, for it now stuck to the book like a leech and stimulated a row about it all over the world. Moreover, in the rush, the small print phrase, 'for three-quarters of the war', tended to get lost. In Britain, the cry was taken up by the *Daily Express*: 'Truth must be served', an editorial statement proclaimed; but, it was asked, was anyone entitled to say that Britain's air strategy had been a 'costly failure?' That, the article continued, was 'the verdict reached by the official historians'. There then followed a not very subtle lecture on how Webster and Frankland should have set about their task. The groundwork for these injunctions had been laid in the *Daily Express* the day before. Under a huge headline, 'Bomber chiefs hit at "this slur" Official War History Starts the Big Row', Keith Thompson informed his readers that Air Vice-Marshal Donald Bennett, the former head of the Pathfinder Force, had 'angrily defended the men of Bomber Command'. The book had dismissed the bomber offensive as a ' "costly failure" except in the last ten months of the war'. Bennett was sure that a 'more accurate and impartial work' could have been produced. Air Marshal Sir John D'Albiac was alleged to have said that the book was a 'slur on the work of Bomber Command and the men who didn't come back'. The upshot of an interview by telephone with me was also printed. I was told that Sir Arthur Harris thought the book had exaggerated errors and decried victories. I said that we had made it clear that the bomber offensive had made a decisive contribution to the defeat of Germany. I was told that I had claimed that German morale was not broken by bombing, and it was put to me that this might have been due to the Gestapo keeping down absenteeism. I replied that the Gestapo had certainly helped to keep things going, but that there was no doubt that the German people, even in the dark days, had backed Hitler wholeheartedly. I was asked why German morale had been under-estimated by British intelligence. I said that in Britain it had been assumed that because there was a corrupt regime in Germany there must also be a rotten core, but that this had proved not to be the case. Had I discussed the work with Sir Arthur Harris? I was asked. No, I had not, I replied, but Sir Charles Webster had. Had I not been too harsh, the man asked, about a form of warfare which was a new concept? We had had that in mind, I told him. The Air Ministry had 'hinted' that it did not agree with some of the salient points in the book and why was that? he asked. I said there had been much discussion with the Air Ministry about the book, but that the view of an historian was different from that of an official.[4]

By printing the questions and answers which had been exchanged with me, the *Daily Express* showed an apparent degree of impartiality, but in truth my answers did little to redress the balance. From the point of view of the substance of the book, they were largely redundant. Anyone who had read it would not have needed to ask them, with the exception of the enquiry about the attitude of the Air Ministry. On this point, however, I was unable to give a substantial reply. What I did know about the Air Ministry's attitude, I could not reveal, because it was contained in documents which at this time were still secret. Moreover, as will have been seen in Chapter 4, there was a great deal relating to the Air Ministry's attitude which I did not at this time know.

Any lapse into the realms of impartiality by the *Daily Express* was quickly remedied by another of Lord Beaverbrook's papers, the *Evening Standard*. This came out on the evening of the same day with a prominent article by Air Vice-Marshal Bennett under the headlines, 'I am angry – and a lot of others will be, too'. Bennett declared that the battle so coldly described by Webster and Frankland was not the one in which he had fought. He conceded that it must have been difficult for 'two learned academic authors' to re-create urgent wartime realities but, he claimed, those who had fought in the air would not only be 'disappointed', they would also be 'angry'. It was a curious article which included the claims that the Battle of Berlin was not a defeat for Bomber Command, that Nuremberg, from which he recorded that ninety-four Bomber Command aircraft failed to return, was a tactical but not a strategic defeat, that the dams raid was not the most precise bombing attack ever carried out, as the authors claimed, because the weapon used was not a bomb, and that Sir Arthur Harris was not a difficult or a tough character. He was simply one whom events usually proved to have been right. But there was something else about this article that was curious. It happened that, on the day of its appearance, Bennett and I took part in a live television discussion with each other about the official history. I think those responsible for the programme were expecting that sharp words would pass between us. In the event none did: Bennett and I conspicuously failed to find anything important about which to quarrel. After the broadcast, I told Bennett that I was not greatly impressed by his article in the *Evening Standard* and I recollect that he told me that not only had he not written it; he had not read it. It was only then that I began to understand the role of a Beaverbrook 'Retainer'.[5]

One of these 'Retainers', I do not know which, but hardly Bennett I think, now offered Lord Beaverbrook a line his servants on the *Daily Express* judged might be useful. This was a return to the hint Sir Arthur Harris had given before the book came out – but after he had made up his mind about it – when he wrote to Sir Maurice Dean that he was 'told' that 'Dr Franklands' had failed to complete a tour of duty as a navigator in Bomber Command.[6]

Someone, perhaps on the basis of this innuendo, had got a snippet from my wartime medical record. The result for me was a series of visits from a *Daily Express* reporter. Each time he came, he started off with the same question. Was it true that I had been grounded during the war? Each time, as it was true, I answered, yes, I had been grounded. Each time, I then explained that this had been in February 1945 after I had completed a tour of operations and when I had become an instructor at number 11 Operational Training Unit. Each time, I told the man that I had been grounded for about eight weeks following an attack of pneumonia and that, after that, I had resumed my normal flying duties. Evidently this was not what he wanted to hear and he came to see me again and again as if he thought he could break me down and win some dreadful admission. Was I sure I had had pneumonia? When was it that I had been grounded? And so on. During the same period, someone from the *Daily Express* started ringing up my wife. The calls always came on evenings when I was going to be late returning home. Did she know where her husband was that evening? I repeatedly suggested to the reporter who visited me that he should ask to see my records, operational or medical, or both, and that, to do so, he should approach the Air Historical Branch of the Air Ministry. On checking with the latter, however, I found that he never did.

Looking back on this, one of the most unpleasant episodes in my life, I ask myself why I did not dismiss the reporter with a Wellingtonian epithet. No doubt, I should have done, but the truth is that I was afraid of him. I had watched my historical efforts being pilloried in press headlines on the basis of things I had never said and I had seen how those headlines had bred and multiplied across the world. I had been brought to realize how even apparently responsible people had taken what the press said I had said to be what I *had* said. I now foresaw headlines to the effect that I was bitter about Bomber Command because I had been grounded LMF (Lack of Moral Fibre). I knew that this was not true, and that I could prove it. All the same, I felt that what I could prove might not make much difference. I had lost confidence in historical fact as a weapon against press hysteria. I therefore received the dreadful *Daily Express* reporter again and again and tried to convince him that his line of thought could not be sustained.

In this, I may eventually have been successful or something else may have happened. Whichever was the case, the telephone calls to my wife suddenly ceased and the *Daily Express* reporter came no more. Instead of a 'Bomber Command coward' headline in the *Daily Express*, my profile appeared in Lord Beaverbrook's *Evening Standard* under the heading, 'Bombing Offensive The Heroes Speak'. I could scarcely have been more surprised to find that I was suddenly proclaimed as one of these, but I have to concede that my understanding of how the press works is no greater than my opinion of what the press understands about how historians work.[7]

What was brought home to me was the extraordinary myopic and vicious resentment that clouded the mind and fuelled the vindictiveness of Lord Beaverbrook. It was Beaverbrook, I was warned, who had ordered the campaign against me for the reason that in the official history I had criticized him for having concentrated, as Minister of Aircraft Production in the war, on the production of light aircraft for too long after the need for heavies had become apparent. Churchill had this same vindictiveness and revealed it in unbecoming thoroughness against people he thought had failed him such as General Sir John Kennedy, General Sir John Smyth, General P.J. Mackesy and even Alastair Buchan, who was no more than the son of his victim, Lord Tweedsmuir. But while Churchill may be excused this unpleasant foible on the grounds that he was the saviour of the nation, Beaverbrook can claim no such dispensation. How could A.J.P. Taylor write so sycophantic a biography of this terrible man? This is a point to which I will return in a later chapter.

In the pursuit of press relations with history, we must now consider how *The Strategic Air Offensive against Germany* fared in some other news sheets. The *Observer* produced a story full of over-simplified assessments of what its reporter thought we had written under the headline, 'End Air Terror said Churchill'. The *News of the World* announced that 'controversy will flare' for the reason that Webster and Frankland had said that Churchill's condemnation of the bombing of Dresden had been toned down in a revised minute. *The People* proclaimed in huge headlines, 'Now it is officially admitted we killed 180,000 German Civilians in vain'. The *Irish Independent* gave headlines to the story that 'Churchill wanted Terror Bombing of Germany but retracted under pressure'. Their reporter seems to have been confused by the stories he had read in other newspapers about Churchill's withdrawn minute after the bombing of Dresden. Even so, he attributed his confused conclusion to Webster and Frankland. The *Daily Mail* produced a large photograph of Sir Arthur Harris in his garden at Goring on Thames with a surprisingly tame-looking bull terrier and accompanied by the headline, 'Bomber Harris blasts back'. Harris was reported to be 'gruffly prepared to fight back' against the charge, said to have been made in the official history, that the bombing offensive had been a 'costly failure'.[8]

Variations on these themes and, in the case of syndicated papers, mirror images of them, quickly spread across the world appearing, for example, in New Zealand, Australia, Canada, South Africa, Northern and Southern Rhodesia, Pakistan, Hong Kong, Trinidad, Malta, Bermuda, Portugal, France, Italy, Ethiopia, the United States of America, Germany and other countries and territories. In some fifty-three newspapers with these origins, of which I received cuttings, substantially the same sensationalized and selective stories about Webster and Frankland were draped across the pages under the same sort of headlines as had appeared – or were simultaneously appearing – in the British press. It was hardly surprising that readers began to argue with me and with each other about what they supposed, on the basis of these articles, was in the official history, and so moved the actual history another step away from public understanding.[9]

Prominent in this process was no lesser a figure than Marshal of the Royal Air Force Sir William Dickson who, not long since, had been Chief of the Defence Staff. In a lengthy letter to *The Times* he sought, to use his own phrase, to put 'into better perspective' the articles and letters which had been and were yet to be written about the official history. As, however, there was a clear indication in his letter that he had not read the book, his 'perspective' in relation to it was of limited value. Moreover, if he had read the book, he would have seen that the whole of his argument that, in the grand strategy of the war, it had never been assumed that victory could be won by bombing alone, had been covered.[10]

A typical example of the process at work was provided by Mr C. Lynefield, who wrote to the *Daily Telegraph* saying that he was 'astounded to read that the bombing offensive had no effect on the morale of the German people'. As a military government officer, he gave the assurance that, when he arrived in Germany, he found that the people had been 'completely cowed' and that they had 'really welcomed' the end of the bombing. Group Captain Houghton, who had been in command of air information at General Eisenhower's Headquarters, told *The Times* that the official historians had created doubts as to whether the 'blanket' bombing of German towns had been worth the cost in lives and effort. He said that at Eisenhower's HQ in Frankfurt in July 1945, there was no doubt that it had been. Mr Dudley Smith, writing from the House of Commons, and also to *The Times*, said that he had been too young to know how operations had been handled in the war but that he was against the debunking, which he considered was now the vogue. By showing that the bombing offensive had been a 'costly failure' Webster and Frankland were joining the unscrupulous band of mostly young writers who, to make their works saleable, were busy producing some 'damning *exposé*, calculated to shock those who still remember'.

G.E. Seager, a former Bomber Command aircrew member, wrote sarcastically to the *Sunday Telegraph* saying that he was 'gratified' to have been told that the bomber offensive had been 'such a wasted effort'. Group Captain Douglas Bader, claiming that he had read the history, wrote in the *News of the World* that the authors had asserted that the bomber offensive had been a 'costly failure' and that this had rightly caused 'distress and anger' among ex-members of Harris's command. No historian, he wrote, was going to convince him that production was not effectively interrupted. This article, which was syndicated abroad, appeared under the headline 'Bader drops a blockbuster on that book'. 'C.G.C.' wrote in the *Manchester Evening News* that the official history was 'just another historian's armchair account of stirring deeds and nobly performed'. To describe the bombing as 'futile and ineffective' was a grave insult to the memory of the 55,000 aircrew who had died in the operations. Air Chief Marshal Sir Philip Joubert asked in the *Daily Telegraph* if any Commander's reputation was safe. He 'understood' that the official history had shown that Sir Arthur Harris had failed to influence the results of the war. This 'biased and unfair' conclusion resulted from the authors having looked at official documents, which supplied the 'statistical record' of actions taken but did not show what had influenced commanders. That could only be determined from 'circumstances' which were not re-corded. Even if we had said what Joubert thought we had said about Harris, which of course we had not, Joubert's argument would still have looked rather strange. Nor was it improved by his final paragraphs. In these, he re-marked that of the two authors, one was dead and must therefore be 'relieved of any responsibility for error'. The other was still alive and was an ex-bomber pilot (wrong) credited with thirty sorties over Germany (also wrong) and was therefore a brave man. But, Joubert concluded, that sort of experi-ence was not conclusive. It still needed to be tempered by judgement and objectivity. Otherwise King Frederick's mule that went on twenty campaigns would not have remained a mule.[11]

Joubert provoked me to reply and I wrote to the *Daily Telegraph* observing that we had not reached the conclusions he said we had and that, in coming to the conclusions we *had* reached, we had had much more evidence to go on than my experience in Bomber Command. Not every news story, however, descended to the level of sensationalism revealed by those to which I have so far alluded. Nor did every comment reach the crass depths plumbed by Sir Philip Joubert. The Defence Correspondent of *The Times*, a Special Correspondent of the *Glasgow Herald*, Ronald Boyle, Air Correspondent of the *Yorkshire Post*, Leonard Beaton of the *Guardian* and George Hunter, Air Correspondent of the *Scotsman*, all took serious pains to convey briefly what the contents of the history were and to comment on some of the more important points made. All of these had evidently read at least parts of it. Even so, it was not until after the worst of the press hysteria had

died down that scholarly appraisals began to see the light of day. On 20th
October there appeared in the *Times Literary Supplement* a long, elegantly
written, and deeply thoughtful and penetrating review. Though it was
splendidly generous to Webster and Frankland, it also contained some
important criticism and many instructive lateral thoughts. Such things in
those days appeared anonymously, but it was not long before I discovered
that it had been written by Michael Howard, who in later years was to be
Chichele Professor of the History of War and then Regius Professor of
Modern History at Oxford.[12]

Howard opened with the suggestion that the term 'official history',
especially if it concerned war, contained a self-contradiction. No government, he asserted, liked to admit the muddle, inefficiency and waste which
is inseparable from the conduct of war. Official histories were therefore
expected to be 'marmoreal monuments' to the heroic men who died in the
campaigns without any blasting of reputations or offence to survivors.
Howard's inference was that this could not be proper history and, more to
the point, he warned that it would be fatal to future military efficiency, which
depended upon correct assessment of past performance. Nor did he believe
that the ghosts of those who had died in the bomber offensive would wish
for anything other than a correct assessment. He wrote that our book, as a
work of dual scholarship, was 'an achievement possibly without parallel in
military history'. The 'chorus of detractors', he believed, could hardly have
begun to read its 'large and closely reasoned volumes' before they began to
decry them. Howard found them to be written with 'magisterial scholarship'
and a 'clarity and elegance of style' which made them a work of 'historical
literature in its own right'. He thought that it was a magnificent ending
to the career of Webster, the most honest and pugnacious of scholars, and
that it provided Frankland with 'a niche of his own among living British
historians'.

Having thus declared his hand, Howard turned to the contents of the book.
Clearly he had read it with a keen eye and it seems that he had also read
some of the stories put about by the 'chorus of detractors'. He boldly pointed
out that the authors had not concluded that the offensive had been a failure.
On the contrary, they had declared that it had made a decisive contribution
to victory. We had, he continued, dealt frankly with misconceptions, disagreements and occasional 'straight incompetence', but, he said, victories
were not won without mistakes and disagreements and it was not wise to
conduct post mortems only after defeats. Even so, he thought we had been
right to point out and stress that the Air Staff had no effective precedents to
guide them in their decisions. 'There had, after all,' he quoted from the book,
'never been a strategic air offensive before.' Nor, looking to the future, did
Howard think there would ever be another. The hydrogen bomb and the

missile, he judged, had placed the mass-bomber raid with the cavalry charge among the 'interesting curiosities of military history'.

Howard succinctly summarized our description of the Trenchard doctrine with its insistence on the long-range bomber as the central instrument of air power and the strategic air offensive as the only proper function of that instrument. He mentioned that some of Trenchard's followers had lapsed from the true faith under the pressure of events, but that others, including Harris, had maintained it to the end. He revealed our explanation of how area-bombing of town centres had, until 1944, become the only feasible operational policy open to Bomber Command and how this conclusion had been adopted by the Air Staff and the Government with the overwhelming support of the British public. He rightly said that we had not criticized Harris for carrying out this policy to the utmost of his capacity until after D-Day, when he had been told to shift his priority to oil and other selective target systems. Only then, when Harris had refused to budge, had we underlined the error of his ways. Indeed, Howard wrote, if there was a criticism to be made of Webster and Frankland, it was that they had 'allowed themselves to become unduly fascinated by the personality of Sir Arthur Harris'. Portal, by comparison, emerged as 'a shadowy background figure' and Harris's other predecessors as C-in-C, Bomber Command as 'transient and em- barrassed phantoms'. Nevertheless, Howard did not find this surprising. He saw Harris as combining the 'obstinate resolution' of Douglas Haig with the 'dynamism' of Jackie Fisher and the 'ruthless insubordination' of Douglas MacArthur. He quoted the tribute we had paid to Harris's 'enduring courage, determination and conviction'. He also observed that we had written of Harris that his prestige 'did not depend on a reputation for good judgement' and that he had 'a tendency to confuse advice with interference, criticism with sabotage and evidence with propaganda'.

I was immensely gratified by this review, not only on account of the won- derfully generous tributes Howard paid to the authors but also because, in grappling with the meaning of the book, he had incidentally wiped out the 'chorus of detractors', which, until it appeared, had largely held the field. Though it was not to be supposed that Sir Philip Joubert, Air Vice-Marshal Bennett, Douglas Bader or Sir Arthur Harris read *The Times Literary Supplement*, and though it was to be assumed that the general public would take their lead from news stories rather than an erudite review, my feeling that our book had been misunderstood was largely dissipated. One of the first to remark to me on Howard's review was Arnold Toynbee. There was also the consideration that I found the review extraordinarily interesting. Howard was still a young man, but he combined the skills of an academic historian with those of a serious journalist. He was also a student of current defence policy. All this showed in his review and gave me the feeling, which

I believe Webster would have shared, that what he and I had set out to achieve by writing the official history of the strategic air offensive had been fulfilled.

Howard was not alone in raising the question of what was meant by the term 'official history'. *The Times* had already taken up the same point in a fourth leader. Having described the trio of Webster and Frankland, as authors, and Butler, as editor, as a strong team, it suggested that if it was playing in its own colours it would 'command as much and as little respect as would any other three men qualified to write history on an ample scale'. But, *The Times* wondered, was the team playing in its own colours? In the four volumes of Webster and Frankland, the work was nowhere described as 'official' although the Prime Minister had referred in the House of Commons to the series as official. Captain Roskill described himself in *Who's Who* as 'official naval historian'. No one, said *The Times* rather optimistically, would dispute the claims of Webster, Frankland and Roskill to be fit to handle their subjects, but 'official history' was a contradiction in terms. History was individual and objective or it was nothing. So, if the 'official historians' were indeed writing under their own colours, would other bona-fide independent historians be allowed to see the source material which had been opened to them? If the thought was slightly muddled, it did invite comment. Sir James Butler replied that 'official history' meant work commissioned and sponsored by a government which then opened its records for the purpose and took responsibility for the competence of the authors and the editor. As was stated in all the volumes and as *The Times* had noticed, the authors and editor were alone responsible for the statements made and the views expressed. Butler was in no doubt that a government would decline to publish anything that was libellous or would cause serious trouble with a foreign power, but so too, he thought, might any other publisher. He could not see why an 'official history' should be 'denied the possibility of being individual and objective and worthy of the name of history'.[13]

Even allowing for the extraordinary pressures which had been exerted upon Webster and myself in the run-up to the publication of our book, to which Butler did not refer, I found, and still find, his explanation entirely satisfactory. But the 'possibility' of an 'official history' being 'individual and objective and worthy of the name of history' was not the same thing as it turning out to be that. This was why Howard's endorsement of the historical value of our work was so welcome. Looked at from the other end of the telescope, it was almost equally satisfactory to read Sir Robert Saundby's verdict that our book was 'disappointing' and did 'much less than justice to a great and successful operation of war. One only has to read,' Saundby concluded, 'the excellent volumes of *The War at Sea* by Captain S.W. Roskill to realize how indifferently the strategic air offensive has been served by its official historians.' In other words, Roskill had marched up and down the quarter deck in accord with the tune of the naval authorities whereas, *mutatis mutandis*, Webster and Frankland had not.[14]

Further evidence in favour of our work being received as independent and objective history came from other important sources. R.B. Wernham, writing in the *Oxford Magazine*, thought that it was natural to 'sniff a little suspiciously at an official history, at least as long as the archives on which it is based are kept officially closed'. Webster and Frankland had, however, produced volumes which, he said, we 'immediately recognize are history and soon forget are official. Their mastery of the subject, insight into the problems, and independence of judgement will be quickly obvious to everyone', Wernham continued, evidently without having paid much attention to the ordinary newspapers. And, 'to crown it all', he added, we had produced 'a most readable book, brilliantly planned, and very clearly written'. D.C. Watt was impressed by the extent to which the air force view of history, propounded by numerous memoirs of senior air force officers, the popular history of the RAF (by Saunders and Richards) and a widely publicized biography of Trenchard had gained widespread acceptance. This view of history had become, so to speak, a court of appeal for the RAF in its quest for government backing and public support of its own particular brand of strategy in the 1960s and as a defence against alternative naval and military ideas. By dismantling this air force view of history, Webster and Frankland had pruned the power of this court of appeal and that, Watt considered, was the reason for the 'furore in service and informed circles' that followed the publication of our book. Without knowledge of the pressure that had been put on Webster and myself by the Air Ministry when they saw the draft of our history, Watt had got to the heart of the matter. His insight enabled him to demonstrate that our 'official' history had destroyed the Air Ministry's official version.[15]

Several other reviewers provided me with interest and gratification. For example, Marvin McFarland writing in the American journal, *Military Affairs*, praised the 'skilful manner' in which we had 'analyzed, digested, evaluated and presented' the complex documentation of the subject and said that we had distinguished ourselves as 'master craftsmen'. A.J.P. Taylor, using as his vehicle the *New Statesman*, spotted several of the key points we had made in the book and was one of the very few to see that one of our principal criticisms of Portal arose from his failure to perceive that a long-range fighter was a technical possibility. But, as I look again at all these reviews with the opportunity to compare and reconsider them so many years after they were written, the operative points seem to me to have been contained in the reactions of Howard, Wernham and Watt and, no less, of Saundby. For it was these that validated Butler's claim that official history had the possibility of being independent and objective, and suggested that the work of Webster and Frankland was such. This was the accolade we had sought from the outset of our endeavour.[16]

R.B. Wernham's assumptions about how Webster and Frankland's official history would be regarded seemed, as I have said, to have been made without his paying attention to what was being said in the newspaper stories on the subject. Knowing, as I do, the pure brand of scholarship that informs the mind of this meticulous historian, it is certainly likely that newspaper stories and television broadcasts had no effect at all on the formation of Wernham's opinion; but they may well have had led him and other reviewers to whom I have referred, to express their views. The press hysteria drew much more widespread attention to the official history than it would have been likely to gain without it. The press distortions, exaggerations and inventions probably caused the more serious reviewers to look more closely at the book than they would otherwise have done. It was also, it seems to me, this publicity rather than the quality of the official history that gave me the *entrée* as a contributor to the *Times Literary Supplement*, *The Times*, the *Daily Telegraph*, the *Sunday Times*, the *Observer* and other papers and journals. It may also explain why many publishers now urged me to write further much shorter books about the strategic air offensive.

I enjoyed my forays into journalism and I did write two further books about the strategic air offensive. The first, which I called *The Bombing Offensive against Germany: Outlines and Perspectives*, was based upon the Lees Knowles Lectures I delivered in Cambridge University in 1963. I adduced no new evidence beyond what was contained in the official history but, by arranging my material under three headings – in prospect, in action and in retrospect – I invited the reader to look at the campaign in the three different perspectives of anticipation, execution and subsequent reflection. This time I was spared the headlines and the news stories, but the book was widely noticed and on the whole very fairly reviewed at a serious level. Sir Robert Saundby returned to the charge. 'Dr Frankland,' he wrote, 'for all his prolonged study of the strategic air offensive does not seem ever to have grasped fully the profound difference between two-dimensional and three-dimensional warfare. The third dimension,' Saundby argued, 'confers upon aircraft the power of avoiding confrontation with most of the enemy's armed forces, and of striking directly at any selected target within range.'[17]

One can readily understand how the Air Marshals, urged on by their wish to demonstrate that their new service had something entirely new to offer, had been led into such a belief before the war. It is harder to sympathize with their adherence to the idea after the war when the historical evidence about what had happened was set before them. Their position had indeed become entrenched and almost mindless. In this particular case, within service circles, it took a general to see what I meant. General (later Field-Marshal Lord)

Carver wrote of my book that I had approached the subject with 'the objectivity of the historian and the down-to-earth reality of one familiar with all the practical factors which theorists can so easily overlook'. He emphasized that my conclusion was that it was the 'failure of the Air Staff to appreciate the classical factors of warfare, in particular the importance of defeating the enemy's forces in order to obtain command of the air, which was the principal failing'. Carver wrote that, from the strategist's point of view, the interest of my book lay in the emphasis I placed on the classical factor, 'bringing one round to the point that every new weapon leads to an opposing reaction; so that, as soon as the initial advantage of novelty is over, balance is achieved and one is faced with the problem of overcoming the enemy's forces as before, with one more complication added'. Carver, for all the originality of his mind, had been brought up in the school of classical strategy and he had not invested his professional reputation in anything so novel and so wrong as the Trenchard doctrine.[18]

My second and last book on the strategic air offensive, *Bomber Offensive: The Devastation of Europe*, was much less ambitious in terms of original thought. I set out to achieve, in the short space of about sixty thousand words, a summarized version of the official history that would include all the principal points and all the essential qualifications. Whether or not I succeeded in the eyes of the critics, I do not know, for there were few reviews. By my standards, however, the book proved to be a best seller: it went into several editions in numerous languages and was bought by nearly a quarter of a million people.

I was by no means the only author to have a second bite of the cherry after the publication of the official history. A number of other writers pillaged it to something like the same extent, which no doubt is one of the reasons why governments commission official histories. Anthony Verrier published his version in 1968. He made massive use of the official history and also of my *The Bombing Offensive* but he was entirely correct in the way he did this, for his footnotes were drenched with references to my work. A.J.P. Taylor commended him for having added some new knowledge through the process of interviewing survivors, but he did not otherwise think that he had added anything to Webster and Frankland – which Taylor added, 'happens to be the most honest and ruthless official history ever written'. Taylor said that he was surprised to learn that Verrier had found some 'flaws and hesitations' in it, but he could not find out what they were because Verrier's jargon was largely unintelligible to him. Taylor thought that Webster and Frankland had been more successful than Verrier in clarifying the issues, and he said that he had only been able to work out what Verrier was driving at by looking up each point in Webster and Frankland. My own view was that Verrier had asked some of the right questions, but that he had failed to answer them.[19]

A much more impressive product of the same kind came from the pen of Max Hastings, whose *Bomber Command* was first published in 1979. The book was widely noticed and at least in journalistic and broadcasting circles, the author was soon accorded the role of leading expert on the subject of the bombing offensive. There were three interesting new points in this book. Hastings observed that Webster and Frankland had failed to notice that the Under-Secretary of State for Air, Harold Balfour, had, during the course of the war, lost confidence in Bomber Command. Hastings was right; we had. He also introduced a chapter on the effects and experience, from the German point of view, of the bombing of Darmstadt, which took place on 11th December 1944. This was brilliant and brought out much more clearly than anything Webster and I had written what it was like to be a German in a big Bomber Command attack. Hastings also discovered a letter from Harris to 4 Group, written on 11th December 1942, from which it appeared that Harris believed that heavy bombers would be able to repel enemy fighter attacks in daylight. Hastings claimed this as an original discovery, which I have little doubt it was. Certainly Webster and I had missed it. Apart from these points, however, and the colour which Hastings introduced by talking to participants, there seemed to me to be little or nothing that had not been covered in the official history. There were also, unfortunately, numerous misunderstandings and errors. For example, Hastings referred to bombers being blown off their course, when in fact they could only be steered off it, to 'Gee' being an improvement on dead reckoning, as though the two were alternatives; to conscripted aircrew, of which there were none; to the Man- chester being grossly underpowered, which it was not; and to well 'armoured' German fighters, when he meant armed. In the context of Hastings's broad and picturesque sweeps, any objection to errors of detail such as these may seem to be pedantic. In my view, however, broad sweeps and general con- clusions, if they are to be illuminating, must be founded on an accurate appreciation of detail and technicality.[20]

In addition to these re-runs of the official history, there have also been some serious attempts to revise it. Group Captain Saward, in his authorized biography of Sir Arthur Harris, repeated some of the proclaimed Harris dogma on the subject of the incompetence and prejudice of Webster and Frankland and took direct issue with us on our verdict on the Battle of Berlin. He claimed that it had not been a defeat and that the reason for its cessation was not that the casualties had become too high, but that the nights were getting too short and that Harris was ordered to turn the weight of his attack against the French railway system. Although the nights were getting short and although Harris was so ordered, the fact remains that the level of casualties in the Battle of Berlin could not have been sustained and the Battle, which had run its course, had not resulted in the German collapse Harris had predicted. Saward's claim was correct dogma but unsound history. Indeed, his argument had been disposed of in advance by none other than Harris himself. On 7th April 1944 Harris had written to the Air Ministry saying that the German defences were approaching a point at which night-bombing could not be sustained. The casualties would be too great. Tactical innovations, which had postponed this outcome, were now, he wrote, 'practically exhausted'. I had quoted this letter in the official history as evidence in support of our conclusion about the Battle of Berlin, but Saward had either not noticed it or had decided to disregard it. His verdict on our verdict did not, therefore, strike me as important.[21]

Denis Richards, also seeking to revise the official history in his book, *The Hardest Victory*, fell more or less into the same error. Accepting our verdict that from the operational point of view the Battle of Berlin was a defeat, he nonetheless went on to claim that the battle ceased, not because the losses were 'insupportable', but because Harris was ordered to bomb France. He too seems not to have understood adequately the effect on Bomber Command of the losses in the Battle of Berlin and to have overlooked Harris's view of them at the time. Richards also found it difficult to accept our view of the results of the dams raid in May 1943. All the same, he failed to produce any significant evidence to rebut the conclusion we reached that the total effect on Germany was small. He also substantially accepted our opinion that the real importance of the attacks lay in the new operational possibilities of precise attack that they opened for the future. In his extensive and important work on air history, Denis Richards has always seemed to me to be looking for the best gloss that could be put upon events from the point of view of the Air Force. His generosity in this sense has, I believe, often carried him somewhat beyond the bounds of what the primary evidence permits and has tended to weaken his criticism of the official history.[22]

The same consideration may be seen to have been at work in Richards's more detailed revisions, which appeared in his biography of Portal. In this work, he makes no mention of the futility of bombing the ball-bearings town of Schweinfurt, even though this was one of the issues on which Portal stood up to Harris, insisting he carried out the attacks, in spite of the expansively expressed opposition to the idea from the C-in-C, who, in this respect, was subsequently shown by history to have been right. Richards also makes no reference to the breach between Portal, as Chief of the Air Staff, and Alanbrook, as Chief of the Imperial General Staff, which occurred in 1942 and undermines the concept of an efficient and smoothly working Chiefs of Staff Committee. He passes over the question of Portal's strong opposition to the American concept of day-bombing without examining the grave consequences that would have ensued had Slessor not talked him out of his position. The fact that Portal was right about what would happen to heavy

American day-bombers once they began to penetrate German air space is not the main issue. Had the Americans been drawn into the night offensive, as Portal wished, General Spaatz would have been denied his opportunity to engage the Luftwaffe in being and so, as it turned out, to win the decisive battle for command of the air. Richards also makes light of Portals's entrenched disbelief in the technical possibility of an effective long-range fighter, which not only proved to be technically possible but became the trump card in Spaatz's hand.[23]

Against this background, it was hardly surprising to find that, when he came to the dispute between Portal and Harris about the oil plan in the winter of 1944–5, Richards was very discontented with the account of it given in the official history. Even after the omission of the full texts of the correspondence and the toning down of some sentences describing it, to which Webster and I had agreed, our judgements did not show Portal in a good light. Though we had acknowledged the great difficulty of his position, we had also made it clear that he had failed to get from Harris the degree of priority for oil bombing he was convinced was necessary to bring the war to a speedy conclusion. We showed that he had retreated behind the suggestion that they should wait until after the war to see who was right. We thus made it clear that, at this crossing of minds, Harris emerged as the stronger character, and that the concentration on general area-bombing continued to be the principal employment of Bomber Command at a time when Portal believed that it should have been overwhelmingly directed against specific oil plants. Richards could not swallow this. He advanced the argument that we had gone 'somewhat astray' regarding the dispute because our statements 'were not subjected to any check by the two protagonists'. Yet he also described how both Portal and Harris had objected strongly to the relevant passages in our book while it was still in draft, how these objections were made known to us and how, in the light of them, we made some changes, not of substance, but to our mode of expression. Thus, in fact, Richards showed that our statements had been checked by the two protagonists. His argument was confused and unconvincing. Nevertheless, it was his spring-board for advancing the claim that, at the time, Portal was 'reasonably content' that Harris was carrying out the policy he had laid down. The inference was that there had never really had been a dispute and that Webster and Frankland had gone wrong in thinking that there had. In this, Richards landed himself in an untenable position. The documentation of the argument, which Webster and I had provided, and which Portal and Harris had tried to prevent us from providing, together with the simple statistics of Bomber Command operations at this juncture, put Richards's claim completely out of court.[24]

So, for all his long acquaintanceship with the problems of air power and his scholarship, Denis Richards's criticisms of the official history did not in my view amount to a valid revision of it. All the same, I do to some extent sympathize with him, as the biographer of Portal, in his wish to redress what he saw as an adverse balance against his subject proceeding from the official history. Years earlier, Sir Norman Brook and the Prime Minister had shown something of the same feeling, but they were not historians and were more concerned with not rocking the boat than historians ought to be. When in a later chapter I come to describe my own experience as a biographer, it will, however, be seen that my motivation is not, perhaps, very different from that of Denis Richards – in which connection, I may now mention that I was invited to write the authorized biography of Portal and I declined the invitation. Portal, I recognize, was of great distinction and eminence, but I did not see him as a figure to the writing of whose life I would have wished to devote years of my own. Denis Richards clearly differed from me in this, which I find not in the least surprising.

To conclude this episode, I must record two vignettes of Portal. Writing to Margaret Kennedy in October 1945, the Warden of Winchester, Harold Baker, gave his impression of Portal when he came to the college *Ad Portas*. 'Perhaps not a great man,' he wrote, 'but the most remarkable I have seen for twenty years or more. He has all the talents and all the desirable virtues harmoniously blended – perfect proportions, with poise and serenity, so that one entirely forgets that he is so remarkably ugly. I still after several months,' Baker continued, 'am filled with admiration when I think of him. He lectured to the school, also, on the Air Force, and added a few words about Winchester which were better than all the books, poems & sermons of others.' The second vignette comes from personal contact. Towards the end of his life, Lord Portal came to the Imperial War Museum to open an exhibition, which I had organized, to mark the fiftieth anniversary of the foundation of the RAF. Though he was by that time a very sick man, he came three times, twice to study the exhibition and then, a few days later, to open it. On his first visit, I drew his attention to the bust of him done by Epstein, which was in the exhibition. For some time he looked at it in silence. I said I thought it was a wonderfully characterful study. 'Yes,' he replied, 'but I never felt as sure of myself as that.'[25]

I now return to the question of people who have sought to revise the conclusions reached in the official history. Between May 1994 and March 1995, Professor Thomas Wilson corresponded with me about a book he was completing on the role and influence of Lord Cherwell in the Second World War, which he later published under the title of *Churchill and the Prof.* Professor Wilson invited me to comment on the typescript of portions of his book that dealt with the strategic air offensive. In the course of our exchanges, he referred to Professor R.J. Overy's new book, *War Economy in the Third Reich*, in which, he said, Overy had challenged the belief that, in the first part of the war, there was a great deal of slack in the German war economy. As Webster and I had concluded in the official history that the 'cardinal error' of British intelligence was its description of the German economy as 'tightly stretched and in decline when it was, in reality, cushioned and increasingly productive...', this observation aroused my keenest interest. I read Overy's book forthwith and also an earlier one entitled *The Air War 1939–1945*, which he had published in 1980.[26]

As fate sometimes decrees, things come in clusters and, at about the same time, I found myself engaged in a symposium at the Royal Air Force Staff College at Bracknell during which both Overy and I read papers. In my opening address, I posed the question of what effect the strategic air offensive had had on Germany's ability to wage war and answered it by saying, 'until July 1944 very little indeed, but afterwards a very great deal'. In his observations, Professor Overy remarked that 'the bombing offensive was probably much more cost effective strategically for the Allies than the popular view would normally concede'. It amused me to find that the 'popular' view now seemed to be that expressed in the official history, which had hardly been the case at the time of its publication. The real interest of the matter to me, however, was the extent to which Overy could sustain his claims. He did not offer much of substance in this respect at the symposium but, having written two books on the subject, he hardly needed to, especially as he was addressing members of the Royal Air Force Historical Society who, at least in theory, were apt to read such things.[27]

My observations are, therefore, based upon the two books by Overy I have mentioned. The most important of these seemed to me to be *War Economy in the Third Reich*, for in this work Overy displays an impressive range and depth of research, including much study of the Speer archives, about which a lot of people talk, but which not so many read. His resulting theory is that Hitler had not planned for war in 1939; he had expected his Polish invasion to amount to no more than a skirmish. He had, however, planned for a big war later. Overy rejects the idea that Hitler had expected the big war to be won by a Blitzkrieg and believes that the plan was for a long war with full mobilization from the outset. Hence his contention that the German war economy was fully mobilized from an early date and that those, including Webster and Frankland – though he did not mention them – who thought that there was a large slack in the economy that enabled Germany to absorb bomb damage and increase production in spite of it, were wrong. Unfortunately for this argument, the evidence Overy goes on to cite overthrows his own claim. For example, he mentions that, in 1940, Germany spent an estimated equivalent of $6,000 million on weapons, and that Britain, in the same period, spent $3,500 million. Britain, he says, nevertheless produced 50% more aircraft than Germany did in this period, 100% more vehicles and almost as many tanks. Not only do these figures not suggest that the German war economy was fully mobilized; they demonstrate that there was a huge slack of unused or wasted resources within the system, which were available to be tapped when harsher times demanded more efficient measures. In other words at this point Overy comes down on the side of the 'slack in the German war economy' theory and against his own contention.[28]

Nor do Overy's subsequent citations of evidence change the picture. For example, he argues that, in 1939, Germany had less non-essential consumer production to cut than had Britain, but he then says that much consumer production was devoted to providing the German armed forces with high standards of dress, which, though he does not say so, was hardly a full mobilization of resources for the purpose of fighting the war. Then again, he states that by the spring of 1941 Germany was nearing a 'situation of full-scale mobilization for war', only to add a few pages later that, in 1944, the German aircraft industry produced almost four times as many aircraft as it had done in 1941 without any substantial increase in its labour force and with a larger component of less productive forced labour. He describes how, in the spring of 1942, Speer inspected twenty major firms in Berlin and found that not a single one was working a double shift, and that, of 117 carpet firms, five accounted for 90% of the output. The remaining 112, with their 10% of the output, were closed and transferred to war production. Was not this a slack in the German war economy? Overy does not tell us. He does, however, explain the habit German aircraft firms had of using surplus aluminium and other materials to produce greenhouses, ladders and mosquito nets. When in 1942, the allocation of materials to the aircraft firms was reduced, the production of aircraft increased by 43%. After studying the book and considering its arguments as well as the evidence, which was copiously displayed, I was unable to see that it constituted a revision of the conclusions on the subject which had been reached in the official history.[29]

Having somehow convinced himself that the German war economy was fully stretched from the outset, Overy was virtually bound to assume that bombing must have been more effective than was supposed in the 'popular view'. After all, if indeed the German war economy had been fully stretched, then holes made in it by events such as the thousand-bomber attack on Cologne and, much more so, the Battle of Hamburg, would have been at least likely to have had serious effects. This, I suppose, must have been the rationale behind Overy's claim at the symposium, which I mentioned earlier, that strategic bombing had been more effective than supposed. I searched his *The Air War 1939–1945* in vain to find evidence to support the contention. Nor did it seem to me that Overy had come to a real understanding of the strategic air offensive, the meaning of air superiority, or the course of events that led to it. I was shocked to find that he thought that *Circus* operations over France in 1941, in which bombers were used to draw up the German fighters, which it was hoped would then be shot down by allied fighters escorting the bombers, were a successful step in gaining air superiority. In fact, as the Germans were not unduly disturbed by what happened to French targets at this stage of the war, they responded only when they saw that the operational conditions favoured them. The result was that the British lost much more heavily than the Germans. It was strange to read that the Casablanca Conference of January 1943 set in train the policy of seeking air superiority over Germany by 'regular fighter intrusion by day'. This policy was in reality set in train only by the American disaster at Schweinfurt in October 1943. It was even odder to learn that the British and American bombers withdrew from the Combined Bomber Offensive in the last part of 1943. The Americans did to some extent, but the British fought the Battle of Berlin which, at that time, was the largest air battle in the history of warfare. Of evidence about the effectiveness or otherwise of the bombing offensive, there seemed to be no trace. But strangely enough, there was much in support of the idea that there was a large unexploited slack in the German war economy for a great part of the war.[30]

If I have laid too much emphasis on the work of Professor Overy, I will excuse myself by blaming Professor Wilson and others who pointed out to me the revisions of the official history those works seemed to have made necessary. My object has only been to show why I do not believe this to be the case. My own view is that the official history needs, not so much a revision, as an addition. It contains insufficient examination of the development of the German night fighter system which, after all, was the principal means by which the Germans held the night bombing offensive in check until the final stages, when the Luftwaffe as a whole began to collapse. If I had my time again, I would wish to remedy this defect but, as I will show, I had moved into other fields and felt that pastures of yesteryear would make unappetizing grazing.

Before leaving the subject of the official history, I must mention two final ironies. The first is that as time has gone on, my work has come in some quarters to be regarded as a whitewash of Bomber Command. For example, in a book published in 1995, John Kegan suggested that it approached the obsequious nature of the official military histories of the First World War and he accused Webster and Frankland of a 'tenderness for reputations' which deprived the narrative of bite. I doubt if Lord Tedder would have agreed with this verdict and I am sure that Sir Arthur Harris and Lord Portal would not. The second irony had arrived earlier. In 1979 a history of *The Royal Air Force and Two World Wars* was published. The author, as he handsomely acknowledged, had consulted me about parts of the book while it was in draft; and in the final version, in addition to making extensive use of the official history and other works by myself, he wrote that, 'One event which did not help the establishment of the truth was the reception given by the British Press to the publication in 1961 of Webster and Frankland's history. The history,' he continued, 'is an exhaustive and scholarly account of Bomber Command's defeats and triumphs, and the final and decisive contribution to the defeat of Germany.' It was difficult to believe, the author added, 'that the reviewers read the history, which indeed contains nearly a million words. Like the Thirty-Nine Articles of the Anglican Church, it remains more often quoted than read and more often read than understood. This is sad because in that book the troubles and the triumphs of Bomber Command are plainly and honestly recorded.' The author of this book and of those sentences was Sir Maurice Dean, the pianist whom he had enjoined Sir Arthur Harris not to shoot because he was doing everything in his power, as Permanent Under Secretary of State at the Air Ministry, to prevent the publication of Webster and Frankland's history. Wonderful are the ways of Whitehall.[31]

CHAPTER SIX

History from the News

One of the disadvantages of being an official historian was that, unless one already had a compatible appointment, such as being the fellow of a college, one wrote oneself out of a job as one proceeded. This prospect caused me anxiety from the outset, especially as there were few positions in the universities open to military historians. Sir Charles Webster was remarkably sympathetic to me in my feelings of insecurity and, although he supported me in my unsuccessful applications for fellowships, which I have mentioned earlier, he believed that the solution to my problem lay in the creation of a new post which would match my interests and qualifications. In November 1951, not long after our partnership as official historians had begun and when he was still Professor of International History at the London School of Economics, he told me that there was a 'kind of examination' in military subjects in the university and that occasional lectures were given. There was, however, no permanent teacher and no organized department. Here, Webster believed, was a potential opening for me. He invited me to meet Colonel S.J. Worsley, who was chairman of the London University Military Studies Committee and who, Webster told me, knew all about the issue and had considerable influence. After the lunch at which I met Colonel Worsley, Webster wrote to tell me that he thought I had made a very good impression, but that Worsley had seemed to him to be too optimistic as to the ease with which a post could be set up. Worsley warned me that the final decision would not rest with him, but said that he 'would be very happy if we could secure your services'.[1]

Webster told me that there would be a contest for the department of military history between King's College and the London School of Economics. He hoped that the latter would prevail because that was where he had the most influence. In the event King's won and, in May 1953, their Principal, Peter Noble, wrote to Butler telling him that it was proposed to set up a Lectureship in Military Studies in the college. He said they already had a good man in their history department, M.E. Howard, who would gladly take on the job. Noble said that he and others in the college were 'favourably inclined' towards Howard, for, though he had not yet published much, they thought he was a good historian, a good lecturer and a very agreeable colleague. A problem had, however, arisen because another name had been put forward, 'a Mr Noble Frankland DPhil' who was, 'I believe', Noble wrote, 'with Sir Charles Webster in writing the history of Bomber Command'. He told Butler that he already had Webster's opinion of me and that he now wanted Butler's. Matters were then handed over to Professor C.H. Williams, who was Head of the History Department in King's. Butler wrote to him saying that he had been favourably impressed by my work and that he had little doubt I would carry out 'conscientiously and efficiently' any work entrusted to me. He said I had had a distinguished career in the Air Force and that my work on the history of the strategic air offensive implied a knowledge of allied general strategy. Williams replied that Frankland was being considered 'very seriously'.[2]

Butler was eventually to play a significantly helpful part in the advancement of my career, but had I at that time known the content of his observations to Professor Williams, which, I did not, I would have thought them rather disappointing. I am sure that Webster, and probably also Wernham, spoke more positively about me; but their letters did not find their way into the public records, as a copy of Butler's did, and I, therefore, do not know what they said. However seriously Frankland may have been considered, Howard was selected.

I have described this episode because, not without a flicker and a hiccup, it directed my career away from university life and into other channels. It appeared to be a serious set-back; Webster was very disappointed. But with the knowledge of hindsight, I can now see how yet again, what looked like a failure was a blessing in disguise. I do not believe that I would have flourished as a Lecturer in King's College, London, and I am sure that I would not have made a success of the appointment in the way Michael Howard in fact did. Today, the Department of War Studies at King's is the most important centre of military studies in the country. This is in large measure to Michael Howard's credit. Moreover, the appointment, in his hands, proved to be the stepping stone to a meteoric academic career, culminating in the Regius Chair of Modern History at Oxford. I am sure that King's made the right decision in 1953 and I am very glad they did.

In those days, all the same, without knowledge or even a suspicion of what was to happen, I had to clutch at such straws as drifted my way. One such was a scheme hatched in the Department of Extra Mural Studies at Oxford that was designed to prepare RAF officers for the Staff College qualifying examination. One of my DPhil examiners, Norman Gibbs, who had now become Chichele Professor of the History of War at Oxford, was in charge and he invited me to participate as a lecturer and tutor. I accepted with alacrity and threw myself into the work to the utmost of my ability. All the action was at the weekends, which was the time when the RAF officers, most of whom were pilots or navigators, could get away from their normal duties. This meant that my contribution did not conflict with going up to London on week days to work on the official history. I hoped that the scheme would eventually develop into a department of military studies on the lines of what had been created in London University and I did my best to promote the success of what I thought might be the foundation of such a development. My designated part was to give lectures to the course as a whole, to assist with the formation of the syllabus, to give individual tuition to a proportion of the students, to set and mark their essays and, at the end of each course, to take part in the marking of the results. I found the work challenging and congenial. The officers, who were Flight Lieutenants or Squadron Leaders, were those who the authorities thought might have an important future, and, though they were somewhat variable in academic ability, all of them were enthusiasts set upon passing into the Staff College.

The courses covered a number of aspects of contemporary international affairs but laid a heavy emphasis on the military aspects and of these air power was the most important, and the one that interested the students the most. As I was the only tutor who had any real knowledge of that subject my position from the outset was pivotal. Also, through the connections I had developed in the course of my research, I was able to attract distinguished figures from the world of action who, at my invitation, came to lecture to the courses. Among these were Marshal of the Royal Air Force Sir John Slessor, whose son, Squadron Leader John Slessor, was a pupil of mine on one of the courses, Air Marshal Sir Robert Saundby, Sir Charles Webster and Group Captain 'Johnnie' Johnson, the top-scoring British fighter pilot of the Second World War, who was also a profound thinker and natural lecturer. In addition, because of my access to the Air Ministry, in which I still had an office, I was able to iron out little matters such as a dispute about the course that arose between the Directorate of Staff Training and the Directorate of Educational Services in the Air Ministry. At any rate, when I was offered an appointment in Chatham House, Professor Gibbs told me that he hoped I would be able to continue with the Oxford scheme. He thought 'it was doing good, & what is being done', he wrote, 'depends on you as much as on anybody'. He said he would do anything in his power to make it possible for me to continue on terms suitable to myself.[3]

I had every intention of doing so. The work had its disadvantages; in particular the intellectual focus of the students was too narrow to be exciting. This was partly owing to the effort they had to make to master and keep abreast of the technicalities of their normal flying duties in aircraft which were already far more complex than those in which I had flown during the war. It was partly the result of the attention they tended to concentrate on the immediate object of passing into the Staff College; and, I think, it was also partly caused by their perception of the kind of mind which, if they were to aspire to the higher ranks of the service, they would have to cultivate. They were disciplined and dedicated men, but they were not free thinkers and their aim was to harness history to the purpose of devising rules that would enable them to solve contemporary and projected problems. In my efforts to persuade them to break out of these bounds, I was badly handi-capped by the almost complete lack of scholarly literature on the subject of air power. There was virtually nothing to compare with the wealth of guidance from the sources one could have offered to the military and naval equivalents of these RAF officers. Nevertheless, the work was reward-ing both in the sense that the students strove to their utmost and the results we got in their examinations were, on the whole, very good indeed. And, as I have mentioned, there was the chance that the scheme would develop into a military department under the Chichele Chair of the History of War.

In those days, it was not much easier to persuade academic historians that air history was a serious aspect of the subject than it is nowadays to get them to accept that royal biography can be too. Moreover, my efforts were crippled by the fact that all my work was classified as secret. My thesis was sealed in the Bodleian Library and secreted in the Air Ministry files. The work I had done on the official history of the strategic air offensive was inaccessible until it had been completed and cleared for publication by the Cabinet Office. The only academics who knew my work at first hand were those within the charmed circle of official history, Butler, Webster, Wernham, Goodwin and Gibbs. When therefore in November 1955, Michael Howard invited me to lecture on the strategic air offensive to his new department in King's College, it seemed to be an opportunity for me to put my name and work into a some-what wider academic context. Webster raised no objection to my accepting, but, before I could do so, I had to seek Butler's permission because what I would say would be based upon the secret work I had done for my thesis and the official history. The reply came from Acheson and, not much to my surprise, it was negative. Acheson wrote that he had talked the matter over with Sir Norman Brook. He said that the latter would not welcome the dis-closure of the substance of the official history in advance of its publication but that was not the only consideration. The subject was controversial and would attract public interest. If there were differences between what was said in the lecture and what later appeared in the official history, it might be concluded that my real view was that given in the lecture and that what was said in the official history was the result of official pressure. No, Sir Norman Brook regretted that he could not agree to my giving the lecture. So that was that as far as my finding an opportunity to disclose some of my discoveries was concerned.[4]

For someone else, however, that was not that, and at the beginning of October 1956 I was quite astonished to read the text of a broadcast made by Professor Gibbs on the BBC Third Programme. Here, to an extent which I could at first scarcely credit, was a summary of several of the main and most original points I had made in my thesis; here was the heart of what I would have said in my lecture under Michael Howard's auspices, had I been allowed to give it. In many instances, even the language in which Gibbs expressed my ideas was almost identical with that I had used. A few weeks earlier, Gibbs had told me he was writing a review of Sir John Slessor's book, *The Central Blue*, and he asked me to lend him a copy of my thesis, of which he had been an examiner, so that he could refresh his memory of it. In agreeing to lend it to him, I had reminded him that it was still a secret document and that he would therefore have to avoid making public use of it. He sent his wife to collect it from my home.

I prepared a memorandum complaining of this plagiarism and wrote Gibbs a letter of resignation from my work for the Oxford RAF courses. Webster read my memorandum and compared Gibbs's sentences with what I had written in the thesis. Having satisfied himself as to my case, he thought it best to send the memorandum to Acheson. He accompanied it with a covering letter of his own in which he wrote, 'I have read Frankland's memorandum and I have, of course, examined the text of the broadcast and compared it with the dissertation. I entirely agree with what Frankland states in his memorandum.'[5]

Acheson showed no stomach for battle and he thought it was a matter for Butler. So Webster wrote to the latter saying that a 'very unpleasant thing has happened'. We had taken the matter up with Acheson, he explained, 'but he says it is a question for you to consider'. At first, Butler was almost as reluctant a hero as Acheson, but eventually he agreed to read my memorandum and the text of Gibbs's broadcast and to re-read my thesis. Meanwhile, I wrote to Sir John Slessor to explain why I had resigned from tutoring the RAF courses in Oxford, to which he had just lectured at my invitation. His son had also just completed one of them. Webster drafted a paragraph which he asked me to put into my letter. It included the following:

> The fact is that Gibbs has published as his own estimate of the bombing offensive the result of the research which I did over a period of years. Sir Charles who fully shares my views of Gibbs' conduct says that he has never in the course of his long career seen a parallel case.[6]

Someone, presumably Acheson, now sent a copy of my memorandum to Gibbs. He conceded that he had examined my thesis and he admitted that he had 'seen the thesis again this summer'; but he had done that only to avoid making howlers in his broadcast about the bombing of Germany and, he claimed, 'I did not use Frankland's thesis'.[7]

I refuted this claim in a second memorandum and, having assured myself of Webster's complete concurrence with everything contained in it, I proceeded to Acheson's office and tried to hand it over to him. He refused to read it or to accept it. He said it was not an official matter and that he could take no part in it. I asked how the use of an official and secret document for a public purpose could not be an official matter. Acheson replied that as Gibbs had denied that he had made any use of the thesis, that situation did not arise. I then reminded Acheson of some of the similarities between the broadcast and the thesis. Acheson said that this evidence was irrelevant and could not be examined. If anything more was said to Gibbs on the subject, he would draw the conclusion that his honour was being impugned and would resign from the Cabinet Office. His resignation, Acheson said, could not be contemplated. I then asked what my position would be in the hypothetical case of my making a broadcast on the basis of, say, one of the secret Air Ministry narratives on Coastal Command. That would be a breach of the official secrets act, Acheson said. So why, I asked, was not Gibbs's use of my secret thesis a breach of the same act? It was not, Acheson answered, because Gibbs had denied that he had used the thesis. In my hypothetical case, I then asked, what would happen if I denied that I had used the Coastal Command narrative. In that case, Acheson informed me, nothing would happen. Webster and I could see that we were not going to get very far on this front, so the matter was left in Butler's court.[8]

At length, on 19th December, Butler handed down his judgement in a memorandum of which he sent copies to Webster, myself and Acheson. He explained that at first he had felt disinclined to intervene in a dispute arising from a charge of unprofessional conduct between two Oxford historians. It had, however, he said been represented to him that, as general editor of the official military histories, he was confronted with the claim that one of the official historians had given advance publicity to arguments and conclusions by another official historian which were contained in a preliminary study and to which he had been given confidential access. He had, therefore, agreed to read Professor Gibbs's broadcast as printed in *The Listener*, Dr Frankland's memorandum, Professor Gibbs's reply and Dr Frankland's rejoinder. He added that he had also read Dr Frankland's thesis and, after doing so, had re-read the documents he had listed.

There was, Butler concluded, 'a very striking similarity between the theme, the arguments, the evidence adduced and the conclusions in the broadcast and the thesis'. He thought that 'Dr Frankland hardly over-states his case in calling the one a précis of the other'. He agreed with me that there were also some 'remarkable verbal parallels'. The question was, Butler considered, whether all this derived from the thesis or was the result of Professor Gibbs's independent thought. Passing on to Gibbs's role as an examiner of my thesis, he referred to Gibbs's claim that within a month the whole thing had gone out of his head. Butler thought this was surprising. He pointed out that examining a thesis for a doctorate involved 'careful and critical reading and checking of argument and sources'. It was quite different from reading examination papers among scores of others and doing it against time. 'Moreover', Butler wrote, 'Dr Frankland's thesis is a work of remarkable ability' which, however much may have become known since, contained 'conclusions which were then original and striking'. He thought it would be 'very surprising' if, at least unconsciously, some of these had not remained in Gibbs's mind. Butler felt that he was not competent to say how far the facts, arguments and conclusions of the thesis had subsequently become known generally and he doubted if reference to an outside expert would serve a useful purpose in trying to resolve that question.

Dealing next with the fact that, at the point he was writing the broadcast, Gibbs had asked to see the thesis, Butler noted that Gibbs had, nonetheless, asserted that he had not used it. He was surprised by Gibbs's statement that he had dealt with the subject of bombing only by 'very occasional reference'. It seemed to Butler to have figured 'fairly largely'. Even so, Butler concluded, Gibbs had said that he had not used the thesis and 'only he can have knowledge on this point'. As to the similarities in phrasing, Butler suggested that the words used were of the sort writers might employ when developing the same arguments and he observed that in some cases there were discrepancies between the two versions. Gibbs, for example, had not used the term *guerre de course*; Frankland had used it several times.

In a final paragraph of his memorandum, Butler summed up by saying that he had been struck by the 'remarkable similarity' between Gibbs's article 'in theme, treatment and conclusion' and Frankland's thesis. He thought that Gibbs owed 'more than he remembered' to the thesis, but he did not think that there was evidence to prove that he had 'deliberately or consciously' given advance publicity to facts and opinions he had derived from his colleague's unpublished work.[9]

Webster was annoyed and I was disappointed by what seemed to us to be prevarication at the end of Butler's judgement, but Webster told me that it had, all the same, convicted Gibbs and that there was nothing more he or I need do except, as we both agreed, point out to Butler that he had not sent a copy of his memorandum to Gibbs. Webster wrote to thank Butler for his analysis of the evidence, which seemed to him to be 'most convincing and to substantiate except in one or two unimportant particulars, the claim which Frankland made'. He confessed that he was surprised by Butler's final decision, but that, he said, was for Butler to judge. He said it was essential that Gibbs should be shown the memorandum so that he would know that 'Frankland had good reason for his view of what had occurred'. If that was done, Webster thought that the 'painful incident' might be brought to a close. I made the same request to Butler, who acceded. Gibbs's response was confined to an acknowledgement of the fact that he had received Butler's 'note'.[10]

Thus ended this 'painful incident'. At the time, it deeply distressed me, and it terminated my endeavour to drive forward the creation of a department of military studies in Oxford. Gibbs's basic mistake was to have allowed himself to be elevated to the Chichele Chair of the History of War, a subject in which he was virtually bereft of original ideas. In retrospect, I feel sorry for him, but I have to admit that during the many years in which I have held my peace, I have found it irritating to sit through lectures and dinner parties at which sycophantic aspirants have poured out eulogies of the great Norman Gibbs. He was alas one of Oxford's greater nonentities, whose conduct, however, was singular in that Webster had met no parallel case since almost the beginning of the century and I have met with none other until almost the end of it, a span of nearly a hundred years.

Before the 'painful incident' had ended my military aspirations in Oxford, another avenue for a continuing career as an historian had been opened to me. As I have mentioned, I was given an appointment at Chatham House in August 1956. This came about in a rather curious way, as things in Chatham House tended to do. For several years I had often lunched with Arnold Toynbee in the Ladies' Annexe of the Athenaeum. His wife, Veronica, was always there. The Club was only a short step from Chatham House in St James's Square, where he held the Research Chair of International History and she was his Research Assistant. There were usually other guests in addition to myself and I used to meet people of great distinction or high promise such as, for example – to name but two – T. Dinison, who, though now a Dane, had won the Victoria Cross as a Canadian in 1918, and young Robert Wade-Gery, who was a Fellow of All Souls and later rose to high distinction in the Diplomatic Service. Having been invited for 1.15 on Thursday 3rd March 1955, I wondered whom I might meet this time. To my surprise, I proved to be the only guest and, more to my surprise, Arnold suggested that I should apply for his Chair, from which he was about to retire. I was astonished. Though Toynbee by now had his critics and was about to be savaged by Trevor-Roper, he was vastly eminent and internationally famous, being known to many as a 'citizen of the world'. That he should be thinking of me as his successor seemed absurd. This, after all, was the Stevenson Research Chair of International History in the University of London, a non-teaching one which was attached to the London School of Economics. The sister teaching-chair was occupied by Sir Charles Webster. The suggestion was that I should not only be Toynbee's successor but also an equal academic colleague of Sir Charles. It was breathtaking.

Webster found it rather breathtaking too. He professed to think little of Toynbee as an historian and still less as a 'citizen of the world', a title he associated more with communism than visionary philosophy. As I saw it, he suffered from bouts of jealousy of the despised Toynbee whose fame, deserved or otherwise, far exceeded his own. This was by no means a rare phenomenon among his contemporaries. Webster was not very enthusiastic about my candidature for the Chatham House Chair – it was there that the Stevenson Research Professor was based. Even so, he generously agreed to be one of my referees. Sir John Slessor and R.B. Wernham, now Professor of Modern History at Oxford, undertook to be the others. That was powerful support and Toynbee was a constant source of advice, information and encouragement, especially when my courage ebbed and I felt disinclined to pursue what sometimes looked like a phantom. At the outset he wrote to me saying he thought I had 'strong cards' as I had been working on nearly contemporary history, which was just the experience needed by the Chatham House Professor whose duties were expected to include the writing of the annual *Survey of International Affairs*. Toynbee also told me that the Director-General of Chatham House, Ivison Macadam, was retiring at about the same time as himself and that he would keep me posted on developments. He thought 'What fun it would be if this did come off'.[11]

It gradually became apparent that there had been something of a bust-up in Chatham House. Toynbee had a while ago given up writing the *Survey of International Affairs* and was, in practice, no more than a titular Director of Studies, which was one of his titles. The Research Secretary, Margaret Cleeve, was not an academic, nor was the Director-General. Peter Calvocoressi, who had lately been writing the *Survey*, had not surprisingly become discontented and he presently resigned. How far Toynbee, absorbed in his philosophy of the study of history, was aware of all this turmoil, I do not know, but bits and pieces of it filtered through and *The Times*, which in those days was much better informed than it was later, seemed to have picked up some of the essentials. Reporting the appointment of C.M. Woodhouse as the new Director-General of the Royal Institute of International Affairs, the formal title of Chatham House, *The Times* observed that the outgoing Director-General had said that there had been criticism of the Institute's activities and that, because of their diversity, there was a 'real need for direction'; and that the new Chairman, Air Chief Marshal Sir William Elliot, would start with 'a new Council and new appointments'. The most important of these was that of the Hon. C.M. Woodhouse. Of Woodhouse, *The Times* said that he was thirty-seven, that he had been educated at Winchester and New College, Oxford, where he had taken a first in Honour Moderations and Literae

Humaniores. He had won the Craven and Hertford scholarships and the Gaisford prize. On the outbreak of war, he had enlisted in the Royal Artillery and was commissioned in 1940. By August 1943, he had progressed to the rank of full Colonel and was in command of the Allied Military Mission to the Greek guerillas, who were fighting against the German occupation of their country and, though *The Times* did not mention it, each other. He later served in the British embassies in Athens and Teheran. He had worked in industry for two years and then became assistant secretary to the Nuffield Foundation. He was elected a Fellow of Trinity Hall, Cambridge in 1949 and had been working in the Foreign Office since 1952. In indicating that Chatham House had attracted to its helm a man of outstanding courage, ability and attainment, *The Times* did not exaggerate. Monty Woodhouse was indeed a star.[12]

Toynbee told me that Woodhouse was a 'notable man and one with whom one would like to work'. He was a distinguished classicist and so, 'like you', Toynbee over-generously wrote to me, 'he combines being a scholar with having practised a dangerous war-time trade'. He would have a 'considerable say' in who was appointed to the Professorship and, Toynbee thought, 'will appreciate qualifications like yours'. He again urged me to apply and offered to advise me on how I should present my case. I accepted this offer and decided to apply. In response to Butler's enquiry, I assured him that, if elected to the Chatham House Chair, I would not set aside my work on the official history until it was finished. Toynbee seemed sure that I would be short-listed and interviewed. He advised me not to mention my connection with him unless it came up incidentally at the interview. He said that he was taking care not to seem to be canvassing for me, but he told me that Woodhouse had asked him if he knew of any promising candidates in the offing and that he had mentioned me, said a few words about what I had done, and said that we were cousins. He said he had spoken in a casual way, but Woodhouse was alert and had probably made a mental note. Toynbee advised that I should talk about my work on the Clarendon Papers at the interview to show that, in addition to being a specialist in the history of air warfare, I was also a diplomatic historian. He thought I should tell the board about the work I had done for the RAF courses in Oxford as Chatham House ran somewhat similar ones. And he wanted me to stress my 'remarkably wide and varied personal contacts, because these, not least the American ones, would be very valuable for Chatham House'. Toynbee certainly did not underestimate the abilities, experience and achievements of his young cousin.[13]

In the light of what Toynbee had said, I was a little less surprised than I would otherwise have been when I received a letter from the Academic Registrar of London University telling me that I had been short-listed, and inviting me to attend for an interview on 7th July 1955. 'What time is the interview?' Toynbee wrote to me, could I come to lunch with him and Veronica after it? The interview was a rather formidable business. It was conducted by a very large board. I immediately recognized which Woodhouse must be because he was so markedly younger than the rest. He seemed to me to be more intent on listening to the exchanges between me and the others than saying or asking much himself. I was pleased to see Sir James Butler at the far end of a long table, near the chairman's seat. His questions were obviously designed to bring out the connections between military and international affairs, and also to show that research experience in the one field could readily be utilized in the other. He could not have been more helpful to my cause. Stormier waters lay ahead. Professor (later Dame) Lilian Penson, who held the Chair of Modern History at Bedford College, London, made it clear that military history was not a serious branch of the subject and that my only qualification was the work I had done on the Clarendon Papers, in which, however, she evinced little interest. Alan Bullock questioned me about my experience of teaching, but when I had finished talking about the RAF courses in Oxford, he concluded that I had had no experience of teaching undergraduates – a conclusion with which I could only agree although I could not understand the relevance of this qualification to a non-teaching chair. I came away with the impression that there was some strong support for me on the board, but that there was also some powerful opposition.[14]

This may well not have been wide of the mark. The next day the Academic Registrar wrote to tell me the board was going to have another meeting and that there would now be a delay as the Long Vacation was imminent. In other words, the board had failed to reach agreement about who was to be selected. My intelligence system told me more. On 24th July, my brother lunched with Arnold and Veronica Toynbee in Barnard Castle, after which they went round the Bowes Museum. My brother said that four candidates had been interviewed, two of them already professors. One of them thought too much of himself to accept an appointment below that level. In view of the possibility that the idea of filling the Chatham House Chair might be scrapped, or at least postponed, this became an interesting piece of news. It appeared that someone might be appointed at the level of a reader to write the *Survey* and that the duties of the Director of Studies, which would otherwise have marched with the Chair, might now be assumed by Woodhouse. Chatham House, my brother deduced, might be glad to save the money that would be required for the professor's salary. Toynbee told him that if a reader was appointed, I would have a very good chance of being selected and that this might in time lead to the Chair. The day before, my brother had discovered that of the four on the short list, two were older and two younger. Apparently Woodhouse favoured youth. Lilian Penson favoured age and someone who had already proved his worth.[15]

Some of the intelligence relayed to me by my brother proved to be accurate and some not quite so. The professorial appointment board took a long time to resolve its difficulties, but at length in February 1956, I received a letter from the Academic Registrar telling me that the Chatham House Chair had been filled by the appointment to it of Professor Geoffrey Barraclough. Brilliant as Barraclough undoubtedly was, a worse choice from Chatham House's point of view could scarcely have been made. Moreover, this seems to have been apparent from the outset, for it was at once decided that the new Professor would not also be the Director of Studies, and this position was now assumed by the Director-General, Monty Woodhouse. Nor was it the end of the saga for me. Woodhouse had already invited me to call on him in Chatham House and had told me that a plan was being considered for the appointment of a Deputy Director of Studies, and that they had it in mind that I should be asked to fill this position. Woodhouse told me that he intended that I should act as his deputy in the direction of Chatham House's studies, that I should work with Barraclough in the writing of the *Survey* and that I should develop a suitable field of research of my own. When Woodhouse confirmed all this in a formal letter and offered me the appointment, I had no hesitation in accepting. The attraction of working as a deputy to Woodhouse was immensely appealing to me, for although I felt much in awe of his astonishing abilities, I found him easy to get on with and suspected that, as Toynbee had predicted, he would also be easy to work with. And he seemed remarkably ready to consider my ideas about the writing of the *Survey* and Chatham House's other studies sympathetically. These advantages far outweighed the problematical issues raised by the prospect of working with Barraclough, whom I had not met, and whose recently published *History in a Changing World* I had found far from impressive.[16]

Thus before he even arrived in Chatham House Barraclough was placed on a short leading rein. He was deprived of the position of Director of Studies which, in Woodhouse's hands, was strengthened by the addition of a Deputy Director of Studies, whom Barraclough had never met. In addition, there was a Research Committee charged with the responsibility of overseeing the research programme, which was now serviced by a recently appointed Research Secretary of marked ability, Shane Olver, and whose chairman was Alan Bullock. Though Barraclough was given a seat on this committee, Woodhouse and I also sat on it. Apart from writing the *Survey*, it was difficult to see what role Barraclough was expected to play. Even the *Survey* was not to be left wholly in his hands: he was told that I was to cooperate with him in writing it. He had not asked for such help and thought that what he would need was 'devilling' by a junior assistant. I explained to Woodhouse that I did not believe in 'devilling', either as to doing it or as to using the products of it: research had to be done by the author himself and, while two or more authors could combine to produce joint or multiple contributions to individual works, as Webster and I were doing, they could not be assisted by 'devilling'. This was especially the case where large masses of material had to be considered, which with recent or contemporary history was inevitable. Help in finding and assembling material as well as, where necessary, translating it, was one thing; 'devilling' was quite another. Woodhouse did not lay down the law but, by appointing me as he had done, he clearly indicated his preference for my view over Barraclough's. Indeed, he told me that he thought the production of the *Survey* would conform more closely to my ideas than to Barraclough's.[17]

It was duly arranged that I would take up my duties at Chatham House on 1st August 1956 and that, until work on the official history was sufficiently advanced, I would work half-time there and half-time in the Cabinet Office. Before 1st August came the situation had changed again. It was decided that I was to be responsible for selecting, editing and explaining the documents for annual publication in the series *Documents on International Affairs*. These volumes of documents had earlier been produced in conjunction with, and in relation to, the *Survey*. Now they were to be produced independently, which was as well since the *Survey* had fallen into arrears and plans for its future were still in the melting pot. For me, this was a fortunate decision. As to my research in Chatham House, I had been given a clear role on which I could embark without hindrance from committees, without pause for higher decisions and without dependence upon what Barraclough might decide, or be allowed to decide, about the *Survey*. It also meant, as the volumes were to be self-contained, that in addition to selecting and editing the documents I would have to explain their significance and set them in the general context of the year. Also, this decision did not override Woodhouse's original instruction that I should develop a specialized field of my own. In due course, I produced and published three volumes of *Documents on International Affairs* and I signified a special field of study by delivering a lecture in Chatham House entitled *Britain's Changing Strategic Position*.[18]

The chief problem in the research needed to produce the volumes of documents was created by the huge mass of material available from which the selections had to be made. But this was a difficulty with which I was already familiar because the history of the strategic air offensive raised the same issue on an even greater scale. There was, nevertheless, a crucial difference between the two tasks. In the case of the official history, all the documentary material, whether secret or not, both German and British, was available as was most of the American too. In the case of the Chatham House volumes, the only documents to hand were those that had been published and, as the chancelleries of the world do not publish their confidential archives, not at least until many years after they have been originated, we in Chatham House, who were trying to write international history almost as it happened, were actually trying to extract history from the news. Barraclough was an optimist about our prospects of success. He believed that the truth of international relations could be inferred from the scholarly study of the news, which was rather surprising because he had built his reputation as a mediaeval historian, who had had access to all the documentary evidence, published or otherwise, and, owing to its relatively small scale, the opportunity to read it all. I was less confident, but confident enough, all the same, to make the attempt.

Looking now at my three volumes of *Documents on International Affairs* nearly forty years later, I find that they do offer substantial historical insights into the course of international relations in 1955, 1956 and 1957. In other words, if those events were surveyed today using what has come to light since I made my selections and explanations, a good deal of the understanding would be the same. At least one could scarcely doubt that there were in 1955 significant moves in the direction of detente in the cold war which were smashed in the aftermath of the twin crises in the Middle East and Hungary in 1956. Nor could it be doubted that the issues of the cold war in 1957 were far more dominant than any calls for international conciliation. But exaggerated assumptions about the importance of the uncommitted 'Bandung' powers and the long-term strength of the Soviet Union, themselves interdependent considerations, would be seen to be historically incorrect. Nevertheless, they do reflect something of the feeling of the time and, in that sense, they are not without historical interest. I think too that my lecture on Britain's strategic position, which I gave in 1957, survives the same test. My analysis of how the advent of the guided missile with a nuclear warhead introduced a strategic revolution and yet left some of the ancient principles of war in place, proved, I believe, to be historically sound at that time and, indeed, for the remaining years of the cold war.

In these senses, Barraclough's optimism about the study of immediately contemporary history with the news as the main source was justified. His own *Survey of International Affairs 1956–1958*, though written by nine hands – including incidentally my own – is further evidence in support of the same conclusion. It is often argued, even so, that worthwhile history cannot be written from the news because the perspective a historian needs is not possible in the case of history that is immediately contemporary. This, it seems to me, is a misconception. The perspective in which contemporary history is seen will be different from that of recent and also that of remote history, but it will not necessarily be inferior. Different need not be worse, and in some respects it may be better. An historian looking back at international affairs of forty years ago would, as I have indicated, attach less importance to the 'Bandung' influence than I did at the time. That is not to say that an historian reviewing the same period in forty years' time may not return to my view of the 'Bandung' influence. Whatever period or subject an historian is considering, he cannot and ought not to escape from what is going on around him. That, after all, is the chief reason why historical interpretations change, and why history is a living subject and not a series of incidents that can be written off as 'done'.

It will be apparent that there was a considerable identity of views between myself and Professor Barraclough as to the value of immediately contemporary history. In fact, the potential for friction between us, which I have explained, was dissipated by this consensus. That was nourished by the opposition to our point of view. Chatham House was not only a centre of contemporary historical research; it was also a talking shop, and it produced a good deal of high-class journalism. I was not opposed to these activities, but I believed them to be secondary to the main purpose which I saw as the production of historical studies that would have a lasting value. Barraclough strongly supported this view, but he was hardly the best ambassador for it.

Physically a small man with a moth-eaten appearance, Barraclough was alert, quick-witted and extremely clever intellectually. He was a remarkable linguist and had achieved considerable distinction as the Professor of Mediaeval History in Liverpool University, where he occupied the chair from 1945 to 1956. He was restless, suspicious and querulous. The establishment, of which there was an influential representation in Chatham House, thought he was a dangerous radical. He had a good deal in common with A.J.P. Taylor, both in background and in ability. He and Taylor were both educated at Bootham School, York; both went to Oriel College, Oxford, where they both shone as outstandingly brilliant undergraduates. They both enjoyed knocking down accepted beliefs and levelling the high and the mighty. I recall standing on a line in the Athenaeum next to Alan Taylor when we were receiving a delegation of historians from the Soviet Union. He had the reputation of taking the Russian side and it was easy to sense the eagerness of the delegates to shake his hand. He remarked to the first that he wanted him to know that he hated Russians even more than he hated Americans. I remember too attending one of Monty Woodhouse's regular staff lunches in Chatham House, at which he told us that Lord Strang had been chosen to be the next chairman of the Institute. One of my colleagues, having evidently forgotten that Strang had been part of the abortive British mission to Moscow on the eve of the German invasion of Poland in 1939, asked to be reminded of what Strang had done in the war. 'He caused it', Barraclough retorted without a second's pause. As with most of his swipes, there was an element of truth in this. That was what made them so amusing and, to some, so provocative.

In Chatham House, I had an office next door to Barraclough's and I learned a great deal from him. I learned, for example, to avoid terms such as 'terrorist' or 'freedom-fighter', for the one could so easily be substituted for the other depending upon who was expressing the opinion. I was also, as I have already shown, more or less convinced through Barraclough's persistence and competence that the art of deriving history from the news, although less authoritative than history from the archives, was nonetheless a worthwhile pursuit. Our alliance, however, was not a natural one. Barraclough was not only much cleverer than I was; he was also much more of a sceptic, and there was no moral centre to his philosophy, a trait he also shared with Alan Taylor. I believe that an historian without a moral centre is like an artist without a colour sense. Like Taylor, Barraclough was too often swept on by the brilliance of his argument and carried out of reach of the tests that should be applied even if they do spoil the wit and pace of a thesis. The alliance between us arose not from real mutual sympathy but from the need, as we saw it, for mutual defence against the opposition.

Chatham House consisted of a number of different islands of influence. The Meetings Department organized a constant series of lectures, which were open to the general membership of the Institute, and also Private Discussion Meetings, which were smaller and more confidential affairs. The Information Department answered enquiries by telephone or in short papers, unless they were about the Far East, in which case they were answered by the Far East Department, whose head was the Research Secretary. The Research Secretary serviced the Research Committee, which had the duty of approving, or otherwise, proposed research projects and taking responsibility on behalf of the Council, which was the governing body of the Institute, for the resulting publications. The Press Library read and clipped the world press for international news, stored the clippings and made them available for research. The Library contained a magnificent and well organized collection of books on all aspects of international affairs. There was an Editorial Department that produced two journals, *International Affairs* and *The World Today*. There was a Membership Secretary and an Administrative and Finance office. In addition to the Research Professor of International History, there was also a Chair of International Economics and one of Commonwealth Relations, the last two being held by Professors F. Benham and C.E. Carrington. Theoretically, all these departments should have been mutually supportive but in practice they engaged in a good deal of rivalry with each other, and nearly all were more or less in opposition to the Barraclough and Frankland school of thought, which advocated a much increased effort in original research on the part of the staff.

There was also the difficulty that most of the senior staff felt Chatham House had lost its way and was in urgent need of fresh inspiration. The appointment of the brilliant Monty Woodhouse as Director-General had raised hopes that, from that point of view, were impossible to fulfil because there was not only no consensus among the staff as to the direction that ought to be taken, but there were quite bitter differences of opinion on the subject. When Woodhouse failed to descend from the mountain with the appropriate tablets, disappointment, hotly pursued by discontent, set in. Nor was Woodhouse's temperament entirely suited to the situation. Two defects among his remarkable qualities were that he tended to assume that his colleagues were endowed with the same ability as he possessed and, second, that they would act in a sensible and logical manner. He was much more inclined to ask what people thought than to say what he thought. He tended to ask them what they believed they ought to do rather than to tell them; and, correspondingly, he expected that if the Council was supplied with the arguments for and against various options, they would select the best one. Even if they did not, he thought it was their role to decide and not his to dictate.[19]

The underlying problem at the Royal Institute of International Affairs had been caused by the Second World War. The initial impetus that had led to the creation of the Institute in 1920, had come from the Versailles Conference, when a number of participants, including Arnold Toynbee, had developed the idea that the systematic and impartial study of international affairs would promote understanding between nations and would help to build a situation in which the disaster of another world war would become impossible. The events of 1939 and the years following crushed this belief and left the study of international affairs at Chatham House without a light at the end of the tunnel. Barraclough and I posited the alternative of considering scholarly historical research as an end in itself.

While Woodhouse was at the helm, I felt that this idea would gradually prevail, not as the sole motivation of the Institute, but at least as a major portion of it. And if Woodhouse was cautious in advancing toward this goal, which it seemed to me that he was too much inclined to be, there were obstacles in our path. The compensation was that working under Woodhouse was agreeable, stimulating and challenging. His marvellously well-lubricated brain machinery and command of language, added to the prestige he had accumulated, made him one of the most memorable people I have ever known.

In 1959 Woodhouse stood and was elected as Member of Parliament for Oxford. He left Chatham House suggesting that I should be his successor. The Council entrusted the selection to a small committee sitting under the chairmanship of Kenneth Younger, who was Vice-Chairman of the Council. Younger, who had announced that he would not stand for Parliament at the general election of 1959, decided to take the job himself. He spoke good German and had been the Minister of State at the Foreign Office in the last year of Attlee's Labour government. After that his political career had entered the doldrums. He told me that he had been warned by Attlee that he would be unlikely to be given office in a future Labour administration and this prospect no doubt made Chatham House seem a suitable alternative. His qualifications for succeeding Woodhouse were obviously much stronger than mine, so that I was not put out of countenance by his selection. He was, all the same, a poor substitute for Woodhouse with whom, in my opinion, he compared as plate does with silver. For a time, I thought I could convince Younger that my aims for Chatham House were sound and attainable. I presented him with a series of memoranda outlining schemes for research programmes, for the better utilization of the existing staff and for the reinforcement of the academically qualified element of it.[20]

The last of these aims was the first to be defeated. On 22nd December 1959, Younger wrote to Alan Bullock, the chairman of the Research Committee, that more than half a dozen candidates for research appointments had been interviewed by a committee sitting under the chairmanship of Professor W.N. Medlicott. At least two of these, he reported, were of 'quite acceptable quality'. The committee had, nevertheless, been unable to agree on any appointments largely because, as Younger explained, he had become convinced, while the candidates were being interviewed, that the whole scheme was misconceived. Anything these candidates could do could equally be achieved, he thought, by commissioning outsiders. There was no need to add to the Chatham House staff. The upshot, Bullock was told, was that the committee broke up after four hours without any appointments being made and with a very angry Professor Medlicott.[21]

This was a serious blow to my plans, but Barraclough and I still hoped that something might be salvaged from the wreckage. I conceded that our scheme had foundered because we had not sufficiently defined a research programme that, had we done so, would have enabled us to relate candidates to specific projects. I also felt that we had failed to reach a clear view of the by-products Chatham House would derive from having more scholars on its staff. Meanwhile, Younger gave a more sympathetic hearing to my ideas on the research programme and, in the first half of 1960, a number of important projects were launched by the process of commissioning outsiders. Barraclough found some good candidates in Cambridge and my enquiries in Oxford, where I had the constructive and well-informed advice of Alan Bullock and Max Beloff, were well rewarded by, for example, U.W. Kitzinger on Anglo-German relations, A.E. Campbell on American attitudes to Europe, W.F. Knapp on general international relations since 1941 and other young historians of outstanding ability.[22]

Good as this was, it was far short of what I had adumbrated in the sketches of research programmes with which I had bombarded Kenneth Younger.

In the last of these I called for a programme that would produce 'definitive works on major international issues of contemporary importance' while seeking to discover the relationship between particular aspects and the generality of international affairs. As to ways and means, I advocated the policy of directing suitable members of the staff to devote part of their time to the production of such work; of the reinforcement of that element in the staff; and, as was already happening, of the commissioning of outsiders. I stressed the importance to the health of the Institute of a greater in-house research effort. That, I argued, would strengthen its standing as a centre of study, it would sharpen its judgement and increase its value as a source of information. It would also develop the possibility of the *Survey* and *Documents on International Affairs* being produced by a larger and more widely equipped team. My memorandum concluded with a list of subjects to be tackled under the headings of contemporary issues, such as the Berlin question and Kashmir, and theoretical and central issues, such as neutralism, trade relations and nuclear strategy and the balance of power.[23]

Except with Barraclough and one or two others, there was, I must admit, little enthusiasm for my ideas among the staff of the Institute. The Research Secretary, Shane Olver, putting his scepticism politely, told me that he took a 'more cautious [? duller] view' of Chatham House's function than I did. I thought too that I detected an increasingly tired look in Kenneth Younger's eye whenever these matters came up for discussion. It was deeply disappointing, and I began more and more to feel that my future in Chatham House was unpromising.[24]

Looking back upon these events from the time-lapse of more than thirty-five years, I am much inclined to think that Olver and Younger were right or, at least, more right than I was. On the evening of 17th February 1960, I had an illuminating discussion of my memorandum with Alan Bullock. He told me that it represented an intellectual exercise through which we had to pass. Though he thought there was room for a certain amount of scholarship in Chatham House, he believed that what was wanted was some vigorous writing on interesting topics without seeking to impose the pretence that the work was based on archives, which, if it was in the contemporary field, it would not be.[25]

The import of this advice came home to me only slowly, but I can now see clearly what it was. My scheme for definitive work in Chatham House was not viable. Books of serious original historical content cannot be written without access to the archives and of these Chatham House had none. All that history could hope to gain from its output was a record of how things looked at the time of their materialization. Interesting as that might be and, as I believe the volumes of the *Survey* and *Documents on International Affairs* demonstrate, it could scarcely be the justification for a major and sustained programme of academic research. Whatever Barraclough might have believed and whatever I might have hoped, history from the news was not a real possibility. It was I and not Kenneth Younger who was barking up the wrong tree.

My time in Chatham House was alas of no long-term benefit to the Institute; but to me, in learning how to combine the art and the business of history, it was of immense value. While working in the Cabinet Office on the official history I had met many distinguished people who had in earlier years made notable contributions to the making of history. In Chatham House I met several more such people, including Lord Attlee, under whose chairmanship I took part in a study group that examined Britain's strategic interests in the post-war world, Lord Shinwell, with whom I had breakfast each morning during an Anglo-German conference in 1959, and Lord Strang, who had been Permanent Under-Secretary of State at the Foreign Office. In Chatham House, I also met several people who were still making important contributions to historical developments and many others who were to do so in the future. Among these, some of the most memorable were Willy Brandt, then Mayor of West Berlin, Lee Kuan Yew, shortly to be Prime Minister of Singapore, Denis Healey, a Labour Member of Parliament with an important political future and an acute intellectual capacity to go with it, Tom Mboya, who was to become Jomo Kenyatta's predecessor as the leader of the Kenya National African Union, and two Algerians, whose names I never knew, who came to Chatham House to explain their war for liberation against the French, or – depending on one's point of view – the terrorist campaign in Algeria.

From these and other such people, I had the opportunity to acquire insights that went beyond what one could glean from the press about the events with which they were connected. Because Chatham House imposed strict rules of confidentiality on private meetings, they knew that what they said would not be attributed and therefore, for the most part, they spoke freely. One such case remains particularly in my mind. Lord Attlee asked me to write a paper on the question of what overseas bases remained as fundamental to Britain's strategic interests. I poured much thought and effort into the exercise and duly presented a report which Lord Attlee circulated to the members of his Chatham House study group. In due course, the group was assembled, as I thought to discuss my paper. Lord Attlee opened the meeting by asking if everyone had received a copy of it. None said that they had not. He then said that he would allow a few moments for the members to refresh their memories of what I had said. The few moments passed and Lord Attlee then said that this item was now concluded and that we would pass on to the next issue. When I later expressed my disappointment to Lord Attlee, he told me that he had made it a principle in Cabinet never to discuss anything about which people had not complained or which was not the subject of an immediate crisis. In a similar aside, one of the members of the group, General Sir Archibald Nye, who had been Vice-Chief of the Imperial General Staff during the war, mentioned to me that he had been quite interested in my arguments, but that he did not believe that there were any bases which were vital to our interests. All we required was an effective mobile force that, in the event of need, could seize what the situation demanded. Certain gaps between theory and practice began to open up in my mind.

Another incident, although in this case a public one, which I found illuminating, occurred in Berlin when I was among the Chatham House delegates to the tenth Anglo-German Königswinter Conference, which took place in March 1959. In the course of this, the Mayor of West Berlin, Willy Brandt, entertained us to lunch. There were fifty or sixty of us and our places were marked with name tabs. I found mine next to a diplomat, who told me he had been the German ambassador in Belgrade in 1941, which made me feel uneasy. We both, however, had chairs on which to sit, which was far from being universally the case. As confusion mounted, Willy Brandt rose to apologize. He said that he had sent out for more chairs. Meanwhile, he told us that before the war, he had given a lunch party for the French Premier, who at the time was M. Blum. The same thing had happened, but Blum had brushed aside his apologies saying that he was delighted to observe how inefficient the Germans were. Up to that time, I had myself tended to be a victim of the myth of German efficiency.

There was a second revealing incident in Berlin. The delegates had been invited to a tea party at the invitation of the Federal Minister for All-German Questions at his Ministry. The invitation was for 16.15. George Brown, already a dominating figure, who was later to become British Foreign Secretary, and I had detached ourselves from the delegation that afternoon and we travelled together by taxi, independently, to the Ministry and arrived there at about 16.20. We were ushered into a large room where chaos prevailed. Numerous caterers were rushing to and fro setting up small tables and laying them. We were given magazines and chairs and asked to wait. After about an hour we heard the approach of the main party, which was easily recognizable from the clamour of conversation dominated by the strident tones of Lady Violet Bonham-Carter, who, as was her wont, was in the vanguard. As the noise grew nearer, the caterers suddenly removed their overalls and several of them formed a receiving line; these were, in fact, Dr Gefaeller, the Chief of Division 2 of the Ministry, and his staff. What George Brown and I had taken to be caterers, were actually our hosts.[26]

Another lesson in the same discipline occurred in Bonn, where we had been invited to a reception in the Redoute by the West German Minister of Foreign Affairs, Dr von Brentano. At this we were to be addressed by the

President of the Federal Republic. We crossed the Rhine in a ferry which was grossly overloaded in order to accommodate the party. An official said we could not sail. Lady Violet Bonham-Carter insisted that we should do so and announced that we would be quite safe as we had an Admiral of the Fleet on board. In spite of the fact that the Lord Jellicoe whom we did indeed have on board was merely the son of an Admiral of the Fleet, the official caved in and we sailed. It was a bitterly cold night, but the Redoute was well heated and we quickly divested ourselves of overcoats, hats, scarves, gloves and so on. There seemed to be nowhere to put these things, but a footman told us to lay them on the floor in an area he indicated to us, and we duly obliged, producing quite an impressive fabric mountain. The moment for President Heuss's entrance now arrived, but he did not. The mountain of our clothing made it impossible to open the door through which he was trying to squeeze. Eventually he entered, not very majestically, through a side door.[27]

These glimpses were more entertaining and more revealing than the conference itself. I failed to make much contact with the German side of the argument, though I did have one or two good talks with some of their delegates. The speeches and debates seemed to be designed more for effect than content. I particularly remember how George Brown constantly intervened, shouting his monologues in a curiously unnatural high-pitched voice, as if he feared his presence might be forgotten. Denis Healey was quite different. His incisive and logical style of argument impressed me profoundly. Antony Head, a former Minister of Defence, was extremely polished and I was struck by the missionary-like zeal of John Strachey. The Germans seemed for the most part to be blinkered and fairly boring. They talked endlessly about reunification, but it was assumed that this was no more than a shibboleth, since the prospect of such a development seemed invisible. I think I learned more about how British politics work than I did about Anglo-German relations, but I also certainly learnt a good deal about Germany.

The Königswinter Conference was a standard part of Chatham House's access to international affairs. It was my second experience of Germany, for a month earlier I had enjoyed a less usual, if more one-sided, opportunity. This was provided by an invitation to lecture on Britain's strategic position to the British Army of the Rhine. Having flown to Düsseldorf in a Viscount, the last wholly successful all-British airliner, I was driven in a staff car to the Commander-in-Chief's house at Rheindahlen, where he had his HQ. I had not previously set foot on German soil and I found it strange to see signposts pointing to such places as Essen and even Hamm, whose marshalling yards became famous at the beginning of the war because of the repeated attacks on them by Bomber Command. The staff major who accompanied me reminded me that these had been largely abortive by informing me that the station master at Hamm had just died in his bed at the age of ninety. On arrival at Rheindahlen, I was greeted by the C-in-C, General Sir Dudley Ward. In addition to commanding the British Army, he was also the NATO commander of the Northern Army Group. He was not, however, empowered to write off the value of a tank, if one should be lost. That was the responsibility of the Command Secretary, a civilian, whom I met together with the British Consul at Düsseldorf at dinner that night. The conversation was agreeable but dull and I discovered that there were no legends about the C-in-C, who apparently had the reputation of being a good administrator.

Sir Dudley Ward told me that, in the event of war, he would make his HQ waterborne on the German canal system. I did not venture to tell him that, in the last war, this had been liable to be drained dry by Bomber Command and I concluded that, in the event of war, another C-in-C would be appointed. Next morning I was driven to the HQ where I was met by a bevy of senior officers in an organization which was obviously top-heavy. From there, I travelled with the C-in-C to the Garrison Theatre to give my lecture. On the way, the C-in-C warned me that there would be some high-ranking German officers in the audience and that they were nowadays our allies. I asked him how he got on with them; he told me that he kept two sets of files, one for the conduct of affairs and the other for German consumption. In the theatre I was confronted by an improbable number of generals and brigadiers, who filled the first four rows of the huge auditorium. After the lecture, they did the talking but the questions were stiff and formal.

In the afternoon I was driven to 1 (British) Corps mess at Bielefeld and, after tea there, to Hoberge House, which was the residence of the Corps commander, Lieutenant-General Michael West, triple DSO, recently knighted, though not yet dubbed, and formerly the commander of the Commonwealth Division in Korea. My escorting officer warned me not to be surprised by anything. He rang the door bell of what proved to be a most luxurious house: it had been built by a German gin manufacturer shortly before the war. The door was opened by a striking-looking man, who wore an open necked shirt and corduroy trousers. This turned out to be General West. Inside, the house throbbed with rock and roll music, which the general later danced to like a teenager. He appeared at dinner in a dinner jacket, but he inveighed against the public school system, having himself been at Uppingham, and in particular against public school girls, several of whom sat round his table. He said that the only merit of Field-Marshal Templer, then at the height of his fame and prestige, was that if he gave the order to advance on the left, one would at least know one had to go on the right. The general's wife perfectly complemented her husband's abilities and eccentricities. She was born an Oppenheim and had a remarkable talent for spotting good works of art before they were generally recognized as such. She had some wonderful modern pictures in the house, including a seascape by Lowry. In years to come, I kept encountering the Wests in various parts of the world and got to know them quite well. They were among the most delightful couples I ever met and he was one of the most gifted and unusual generals of his generation. On this occasion, however, that was all I saw of them. General West excused himself from my lecture the next morning on the ground that he was opening a major mock-battle against the Russians.

The Chief of Staff was in the chair at the lecture which I gave in 1 Corps HQ. It was a much livelier affair than the one at Rheindahlen, and the audience of brigadiers, colonels, lower officers and sergeants spoke and questioned with far greater spontaneity. Although not universally popular, the Corps Commander was the object of a good deal of hero-worship, and legendary stories of his doings and sayings abounded. Afterwards I asked to be taken out to see the Bielefeld viaduct. I stood in awe of the enormous strength of the huge structure, which had been breached by Bomber Command in the war and which was still breached. A by-pass railway had been built round it. I was then driven to Osnabrück, where I spent the night at Talavera House as the guest of Brigadier and Mrs Dickson. Dickson commanded the 12th Infantry Brigade, which was in the front line. He told me that, if he was attacked, each of his soldiers would have to face six or seven hundred Russians. He seemed to think that a holding action would be impossible, which was bad news since the next step would be the use of tactical atomic weapons. All the same, the soldiers seemed to me to be thinking in conventional terms of mountain ranges and rivers, mainly the Rhine, I thought. The lecture did not go as well as at Bielefeld. One of General West's qualities was shown by his encouragement of independent thought, in which he was less than wholly typical of the Army.[28]

I have described these experiences with their sidelights on Anglo-German relations and the cold war to show that, among the cons of Chatham House, there were some pros. The principal con from my point of view was Kenneth Younger's increasingly evident wish to rid himself of my schemes for the future of the Institute and, I foresaw, of me with them. Indeed, within a few years of my departure from Chatham House, Barraclough and his research chair were shed, as also were both Benham's and Carrington's. The *Survey* and *Documents* were both discontinued after the volumes for 1963 were published in 1977 and 1973 respectively. In my place as Deputy Director of Studies, Younger appointed as Director of Studies an eminent journalist, Andrew Shonfield. Not much of the Chatham House which I had joined was left. Shonfield in due course succeeded Younger, but not without the irony of Younger having first asked me if I would stand. I told him that I was otherwise engaged on the other side of the river. My move was from the attempt to get history from the news to that of demonstrating it in the gallery.[29]

CHAPTER SEVEN

History in the Gallery

In the early autumn of 1955, I spent a short holiday in London visiting several of the capital's institutions which, had they been in Paris or Washington, I would surely have taken in long before. Being in London, however, these had, so to speak, been too near to see. Now I sought to repair this oversight and among the places I selected was the Imperial War Museum. I went there on a fine sunny afternoon near Battle of Britain Day. As I walked up the steps to the entrance, trying to translate a Latin inscription about Henry VIII, my attention was caught by a lone Hurricane flying directly above. My introduction to the museum of the two world wars was thus vividly and memorably celebrated by an animated artefact. Hurricanes had long since become 'museum pieces', but this one, already a very rare bird, was still flying to remind onlookers of a decisive British victory in 1940, otherwise a year of almost unrelieved defeats. The rest of my visit produced a severe anti-climax.

The galleries of the Imperial War Museum had a dingy and neglected air. They were crowded with masses of mostly quite small items arranged in congested groups unrelated to each other and disconnected from any discernible historical themes. I remember particularly a large case of shell fuses each of which looked very much the same as the others. The subtle differences between these only moderately interesting public exhibits were explained in lengthy hand-written captions most of which were much larger than the objects described. Both fuses and captions were covered in dust, a theme that was reflected in displays of very small, badly faded photographs. Amongst the debris, it is true, there were numerous stunning exhibits such as the Sopwith Camel in which Lieutenant S.D. Culley had shot down a German Zeppelin over the North Sea on 11th August 1918, a German V1 flying bomb, an Italian human torpedo and the forward section of a Lancaster bomber. But the historical impact of these and many other remarkable objects was lost in the crush of matter which gave the impression of having been dumped in a warehouse rather than installed in a museum. Indeed, the extent to which the jumble was rationalized was indicated in a typical sentence in the guide book. Under the heading of the Army Gallery, this read,

'Along the right-hand wall is a frame containing photographs of all the Army VCs of 1939–1945, and a model of a Nissen Hut'.[1]

I left the Museum with a keen sense of disappointment, but, after ruminating briefly upon the question of how such an institution could demonstrate any of the truths of twentieth-century warfare, I substantially dismissed the issue from my mind. But then, towards the end of my labours on the official history, I returned to it for a second visit, this time to select photographs to illustrate that history. Behind the scene of the public galleries, I now found a vein which was rich indeed. The Museum's photographic library already possessed about three million classified photographs, but the means of finding what one wanted were ill-organized and, as I later discovered, many of the captions were inaccurate or misleading. Once again, having done the best I could, I dismissed this vast and substantially untapped historical source from my mind. I had not yet understood the potential of visual evidence, not merely as a means of illustrating points made on the basis of other evidence, but as a primary source in its own right. Nor had it occurred to me that I would ever work in a museum, least of all direct one.[2]

All this was changed on 16th May 1960 by what for me was a most fortunate omission. That morning, I left home as usual to catch the train from Oxford to London, but I forgot to take with me my brief case which contained the Chatham House papers I had intended to read on the journey. Having nothing better to do, I read *The Times* much more thoroughly than usual and it was, I believe, this that caused me to notice an advertisement inviting applications for the post of Director of the Imperial War Museum which, it was announced, would fall vacant on the forthcoming 30th September. Candidates, it was said, must have a knowledge of the literature relating to the two world wars, they should have had experience in a position of authority and of museum administration and practice and they should preferably have done war service in HM Forces. They had to be at least thirty-five and preferably not more than forty-five. Despite the bit about museum experience, of which I had none, I immediately decided to apply. Suddenly the idea of attempting to breathe new life into what I had seen was a decaying institution seemed infinitely attractive. I knew too that my time was running out at Chatham House. Nor did I prove to be wrong in anticipating that my chief there, Kenneth Younger, would strongly back my candidature. For him, the prospect of my voluntarily crossing the river to the Imperial War Museum was likely to be much more attractive than the awkwardness of having to sack me.

My chances of being appointed, it seemed to me, would depend on the extent to which the selection board would reckon that my standing as a military historian would qualify me for the post, and whether or not that estimate would outweigh the disadvantage of my having no museum experience.

I was well content to confront the issue on those terms because it was historical ideas rather than museum doctrines which I wished to pursue, although, as I have said, the challenge of attempting to revive a moribund organization also had a strong appeal. My main handicap was that the official history of the strategic air offensive had not yet emerged from the Air Ministry imbroglio into the light of day and, in fact, it was not to be published for another seventeen months. The three volumes of *Documents on International Affairs*, which I had published, were but slender evidence of my capacity as a military historian. Everything appeared to depend, therefore, on the word of those who knew my work in advance of its publication.

Webster and Butler proved to be strong and influential supporters, as I expected. Webster in particular was quick to see that the Imperial War Museum had a potential far beyond its existing status and he freely expressed his opinion that I was the man for the job. As was not unusual, his voice carried and, as I subsequently learned, the chairman of the trustees of the Imperial War Museum, Admiral of the Fleet Sir Algernon Willis, soon heard from a fellow trustee, Sir Cosmo Parkinson – who had heard it from Webster – that I was a candidate worth consideration. Butler's quieter style proved to be at least as effective for, as it turned out, he was a member of the selection board and the one who was there to provide the others with historical know-how.

To strengthen my hand as much as possible, I sought to mobilize two members of Butler's Panel who knew my work and conjoined high rank with marked intellectual characteristics. These were Lieutenant-General Sir Ian Jacob and Air Chief Marshal Sir Guy Garrod. Jacob readily agreed to act as a referee and, wishing me good luck, he added that the Imperial War Museum was 'a very interesting place', which he thought would 'absorb a lot of energy'. Garrod took a rather different view. He told me that he knew little of the Imperial War Museum and that he had never visited it. He felt that the post of its Director was a backwater; if it was a stepping stone to the British Museum or the V & A that would be a different matter, but he wondered if I wanted to spend twenty-five years at the Imperial War Museum. He thought I would do better to seek a university chair or a directorate of education somewhere. 'But,' he concluded, 'do not go for something that (I would say) has no prospects.'[3]

These contrasting views represented a big part of the problem with which I became all too familiar in the opening five or six years of my directorship and, as an *hors d'oeuvres*, an opinion of them was elegantly epitomized in a note written to congratulate me when I got the appointment by my former mediaeval tutor, Michael Maclagan. 'Long years ago,' he recalled, 'when your new charge was in Imperial Institute Road, SW7 and I lived nearby I was a keen "aficionado" of the War Museum, somewhat to the disgust of my father who then ruled the V & A.'[4]

Despite my lack of qualifications, I was duly summoned by the Civil Service Commission to appear before an appointment board on 11th July 1960. My memory of the interview, which took place in a splendid room at 6 Burlington Gardens, subsequently occupied by the Museum of Mankind, is somewhat hazy. I do recall, however, that the board was unwieldy in size and consisted of fifteen or more members. Apart from Sir James Butler, whom I naturally recognized at once, I could not put names to any of the faces. I assumed that the man in the chair was Admiral of the Fleet Sir Algernon Willis, the chairman of the board of Imperial War Museum Trustees. His rather rumbustious countenance and commanding manner suggested that this was right, but it was not. This character, I later learned, was the First Civil Service Commissioner, Sir George Mallaby. The less colourful and more studious looking man on his right, who I thought was the First Commissioner, was the Admiral of the Fleet. I was later also able to identify who some of the others were. They included Priscilla Lady Norman and Major-General R.F. Johnstone, who turned out to be trustees of the IWM, and Sir Trenchard Cox, who was the Director of the V & A. The identities of the others I never knew or have since forgotten.

The interview passed off very pleasantly and I came away feeling that my qualifications, such as they were, had had a good airing. As when I was interviewed for the Chatham House chair, Sir James Butler proved to be a friend in need; his questions were obviously designed to enable me to bring out any historical strengths I had got. Unlike the Chatham House board, this one did not seem to harbour an opposition; everyone, so far as I could judge, appeared to be placing a favourable interpretation on their exchanges with me. It was as though they had recognized in advance that I was the best candidate and it was not entirely a surprise when I was told a few days later that I had got the job.

It may be that the other candidates were not tremendously impressive, although I was later given to understand that they included three members of the IWM staff, one of whom was strongly backed by the outgoing Director; Charles Gibbs-Smith, a noted historian of aviation, who was a Keeper in the Victoria and Albert Museum; and another, who was a naval historian. No doubt many people were deterred from applying by the dismal state of decay which beset the IWM.

This state of decay was the challenge that now confronted me. The outgoing Director, L.R. Bradley, had been on the staff of the Museum since its inception in 1917 and had worked his way up from his initial post as a glorified store-keeper to that of Director, which, he told me, he should never have been. His empathy was almost wholly with the First World War, in which he had served as a subaltern in the Middlesex Regiment until being invalided out. To him, the Second World War was a nuisance which deposited masses of material in the Museum, squeezing its already restricted space and disrupting such order as its exhibitions had earlier had. When commenting on a staff inspection by the Treasury in the penultimate year of his Director-ship, one of his recommendations was that the rank of the next Director should be downgraded. He thought this would facilitate the gradual phasing out of a museum whose usefulness was diminishing in step with the passage of years since the end of the Great War, and whose significance had been modified by the Second World War.[5]

Mr Bradley continued to see the Imperial War Museum through the eye of its original beholders and those who had founded it. They had believed that the Great War must be the war which ended war. They, who had laid their plans in the year of Passchendaele could be excused for believing that there would never be another world war. Their requirement for the museum they created was that it should stand as an enduring memorial to the horrors of war, as a warning and a reminder to subsequent generations who would never experience such horrors themselves. The coming of the Second World War shattered this illusion, as it had done for the Royal Institute of Inter-national Affairs. In that context, it was not wholly illogical for Mr Bradley to believe that the best course was to arrange for a gradual and dignified decline towards extinction for the museum which history had turned on its head. It did not occur to him that there was an alternative, or if it did, it was not one which he wished to embrace. He gave the impression of hoping, as he approached the grave, that the museum, which he had served for so long, would do the same.

Even the Treasury took a more positive line than that and had hinted that it might entertain a plan for the modest extension of the Museum. Mr Bradley had responded with a hastily conceived scheme envisaging the building up of one wing to provide a little more space for exhibitions, a little more for the library and a little more for the photographic collection. The plan could be given high marks for simplicity, but not many for imaginative innovation. In any case, when discussions were opened with the Treasury, Mr Bradley more or less told them that extending the Imperial War Museum would be a waste of money. This disappointed the Chairman of the Trustees and caused him to look up Mr Bradley's age. Finding that it was sixty-seven, he decided that it was time to seek a new Director.

This was undoubtedly a severe blow to Mr Bradley, for despite his view of the future of the Museum he was utterly devoted to it in its decaying form. He not only worked but also lived in it, spending most nights in a tiny room off his office and only occasionally going home. He scarcely ever took a holiday. He had a line strung up in the Board Room on which he dried his washing and on one occasion, having forgotten to remove it on a board day, he was narrowly saved by a loyal member of the staff, who took it down just in time. Mr Bradley kept himself to himself and had as little to do with the staff and the outside world as he could manage. Some members of the staff did not even know him by sight and there was an occasion when someone who worked in the Establishment Office stopped the strange old man wandering about in an area of the Museum that was closed to the public and asked him who he was. There were other members of the staff with whom Mr Bradley was not on speaking terms. He himself told me that there would be no need for me to have anything to do with the Art Department because it had its accommodation at the far end of the corridor from the Director's office. This life in the Museum, however, entirely suited Mr Bradley and, sensing what a deprivation retirement would be, the Trustees re-engaged him on a part-time basis to weed the Museum's film collection, which, it seemed, had grown too big for its boots.

That arrangement was the product of an uncharacteristically weak decision by an otherwise notably strong Chairman and it caused me much anxiety. This was not diminished when Mr Bradley told me that one of his initial decisions was that all film coverage of the Royal Air Force could safely be scrapped because the air force had come into being only seven months before the Armistice and had not had much effect on the Great War. He seemed undeterred when I mentioned that the Royal Air Force had been in being throughout the Second World War but, as Mr Bradley invariably treated me with the utmost courtesy, it behoved me to respond in kind. I chose subterfuge rather than confrontation; I acceded to Mr Bradley's idea but only after I had instructed the appropriate members of what was now my staff to remove all film placed by Mr Bradley in the destruction bins and return it to the Museum's film-storage vaults at Hayes. This had the advantage of saving the coverage of the Royal Air Force and also a great deal of other historic film and at the same time enabling my relations with my predecessor to continue on an entirely cordial basis.

Mr Bradley was far from being the sole or the greatest problem I encountered when I came to the Imperial War Museum. Not surprisingly, the staff was heavily demoralized and I was repeatedly and anxiously questioned by members of it as to the likelihood of the Museum's survival. Nor for the most part was the staff well qualified. Only one member had a university degree. But though this character had a first degree and a doctorate, he was employed in the film vaults on the repetitive task of checking nitrate film for stability. I could not make better use of him as he did not wish for promotion and greater responsibility. He had in fact settled in to a therapeutic monotony. There were other more adventurous members of staff who were clearly in the wrong places. For example, C.V. McCann, who later proved to be an outstandingly brilliant aircraft model-maker, and clearly needed to work among three-dimensional exhibits, was employed in the photographic section carrying albums to and fro for the use of the public. If, as I was determined it should be, the Museum was to be transformed into an institution of historical enlightenment, the staff had to be substantially reinforced by people with trained minds in various disciplines. By no means the whole of the old guard welcomed the prospect and it was in any case difficult to achieve because I was only allowed to create new posts with the approval of the Treasury, which was extremely parsimonious in such matters.

There was also, as I have indicated, an urgent need to release specialized skills by the organization of departments in the Museum. Apart from a reasonably coherent Art Department, under W.P. Mayes, albeit with a staff of only one in addition to himself, the rest of the Museum's collections and activities were very loosely structured. Moreover, there were several areas of prime importance for which there was no provision whatsoever. There was no department of documents and, amazingly I thought, there were hardly any documents. There was no provision for school parties and other educational activities. There was no department of publications, and it was anybody's guess as to who was in charge of exhibitions. There was a fine library but the management of it was amateurish and there was neither money nor planning for acquisitions. There was a huge film collection but there was no cinema in which any of it could be shown, and much of the film was on the highly dangerous medium of nitrate base. The great collection of photographs was wreathed in mystery, as only the most primitive of finding aids had been devised. Not many of the wonderful pictures in the Art Department could be displayed to the public since there was but little space to hang them in the crowded and often damp galleries. The bulk of the collection, indeed, was stored in such high density that the viewing of a given picture often involved an operation akin to furniture removing. The reserve collection of three-dimensional exhibits was kept in a disused torpedo factory at Crayford in Kent. This was not publicly mentioned; the place was often flooded and some of the larger exhibits had been walled in, Egyptian tomb-style, when some carelessly designed structural alterations were made.

Nor was the Crayford store the only part of the Museum liable to floods. The lower exhibition galleries of the main building in Southwark were below the level of the ground in front of the Museum, and whenever sudden heavy rain fell a good portion of it poured mercilessly past a line of warders armed with mops and down into these galleries, where it fanned out amongst the crush of exhibits. The galleries were also vulnerable to ordinary rain, for they lay under glass roofs which had been erected over the open central court of what, before the Imperial War Museum moved in, had been the Royal Bethlehem Hospital for the insane, or, colloquially, Bedlam. These roofs leaked like antiquated greenhouses and the result, in truth, was worse than Sir Guy Garrod's vision of the Museum as a backwater. Mr Bradley's extreme re-

luctance to receive any new acquisitions was thus to some extent, understandable.

In short, the accommodation was bursting and leaking at the seams, and
the staff, numbering less than seventy in total, nearly half of whom were
needed to ward the building, was insufficient in size and inadequate in
scholarly capacity. The task of retrieving the institution, let alone developing
it into an historically useful one, was daunting. But on my side there were
some powerful advantages.

One of these was the Chairman of the Trustees, Admiral of the Fleet Sir
Algernon Willis. He was a remarkable and unforgettable man, the likes of
whom have been conspicuously absent since. As he played an important if
improbable part in enabling me to achieve my initial ambitions for the
Museum, some description of him finds a proper place here. Before taking
up my post, I had been warned by more than one friend that Admiral Willis,
a formidable disciplinarian with somewhat blinkered views, would be very
difficult to work with in a museum context. In theory this should have been
so. Though married to the twin-sister of the former Prime Minister Attlee's
wife, his outlook was somewhat circumscribed and did not much extend
beyond the welfare of the Royal Navy, in which he had spent almost the
whole of his life. He had been present at the Battle of Jutland and in the
Second World War had been Chief of Staff to Cunningham in the Mediterranean Fleet. It was said that he had worked himself to the point of collapse
and that he had stood for endless hours on the bridge of the flagship in an
effort to discharge to the full every detail of his duties. It was said, too, that
he expected all his subordinates to do likewise. Yet there was another side
to this demanding and austere character. On one occasion, when the Fleet
was coming in to Malta after a particularly arduous period at sea, Cunningham gave orders that a signal should be made requiring ships' sides to be
manned by sailors in best whites. Willis recognized that this would impose
another and in his view inessential burden upon nearly exhausted sailors,
who would have to wash and press their uniforms and then postpone
the time when they might have expected to relax. Disciplinarian as he was,
and much in awe of the C-in-C as he also was, Willis conveyed his view
to Cunningham, who then thought better of his order and cancelled it.
Cunningham thought highly of Willis and, when his own term of office as
Chairman of the Trustees of the IWM came to an end, it was Willis whom
he nominated to succeed him.

From the point of view of the Museum, this may not have seemed a particu-
larly good choice. In terms of what subsequently became known as heritage,
Sir Algernon Willis had a well-known but not very satisfactory reputation.
A few years earlier, when he was C-in-C at Portsmouth with his flag in HMS
Victory, he had reported to the Admiralty that the old wooden warship

Implacable was surplus to requirements and he had her towed out to sea and scuttled. This was thought dreadful. *Implacable*, as a French ship under her original name of *Duguay-Trouin*, had fought in the Battle of Trafalgar. This episode conveyed much of the essence of Sir Algernon's attitude to expensive luxuries. Also, even HMS *Victory* had not been entirely in safe keeping. Sir Algernon found that the galley was not economical. Its arrangement devoured unnecessary man hours and he wished to have it remodelled. Someone fortunately prevented this and Sir Algernon, much to his discontent, was forced to continue to preside over a waste of public money.[6]

Public expenditure, unless it was for the maintenance and improvement of the Royal Navy, tended to excite Sir Algernon Willis's suspicion and often disapproval. Any wastage of public money aroused his hackles to an extreme extent; he came, after all, from Aysgarth in Yorkshire. This frugality was reflected in his personal life, an instance of which was provided by the fact that his full-dress uniform as an Admiral of the Fleet was the same suit that had been made for him when he became a Lieutenant in 1909. The only modifications to it were an increase in the number of gold rings on the sleeves and the insignia of higher rank on the epaulettes. The elderly Admiral of the Fleet within retained the same figure as that of the twenty-year-old Lieutenant.

Another instance of his frugality was provided in a social context when it was Willis's turn to retire from the chairmanship of the IWM Trustees. He told me that he favoured Admiral Sir Deric Holland-Martin as his successor, but that I should meet him before a final decision was made. This showed great consideration for me, but must have been rather confusing for Holland-Martin, who was told to meet Willis in my office at 12.30 or thereabouts. Holland-Martin must have assumed that he would be offered lunch or at least a glass of sherry. However, after ten or fifteen minutes of fairly clipped conversation – Sir Algernon disapproved of lengthy exchanges – he announced that the end of the meeting had come, that he had brought only enough sandwiches for his own lunch and that he could therefore give none to Holland-Martin, who was thus given his congé.

These characteristics had their awkward side for me as Director of the Museum. I was determined to redevelop it and I knew well that one of the pre-conditions of success was a substantial increase of the government financed budget. I aimed to convert the Museum into a centre of historical study, but I also sought to soften its forbidding impression by the introduction of a measure of socializing and, by this means, to enlist the support of people of influence and of learning. Under Sir Algernon's aegis, I initially dared not give parties in the Museum at its expense, so I had to pay for them myself. I also felt the force of Sir Algernon's gaze when I explained the financial proposals I intended to put to the Treasury.

All this, however, worked to my ultimate advantage. Sir Algernon's critical scrutiny of my financial proposals sharpened my wits and meant that, when the matters came to the Treasury, I had built a better case than I would otherwise have done. Of course, I lost some of the arguments. For example, I wanted to apply for a special grant to buy a picture by C.R.W. Nevinson, which could have been acquired for £500. The subject of the painting was nothing grander than an army lorry, but the painting in my view was great. I needed the Chairman's support to obtain the grant. Sir Algernon enquired if we had a photograph of this type of vehicle and, on being told that we had, decided that we did not need the painting. Surprisingly he fully backed my plan for a major extension and redevelopment of the Museum building and my gratitude to him for this far exceeded the regret I did feel about the Nevinson painting.

Sir Algernon's dislike of discussion and debate also proved to be a sovereign advantage to me. He expected me to keep him informed in the briefest possible terms only on points of major importance. Most things he left entirely to me, and my experience of major questions was that he almost invariably supported my aims provided my argument was sound and brief. One of the great advantages of being a chief executive under the chairmanship of an admiral is that admirals know the difference in function between themselves and the captains of ships. Another advantage arising from the same trait was that the Board of Trustees was kept in very good order. Having satisfied himself as regards my agenda, Sir Algernon Willis would brook only brief discussion and that only if it introduced points of substance which neither he nor I had thought of. All petty manoeuvring and attention drawing, to which museum trustees are especially prone, were mercilessly and rapidly crushed. This meant that my belief that the Trustees should act as an enabling body, and not as an initiating one, and that above all they should be denied all executive functions, came fully to fruition in the Imperial War Museum. This was of great benefit to the Museum. The reverse tendency has brought many museums to the point of paralysis, not least the British Museum.

Though I always regarded Sir Algernon as a father figure and never addressed him otherwise than as 'Sir', it was more than merely a good working relationship that developed between us. From an uneasy and stilted opening experience, there came into being an affectionate friendship with all the advantages that mutual concern for one another's welfare and respect for each other's qualities bring.

Another advantage that favoured my endeavour was inexperience. Had I appreciated in advance the full extent of the Museum's decay, both as regards its accommodation and the abilities of its staff, had I known the extent to which the staff at all levels were unionized and understood the policies of the unions involved, had I appreciated the far-reaching and constricting effects of the Treasury's financial controls and a host of other difficulties, I might have hesitated to undertake the task. As it was, I knew enough of the problems to be outside the frontiers of cuckooland but not enough to be in the realms of despair.

In addition, there was a perception in the Treasury, the Ministry of Works and other government agencies, with which I had to deal, that the time of make or break had come for the Imperial War Museum. Parsimonious as they were about permitting anything costing money, I could recognize their feeling that the dissolution of the Museum might create awkward problems and that these might be more embarrassing than the acceptance of modest proposals for resuscitation. In the chain of negotiations I embarked on to gain acceptance of an extension and improvement plan for the building and the reinforcement of the staff, this climate of semi-tolerance was a marked advantage to me. Also, as the Treasury knew all too well, one thing leads to another. Once I had won acceptance of my scheme for the building and money had been allocated for it, my argument about the staff became more powerful. Within six years, the main building in Southwark was repaired, redeveloped and considerably extended and the level of staff competence and initiative had risen more than in proportion.

On 2nd November 1966 the Queen accompanied by the Duke of Edinburgh and the Royal President of the Museum, the Duke of Gloucester, came to the Imperial War Museum and declared open the new and modified premises which my extension and improvement plan had yielded. The event was unparalleled in the history of the Imperial War Museum since King George V had opened the original displays in the Crystal Palace in June 1920. In his speech of welcome to the Queen, Sir Algernon Willis announced that the extension and improvement plan had been put forward in 1961 and that five years later despite 'economic crises, freezes and squeezes' the work had been completed. The product, he told the Queen, included a library reading-room in the previously derelict chapel under the Dome, a properly equipped cinema, three new large exhibition galleries capable of displaying heavy equipment such as tanks and aircraft and a new wing of five floors offering, on the ground floor, another exhibition gallery and, above, accommodation for nine thousand works of art on sliding frames giving easy access to any of them, three million photographs, 4,260 miles of ciné film and more than 100,000 books.[7]

The new and modified accommodation provided adequate space fitted out to modern standards for the Museum's reference material for a period ahead which I estimated to be twenty to twenty-five years, and this provided a sure base for the development of the Museum as a centre of research and education. It also liberated other substantial areas in which further public exhibitions could be developed. The completion of the project was the hinge upon which my design for the Museum turned. I could not, however, have proceeded had not my programme for the development of the staff been correspondingly successful.

The extension plan had yielded everything I had asked for. Even at the time, I found this gratifyingly surprising, especially as I had heard Jennie Lee, the first Minister with specific responsibility for the arts, asking one of her officials if she could stop the works, which she had come to inspect, on the grounds that nobody wanted another war. My plans for the staff in terms of numbers and to some extent ranks, had not matched that standard. But despite some failures, the quality of what I got enabled me not only to realize my initial objects, but to aim at others I had not envisaged in the early years. Among many splendid recruits, were a number of brilliant people, who had already joined or were about to do so. Among these were Christopher Roads, Peter Simkins, Edward Inman, Roderick Suddaby, Gwyn Bayliss, Clive Coultass, Roger Smither, Christopher Dowling and, as it turned out, the star of them all, Robert Crawford.

My recruitment policy was to look for candidates fired with enthusiasm and equipped with demonstrably trained minds. I was not particularly interested in, or necessarily impressed by, previous museum experience or qualifications. Candidates with those qualifications tended to be tired failures from other museums or aspirants who had become desperate at failing to get into the V & A, and such like. The Civil Service Commission, which supervised recruitment for all the national museums, did not approve of my ideas, but they stopped short of blocking them. The underlying strength of my position was the unfashionable nature of the Imperial War Museum. Though the climate began to improve in the 1970s, that of the 1960s did not recommend the IWM to the art and museum world. In such quarters, the general impression seemed to be that the IWM was there to glorify war, to prove that one Englishman was worth ten Germans and that I was a retired colonel. Indeed, I recall one young candidate who, at the beginning of his interview, placed his feet on the table behind which I and the other members of the appointment board were seated and who in the course of it told us that he was not enthusiastic about working in a museum which was directed by a clapped-out colonel. There was also an abiding impression that the Museum was concerned with 'Imperial wars', by which was understood colonial wars. This arose from a failure to grasp that the word 'Imperial' in the Museum's title referred to the composition of its Board of Trustees, which included representatives of the Dominions and India, and not to its terms of reference. Many of the educated candidates of the 1960s did not wish to work in a militarily aggressive and imperialistic organization, especially if it was directed by an ex-Army martinet. The general public was perhaps not quite so stupid, but there was all too often the same impression there and in the press. The result was that, most fortunately, I was driven outside the magic circle of museumry for the sources of my recruits and that they had to develop their specifically museum skills after, instead of before, they arrived. I myself had had to do the same.

The success of this policy for recruitment meant that, as the years passed, I came into control of a staff capable of providing expert management of the library, the film and photographic collections, the three-dimensional objects and the several specialized collections ranging from firearms to postage stamps. In addition, I was able to organize these areas into coherent departments with systematic staff structures. It also became possible for me to create new departments to deal, for example, with education, publications, research, data retrieval, sound records and exhibitions. Above all, in the scale of my priorities, I was able to bring into being a Department of Documents to collect and make available for research the retained photocopies of the captured enemy archives of the Second World War and the influx of mainly British private papers, which the now more widely known Museum attracted. The vigorous and effective efforts of this new department within a decade built up a major source of research, which became indispensable to anyone seriously concerned with the two world wars and subsequent conflicts in which Britain and the Commonwealth have been involved. In this particular venture, I owed an incalculable debt to Sir John Wheeler-Bennett, Sir William Deakin and Lord Bullock, whose support lent credibility to the plan, and to the Leverhulme Trust, which financed the nucleus of the Department when the Treasury declined to do so.[8]

An historical museum cannot, however, depend for its validity entirely upon the wealth of its conventional resources, in this case, its printed books, documents, photographs and films. It must also demonstrate history in its public exhibition galleries. My task here was to convert a warehouse full of curiosities into an historical display. Initially I was restricted by space and staff resources to a limited programme. Until the extension plan was completed and my recruitment policy had borne fruit, I could only nibble at the problem. I decided to announce my intentions as to what was to follow by mounting a series of temporary exhibitions on reasonably small scales which would illuminate selected aspects of the whole subject. By this means, if only in small fractions of the whole, I hoped that the IWM might begin to show and explain history.

My first endeavour was such an obvious project that I myself had overlooked it and might well have missed a golden opportunity but for the advice of one of the old guard, the Keeper of the Art Department, W.P. Mayes. Though he and I unfortunately never achieved a satisfactory working relationship, I was, and remain, deeply grateful to him for spotting the opportunity. He pointed out to me that in a small gallery, long since closed to the public, there was a remarkable collection of exhibits concerning the Zeebrugge Raid of April 1918, which were stored there cheek by jowl, having been squeezed out of the naval gallery by the advent of Second World War material. Mayes thought that my objective could be met simply by thinning out and rearranging this material to allow public access. By this extremely simple method, which was the most we were at that time capable of, a valuable footnote to the history of the war at sea was 'written' in captioned authentic three-dimensional objects supported by contemporary photographs. This was the first such special exhibition ever staged in the Imperial War Museum. Its inauguration by the then Civil Lord of the Admiralty, C.I. Orr-Ewing, attracted a distinguished company, many of whom had taken part in the Raid, it produced notices in the press and then a very satisfactory attendance by the general public. It also led to a succession of similar but increasingly ambitious exhibitions on such subjects as the origins of military aviation, which was put on in 1962 to coincide with the fiftieth anniversary of the foundation of the Royal Flying Corps, Women at War, the German occupation of the Channel Islands and Colditz. We also mounted a series of special photographic exhibitions dealing with subjects where visual evidence was specially telling. These included a particularly successful series of *Fifty Years After* displays, which matched photographs taken during the Great War with re-takes of exactly the same sites shot fifty years later. Peter Masefield, who was later to join the Board of Trustees, travelled the Western Front from 1964 to 1968 seeking out the places and taking the matching photographs. The result was an interesting comment on the impact of war upon the landscape and the power of subsequent healing and reconstruction.

These temporary exhibitions served a critically important role in my plans for the Museum. They focused the minds of the staff on the object of displaying history as opposed to collections of curios. They also signalled to the public what the purpose of the Museum now was. They attracted attention in the press, on sound broadcasting and on television and this initiated an upward turn in the number of visitors which, for these and other reasons, increased from 300,000 to over a million a year during the period of my directorship.

Alongside, and sometimes arising from, these temporary exhibitions, a concerted programme for the reorganization of the permanent displays was brought into being. My first object was to break down the barriers imposed by the existing exhibitions between naval, military, air and civilian activities, and between allied and enemy materials. The conduct of war depended upon the relations between them and I wished to move the exhibits accordingly. The achievement of this reform was necessarily a protracted business, involving much research and careful thought about the repositioning of exhibits, as well as the introduction from storage, or the acquisition, of others, which were often very awkward in size, shape and weight. As the staff grew in size from the seventy I inherited to the 343 who were in post when I retired, and as the quality of its individual members increased, more and more became possible. The culminating point of this prolonged effort, in so far as exhibitions were concerned, was reached on 27th March 1980 when the Prince of Wales opened the *War Exhibition* in the central galleries of the Museum.

The underlying rationale of this exhibition was that war was endemic in society in the sense that it not only arose from but also moulded it. To show the foundations from which sprang the extended scale and scope of warfare which had characterized the twentieth century, we went back to before the Museum's technical terms of reference, which began in 1914, to the period of the American and French revolutions, and we carried the narrative on through both world wars to the conflicts subsequent to 1945 and the threat then posed by the nuclear stalemate. We took infinite pains to secure historical accuracy and even, to some extent, verisimilitude, in the manner in which the exhibits, numbering over a thousand, were presented and the way they were related to each other. The overall aim was to reveal to a general audience the principal factors that had activated the vast development in warfare which this period had witnessed and which we categorized as military, civil, political, economic, technological and artistic. My role in the development of the *War Exhibition* resembled that of the general editor of a written work. The exhibition was brought into being by the Museum's Keeper of the Department of Exhibitions, Mike Houlihan, and his talented staff. Much of the historical research and supervision was done by the Museum's historian, Peter Simkins.

The *War Exhibition* was the most ambitious historical project of its kind I have ever seen in any museum. One could walk through a trench on the Western Front in the First World War, the forward section of a Halifax heavy bomber of the Second and over the camouflaged dugout of a Vietcong sniper in the Vietnamese war. One could examine objects varying in size from a British Mark V tank of the First World War to an escape compass disguised as a button issued to RAF Bomber Command crews in the Second. The authentic exhibits were placed in constructed settings such as the trench and the dugout, but we halted at the threshold of simulated realism. There was no mud in the trench, the Halifax bomber, though authentic, was silent and rigid. The viewer who could make the leap of imagination was allowed to do so and those who could not were left to see only the stark and static objects.

In this last respect, the exhibition might be said to have fallen short of, for example, the Jorvic Museum in York or the *Blitz Experience* and the simulated Mosquito sortie, which were installed in the Imperial War Museum after my time there. It did fall short of these, but in my view, only technically and not historically. Jorvic in York is a splendid technical achievement and it is highly entertaining to be taken through what was apparently England in the times of the Norse raids. But it is fiction and not history. Few of the objects to be seen are authentic, the smells are not the smells the people smelt at the time, the voices are not their voices and probably do not give vent to the words they spoke. The whole thing is an imaginative reconstruction and, as such, is most arresting; but it is not history. In the Imperial War Museum, the *Blitz Experience* is likewise not history. The Air Raid Warden is not an Air Raid Warden; he is an actor giving an impression of what an Air Raid Warden might have said but probably never did. The crunch of the bombs does not impinge on the ear drums, the aftermath of dust does not penetrate the lungs, and the warning of broken glass littering the street can safely be disregarded. The Mosquito sortie is quite a rough ride, but the conveyance is not a Mosquito, nor does it vibrate or smell like one and the visitor always comes home alive.

These so-called 'virtual reality' experience exhibitions, however thrilling they may be, are the stuff of theme parks rather than historical museums. Moreover, in the case of the Imperial War Museum, there is an additional moral point. Before entering the *Blitz Experience* or embarking upon the Mosquito sortie, the visitor knows that he will not be killed. The experience is, therefore, bogus and perhaps even dangerously so. The visitor who thinks he has had the blitz experience or the sensation of the Mosquito sortie is sadly misled and the spirit of war is devalued. This kind of reality does not serve to avert the glorification of war by presenting it full front; it serves to make war seem entertaining like the big dipper at the fun fair.

When once it was suggested to me, when I was in charge, that there should be more realism in the Imperial War Museum, I replied that it should be suggested and not simulated. An honest attempt at realism, I said, could well be achieved by concealing a machine-gun in the sales stall, which, in those days, was on a mezzanine floor overlooking the entrance hall, and advertising the fact that this would open fire at random times on random days. The experience of entering the Museum would then convey at least something of the chances of war. My interlocutor did not think that this was a good idea, but his hesitation as to alternatives conveyed the essential problem of displays in the Imperial War Museum.

In the realization of that problem, I recognize that the exhibitions in the Imperial War Museum for which I was responsible did fall far short of the ultimate in historical truth. I claim, all the same, that they made a substantial contribution to a better historical understanding of the subjects with which the Museum was concerned. Seeing the whole length of a fifteen-inch naval

gun enables one to understand better the complexities of the Battle of
Jutland; the spectacle of an intact German V2 semi-guided missile gives more
substance to an account of German resilience in the closing stages of the
Second World War than a mere photograph, or even a ciné film, can do; and
a simple wooden cupboard, in which Belgian patriots secreted a British
soldier for much of the First World War, speaks vividly of resistance movements. The cockpit section of a heavy bomber of the Second World War at
least helps to make the distinction between flight in those days and under
those conditions and flight as everyone has since experienced it in modern
jet airliners. Moreover, the arrangement of such historical artefacts in relation to each other presents admittedly limited but nonetheless true vignettes
of history.

My own disappointment at not being able to achieve more than this in the
gallery by the use of artefacts is tempered by two considerations. First, it
must be admitted that no form of historical presentation is historically comprehensive. Neither the descriptive written passage, the reproduced original
document, the illustrated point nor the authentic artefact, nor all of these
placed together, can succeed in telling the whole story. An historical event
is necessarily something of the past and the whole of the past and, in many
cases, most of it can never be recovered. The historical limitations of exhibitions in the gallery are not unique to that particular form of expression
and, though they cannot be regarded as more than aspects of evidence, that
evidence is primary and can only be supplied in significant mass by substantial museums. Second, I did not believe that the gallery was the limit of
the potential for exhibitions open to the Imperial War Museum. In the
following chapters I will describe how we broke out of the gallery and onto
the screen and the site. In the meantime, I must consider another aspect of
history in the gallery that is fully as important as any I have described so far.
This is the use of art.

Art is not, or not usually, created as a source of history. Whether or not
an artist has a sense of history does not alter the fact that what he teaches is
how things appear and what he feels about them. Paul Nash's views of the
Western Front in the First World War, for example, do not record the extent
and effectiveness or otherwise of the artillery barrages; they do not comment
on the military results of the destruction or even, for the most part, on the
conditions of the troops fighting from the trenches. It is documentary
evidence, photographs and ciné films which tell about those things. All the
same, in addition to its value as a work of art, the painting can tell historical
things in a way no other medium, save perhaps, poetry, can. Nash's First
World War paintings reflect his horror at violence to the landscape and
especially the trees. The power of his work was such that it beckons one to
share that feeling, to enter into his view of the battlefield unto the fourth

generation. For the student of history, this is an additional piece of historical evidence. It gives him the opportunity to understand otherwise unknowable things.

The Imperial War Museum possesses some ten thousand works of art relating to the two world wars and subsequent conflicts. Many of these works are by great and famous artists such as Paul and John Nash, Eric Kennington, C.R.W. Nevinson, Stanley Spencer, Lavery, Graham Sutherland, Albert Richards, Epstein and Henry Moore. This means that the Museum is also an art gallery but, because of the nature of the paintings and sculpture, it also means that, in this art, there is an important additional source for history in the gallery.

When I took over as Director of the Museum, the Art Department under W.P. Mayes was virtually the only part of the Museum which was up and running, as I have noted earlier. Its problems were largely that the previous Director had not regarded it as a true element in the Museum, that it had but little space in which to display its treasures and none to make them available for inspection while in reserve. All three of these problems, if not eliminated, were certainly alleviated during my regime. My extension and improvement plan, as I have already described, provided at least a minimum of adequate space for exhibition, and the pictures in reserve were also made fully available for inspection. I was, however, much less successful in convincing Mayes, and more particularly those who succeeded him and reinforced the size of the staff which had been at his disposal, that the Director now really did regard the Department of Art as a true and highly important element in the Museum. This was probably due to a degree of mutual suspicion. My people in the Art Department felt, I think, that my competence regarding the works of art lay, not in their merit as works of art, but as sources of history. They distrusted my judgement rather as pure scientists used to look askance at applied scientists. On my side, I feared that most of them would have been happier to have appointments in the Tate than in the Imperial War Museum. The Tate was, after all, more fashionable and it did not embody the competition between space for paintings and space for large, heavy three-dimensional objects that inevitably characterized the IWM.

Nevertheless, the Art Department, in addition to its role as a purveyor of art for the sake of art, made a highly significant contribution to the work of the Museum as an historical institution. This was achieved through an enlarged 'permanent' – though in reality constantly changing – exhibition and through a regular series of special temporary exhibitions showing the work of individuals, such as, to name a few, Orpen, Graham Sutherland, Henry Moore, James McBey, Richard and Sydney Carline and Albert Richards, or groups of artists arranged on the theme of some particular aspect of war. Henry Moore's shelter drawings express, as the artist himself told me, his preoccupation with the underground which derived from his childhood as the son of a coal miner, but they also speak eloquently of the threat from the air to city dwellers in the Second World War. An historian cannot tell the viewer of an art exhibition how to interpret the pictures he sees, but from his own understanding of them he can begin to assess their historical value. In this respect, I have found the works of Albert Richards are a catalyst.

Richards was not an artist at the front observing the battle; he was an active soldier who was also an artist. He did not paint pictures to record events; he painted to reveal his idea of art and incidentally recorded events. His work brings one nearer to battle than does that of his mentor of earlier years, Paul Nash, for one can almost believe that he painted as he descended on his parachute into the cauldron of Normandy during the allied invasion of Europe. The immediacy of the works is stunning, yet they were in fact the products of more mature impressions. 'I have always felt,' he wrote in July 1944, 'that if the subject was good enough, it would still be as fresh months after seeing it, and probably would have developed in one's mind during that time.' Having myself known the colour of war, I can readily understand the particularly vivid use of paint which characterizes Richards's work. Equally, though I have never myself made a parachute descent onto a field of battle or engaged an enemy on the ground, I have a powerful and intelligible impression of both activities from looking at and thinking about Albert Richards's battle scenes. They are something apart from the stereotypes of conventional military painting and they are something apart from the imaginative reconstructions, which are as far as many of the official war artists ever got. They offer more than the written account of an eye-witness could convey, and they have more movement in them than a ciné film could show. In short, by altering reality, as an actor does on the stage, they convey reality more truly than realism can. Such in my view are the senses in which Albert Richards's war pictures are at the same time great works of art and important pieces of historical evidence. Thus the art exhibitions in the Imperial War Museum had the potential of bringing before people's eyes the realities and the experience of war. Many of them I believe did so.[9]

Not the least of the advantages of art exhibitions is that, despite the heavy weather made of it in such institutions as the National Gallery or the Tate, the hanging of pictures is child's play by comparison with the display of heavy three-dimensional artefacts. All that is needed is wall or screen space, viewing distance, the right light and ambience and well-placed captions. There is the same basic simplicity about the display of ciné films, to which I now turn.

CHAPTER EIGHT

History on the Screen

I had my introduction to Catherine the Great when I was eleven. I saw her on the screen in the well-known film of that title: she was played by Elizabeth Bergner. Though I have since been told that Bergner was not a great actress, she was – to my eye in 1933 – so good that I almost imagined that I had seen, not her, but the Empress herself. By the 1950s, I was somewhat less gullible, but even so, having seen *The Dam Busters*, I almost imagined that I had seen Guy Gibson. I think I was not alone among the British public in feeling that Richard Todd was more like Gibson than Gibson could have been. Some twenty years later I remember watching the filming of a sequence of *Edward and Mrs Simpson* on board HMS *Belfast*. When Edward Fox came up the side of the ship and stepped onto the deck, dressed as an Admiral of the Fleet and fingering his tie, I felt inclined to pay him the respects I would have offered to my sovereign. Nor was this feeling wholly dissipated when, in an interval in the shooting, I lunched with Fox in the wardroom of the old cruiser.

These are some indications of the power of dramatic historical films to inform or to beguile. Of course, the more one knows of a subject, the less a film drama about it is likely to succeed in beguiling. All the same, though I sat next to Lord Dowding at a preview of the film *The Battle of Britain*, the on-screen Dowding was altogether more convincing than the real one beside me. What is more the real Dowding did not seem to dissent entirely. There was a scene in the film where two of Dowding's antagonistic sub-ordinate commanders, Park and Leigh-Mallory, were unhistorically shown slanging each other in front of their Commander-in-Chief. I remarked to Lord Dowding that this elision of events was unfair in that it represented him as feckless and clueless. Oh yes, he agreed, it was unfair, but what mattered to him was not that but the good publicity the film gave to Fighter Command. This raises a slightly different point, because Dowding was not beguiled by the film's historical inaccuracies: he was simply enchanted by the image it gave of the victory he had won. Just as Harris and Portal had hoped that they could modify the account given by the official historians of the strategic air offensive to bring it more into accord with the images of the campaign they wished to be projected, so in the case of the film, *The Battle of Britain*, Dowding was essentially concerned with the appearance and not the historicity of what he saw.

The Dam Busters produced an apparently different reaction from Sir Arthur Harris. When shown the draft script of the film, he stressed that the story was that of an actual operation and that it should therefore stick to the facts. He warned against exaggerating the strategic results of the attack: false claims, he said, could easily be refuted. He also thought it ridiculous that Barnes Wallis was portrayed disclosing the secrets of the operation to his doctor when in real life he could never possibly have done such a thing. He objected to the portrayal of himself as an 'irascible, unapproachable moron'. On these points, or at least on the first two of them, Harris was on good historical ground. On the third, which had some justice in it, he was, how-ever, in a less secure position and from that point he developed others which placed him firmly on the side of myth and against that of history. He claimed that he had supported Barnes Wallis throughout, giving him the best crews and applying pressure in the highest quarters. Though he said he was used to being pestered by inventors of such schemes as the mounting of anti-aircraft guns on frozen clouds, he asserted that people of Wallis's calibre had had unobstructed access to himself. Some substance could be given to these claims by referring to Harris's own published account of what happened in his *Bomber Offensive*, but as was later to be shown in the official history, the primary records of the time presented quite a different story. In fact, Harris had strongly opposed the plan to form a special squadron to carry out the dams raid; he had dismissed Wallis's conception of the bomb as 'just about the maddest proposition as a weapon that we have yet come across'; and he had warned that low level operations with heavy bombers had 'almost without exception' proved to be 'costly failures'. He thought that Wallis and company should be given one aeroplane and told to go away and play while 'we get on with the war'.[1]

Whatever corrections or distortions may have been introduced to the final version of *The Dam Busters* by Harris's observations, the film came across more as a celebration of myth than an illustration of history. As his biographer has told us, the real Gibson was an entirely different character from Todd's version. Todd's Gibson was a clean-cut natural leader, a brilliant pilot who knew his men and inspired them by personal contact. The real Gibson, exhausted by responsibility and hazard, had developed a carbuncle on his face, was afflicted with arthritic feet and, on the morning of the dams raid, was declared by the medical officer to be unfit to fly. So far from in-spiring his men by personal contact, there were many men who flew on the dams raid that he had never spoken to, and he only distantly knew even the members of his own crew. Todd's portrayal omitted the coarse side of the man. That would have been better displayed, Ann Shannon thought, by Micky Rooney; and Ann Shannon, the wife of one of Gibson's ablest and most gallant lieutenants, knew Gibson better than most.[2]

There are other massive historical distortions in *The Dam Busters*; indeed, the film would not have made much sense to cinema audiences if it had been shot under the conditions of visibility which Gibson and his crews had had to face, despite the almost full moon that night. For what was regarded as security reasons, the shape of the bomb was changed from cylindrical to round and from time to time the aircraft lacked credibility. All the same, the greatest distortion lay in the changing of Gibson's character and appearance. Todd could no doubt have acted the real Gibson as faithfully as Fox did Edward VIII. So why was he not asked to do so? The answer lies in the fact that R.C. Sherriff, who wrote the script, was a dramatist and not an historian. The unfortunate consequence is that the public impression of Gibson pays less tribute to the hero than the real man deserves. To have achieved what Todd's Gibson did would have been truly remarkable; to achieve what the real Gibson achieved was far more so.

Drama, it may be argued, depends upon distortion. A playwright or novelist changes reality to make it dramatic, much as an artist changes the actual scene to fit his composition. As I have argued in the previous chapter an artist's changed scene may present a more fundamental truth than an actuality drawing or photograph is capable of doing. Perhaps an historical drama has the same kind of potential, but whether it does or not, war films such as *In Which We Serve*, *Reach for the Sky*, *The Battle of Britain* and certainly *The Dam Busters* do not seem to. The best that these dramas have achieved is to some extent to fill the gaps left by documentary films. There is after all no documentary film of the dams raid; nor of the sinking of HMS *Kelly*; and the camera-gun evidence of the Battle of Britain does not add up to a picture of the battle. Even so, documentary film, to the extent that the coverage exists, does in the hands of responsible producers have the power to convey history, and especially the history of war, beyond the perceptions of other media. The proof of this thesis, I venture to claim, lies in the twenty-six episodes of *The World at War*, produced by Jeremy Isaacs with myself as the chief historical advisor. This, however, it to leap towards the end of my experiences in creating history on the screen. The beginning was in the film department of the Imperial War Museum.

Among the first things I learned when I took over as Director of the Museum was that the floor of the Board Room where the Trustees were accustomed to meet was unsafe. Until I could get the matter attended to, I had to restrict the number of people occupying the room at one time to twenty, which was fewer than the total number of trustees. Later I learned that the film collection was unsafe. It was rather alarming when I had assumed responsibility for thousands of miles of film, much of which was on a nitrate base, to be told that this was liable, when unstable, to self-combustion or even explosion. But as the film was stored in modern vaults fitted with flues to enable film which caught fire to burn out locally and so prevent a misfortune from developing into a disaster, the threat was somewhat less than it might have been. Avoiding a disaster, however, was not the same thing as preserving an historic film collection. My first task in the field of history on the screen was, as I have already described, to defend the collection from the threatened depredations of my predecessor, L.R. Bradley, and then get the nitrate film copied onto an acetate base. This latter step was costly and tedious, but it did in time secure the entire collection on a base that made long-term preservation and projection onto screens or viewing machines possible. This in itself was a considerable saga, as was the provision of finding aids to bring the collection within the grasp of research.[3]

When these measures began to show dividends, film researchers and television producers took to arriving in increasing numbers in the Museum. Among them was Tony Essex of the BBC, who came with the idea of producing a film history of the Great War in twenty-six episodes that would appear in 1964 to mark the fiftieth anniversary of the outbreak of that calamity. He rightly appreciated that a large part of his raw material lay in the film collection of the Museum and that, though the BBC was willing to devote some £100,000 to £300,000 to the making of his series, the charges the Museum would be entitled to levy would carry him beyond even the highest estimate for that allowance. It seemed to me that if I insisted on charging the full rates, either the series would be scrapped or else it would be constructed from inferior material. I therefore proposed that the Museum should reduce its charges in exchange for the right to exercise a considerable degree of control over the quality of the programmes. In those days, one had to consult the Treasury before entering into the financial aspects of such agreements, so on 13th June 1963 I wrote to the Treasury setting out what I had in mind and asking if there was any objection in that quarter. As by 3rd July the Treasury had not answered my letter, I took it that I was free to proceed as I thought best. In August, an apparently satisfactory agreement was reached with the BBC, by which time I had also secured my flanks by obtaining general approval for my plan from the Trustees and I was now supported in my endeavours by an exceptionally able and exceedingly vigorous recruit to my staff, Dr Christopher Roads, whom I had appointed as Keeper of the Department of Records. It was thus that I came directly into the business of making historic documentary film programmes.[4]

I was soon to learn that I was not as clever as I had thought and that the BBC, as represented by Tony Essex, had less integrity than I had expected.

Though wonderfully evocative and historically impressive scenes were put together, things tended to be left to the last minute in journalistic style. The result was that the quality control by the Museum, which I had made a condition in the agreement, was impossible to exercise. Over and over again the commentary was recorded before we had seen or heard the text for it, and invariably the film assemblies were shown to us only a day or so before they were broadcast on the new BBC 2 channel. I tried to tolerate this situation in the belief that BBC 2 did not yet have many viewers and that proper revisions could and would be made before the programmes went out to the mass audience of BBC 1. When I was told that there would not be time in the interval between the two transmissions for this to be done, my patience was exhausted and after stiff but unavailing arguments with Tony Essex, I protested to the Director-General of the BBC, Sir Hugh Greene. In my letter, I stressed a ground of objection about which Roads and I felt particularly strongly. This concerned the use of 'reconstructed' material without identification.[5]

Much of the film footage of the First and also the Second World War shows reconstructed scenes. For example the famous films, *The Battle of the Somme* and *Desert Victory* (of the Second World War) are based upon operations re-enacted by troops, who had often taken part in the real battles, after those had taken place. For the most part, therefore, they are not what they appear to be: they are not genuine records of these major operations of war. As there are in these cases and in many others no genuine film records, these reconstructed scenes do have considerable historical value all the same. That value nonetheless depends upon honest declaration. When, as happens in *Target for Tonight*, a bomb-aimer is seen from outside the aircraft as it runs up on the target, it is obvious to any viewer that the scene must have been reconstructed; but when a mass of infantry rise from their trenches and advance into no man's land, the fact that the scene has been reconstructed may not by any means be obvious. Yet precision and the integrity of the sources is no less important in the visual expression of history than in any other historical form.

It was a relief to find that Sir Hugh Greene sympathized with my discontent. He said that he would arrange for Mrs Wyndham Goldie, Head of the Talks Group of BBC Television, to meet me together with members of *The Great War* production team so that steps could be taken to settle my complaints before the series was put onto BBC 1 air. The BBC in those days was a strongly hierarchical organization and Mrs Wyndham Goldie promptly got in touch with me, made herself as pleasant as could be and seemed willing to agree to any sensible suggestions. Moreover, she gave every appearance of having the power and personality to enforce whatever was agreed. A number of hard-looking men stood around her in apparently deferential modes, and although I thought they would stab her in the back if ever she looked away, she never seemed to do so, and I became hopeful that *The Great War* series would in future be screened, if not with our entire approval, at least without disgrace to the Imperial War Museum. Something of that order was eventually achieved, but everything negotiated with Mrs Wyndham Goldie had to be watched onto the screen by us, in case Tony Essex modified the terms on the way, and everything negotiated was subject to the ruthless time schedule, which was always too short.[6]

The main bone of contention continued to be the use of reconstructed material without declaration or, to put the matter more bluntly, the pretence that reconstructed material was actual battle coverage. Mrs Wyndham Goldie accepted my demand that announcements should be made in each programme indicating the extent to which the sequences were reconstructed. Tony Essex then began to argue that sequences which we knew were reconstructed were, in truth, actuality film. He obviously did not want the impact of his programmes to be diminished by pedantic statements about their authenticity or otherwise. Dr Roads and I had to beard him in Mrs Wyndham Goldie's television lair on, as luck would have it, Friday 13th November 1964. As we made our way to this seat of power in the falling darkness of the evening, the heavens opened and we were both soaked to the skin. We knew there was no hope of achieving radical reforms, but we succeeded in getting a series of saving excuses placed upon a firm footing. Shortly afterwards, the need for these was made publicly apparent by a perceptive letter in the *Daily Telegraph* from John Brophy in which he pointed out some of the ways in which viewers could distinguish between reconstructed and actuality sequences. It seemed appropriate that the rationale of our saving excuses should be published in the same paper and this was duly done in a letter signed by myself and Mrs Wyndham Goldie, which was also published in the *Daily Telegraph*.[7]

As I look at it again, after an interval of more than thirty years, this letter makes rather feeble reading. It shows that Mrs Wyndham Goldie was posing as an honest broker of television truth who needed at the same time to command the allegiance of her hard and cynical subordinates and avoid strictures from her more idealistic superior, Sir Hugh Greene. I on the other hand come out of it little if at all better for it is apparent that, in the interest of keeping the programme going, I was prepared to say that it was historically valid because the face-saving announcements, which it was now agreed would be broadcast, said that it was not. Although Tony Essex's *Great War* series was a break-through in the presentation of history on the screen and although a second bite at the same cherry by the BBC made in 1996 was not only not better than but not as good as Tony Essex's version, I do not feel proud of my part in the *Great War* series. From the point of view of the ulterior aims

I had in mind, however, it proved to be a great success. It launched the idea of history on the screen more surely than I realized at the time.

I was already eager for further and I hoped better opportunities when, towards the end of October 1965, a letter arrived for me from Lord Mount-batten, whom, over the previous four years, I had got to know quite well. He told me that a television series of his *Life and Times* was to be produced by Peter Morley and he sought the cooperation of the Imperial War Museum. I thought this was a golden opportunity: Mountbatten had been at or near the centre of great international events for sixty years, for much of the time in a dominating role. He had stood with Nicholas II on the bridge of the Tsar's yacht before the Great War, and during it he had seen the trenches on the Western Front, he had been on board Beatty's flagship immediately after the Battle of Jutland, and he had himself embarked on a naval career which, in the Second World War, brought him distinction and fame. He had then been Chief of Combined Operations, Supreme Commander in South East Asia and, after the war, Viceroy of India. After resuming his naval career, he had become First Sea Lord and eventually Chief of the Defence Staff.[8]

Already by 1965 it had become quite fashionable to laugh at Mountbatten, though strictly behind his back. He had some characteristics which invited this. He was egocentric to a degree and he took the interpretation of himself and his achievements with the deadly seriousness only possible for one who totally lacked a sense of humour. He was preoccupied with recognition for his services and was resentful of the very few honours that had not been conferred upon him. To his annoyance, he was not made a Field-Marshal, nor was he awarded the Royal Air Force pilot's brevet. To gain it, he had asked Lord Portal to teach him to fly, but Portal had turned him down. Almost everything else he had been given but for Mountbatten enough was never quite enough. I never belonged to the fashionable school of cynical comment; I admired Mountbatten and saw him as a major figure in the history of the twentieth century.

Though he was willing to acquiesce in the plan to make a television history of his life and times, the driving force behind the project was his son-in-law, Lord Brabourne, and it was with Brabourne that I negotiated an agreement for the production of the series in cooperation with the Imperial War Museum. Brabourne was a shrewd and meticulous negotiator and, as a highly distinguished film producer himself, was well equipped for the task. Our agreement produced none of the unpleasant consequences that had followed my initial sortie into that kind of world with the BBC for the production of the *Great War* series. Brabourne proved to be a much more solid and reliable character than Grace Wyndham Goldie and was far more in touch with day to day developments than Sir Hugh Greene had been. Also the producer, Peter Morley, was vastly superior in integrity and skill to Tony

Essex. John Terraine, who wrote the script, provided a scholarly input which I could not fault. It is true that Terraine had written much of the script for the *Great War* series, but it is also true that, however good a script may be, the ultimate judgement of visual history must depend on the pictures. The key difference in quality between the *Great War* series and *The Life and Times of Lord Mountbatten* was the difference between Peter Morley and Tony Essex. Another difference of great importance was that Terraine had a much more single-handed grip on the Mountbatten script than would have been possible for any single writer in the case of the far wider subject of *The Great War*. Even if, as in the case of the Mountbatten series, the subject is set in the context of world events, the approach to history through biography has the advantage of providing a defined and reasonably restricted viewpoint. A sharp picture of limited size may be able to shed light at least as interesting as that from a larger picture with a more blurred image. This is a matter to which I will return in a later chapter so it may for the time-being, be left on one side.[9]

Perhaps the greatest hazard in the making of the Mountbatten series was Mountbatten himself. He was not naturally disposed to the idea of history in which he had been involved being unfolded on purely objective grounds. He expected it to be rendered in terms which would show his contribution in the most favourable light. He had spent a good deal of time generating 'archives' which would help to achieve that result. I recall seeing evidence of this when, on one of my visits to Broadlands, Mountbatten showed me round his archives. His method was to write to prominent contemporaries asking for their judgement on questions which were crucial to his reputation. Naturally, such people normally replied in complementary terms. The answers were then filed as evidence of how right Mountbatten had been, even about such controversial matters as the Dieppe raid. For a great man of action and high achievement, there was nothing unusual about this. It was simply that Mountbatten was more thorough, more persistent and more sensitive in such matters than any one else I knew, apart perhaps from Lord Montgomery.

That Morley and Terraine – especially, I believe, Terraine – circumvented this hazard was immensely to their credit. Mountbatten was after all a towering personality. Yet circumvent it they did. Though they adopted a sympathetic attitude to Mountbatten throughout, which is a perfectly legitimate attitude on the part of a biographer, they still produced, not a hagiography, but a serious historical study. When I introduced the preview of *The Life and Times of Lord Mountbatten* in the cinema of the Imperial War Museum on 19th December 1968, I declared that the angle of vision was Mountbatten's. The series, I said, would show the First World War through the eye of a young prince seeking to serve his country in junior and hazardous roles. We would see the Second World War from the viewpoint of command, first of HMS *Kelly* and ultimately of the Supreme Commander, South East Asia. After the war we would see the devolution of Empire through the eye of a Viceroy. Although the combination of these angles and many others, I said, was wholly unique, there was much more than that to the series. I praised Mountbatten for the free rein he had given to John Terraine and Peter Morley, which had enabled them to combine the evidence of actual experience and personal recollection with a 'broad sweep of brilliant historical application and a film artistry of inspired proportion'.[10]

I entirely meant what I said, but I do not know how far my claims were accepted by my audience, the like of which I have never again seen. It included the Queen and Prince Philip, the Queen Mother, the King and Queen of the Hellenes, most of the rest of the British Royal Family, the Prime Minister, Harold Wilson, and many members of his government including even, on one of his last public appearances, John Stonehouse. I remember noticing that as I opened my mouth to start speaking, the Prime Minister fell asleep. Mountbatten, on the other hand, sat there, head slightly on one side, with a fixed look of concentration on his face. Another angle on the occasion was provided by the Secretary of the Cabinet, Sir Burke Trend, who was overheard by a friend of mine remarking of the series that 'only a Kraut could have done it'. Some may have thought I was too deferential.

No one, however, could have thought that of Professor Arthur Marwick, a radical exponent of historical truth. Yet he was much more impressed by the series than Sir Burke Trend had affected to be. If he thought that the biographical approach, which had provided the unity of the series, had overblown the historical significance of Mountbatten, he nonetheless believed that the filmed sequences of Mountbatten himself, which he calculated had occupied about a third of the total footage of the series, would be valued by historians in the future. He also thought that the 'relatively untrammelled collaboration' between John Terraine and Peter Morley, assisted by the 'skilled archive research' of John Rowe, had produced a 'pleasing sharpness of focus'. In essence, Arthur Marwick and I were much of the same opinion about *The Life and Times of Lord Mountbatten*. Moreover, in the article in which he expressed these views, Marwick drew comparisons with other examples of history on the screen, including *The Great War*, about which he was more complimentary than I would have been. But he did observe that in that series the 'faked stuff' should have been more clearly distinguished from the authentic.[11]

Marwick's carefully considered and deeply informed article on what, in those days, was called video history, carried a note of correction for myself. A few weeks earlier, having been somewhat disappointed by the paucity and superficiality of such reviews of *The Life and Times of Lord Mountbatten* as I had seen, I had written to *The Times* to complain. I remarked that as academic historians were only just beginning to recognize the value of photographs as historical evidence, it might be too much to hope that they would appreciate the relevance of films and television techniques to the art of history. I had sought to protect myself by conceding that there were 'a few notable exceptions', but Professor Marwick evidently felt that this was insufficient and promptly responded with the news that historians were 'very fully aware' of the significance of film. He referred to the Film Committee of the Historical Association and the University Historians' Film Committee. More important than these bodies, he said, was a consortium of university history departments that had already entered the field of the film-making business with Professor J.A.S. Grenville's brilliant *Munich Crisis*. He added that historians did appreciate the 'virtues of the excellent Terraine-Morley *Life and Times of Lord Mountbatten*' which he hoped would become available for use in universities and school classrooms. He accused me, perhaps not wholly without justification, of believing that all academic historians were 'outmoded fuddy-duddies', which he set in counterpoint to the suspicion amongst academic historians that all television producers and scriptwriters were charlatans. Though neither a don nor a television producer, I certainly did recognize that Marwick was not a fuddy-duddy and equally that Terraine was not a charlatan and I derived much scholarly benefit from continuing contacts with both of them.[12]

In the course of these excursions in the press, Marwick had commented on the fact that the BBC had abandoned their plan to make a television series to do for the Second World War what *The Great War* had done for the First. Marwick suspected the reason was that the BBC had feared that the programme would flop without the presence of Tony Essex at the helm; he had moved into commercial television. Marwick believed that no purely academic team could handle a project so massive as the Second World War, yet, he wrote, 'what a marvellous one it would be for genuine co-operation between the academics and the television professionals'.[13]

I had already got wind of the Second World War project, in which Terraine was likely to be involved, but I dreaded the prospect of working again with Tony Essex; and I doubt if I would have risked associating the Museum for a second time with a production of his. Fortunately, however, I was saved from the awkwardness of such a decision by Tony Essex's withdrawal from the battlefield and the arrival of a radically different proposal that offered me, both in my official and private capacities, a real influence on the making of a major television series. Thames Television, the company which had produced *The Life and Times of Lord Mountbatten*, decided to make a twenty-six part series on the Second World War. It was to be produced by Jeremy Isaacs and it soon emerged that massive financial provision was to be provided. Before any public announcement was made, I was invited, in my official capacity, to associate the Imperial War Museum with the project and, in my private one, to act as the chief historical advisor to the producer of the series. I already knew enough of what was planned to enter immediately and positively into negotiations, which quickly resulted in satisfactory agreements. These were not only good in themselves, but they were honoured throughout the following three years, both in the letter and the spirit, by Thames Television in general and by Jeremy Isaacs in particular. My part in helping to make the twenty-six episodes of what came to be called *The World at War* was by far the most important foray I made into the field of history on the screen. It was also a thoroughly happy sortie. In all my experience of television, before and since, I have never again encountered a producer of such brilliance and integrity as characterized Jeremy Isaacs.[14]

Even before we had reached the necessary formal agreements, Isaacs and I had begun to map out the structure of the series. My first contribution was to observe that the original outline was far too much Europe-orientated and far too little directed towards the problems of the war in the Far East. I also warned that the relationship between programmes dealing with all-embracing subjects, such as the Battle of the Atlantic, and those covering episodes of short duration such as the first arrival of American troops in the European theatre would create problems of balance for which we would have to find solutions. I urged too that we should break away from received British prejudices about the war and that, for example, the series should make it clear that the civilians who suffered most were not Londoners nor the people of Coventry, but the Germans from bombing, the Russians from siege and occupation, and the Japanese from both conventional and atomic bombing. I also wanted it to be made clear that the land operations which decisively exhausted the German army were not in Africa, Italy or France, but in Russia. As to details, even at the outset, I applied the heavy hand to loose drafting. For example, the Germans did not break through the Maginot Line; they circumvented it. Italian naval strength was not destroyed at Taranto; it was reduced, and so on.[15]

Jeremy Isaacs's immediate willingness to take on board all these and numerous other ideas with which I loaded him, was a huge encouragement and one which prompted me from then onwards to put forward my judgements without fear or favour. Moreover, even though the schedules were necessarily often tight, I was always shown the draft film assemblies and the accompanying scripts in sufficient time to enable me to comment and to allow the opportunity for Jeremy Isaacs and those others working under him on the particular programme in question to make revisions before the final recordings were made. I recall one occasion when, through an oversight on my part, I had passed an assemblage as actuality only to discover, after it had been put into the can, that it was reconstructed. Isaacs grumbled mildly about the costliness of the mistake, but he had no hesitation in scrapping the offending passage. My apprehensions, based upon my experience of the *Great War* series, soon evaporated and there was not even a Mountbatten to threaten our independent judgements. By the same token, the professional observations of the film department of the Museum were also fully taken into account.[16]

If Jeremy Isaacs and I occasionally had disagreements, these were always resolved by discussion and I can now only recall one point upon which he entirely rejected my advice. I did not want the commentary to be spoken by the voice beautiful of Laurence Olivier. I thought an anonymous voice would be much more appropriate to the occasion, but Jeremy Isaacs was determined that Olivier's voice it should be, and it was. This was not exactly a proper matter for the historical advisor, so I was content to be rebuffed. I was not consulted about the music. All the same, I did think that Carl Davis was an inspired choice as the person to compose it, and his contribution, in my view, was prominent in the overall television artistry that embellished the series.

At last the years of creative endeavour were rewarded by the completed twenty-six part series. The European preview of *The World at War* took place in the Imperial War Museum on 30th October 1973 in the presence of the President of the Museum, the Duke of Kent. In the brochure which was handed out on that occasion, Thames Television declared that the series was not a 'war film' nor a nostalgic indulgence: it was simply information. But, the statement continued, it was 'information portrayed in a manner and on a scale that only television can achieve'. The series, it said, made use of real film of real events. It did not illustrate one battle with film of another, nor did it 'compile for dramatic effect sequences of material from widely varying dates and places'. Much of the responsibility for ensuring the accuracy of historical fact and film had, it said, fallen upon me and my staff. Thus, in measured and agreeably low-key terms, was launched *The World at War*. From that time to this, it has been shown again and again all over the world. My doubtless myopic vision has led me to think that Jeremy Isaacs was thrown away on the Royal Opera House when he might have stayed in action on the television front.[17]

Shortly before beginning to write this chapter, I again viewed the whole of *The World at War* so that I could attempt some conclusions about it almost a quarter of a century after it was made. History reflects the age in which it is written as well as that of its subject. In this respect, *The World at War* is no exception. While we were making the programmes, Soviet military might and the division of Germany between East and West seemed destined to last forever, and the killing in Indo-China had gone on 'to this day'. The possibility of a major nuclear exchange between the two super-powers, though diminished by a balance of terror, was ever present. The canvas on which we attempted to sketch the Second World War was of a different texture from what it would be if we were to attempt the same task today. While this long perspective undoubtedly has an effect on one's view of *The World at War*, it does not seem to me seriously to date it. This is because the series does not adopt a strong point of view. It consists essentially of sequences of visual documents of mainly primary evidence which are allowed to impact on the viewer without the distraction of more than a minimum of explanatory narrative. Although there was a certain basic reliability about the judgement of Nazi ideas, which was guaranteed by a notable Jewish influence on the programmes, the editorial line, in so far as there is one at all, is substantially objective. The tenacity, skill and courage of German troops, for example, is fully recognized and revealed as also is the utter self-sacrifice of the Japanese troops. The production was British. But it is not anti-American.

As to the bedrock of the programmes, the primary evidence was of two kinds. First, there was the film of actual operations and situations. This is highly authentic material, but for that very reason, it is often confusing. Second, there were the talking heads, almost all of whom took part in the war. They range from Eden, Avrell Harriman, Lord Mountbatten and Robert Boothby to ordinary fighting men from the sharp end, including myself. All these provide primary evidence, but it is primary evidence, not about the war itself, but about how it appeared to these people in the period 1971–3. The secondary evidence was also of two kinds. First, there was reconstructed film as, for example, in episode 2, when the Battle of the River Plate was described, or, in episode 12, when clips from *Target for Tonight*, were used to convey the sense of a Bomber Command night attack. The fact that these were reconstructed scenes was systematically drawn to the attention of the viewer. Second, there was the spoken narrative, the scripts of which were compiled by a team of able and often quite young writers, and which were scrutinized by myself. This narrative often brings to intelligibility the more confusing actuality battle film and the talking heads usually do the same. But, of course, the talking heads and the narratives convey the subjective views of the speakers and the writers who made the contributions.

It seems to me that the initial claim by Thames Television that the series was simply 'information' has largely been justified by the test of ageing. But they also claimed that it was information 'portrayed in a manner and on a scale that only television can achieve'. Presumably, the same thing could be done in the cinema, even if it is hard to see people trooping out thither week after week twenty-six times. Otherwise, it seems that this claim has also been justified. The ability to use both still and moving pictures offers the prospect of anchoring the moment or the detail, while the moving picture reclaims the exact past in more frightening reality than can otherwise be achieved.

These possibilities, however, relate more readily to the conditions of the war than they do to its tactics and strategy. Indeed, in *The World at War* there is not a great deal about tactics or strategy. Most of the series is about the conditions of war and provides a better insight into what it was like being at war on land, at sea and in the air than can be obtained from any single personal experience account; It is also more graphic than any written description. While a strategic account of how the atom bombs came to be dropped in action, and a tactical one of the German air defensive system known as the *Kamhüber* Line were included, these do not depend on television for their messages. They could equally have been provided by other means. That is not the case with the episodes dealing with conditions. These tend to mark out television or – on other screens – films not simply as the best means of expression but, as far as actual record is concerned, the only effective ones. Outstanding examples in *The World at War* of this are to be seen in episode 9 dealing with the Battle of Stalingrad, episode 12 about the American day-bombing of Germany, episode 21 which shows the Russian advance into, and capture of, Berlin, and episode 23 which records the American Pacific island-hopping campaign. Probably the best explanation of the historical success of *The World at War* is that Jeremy Isaacs thoroughly understood the historic strengths of television and played to them.

Although I never again operated in the field of history on the screen on anything approaching the scale of *The World at War*, I did take part in a number of other endeavours ranging from a very satisfactory series of appearances on *Pebble Mill at One*, in which I was able to present exhibits from the Imperial War Museum and comment live upon them, to a disastrous programme in which I was supposed to provide historical balance in a news item that was distorted to such an extent that my complaint to the Broadcasting Complaints Commission was upheld. The apology and correction which was then broadcast came on the air so long after the event, however, that I cannot imagine that many people, if any, made the connection. For a retraction of that sort to have much effect, the person being apologized to must be very well known which I was not.

The Pebble Mill studios in Birmingham had singular advantages for the purposes with which I was concerned in these programmes. Space was virtually unlimited and existed both inside and outdoors, so that I was able to have the cameras brought to bear on a variety of objects ranging from Queen Mary's wartime ration book to the forward section of a Lancaster bomber. The production team, which included Roger Laughton and Pam Creed, spared neither time, effort nor money to make all this possible. As my contributions were on a weekly basis and continued for a substantial time, I was able to establish a style of showing exhibits of many different kinds and relating them to a series of historical themes that, because of the frequency of the programmes, could be connected to each other and to the general development of the war. Thus, for example, I showed civilian gas masks, ration books and so on to make points about civilian life during the war; the Lancaster fuselage as the setting in which I described some aspects of Bomber Command operations; Field-Marshal Montgomery's caravans as that for discussion of the exercise of command in battle; and objects from, as well as film of, HMS *Belfast* to set the scene for an examination of the role of cruisers in naval warfare.

The *Pebble Mill at One* series offered me the ideal opportunity for demonstrating museum artefacts and allowing them to tell history. I could have done this without television in front of a live audience as, indeed, was impressed on me by the fact that the Pebble Mill programmes had such live audiences. But while the live audience in the studio had the advantage of providing immediate audience reaction and thus an awareness of when a particular point had been sufficiently emphasized, it was the TV cameras and their connection with the distant audience that, by generating their own particular brand of adrenaline, set the tone and the pace of the proceedings. As the programmes were live and were not taped, I necessarily never saw them, but, in the light of the feed-back that reached me, I venture to claim that they were highly successful. Essentially, this was because their formats played to the strengths of television.[18]

This last point also applied to a different kind of television opportunity that occurred when I was asked to do a programme on the bombing of Dresden for Channel 4's *Diverse Reports*. This was prepared and recorded in good time without undue rush ahead of the broadcast date, which was 13th February 1985, the fortieth anniversary of the attack. I had made numerous attempts to explain the highly complex issues on television on earlier occasions, but invariably the results had been virtually useless, either because the time allowed was wholly insufficient or because of the intervention of editorial prejudice, or both. In the *Diverse* programme, however, there were none of these obstacles. My script was not cut or distorted; there was ample time in which to deploy it; and though I know that the producer, Nigel Maslim, regarded the attack as highly immoral, he did not allow his own views to impinge upon those of the historian whom he had invited to explain and balance the evidence we displayed. This included much documentary film of the operation both from the attacking and receiving angles, and also about the aftermath. There was in addition a good selection of documentary film dealing with surrounding circumstances, such as the Ardennes offensive and the German V2 campaign. In the form of talking heads, we also introduced survivors from among the citizens of Dresden who had been there during the raid, some members of Bomber Command crews who had delivered it, and some survivors of the high command at the time.

I felt thoroughly satisfied that the full range of viewpoints from condemnation of the attack as a war crime to the belief that it was necessary and productive had been explored and related to an objective historical analysis, and that this had been done in strongly visual terms playing to the strengths of television. More to the point, was the gratifying response from many viewers. I think this programme produced a larger volume of letters from viewers than any other comparable endeavour in which I took part. The Chief Executive of Channel 4 was pleased and I was particularly glad that he was, for his name was Jeremy Isaacs. Nigel Maslim was also pleased, if partly because, in his view, my balancing act was 'diverse'. Despite these grounds for satisfaction, the fact remained that most of those who wrote to me came down on one side or the other, which one could infer would have been the side on which emotion had placed them beforehand. Understanding the issues, I wrote to Maslim, depended upon the extent to which people could empty their minds of inherited notions and preconceived ideas. For the most part, I thought, whether they belonged to the bulldog or the liberal-sop schools, they seemed unable to do so. The facts and their contexts seemed to have come in for little consideration. I told Maslim that I was glad to be in the business of explanation and analysis and not that of persuasion.[19]

As far as production was concerned, I had a similarly rewarding experience with the German broadcasting company *Sudwestfunk* which invited me to provide the framework for a wide-ranging programme looking at the whole of the allied bombing offensive against Germany. Having thoroughly and intelligently digested my written outline of the subject, Erich Bottlinger brought a television entourage to my house which planted their cameras in the drawing room and more or less converted the rest of the accommodation into a television studio with its ancillary offices. This invasion was well rewarded because, though I did not see it myself, the programme, which was only broadcast in Germany, was seen by Leonard Cheshire whom I had secured as one of the talking heads. Despite some initial doubts, he later told me it was well balanced and informative. I had always believed that good relations between the British and modern Germans did not depend upon misrepresentations of the history of the Second World War and I was, therefore, especially pleased that this fair representation of a potentially divisive issue was produced by a German company for German consumption.[20]

How ill so many other programmes in which I took part compare with these experiences! A striking example of the downside of history on the screen is provided by a programme entitled *The Battle of the Bombers*, which was broadcast on BBC 2 in 1993. The producer, Helen Bettinson, invited my participation and told me that, in her opinion, attention had been too much concentrated on the bombing of Cologne and Dresden. She proposed to make a programme about the offensive as a whole, but with its focus on the bombing of Essen. She discussed her plans with me at length and in considerable detail. I was impressed by her intelligence and grasp of the subject and I accepted her invitation to provide a commentary on her assemblage of documentary film and talking heads that would explain the historical setting of the offensive and, in particular, the reasons why it was launched and sustained. The resulting film was then to be shown to a studio audience which was to debate the issues raised under the chairmanship of Jonathan Dimbleby. In short, the programme was designed to provide the background for what it was hoped would develop into a balanced debate. The camera team duly arrived in my house and I provided historical answers to a wide range of very intelligent questions put to me by Helen Bettinson. When, however, the programme went out in front of the studio audience, my contribution was cut to four brief extracts, which met virtually none of the objectives for which I had made the recording. Instead of a balanced debate, there then followed a general shouting match, mostly about the bombing of Dresden, between very excited contenders, none of whom seemed to know anything at all about the bombing offensive. In so far as there was a conclusion, it appeared to be that the British should have confined their methods of warfare within constraints not observed by Hitler, which would have enabled him to win the war without undue inconvenience or ill-consequence to the Aryan element in the German nation.[21]

Uninformed democratic opinion is sovereign when it comes to parliamentary elections, the presumed protection being that one silly idea cancels another. When it comes to historical debate, it is not helpful; having listened to the studio debate about the bombing offensive, I can imagine that if a seventeenth-century version of Jonathan Dimbleby had presided over a similar debate about Galileo's thesis, the conclusion would have been that the sun rotates around the world. History on the screen is not well served by such populist stunts.

CHAPTER NINE

History on the Site

While the screen provided an opportunity for history to break out of the confines of the gallery, there was another form of historical display which could not yield to the constrictions of a museum in the sense of gallery spaces: this was an object, or a building, or a group of buildings, extensive enough to be defined as a site or 'out-station'. That the Imperial War Museum had no such 'out-station' seemed to me, from the first days of my directorship, to be a grave and limiting handicap.

Unlike the initiation of my idea of history on the screen, which came when I was eleven years old, my vision of history on the site came to me only a few months before I entered the museum world. For rather the same reasons as those that had led me to make my first visit to the Imperial War Museum, I set off to Portsmouth to remedy an extraordinary lack in my cultural experience, namely, that I had never seen HMS *Victory*. Guided by her mastheads, so much taller than I had expected, I came round a corner of buildings and there before my eyes was the Royal Navy's most famous ship. Beyond her there lay HMS *Vanguard*, the largest battleship ever built for the Royal Navy against whose grey mass *Victory* stood out dramatically. The contrast between past and recent past was stunning. This was history on the site to perfection. I knew of course that *Victory* had been laid down in 1759 and, after work on her had been suspended for a time, had been launched in 1765. I knew that this ship, forty years old at the time of Trafalgar, had continued in active service for another thirty years after that. I knew that she was of about two thousand tons and that fifteen or twenty of her like had had the capacity to change the course of world affairs. I knew that *Vanguard* had been laid down in 1941, launched in 1944 and commissioned in 1946, and that she was of about forty-two thousand tons. I knew too that, before she sailed, she was virtually obsolete as a weapon of war and that as I gazed on her after no more than fourteen years of active life, she was about to be towed away to the scrap yard. She had never had – and her like no longer had – the power to exert any real influence on the course of world affairs.

These elementary historical facts, written on the page, may seem almost too obvious to be worth recapitulation; the recollection of them within sight of the two ships, however, especially with the one superimposed upon the other, was electrifying. History on the site has the power to invest ordinary facts with larger significance and to bring to mind a deeper awareness. The Ironbridge Gorge Museum, for example, explains the location and working of machinery that generated the industrial revolution more emphatically and in more dimensions than the printed page can. At Quarry Bank Mill, Styal, one can see not only how the looms were powered and how they worked, but also precisely why child labourers were needed and the extreme hazards to which they were exposed. Seeing real things is different from having them described.

History on the site is as intricate and complicated a form of expression as any other historical or museum technique. The preservation and presentation of a site as large as Iron Bridge Gorge or as small as *Victory* or Quarry Bank Mill amounts to much more than stopping things falling down or keeping them afloat and giving access to them. Also, and particularly with history on the site, theory is one thing and the practical achievement of one's aims quite another. I now come to my practical experiences in trying to present this form of history.

On 14th April 1967, accompanied by Peter Simkins, Martin Brice and Ray Freeman of my staff, I visited Portsmouth. Our mission was to investigate the possibility of acquiring for preservation one of the six-inch gun-turrets on board the cruiser, HMS *Gambia*. We found her, a pitiful figure, lying in 'death row'. Age and vandalism had reduced her to a travesty of her wartime splendour. We had to walk the decks carefully. All of them were in danger of collapsing; rusty steel was everywhere to be seen; and broken glass abounded. As the ship was unmanned, the local vandals had taken the opportunity to come on board in the evenings for the enjoyment of smashing things up. Poor *Gambia* was in this state because she was about to be scrapped. No one other than ourselves had any interest in preserving any part of her. I thought that we might well remove a gun-turret before the rest went into the melting pot, but Peter Simkins suggested that a better plan would be to save a whole cruiser, guns and all. He knew that *Gambia* was too far gone to be that cruiser, but nearby, riding at anchor, we could see a similar vessel, HMS *Belfast*. It was to her that we presently repaired to accept an invitation to lunch from the Senior Officer of the Reserve Fleet, Captain T.E.B. Firth, who had his headquarters on board.[1]

My immediate reaction to Simkins's suggestion was that he had gone over the top, but even before we reached the quarter-deck of *Belfast*, I had come to think, why not? Like *Gambia*, *Belfast* had finished her sailing days and, though she was still in commission as an accommodation ship, we knew that she too would shortly be moved into 'death row' and soon after that scrapped. Unlike *Gambia* she was still in excellent condition. There was no rust to be seen and, in place of the evidence of vandalism on *Gambia*, there was the gloss of naval spick and span. Captain Firth and his officers showed us all over the ship and we noted much equipment we thought we might be able to remove and preserve. My thoughts, however, were now consumed by the idea of preserving the whole vessel.[2]

Belfast had been laid down in 1936 and completed in 1939. Together with her only sister, HMS *Edinburgh*, which was lost in the war, she was the largest cruiser ever built for the Royal Navy. She was an early victim of German magnetic mines, which broke her back in November 1939. She was reconstructed and adapted to some of the necessities, such as damage control, that war experience had dictated and at the end of 1942 she rejoined the Home Fleet. In 1943, she sailed with two Arctic convoys to Russia and on 26th December was prominent in the last of the Royal Navy's capital ship gunnery actions, which resulted in the sinking of the German battle-cruiser *Scharnhorst*. She took part in the opening bombardment of the Normandy coast on D Day, 6th June 1944. Following a second refit, she proceeded to the Far East. She was repeatedly in action during the Korean war, bombarding shore batteries and beach-heads and enforcing the blockade. She was reconstructed and modernized in 1955 and again in 1959. When she retired from the fray in 1966 to become an accommodation ship, *Belfast* contained within herself unique evidence of the development of naval thought over a period of thirty years. Commissioned when the naval view seemed to be confined to the horizontal through binoculars, she retired with sophisticated radar, damage control and an obvious awareness of the threat from the air.[3]

If not the most distinguished of the Royal Navy's Second World cruisers – *Belfast* could not, for example, rival the battle honours and fame of HMS *Sheffield* – she was about to become the only one left. Indeed, in completely authentic form, she was the sole British survivor of the 'Dreadnought' age. We were confronted not with the question of why *Belfast* should be chosen for preservation but rather with the challenge of grasping a last opportunity. Having put this to my Trustees and gained their support, I proceeded with my Chairman, Admiral Sir Deric Holland-Martin, to the Navy Department of the Ministry of Defence where we had a meeting with the Permanent Under Secretary of State, Sir Michael Cary. The object was to persuade the Navy to hand over *Belfast* to the Imperial War Museum for permanent preservation. We also had to convince Cary that the cost of fitting up and maintaining her as a museum ship would not be prohibitive. We knew that the naval authorities would have to be assured that *Belfast* in our hands would not become as discreditable to them as *Gambia* had in their own.[4]

Sir Michael Cary was an engaging character and a man of great charm. He was also highly cultivated and frighteningly clever. Holland-Martin, who knew him well, both liked and admired him; but I had reason to know that Cary did not entirely reciprocate these feelings. He had some of the mandarin's condescension towards senior service officers which was common in Whitehall. I was apprehensive about the outcome of the meeting. In the event, it passed off agreeably enough. The civil servants in the Navy Department, however, felt that I had underestimated the problems and the costs of my scheme, and it was agreed that a committee should be set up to examine the possibilities in greater detail. The Navy Department undertook to send two representatives to sit on this committee and, most important of all, they agreed to stop the 'destocking' of *Belfast* in preparation for her scrapping until the committee's report had been completed. My first move was to invite the participation of the National Maritime Museum.[5]

The Committee which thus came into being proved to be a very strong one. Basil Greenhill, the Director of the National Maritime Museum, not only agreed to participate, but joined the Committee himself and generously undertook to serve as vice-chairman. In addition, he nominated a member of his staff, G.P.B. Naish, as another member. I, having appointed myself to the chair, nominated as further members Peter Simkins and Martin Brice, both of whom it will be remembered had accompanied me on the visit to Portsmouth that had triggered these developments. The Navy Department representatives, Commander H.K.J. Cock and C.J. Pollitt, proved to be of the utmost value. Commander Cock had naval knowledge that immensely enhanced the authority of our report and Mr Pollitt, who served as Secretary of the Committee, knew the ways of Whitehall better than any of the rest of us.[6]

As the work of our Committee proceeded, it began to appear that we might achieve a workable plan for the preservation of *Belfast* and also create an unprecedented system of cooperation between two national museums. We now planned that the ship should find her permanent mooring at Portsmouth and that she should be provided for and administered jointly by the Imperial War Museum and the National Maritime Museum. These two ideas found a prominent place in the Committee's report, which was completed, after eight meetings, on 18th June 1968. We knew that our recommendations would not be accepted if we did not propose a viable and economical form of administration for *Belfast* as a museum ship. We unanimously reported that, under these arrangements, the preservation of *Belfast* as a logical development of the two Museums was technically, economically and administratively feasible. Basing our estimates, where naval technicalities were concerned, on figures given to us by the Dockyard Department of the Ministry of Defence, and where museum matters arose, on the experience of the two museums, we showed that the annual running cost of the proposed museum ship would be only ten per cent of the current running costs of the two museums, despite the fact that we had made an allowance for a sinking fund to provide for periodic dry-docking. We also took account of the one-off expenditure that would be needed to adapt the ship to museum purposes, but we stressed that the excellent condition of the hull and the high quality of the pre-war steel of which it was constructed were favourable factors. We recommended that, despite the fact that the ship would be a part of the two museums which at that time were not allowed to levy admission charges, there should, notwithstanding, be a charge for visiting *Belfast*.[7]

It seemed to me and, I think, also to my colleagues on the Committee that we had produced a strong case for seizing this last opportunity to preserve a heavy naval unit of Second World War vintage. Even so, we would first have to persuade the Navy Department to hand the ship over to us and thus forego her scrap value. We would then have to persuade the Ministry of Works that the cost of preserving and adapting her to museum purposes was estimated with reasonable accuracy. Finally, if we could surmount these obstacles, we would have to persuade the Department of Education and Science to authorize the scheme and provide us with the additional establishment needed to man the ship. This was bad enough. What was worse was that unknown hands were turned against us.

I noticed that Lord Mountbatten, with whom I was constantly in touch about the production of his *Life and Times*, was distinctly lukewarm about *Belfast*. He told me that the scheme for the preservation of HMS *Warrior* was justified on the ground of her being the first of her type. I replied that the same could be said of *Belfast* on the ground that she was the last of hers. Evidently, this did not much impress Mountbatten, because the next thing he told me was that *Belfast* was rusted through and would be impossible to preserve. I categorically denied this, only to hear a few days later that Prince Philip had called a conference in Buckingham Palace to discuss ship preservation. This, I was told, concluded that the *Belfast* scheme was not practicable because the ship was rusted through. I was unable to correct this impression, as I had not been invited to the conference. I fear that Prince Philip retained this belief in rust for some while to come and that, partly in consequence, others had the same view. This was very damaging. I never discovered who started the rust scare, nor how it came to the ears of Lord Mountbatten and Prince Philip. Once there, however, it was hard to dislodge. The difficulty in such cases is that princes have to be aware of so many disparate matters simultaneously that it is impossible for them to examine the credentials of those who brief them to a sufficient extent.[8]

As a compensating if not a balancing factor in the face of these adversities, I was establishing contact with Rear-Admiral Morgan-Giles, the Member of Parliament for Winchester and a former Captain of HMS *Belfast*. Though I did not then foresee it, this was to prove in the long run to be one of the decisive factors leading to the permanent preservation of *Belfast*. Meanwhile, there was a long pause as arguments and counter-arguments about the recommendations of the *Belfast* Committee were marshalled and rehearsed. Suddenly in February 1969 the clouds lifted and I was given the astonishing news that the Department of Education and Science had decided to support the *Belfast* scheme as proposed in my Committee's report, and that they would recommend to the Treasury that the funds should be provided.[9]

More good news came in hot pursuit. The Navy took *Belfast* into dry dock, which they would hardly have done had the ship been about to be scrapped. This also meant that we would get a ship in much better order than her existing good condition and that there would be an opportunity for blocking off ports that would no longer be required and that tended to be sources of corrosion. On 20th August 1969, Greenhill and I went to Portsmouth to see what was going on. There we met Sir Victor Shepheard, the eminent naval architect and former Director of Naval Construction at the Admiralty, who was now a Trustee of the National Maritime Museum. We lunched on board *Belfast*, high and dry in her dock. Afterwards, we crawled along the keel and listened to Shepheard's comments. Although there was a good deal of pitting to be seen, Sir Victor was perfectly confident that the general condition of the hull was excellent and much better than he had expected. His authoritative opinion extinguished the rust scare and was a great relief to me for, as I admitted to Holland-Martin, I had for some time been stating that the underwater condition of the ship was excellent.[10]

We had hoped that before 1969 was out, we would get a favourable decision from the Treasury, but March 1970 came round and we still had no news. On the other hand, the Ministry of Works had agreed that they would accept responsibility for the maintenance of the ship in the same sense as they did in the case of the buildings that accommodated the national museums. This seemed to be yet more good news but, as we were presently to learn, it was not.[11]

Before we could understand the significance of the decision by the Ministry of Works, there was another huge delay, and it was not until February 1971 that the awful truth began to emerge. Rumour now had it that the Ministry of Works had put so enormous a sum against the cost of preparing and maintaining *Belfast* as a museum ship that the Treasury would be bound to refuse to sanction it. It was also said that the Treasury was reluctant to sacrifice the £350,000, which was thought to be the scrap value of the ship. Some of this news found its way into the *Guardian*, which adopted a strongly pro *Belfast* attitude and gave space to my assertion that rejection of the scheme for the preservation of our last large warship of the Second World War would be a 'major tragedy' comparable to the pulling down of the last Norman castle. This made no difference and, a few nights later, while I was at an evening party in London, I heard that the scheme had been rejected on the grounds that the Ministry of Works' estimates were unacceptably high. I felt utterly defeated and dejected. But I did not have much time to nurse my bitter disappointment.[12]

Indeed, during the months when the *Belfast* drama had unfolded, I had had much else on my mind such as the production of *The Life and Times of Lord Mountbatten*, the mounting of a special exhibition about the Victoria Cross and the George Cross, which was opened by the Queen, the development in the museum of a Department of Documents, the launching of the Imperial War Museum Trust, the installation of two fifteen-inch naval guns in front of the museum's facade and so on. There had also been the problem of dealing with the aftermath of a serious fire in the Museum caused by a misguided but very courageous pacifist, who scaled the building by night and deposited an incendiary device in the library reading-room in the dome. On the morrow of hearing that Lord Eccles, the Minister with responsibility for the Arts, had rejected the *Belfast* scheme, I flew off to Australia in response to an invitation from the Federal Government to advise on museum matters. On this trip, during which I circumnavigated the world in twenty-seven days, I inspected museums in Canberra, Wellington, Auckland, Los Angeles, Chicago and New York. While I was so engaged, the Deputy Director, Dr C.H. Roads, acted for me in the Imperial War Museum.

I hope that my report on museums was useful to the Australian Government; I know that my absence from London did no harm to the *Belfast* scheme. I came home on 6th March 1971 hardly daring to ask for news of what had happened to it. The National Maritime Museum had abandoned ship, but Christopher Roads had not. In consultation with Admiral Morgan-Giles, he was already well on the way to the establishment of a charitable trust designed to take over *Belfast* and run her as a private museum ship. Roads was not exactly an expert on the distinction between the arts of the possible and the impossible and this advantage had no doubt sustained him in the tenacious and audacious stand he had taken. I hope that, had I been in London at the time, I would have taken the same line; but I am not sure that I would have. Though the Minister for the Arts had ruled that no further official museum time should be devoted to *Belfast*, neither Roads nor I seemed quite able to understand what he meant. A month later, Morgan-Giles, Roads and I were on our way to the Navy Department to put our case to the Navy Minister, Peter Kirk. This time we did not have to bother about the Department of Education and Science, the Ministry of Works or the Treasury. We did, however, have to raise some money.

Everything now moved at high speed. We established a *Belfast* Board with Morgan-Giles as Chairman and myself as Vice-Chairman; we launched a public appeal for money; and Morgan-Giles succeeded in interesting his

Parliamentary colleague, John Smith, in our project. The latter's munificence now became the key that turned the lock in our favour. We gained access to about £170,000, which we reckoned – correctly as it turned out – would be sufficient to bring *Belfast* under tow from Portsmouth to Tilbury, dry dock her there, carry out modifications to make a first stage of public exhibition access, and then bring her up the Thames to the Pool of London where, off Hays Wharf, we had arranged a permanent berth. We had also been extremely fortunate in obtaining the services, as Director of the Trust, of Vice-Admiral Sir Donald Gibson, who had recently retired from the service but retained the cheerful gusto of a cavalier that had made him so well known in the Navy, and who was a shrewd judge of awkward problems. The Navy Minister having accepted us as competent, we were given the ship and, in what seemed to be no time at all, our day of triumph arrived.

This day was 15th October 1971. Our party, consisting of Peter Kirk, Admiral Morgan-Giles, Admiral Gibson, Christopher Roads and myself, assembled at Tilbury before first light. To reach the Pool of London at the speed to which we were restricted by the need to protect our underwater preservative epoxy resin, required an early start. We had to keep to an exact schedule to ensure our arrival at Tower Bridge at low water so we could pass into the Pool of London without our masts fouling the superstructure of the bridge. We were all too conscious of the fact that, if we succeeded, ours would be the largest ship ever to come into the Pool of London. Pulled, pushed and nudged by tugs, we crept up the Thames and past Greenwich where, as the sun rose, we saw that the cadets were drawn up on parade to salute *Belfast*. As there was no electric power on board, we had lit the bridge by candlelight and another anomaly was the sight of our two admirals hauling on ropes and carrying out other duties not usually performed by flag officers. These two expedients characterized the way in which the *Belfast* Board functioned. On our journey, we passed nervously through locks, hoping against hope that we would not inflict damage that we could not afford to repair. As we approached Tower Bridge, an old Swordfish of the war-time Fleet Air Arm, appeared overhead and escorted us to our destination. At the same time, the River Fire Brigade pumped a salute of water into the air. And so we came successfully onto our berth off Hays Wharf. Six days later, on Trafalgar Day, we opened the ship to the public, although at first they had to be restricted to the open decks.[13]

The last leg of our journey had presented us with some formidable problems. To provide sufficient depth at our mooring, we had had to dredge out a hole in the river bed so that we could still float at low water. Also, to make the ship completely secure along her whole length, we had to fasten her to specially constructed dolphins, which allowed for a rise and fall of the water of some twenty feet. To bring the public safely on board, we had provided

a flexible gangway. All this accomplished, we set about a systematic programme of opening up more and more of the ship until ultimately everything
from the bridge to the engine-room was open to visitors. We decided not to
restore the ship to any one particular period of her history but instead to
present one compartment in the condition of one period, another in another
and so on with the object, which we ultimately achieved, of showing all of
Belfast's development over the whole period of her life from the time of her
first commissioning until our acceptance of her. Thus, we released *Belfast*'s
capacity to present, not just one period of historical evidence, but a whole
generation of it.

The *Belfast* Board, under Admiral Morgan-Giles's chairmanship and with
the added value of *Belfast*'s two able successive Directors, Vice-Admiral
Gibson and Rear-Admiral Philip Higham, made a brilliant and unique contribution to the presentation of history on the site. Even so, as time went on it
became apparent that the preservation of the ship in the long-term depended
on the creation of a wider financial base than the *Belfast* Trust alone could
provide. It seemed to me that the solution could best be secured by absorbing
the ship into the Imperial War Museum so that its profit and loss accounts
could be entered into those of the Museum as a whole. The realization of
this idea depended on convincing the Minister with responsibility for the
Arts that it was viable. Fortunately for my plans, that Minister was no longer
Lord Eccles. He was now Lord Donaldson. Also fortunately, the Chairman
of the Imperial War Museum's Trustees at this point was Sir Peter Masefield.

Lord Donaldson had what must have seemed to his civil servants the
disquieting habit of listening to advice from without as well as from within.
Sir Peter Masefield was a skilful negotiator endowed with unusual degrees
of patience and persistence. He gradually wore down the obstruction of
the civil servants and got his message across to the Minister. In 1978, HMS
Belfast became a department of the Imperial War Museum. On the eve of
my retirement from the directorship of the Museum, I saw *Belfast* into dry
dock at Tilbury for the second time. My successor, Dr Alan Borg, received
her back with her underwater parts viable for the rest of the century. *Belfast*'s
continuing life afloat in the Pool of London affords visitors insights into
naval history which, as I have said, are unique. As the years advance those
insights become more and more remarkable because as naval development
continues, *Belfast* becomes less and less like contemporary warships. In time
to come, she will resemble them no more than *Victory* does today.

In the report of the *Belfast* Committee, we had included the calculation
that, as a museum ship, *Belfast* would yield some 17,500 square feet of
exhibition space. We saw this as a useful extension of the exhibition areas
in both the National Maritime and the Imperial War Museums. In the event,
though it was only in the Imperial War Museum, it did make possible a

marked improvement in our ability to present the twentieth-century history of sea power in the gallery. This was no more than a welcome by-product of the successful preservation of *Belfast*. Obviously, by far the most important product was the ship herself as an artefact of history on the site. I mention this to show that *Belfast* did little to soothe my feelings of claustrophobia about galleries. My anxiety arose, not from the prospect of there being no scope for the further enlargement and redevelopment of the main building in Southwark, which I knew there was. It came from my belief that a museum of twentieth-century warfare could not discharge its role properly within conventional galleries. Much of the most important evidence was substantially too large to make that possible.[14]

One Friday evening, which I cannot date, I remember talking of such matters to Dr Roads. I said that we ought to look out for a disused airfield, which would in itself be an historic site and which would enable us to deploy heavy weaponry. Roads seemed to agree, but he did not add much to the burden of my argument. I thought I had lodged an idea which might someday be brought to fruition. On the following Monday, Roads appeared in my office and told me that he had found 'your aerodrome'. It was the former Royal Air Force Station, Duxford.

There were some difficulties. Although Duxford had been declared surplus to requirements by the Ministry of Defence in 1968, it was not exactly disused. The County Authority had produced a plan to create a sports and recreation centre on the site and the Home Office wished to build two prisons on it. Meanwhile, vandals were systematically setting about its destruction. Both proposals for the future of the place, however, were eventually thrown out by the Government after a public enquiry. But that did not mean that the site could now be turned into a museum. Had we submitted an application for such a purpose, I have little doubt that it too would have been turned down. Instead, we timidly applied for permission to use part of one of the hangars for the temporary storage of some of our aircraft, which for the time being we could not accommodate elsewhere. Two years later, we had moved in some ten aircraft and had made an alliance with the East Anglian Aviation Society, whose skilled members were working, without pay, on the restoration of these machines.[15]

I took the view that, if an aircraft was worthy of preservation in the Imperial War Museum, it was too valuable to fly. There was also the point that, in order to put an old aircraft into flying order, it had to be modified to meet contemporary safety standards. The East Anglian Aviation Society and its successor body at Duxford, the Duxford Aviation Society, while fully accepting my views with regard to the Imperial War Museum's aircraft, did not share them with regard to their own. Also, nearby there was the Shuttleworth Collection, which had been established for the primary purpose of flying rather than merely preserving vintage aircraft. Close alliances with these bodies enabled us, without jeopardizing the Museum's aircraft, to introduce flying displays of historic aircraft at Duxford. From small beginnings in 1973, these air days grew in scope and frequency until, in June 1976, we and the Duxford Aviation Society organized a flying display, that attracted an audience of some 45,000 people.[16]

The revenue produced by these flying displays and others which followed them, enabled us to drive forward the conservation and display at Duxford not only of aircraft but also of military vehicles and other large naval, military and air exhibits which would not fit into galleries in London. The dedicated work of many highly skilled but unpaid technicians, who were members of the Duxford Aviation Society, made possible an expanding programme of ambitious projects at astonishingly low cost. We also made productive agreements with the Cambridgeshire County Council, which owned the runway at Duxford and whose cooperation was essential to the success of our enterprise. Another great advantage that flowed from our association with the Duxford Aviation Society was their interest in civil as well as military aircraft. Its terms of reference denied the Imperial War Museum the opportunity of collecting civil aircraft unless they had military significance. No such restriction impeded the Duxford Aviation Society, which collected and displayed at Duxford many highly important civil aircraft, including the prototype Concorde 01, which had flown faster than any other version of that aircraft.

Emboldened by these developments, I sought to convert our permission from the Government to use part of one hangar for temporary storage, into a permanent grant of the whole site for the purposes of the Imperial War Museum and the Duxford Aviation Society. I dreaded entering into negotiations with the chief civil servant in the Ministry for the Arts, C.W. Wright, who I thought had been one of the great obstacles to my plans for HMS *Belfast*. Holland-Martin did not trust him and my feeling was that he regarded my ideas as outrageous or frivolous or both. I was therefore most agreeably surprised to be told in February 1976, after much less than the usual manoeuvring, that the Minister for the Arts, Hugh Jenkins, had approved my application. Thus, Duxford airfield became a permanent element of the Imperial War Museum, and a solid foundation was laid for the further and rapid development of the site. I was now able to open Duxford to the public on a daily basis in the season March to October. In the first full season of 1977, 167,000 paying visitors came. In the second season, there were 340,000, and by 1982, when I retired from the Museum, two million people had visited Duxford. The small temporary space in one hangar grew into one of the finest air museums in the world, one also containing major exhibitions of naval and military content.[17]

The main credit for this achievement must be divided between C.H. Roads, who seized the opening initiatives, Edward Inman, who as keeper and subsequently director of Duxford consolidated the original gains and then drove the project forward in huge steps, and the Duxford Aviation Society whose members provided a skilled workforce without which none of this could have been done. There was, in addition, another factor that contributed decisively to Duxford as an outstanding example of history on the site. This was the site itself and its past associations.

The original aerodrome at Duxford had been built during the First World War and it was among the earliest RAF Stations. Three of the original timber-trussed hangars survived to yield for museum purposes more than 100,000 square feet of exhibition or conservation and restoration space. Though a fourth hangar was blown up in the process of making the film *The Battle of Britain*, these three surviving hangars suffice to convey the appearance of the aerodrome in its original form. Further building from then until 1961, when the RAF left, now records the development of RAF requirements and the methods of meeting them over a period of more than forty years, including a little of the First World War and the whole of the Second. This offers the ideal setting for the display of aircraft and other artefacts representing the same period of time. Since Duxford became a museum, much further building has been undertaken and by 1986 more than another 100,000 square feet of space under cover had been provided. Subsequently, a land warfare hall and the American Air Museum have been built. These additions have given Duxford a total of over 300,000 square feet of exhibition, storage and restoration space under cover. This has made it possible to carry on the presentation of the history of aviation beyond the period of Duxford's historic buildings and up to the recent past, without incurring anachronistic penalties. It has also enabled the very largest aircraft such as, for example, Concorde and even the huge American B52 bomber to be displayed under cover – and yet with many good viewing angles for the visitors. It means too that, in many cases, the work of restoration and maintenance can go on in view of the public. The displays at Duxford are far removed from the show-room conditions of the conventional gallery and are much more akin to the service hangars of air force stations.[18]

Duxford's past associations greatly enhance the value its physical attributes give it as the scene of history on the site. It has often been at the centre of important historical developments and twice of decisive ones. It was from Duxford that the 'big wing' tactics of 1940 were evolved; and it was from Duxford that Douglas Bader flew to lead the massed squadrons of Fighter Command's 12 Group in the execution of these tactics by concentrated attacks upon the Luftwaffe in the Battle of Britain. The success of these operations was a key factor in the outcome of the battle. Three years later,

Duxford was allotted to the United States Army Air Forces and became one of the bases of the American long-range fighter offensive against Germany. In the course of the following year, these operations, in combination with the American long-range day-bombing offensive, achieved a decisive degree of air superiority over Europe. This, like the Battle of Britain, changed the course of the war.

It may be that the majority of the four million people who had visited Duxford by 1989 did not reflect upon these historical matters. It may be that most of them came simply for the excitement of seeing aircraft, tanks and guns, or for the thrill of flying displays. If so, this does not change the fact that history on the site is available at Duxford in scope and depth. Conventional historians do not expect everyone, or even very many people, to read their books. Nevertheless, their better works do contribute to the sum of human wisdom, from which those who reflect upon these things and those who do not all benefit. So it is, I believe, with history on the site. Learning and entertainment are not necessarily antagonistic: at Duxford, as also on board *Belfast*, the two can be dispensed at the same time without harm to either.

Splendid as Duxford is as an example of history on the site, it is not pure history. The fact that it offers so much space as an outstation of the Imperial War Museum, which embraces all aspects of twentieth-century warfare, means that many of the artefacts there have been installed because there is ample space for them and not because, by historical association, they should be there. In this respect, Duxford compares ill with *Belfast*, but that is a small blemish to set against the advantage of the sheer weight and size of what can be shown at Duxford and the large conservation, repair and reconstruction programmes that can be achieved.

In purity of history on the site, *Belfast* compares well with Quarry Bank Mill or the Ironbridge Gorge. All the same, none of these can rival, in that particular respect, sites which remain intelligible without reconstruction or even restoration. Among the most striking of such sites I have seen is the Phrygian city of Apamea in modern Syria. Here, in the Second century AD the Romans built a fine city in what today appears to be the middle of nowhere. Walking down the paved main street flanked by magnificent colonnades with parts of their entablature still in place, there is not a sound, and you can see no reason why a city on this scale should have been built here. Yet the grooves in the paving tell of the chariot-wheels which must have passed often to cut so deeply into such hard stone. Nearby, are the remains of a grand governor's palace. Not far away, are those of a dingy and mean mediaeval town. What did the inhabitants of that make of the Roman city? Maybe, they saw it as no more than a source of stone for their infinitely less ambitious buildings. One then learns that Apamea used to be the pivotal point on the east-west trade route. The stone that is believed to have been the town-crier's platform, from which he would have proclaimed the arrival and departure of the merchant convoys, is still there. Now one can hear the hustle and bustle, now one can understand why the city was founded here; the significance of the *pax Romana* is brought home by the contrast between the rich city, built on open land without defences, and the mediaeval town huddled behind its defensive walls on a rocky promontory. Then the trade route changed and the city began to decline towards the deserted, collapsing shell which it is today.

Pure history on the site is not necessarily better than the versions which are compromised by reconstruction, as in the cases of Ephesus and the Iron Bridge Gorge, or supplemented by additional material, as is the case at Duxford. But it is different, and it raises the question in relation to purveying history on the site of how far things should be explained by reconstruction, or the story enlarged by supplementary means. I judged these issues quite differently in the cases of *Belfast*, which I wished to be as 'pure' as possible, and Duxford, which I wished to contain as much as possible.

CHAPTER TEN

History through Biography

In 1957 Sir Arthur Bryant published a study of Field-Marshal Lord Alanbrooke based upon his diaries and autobiographical notes. I was asked to
review the book on the BBC's Third Programme. The broadcast was produced by Ian Grimble, who worked for the Talks Department. This led indirectly and through a series of strange chances to my entry into the field of
biographical history. The chances were strange, because what I was to write
had nothing to do with Lord Alanbrooke and, though it was suggested by
Ian Grimble, it had nothing to do with the work he was doing for the
BBC. It arose simply from the chance fact that when I had finished the
broadcast about Alanbrooke, Grimble mentioned the case of 'Anastasia'
which, at the time was getting an airing in a German court. For no particular
reason, he asked me if I thought 'Anastasia' was indeed the Grand-Duchess
Anastasia. I said I was sure she was not. I told him what I knew of the last
days of the Imperial Family and how the Tsar, the Tsaritsa and all their
children had perished in the night of 16–17th July 1918. Grimble's question
had struck a response more highly charged than I think he had expected and
the response moved him more profoundly than I had foreseen. He asked me
to write a play about the murder of the Tsar, which he would produce for
broadcasting.

I had not previously thought of writing a play; nor is that quite what I did
in response to Grimble's invitation. I produced a narrative punctuated by
spoken parts representing the Tsar, the Tsaritsa and other protagonists in the
plot. The narrative, which in the broadcast I spoke myself, was based upon
my reading of the historical evidence; the 'punctuating' sections were produced from the words used in correspondence and memoirs of the period.
The result was intended to be historically valid in the sense that I restricted
the narrative and the acted parts to the confines of the sources from which
I worked. But it was not of course history, for I had, for example, used words
which had been written and made them oral. The BBC called it a reconstruction and Michael Swan, writing about it afterwards, said it was a documentary. I thought it was an historical play.[1]

Three actors, Mary O'Farrell, Stephen Jack and Denis McCarthy, played all the many parts with a brilliance which astonished me. After I had told them about the characters they were representing, they produced what I wished more perfectly than I had thought possible. I remember in particular how, with utter conviction, Mary O'Farrell transformed herself from the Tsaritsa to a lady-in-waiting and to a peasant woman without, so to speak, batting an eye-lid. These were the great days of radio acting and I was fortunate to be allotted such a cast. The broadcast, which went out twice on the Home Service, attracted a good deal of interest and, among those who listened to it, was a publisher who asked me to turn it into a book. The result was *Crown of Tragedy, Nicholas II*, which was published in 1960.

The book like the play was designed to be historically valid, but unlike the play it was as true to its sources as I could make it. It was not a biography of the Tsar and still less was it a history of the Russian Revolution. It was, however, history through biography, if only a vignette of it. It surveyed the final stages of the decline and fall of the Romanov dynasty and the initial course of the Revolution, but it did so through the eyes of the Tsar. The focus of my interest was the Tsar, and not the Revolution. If I wrote entirely from printed sources, much of the material was nevertheless primary in that it consisted of journals, correspondence and depositions. As secondary evidence, there was a gold mine of memoirs and, among some important histories, there was the magisterial work, *The Fall of the Russian Monarchy*, by Sir Bernard Pares. Finally, there was the *Enquête Judiciare sur L'Assassinat de la Famille Impériale*, loosely known as the Sokolov Report.

The Sokolov Report was in those days a rare book, available only, so far as I could discover, in French. It may still be so, for much of what has been 'discovered' in the 1990s about the fate of the Imperial Family is clearly related in the Sokolov Report. It was written immediately after the murders on the basis of a systematic investigation on the spot in the interval of time between the capture of Ekaterinburg by the Whites and its recapture by the Reds. It provides first-rate evidence, which has stood the test of time. *Crown of Tragedy*, therefore, contained most of the essential information about what had happened to the Tsar, the Tsaritsa and their children in July 1918. Yet, as I write, this is now held to be something that has only come to light in the last few years since the collapse of the Soviet Union. In the interval, a surprising body of opinion continued to wonder if the Grand-Duchess Anastasia had survived and if she was, in fact, Anna Anderson.

To some, the fate of the Imperial Family and the stages by which it came about, may seem to be of paltry importance in relation to the vast historical shifts that encompassed it. In absolute terms this must be so. And yet, as seems to have become increasingly apparent in Russia and elsewhere, the death of the Tsar and his family has a symbolic significance which far outstrips the mere fact of the event itself. This at any rate is how I saw it, and that was the reason why I wrote *Crown of Tragedy*.

In his review of the book, Lord Birkenhead obviously sensed this point. He was generous in praise of my work, which he described as 'unpretentious and absorbing' and hard to put down. He said that I had told the story with due sympathy for the Imperial Family, but that I had not glossed over the characters of the Tsar and the Tsaritsa, who had contributed so much to their own fate. It would have been too much to expect A.J.P. Taylor to take the same line. Even so, he too was generous in praise of the 'admirable sympathy and careful detail' with which I had described the fall of the Tsar. He was less impressed by my knowledge of the historical background. He condemned me for calling the Bolsheviks 'social revolutionaries'; he thought they were 'social democrats'. This comment caused me no undue distress, but I was puzzled by it, and I still cannot see how Taylor could think of the Bolsheviks as democrats. He also thought it very ignorant of me to say that the Petrograd Soviet had a majority of Bolsheviks from the outset, when in fact they only gained a majority in September 1917. Here I was, I believe, guilty of an error, but hardly one of sufficient gravity to justify Taylor's conclusion that it made it hard to recognize in me the 'trained historian' of the dust jacket.[2]

Of these two reviews, I preferred Birkenhead's to Taylor's, although I knew some would say that the first was by an amateur, and the second, a professional. Even so, Birkenhead, amateur or otherwise, proved to be a much more honest and conscientious biographer than Taylor, a matter to which I will return later in this chapter when I come to the Duke of Connaught. Anyhow, Taylor made it up to me when he presently wrote so admiringly of the skill and integrity with which the official history of the strategic air offensive had been written. Perhaps he only said this because he thought Webster had written what I wrote.

While *Crown of Tragedy* nourished my idea of history through biography, I did not think of myself as a biographer. Indeed, I declined a number of invitations to become one. Among these, the most interesting was from Ronald Lewin on behalf of the Hutchinson Publishing Group. He urged me to write the life of Lord Portal; but after anxious thought I declined that too. Knowing what I now do about Portal's attitude to the official history of the strategic air offensive, I am glad that he was not burdened with this particular suggestion. In any case, writing the lives of people who are still living places the author under a double disadvantage. He cannot complete his work because the story is not finished and he will be aware of the sensitivities of his subject.[3]

In 1974, Prince Henry, Duke of Gloucester, died. He had been President of the Imperial War Museum since 1936 and, from 1960, when I became director, I had met him at regular intervals. He was not a conversationalist and gave the impression of thinking that everyone else was more important than he was. His lack of small talk and nervous habit of seeming to giggle made him rather hard going, but I saw in him some attractive qualities. Among these was his preference for talking to underdogs rather than top cats. In the Museum, he tended to sheer off the Trustees and make a bee-line for the warders. There was also an underlying common sense about the man which somehow I had not expected to find in a prince. I think that he thought I was too punctilious and respectful towards him; I thought he was very unbending and kind to me. After his death, I was invited by Princess Alice to advise about what was to be done with his uniforms.

I was not an expert on uniforms but, being director of the Imperial War Museum, I suppose I was taken to be. One did not have to be an expert, however, to see that Prince Henry's array was a very splendid one and it straightaway occurred to me that they would make the heart of a wonderfully picturesque exhibition in the Museum. It would add a touch of colour and romance to the grimmer business with which we were normally preoccupied. This was approved and we put on the *Soldier Royal* exhibition in which all Prince Henry's uniforms, all his orders and medals and other personalia were displayed alongside the linking thread of a photographic narrative of his life and service. The exhibition was a huge success, thanks to the skill of Mike Houlihan, Keeper of my Department of Exhibitions, and his staff. The public entirely took the point of a touch of colour and romance.

I knew that Princess Alice was satisfied with the result, but I was taken entirely by surprise when she suddenly asked me to write the life of Prince Henry. I was full of apprehension; I still did not think of myself as a biographer and even as I tried to do so, I thought there would not be much primary material on which to base such a book. I did not expect Prince Henry to have been much of a correspondent and I had no desire at all to write a royalty-watcher book. My first biographical lesson about Prince Henry was now at hand. Brief enquiry quickly showed that my impression of him as being unlikely to have written many letters was wholly wrong. His valet, Amos, staggered under the weight of boxes of correspondence which he brought up from somewhere understairs in Kensington Palace. Much more came to light at Barnwell Manor and in the Royal archives in Windsor Castle. The problem was not how to find primary material but how to digest it.

Prince Henry was the third son and fourth child of King George V and Queen Mary. At his birth, he seemed to be comfortably remote from the throne and he was thus brought up in slightly less stringently conditioned circumstances than his two elder brothers. He was, for example, sent to school instead of being educated within the confines of the court. He was in fact the first son of a British King to go to school. He then pursued a career to a greater extent than was permitted to the Prince of Wales or the Duke of

York. When his father died in 1936 and his eldest brother came to the throne as Edward VIII, Prince Henry was nearing the stage at which he might have expected to be given command of his regiment; the career he had followed was in the Army. The abdication of Edward VIII ruined this prospect. Prince Henry suddenly found himself as the next adult in line of succession to the throne. He became Regent Designate and remained so until Princess Elizabeth reached the age of eighteen some eight years later. To his bitter disappointment – the Duke of Connaught wrote him a letter of sympathy about it – he was promoted from major to major-general and given a heavy load of ceremonial duties in support of King George VI. Such were the salient factors that conditioned his life. There was no escape for Prince Henry from the scene of great events and the company of great men.[4]

An ordinary man in an extraordinary position, which is so often the lot of a prince, makes an interesting subject in itself and, for a biographer, an unusual one. Most biographies are about extraordinary people and are full of explanations as to how it came about that they achieved whatever it was that caught the eye of history and attracted their biographers. The tensions in such studies are often concerned with ability and ambition, and how people outdo or out-achieve each other. In the case of princes, and notably in that of Prince Henry, quite different considerations prevail. Here the tension is about how the ordinary man adjusts to the extraordinary position into which he is born. Moreover, the factor of royalty is a levelling one, for whatever may be the talent or lack of it in the prince, he will still have the problem of adjusting to his position. The conventional biographer has the task of discovering how his subject achieved the position of eminence that caused the biography to be written. The Royal biographer has approximately the opposite one of finding out the extent to which the subject succeeded in filling the position that birth conferred upon him. Neither the one task nor the other seems to me to be more or less interesting. The answer to the question, was Prince Henry worth a biography? is obviously that he was; he was the son of a king, the brother of two kings and the uncle of the present Queen. The interesting question is, what sort of a fist did he make of that?

This question is of interest to people who believe in the efficacy of a constitutional monarchy, which entails a Royal Family, and to those on the lunatic fringe who think that some other type of head of state would be better. Either side can use the same information to defend themselves or to attack each other. Both require royal biographies as ammunition. Then there is the further interest, as I have already mentioned, in that the prince usually plays his part on the stage of great events and amidst the great men and women who have helped to mould them. Even if he contributes nothing to the making of history, he is hard pressed not to reflect it. If these considerations are taken to be valid, Prince Henry seems an excellent subject for a biography.

And there was in his case, as I have mentioned, the added advantage of the copious documentary evidence of his life which survived him.

Prince Henry died in 1974. My biography of him was published in 1980. It may be thought that my study was written too soon after his death. This is not a question of perspective. My perspective of Prince Henry in the years immediately following his death may be somewhat different from one that might be seen twenty or thirty years later, but it will not necessarily be better or worse. The question which does arise concerns the feelings of his family and friends who lived to see the book. This could well have raised insuperable difficulties. That it did not was owing to the attitude of his widow and his son who, whatever they may have thought of what I wrote, showed no propensity for censoring or even influencing it. Also, although I had no wish to gloss over Prince Henry's warts, I equally had no wish to be harsh about them. A biographer has no need to be hostile to his subject and, in my opinion, he usually does better to be sympathetic. I admit that this does not deal with Alan Bullock's problem in writing about Hitler and Stalin but, for my part, I have never wished to write about people whom I dislike.

The advantage of writing about Prince Henry so soon was that I could pick the brains and memories of many who knew him well, and some very well. Particularly interesting among these were his wife's sister-in-law, Rachel Scott, his valet, Amos, his chauffeur, Prater, and several of his comrades from his early days as a young cavalry officer. Then there was Wilfred Thesiger who, though still an undergraduate at Oxford, had joined Prince Henry's entourage for his visit to Abyssinia in 1930 to represent the King at Haile Sellassie's coronation. From these and many others, I was able to obtain a spectrum of impressions of Prince Henry in many different settings and at the various stages of his life. The facts, as remembered by these people, often conflicted with those indicated in the documents, but while memory may often deceive as to facts, it may equally be superior to documents in conveying impressions. The ideal is to have both sources, and here they were.

For the most part, Prince Henry filled the role of an understudy. His independent military career was abruptly truncated in 1936 and he was not required as Regent, since George VI survived until after Princess Elizabeth had attained her majority. His duties during the war, if at times extremely hazardous, were limited by the fact that, trained to the level of a major, he had become a major-general. His one exercise of independence was as Governor-General of Australia, to which he was sworn in in January 1945. But even this appointment was of shorter duration than he wished because the King required him at home in 1947 so that he himself could visit South Africa. Nevertheless, Prince Henry's role as an understudy carried him on royal duties all over the world from Tokyo to Addis Ababa, from Freemantle to

Nairobi, from Habbaniya to Colombo and from Kuala Lumpur to Belfast. The study of his life produces vignettes of the history that summoned these and many other missions; it also produces unique angles on the history of the monarchy in the first half of the twentieth century. While Prince Henry had hardly any personal role in the making of history, the study of his life affords illuminating sidelights upon it.

As my work on the life of the Duke of Gloucester drew to a conclusion, the Registrar of the Royal Archives, Miss Jane Langton, gave to me her informed opinion that his great uncle, the Duke of Connaught, was the most documented British prince of any age. I took this as a challenge; I sought and was granted access to the material with a view to writing the life and times of Prince Arthur, Duke of Connaught.

Prince Arthur lived from 1850 until 1942. A godson of the Duke of Wellington, he died in the year of Montgomery's victory at Alamein. He was the third son and seventh child of Queen Victoria and Prince Albert, but unlike Prince Henry he was always comfortably remote from the succession to the throne and the position of Regent. On the other hand, he was the acknowledged favourite son of the Queen, which had its awkward side.

From his earliest days, Prince Arthur was destined for the Army and, as soon as he was old enough to join it, he took up the profession with the utmost enthusiasm and dedication, which proved to be enduring. His military career was hampered by the imposition of ceremonial royal duties from time to time, by over-rapid promotion, and by the Queen's intention that he should eventually succeed her cousin, the Duke of Cambridge, as Commander-in-Chief. Nevertheless, Prince Arthur was able to match the skills required to discharge all the military appointments he received, although these came to him earlier than they would have done had he not been a prince. When, in 1876, he was promoted lieutenant-colonel and placed in command of the 1st Battalion, the Rifle Brigade, he was perfectly competent to carry out his duties. Yet more impressively, when promoted major-general in 1882 and placed in command of the Guards Brigade in the Egyptian Expeditionary Force, he exactly met what was required of him by the Commander-in-Chief, Sir Garnet Wolseley. This was the execution of a hazardous night march on the eve of the Battle of Tel-el-Kebir and the movement of his brigade into action at the right point and at the right time. As a lieutenant-general in command of the Aldershot Division, he got the better of Sir Redvers Buller in the manoeuvres of August and September 1898 and he achieved this in spite of the fact that Buller was deemed to have had the better staff.[5]

Nor when he reached the higher ranks of the Army, was Prince Arthur prepared to coast as his superiors often expected him to do. As Commander-in-Chief of the Bombay Army, he constantly sought its modernization and he was an early advocate of a unified Indian Army. His recommendations, however, fell on deaf ears, both in the Indian Government and the War Office. When, in 1904, he was appointed Inspector-General of the Forces with instructions to advise the new Army Council on how the so-called army reforms were working in the field, he did so, which they had not expected, and which caused them much embarrassment.[6]

Important and interesting as was Prince Arthur's military career, it was not the most significant or the most interesting element in his life. His greatest and most historically important position was as Governor-General of Canada from 1911 to 1916. Those years saw a great leap forward in Canada's awareness and assertion of her position as an independent state. Prince Arthur, who welcomed and encouraged the development as much as any Canadian, paid scant attention to outmoded directives from the Colonial Office in London, and acted the part of a constitutional Canadian sovereign, advising and warning and watching with pride as Canada advanced towards adulthood. He also watched with alarm when the Canadian war effort fell under the direction of Sam Hughes, the Minister of Militia and Defence.[7]

These exemplary observations of some of the principal aspects of Prince Arthur's long life suffice to show that, if not quite so near the front line of royal function as Prince Henry, he was more gifted and lived much longer than his great-nephew. This gave his biographer a longer view of his place in history and especially the development of the monarchy than had been provided by Prince Henry. His considerable talents and his opportunities to concentrate also meant that his direct contribution to the making of history was significant. As a figure of historical interest, then, Prince Arthur was more prominent than any other British prince of modern times, apart from those who came to the throne. As an exemplar of the royal function and the royal career, Prince Arthur occupies a position of unique eminence.

This was a large part of his attraction to me as a biographer. The rest of it lay in the wealth of the sources for the study of his life which survived him and about which Jane Langton had spoken. This material proved to be even more extensive than she had imagined. In the Royal Archives, I found and read some fifteen thousand items concerning Prince Arthur. In this context an item, it should be noted, meant something ranging in scope from a single telegram to a long series of journals. There were five major classes of relevant documents in the Public Record Office and ten in the Public Archives of Canada. Further important material came to light in the Hove Central Library, National Army Museum, Wiltshire Record Office, Durham University Archive, National Library of Scotland, Churchill Archive Centre, University of Sussex Library, School of Oriental and African Studies, Royal Commonwealth Society Library, Nottinghamshire Record Office, House of Lords Record Office, Imperial War Museum, British Library, Cambridge

University Library, West Kent Archives Office, India Office Library and Records and the Bodleian Library.

I mention these sources to indicate the breadth as well as the volume of the material and also to show the extent to which Prince Arthur's activities imprinted themselves upon the historical record. Yet before my biography appeared, little of consequence had been published about him, and what had, largely traduced him. One of the reasons for this apparent lethargy was that, at the time of his death in January 1942, Britain was in desperate straits, having faced defeat on nearly all fronts. There was much for the King and the nation to think about other than the passing of the old Duke, who had been out of the public eye for the last few years. Queen Mary was one who did think of him, but she was told by the Royal Librarian that little material upon which a biography could be based had survived. He understood that Prince Arthur had been in the habit of burning all his letters as soon as they were answered. So, nothing had been done and the field was left open to those who wished to construct their own images.

In Canada, a legend arose to the effect that Prince Arthur had treated the Dominion as a colony and that his haughty royal eye had been displeased by the raw Canadian patriots who crossed his path. In particular, rumour had it that he had arrived in Canada with his mind already poisoned against the Canadian folk hero, Sam Hughes, by his predecessor as Governor-General, Earl Grey. In fact, Prince Arthur's conduct and attitudes in Canada are fully documented virtually on a day to day basis. From this evidence, it is clear that he had had no such prejudices and that the reverse was true. He welcomed Canadian patriots with sincere warmth and rejoiced in the informality and directness that characterized their style. In particular, he was initially perfectly content with Sam Hughes, the Minister of Militia and Defence and, unfortunately for the legend, he wrote to the King at the time saying so.[8]

What Prince Arthur had said to the King, and the other massive evidence about his attitude to Canada in general, and Sam Hughes in particular, was, however, still buried in the Royal Archives when the legend passed to the second generation, where it was taken up by Dr R.G. Haycock. As lately as 1986, Dr Haycock published a biography of Sam Hughes, who, in the title of the book, was announced as a 'controversial Canadian'. It is noteworthy that this book was published by the Wilfrid Laurier University Press in collaboration with the Canadian War Museum, the Canadian Museum of Civilization and the National Museums of Canada. Together with this authentication and its array of footnotes, it might well be taken to be authoritative. Alas, Dr Haycock was convinced that Prince Arthur was prejudiced against Sam Hughes even before he met him and that thereafter his attitude was 'overbearing and arrogant'. Building on this assumption, Dr Haycock went on to paint a picture of a dispute between an apoplectic old royal field-marshal, whose uniform collar was too tight, and whose view was that of a stuffed-shirt English 'aristocrat' on the one hand, and a good, bluff, self-made Canadian, whose worst fault was impulsiveness on the other.[9]

Dr Haycock may have thought that it was this impulsiveness that led Sam Hughes to demand of Prince Arthur that he should be awarded, not just the VC, but the VC and bar for services he claimed he had rendered in the South African War some eleven years earlier. Dr Haycock described this demand as 'wearisome'. Prince Arthur, at the time, took it to be a sign of conceit and madness. It was such conceit and madness which caused him to lose confidence in Sam Hughes and, when the war came, to wish to have him dismissed from the government. This arose, not from Prince Arthur's dislike of self-made Canadians or his overbearing and arrogant attitude, but from his fear that a mad and corrupt minister in pursuit of glory on the battlefields of the Western Front would bleed Canada white. The burden of Dr Haycock's biography of Sam Hughes is, indeed, that the man was mad and probably corrupt too; the rest of the proof of the matter is to be found in the documents he cited. It has long since been entirely apparent, even from published material alone, that Sam Hughes's involvement in the Ross rifle scandal and associated scandals connected with the equipment of Canadian soldiers in the First World War wholly justified Prince Arthur's wish to have him dismissed. Dr Haycock, who knew all this, nevertheless failed to qualify his harsh judgement of Prince Arthur, even though he was quite unable to document it.[10]

A.J.P. Taylor outdid Dr Haycock in that he convicted Prince Arthur of bad conduct by citing, as a letter of Prince Arthur's, a minute written by another hand which had nothing whatsoever to do with the prince. Though this was about the rather boring matter of an honour for Max Aitken, later Lord Beaverbrook, it serves to show how history is distorted by those who enjoy perpetuating legends and are unscrupulous about the use of their sources. It also shows that the sport of traducing Prince Arthur was popular.

In his biography of Aitken, Taylor accused Prince Arthur of lying to the King about the granting of an honour for his subject, or should I say his master? Certainly, Prince Arthur did not wish an honour to be conferred on Aitken, whose reputation in Canada, he thought, was unsavoury. As the Prime Minister, Robert Borden, left the decision to the Governor-General, Prince Arthur excluded Aitken from the Canadian submissions. This was annoying for the Colonial Secretary, Bonar Law, because he had a debt to Aitken to repay. He did not, however, want to be seen to be doing so. He had hoped that the reward might come from Prince Arthur's Canadian list. When it did not, he put in the recommendation on the British Prime Minister's list and Aitken was created a baronet in the Birthday Honours of 1916. Taylor, in describing this episode, stated that Borden made the recommendation for the honour to Prince Arthur (which he did not) and that Prince Arthur forwarded it to the King with an accompanying letter. In this letter, Taylor claimed, Prince Arthur told the King that Borden had 'regretted an honour being conferred on a man with a Canadian reputation such as the particular individual possessed'. Taylor did not believe that Borden would have said that and he concluded that Prince Arthur had lied to the King and was not 'over scrupulous when his personal feelings were involved'. The shocking facts are that this 'letter' was not written by Prince Arthur, it was not written to the King, it was not written in 1916 and it was not a letter. The exact phrase, which Taylor attributed to Prince Arthur, belongs in an internal minute addressed to Bonar Law, probably by his Private Secretary, but certainly not by Prince Arthur.[11]

I first heard A.J.P. Taylor lecturing when I was an undergraduate at Oxford. He used to appear gownless and without notes of any kind. All the others I heard wore gowns and consulted notes. Taylor would perch on a table and hold forth about Bismarck, or some such subject, in a series of short, epigrammatic and often startling sentences. While doing this, he was quite still; he did not use hand movements to emphasize points nor did he wag his head about or laugh at his own jokes. He was the most brilliant lecturer I have ever heard. Even so, on returning to my rooms, I sometimes found that things Taylor had announced as facts did not always seem to be confirmed as such by the books I had. Later, he used exactly the same technique in delivering his televised history lectures. The huge success of these was owing to his ready flow of spontaneous language and, I believe, to his ability to move from the lecture rooms of Oxford to the television studios without any change of style. Brilliant he undoubtedly was, but historically minded – in the best sense of that phrase – he was not. Taylor was more concerned with the impact of what he said and wrote, than with its historical validity. What he wrote about Prince Arthur in his biography of Beaverbrook, though it was about a trivial matter, shows that he was willing to cook the books as well.

The study of Prince Arthur's functioning as Governor-General of Canada is valuable for reasons that are much more weighty than the correction of unjustified criticism. The documentation of his work provides a panorama of Canadian politics and society, and a picture of the Dominion at large which is unique. It is not just the qualities and activities of Sam Hughes that were thrown into stark relief by the Governor-General. There is also ample evidence of the strengths and weaknesses of the Borden Cabinet and especially of the Prime Minister himself. Prince Arthur and Borden got on well for the most part and found much in each other to respect. Even so, Borden's weakness when confronted with an increasingly mad Sam Hughes becomes horribly apparent through his dealings with the Governor-General. Also, the Governor-General can be seen to have lost some of his customary poise in the face of the same problem.

Prince Arthur's constant and extensive touring carried him, often several times, to every quarter of the huge Dominion. He certainly travelled more widely than any previous Governor-General and, it is safe to say, much more so than Borden or any member of his Cabinet. Beyond its picture of politics and society, the documentation of Prince Arthur's work as Governor-General provides a view of the dramatic developments occurring in so many parts of the land during his term of office. His life during these years intermingled with the history of Canada and is a striking example of the significance of history revealed through biography.

If historians ignore Prince Arthur's part in the aftermath of the army reforms in Britain, as they largely have done, their appreciation of the efficacy of these reforms will be defective. The same principle applies to the history of Canada in the crucial period from 1911 to 1916. By neglecting Prince Arthur, Canadian historians have missed important and revealing evidence. Strangely, however, there is resistance in Canada to this method of revision. Apparently there are still many tracts in the land where criticism of Sam Hughes is frowned upon. The madness of the man and the corruption of his administration, which landed Canadian troops in France with rifles which jammed, boots which disintegrated and shovels which broke, seem, in the distance of time, to matter less than his proclaimed view that a Canadian was altogether a better thing than an Englishman.

Of the three figures on whom I have focused in my attempt to get at history through biography, the Tsar Nicholas II was the most important. His importance derived from the fact that fate placed him on the throne of Russia in 1894. There was also his indecisive nature and his anxiety about his wife and son. Chance made him a king. Character made him a pawn. The view of Russian history as seen through his eyes is nevertheless pervasive and illuminating. The interest of the subject arises from the contrast between Nicholas's qualities as a man and his defects as a sovereign. Prince Henry was the least important of the three figures because fate decreed that he should remain in reserve. Had he been further from the throne or had he come to it, his life might have been more rewarding. As it was, his opportunities and his talents restricted his role to making a dogged journey along the path of duty. This he followed, sometimes in the face of great danger and often under considerable difficulty, until illness brought an end to his active life in 1967. The chief importance of his life is the light it sheds on the functioning of the modern constitutional monarchy in a succession of crises. Prince Arthur, further from the throne than Prince Henry and much less important than Nicholas II, presents a richer harvest of history through biography than either. His field was wider and his life much longer. His ability to play the full part of a prince and at the same time pursue an important career mark him as distinctly unusual. His gift for public speaking, his social charm and his diplomatic skills were the ideal equipment for his many royal roles. Though by no means brilliant, he was essentially competent, or at least competent enough to make a substantial success of an important public career as a soldier and a proconsul. The interest of Prince Arthur lies in his life and its influence upon and its reflection of his times.

Finally, in the case of Prince Arthur there is an added bonus. I completed my exhaustive study of the documentation of his life within eleven years. Working on the same scale, I could not have done that for Queen Victoria's life in fifty years. Indeed, the surviving amount of primary evidence about her is so vast that an authoritative biography is virtually beyond the reach of any writer who starts work over the age of thirty. So far, no authoritative biography of her has been written. The best attempt was made by Cecil Woodham-Smith, but time ran out for her long before she had completed her task. Perhaps the only living biographer with the intellectual stamina to finish such a study is Martin Gilbert. But he started work on Churchill in his mid-twenties and even if he had the inclination, he could not hope to have the time in which to do full justice to Victoria. The bonus provided by Prince Arthur's life is the sharp reflections it casts on his mother's life. From this source, there is much to be learnt about her character as wife, mother and sovereign, which is not in her biographies.

It may well be thought that my choice of subjects for biographies is strange. As I have indicated, none of them was a great man and none had more than a limited effect on the course of history. Instead of Nicholas II, why not, for example, choose Stolypin? Instead of Prince Henry, why not choose Sir Gilbert Laithwaite? Instead of Prince Arthur, why not choose Field-Marshal Wolsley? The answer is that I am fascinated by the role of princes and the nature of their functions in the modern world. My reward is that this preoccupation often opens my eyes to an aspect of history which I would otherwise have missed and which other historians have not seen. It should be recognized that, if one wishes to see something in the dark, the best course is to look at something else slightly to one side of it.

A splendid example of this truth is provided by Sir J.E. Lloyd's biography of Owen Glendower. Necessarily, this can only give a sketchy picture of Glendower, about whom so few basic facts have survived. In his attempt, however, Lloyd casts brilliant shafts of light upon late mediaeval Europe in general, and upon the court and rule of Henry IV in particular. Who would expect to find such strange repercussions of Papal rivalries in the fastnesses of Wales in the second half of the fourteenth century?[12]

Conclusions
and Comparisons

Historians have often written about the art of history. They have generally done so in theoretical terms that are far removed from practicalities. As their theses are often based on lectures, which do not easily turn into good books, their observations are usually conveyed in language designed to be heard rather than read. What they produce may well be vastly stimulating and entertaining for undergraduates. Whether it has much value for those who have advanced a little further, or for the general public, is another question.

I think historians can get themselves into an unnecessary muddle; and because of their detachment from actualities they have a tendency to come down on the side of rather silly propositions. Professor Geoffrey Barraclough's *History in a Changing World*, for example, stands condemned by its own title. When in all history has the world not been changing? Professor John Vincent tells us that history is confined to what has been written down. Does he then expect historians to ignore evidence such as that provided by the iceman recently discovered in the Alps, who belonged to a society that could neither read nor write? Even Professor E.H. Carr, in his *What is History?* gets into a muddle about the answer to his question. He mentions the case of a gingerbread vendor who was kicked to death in 1850. He thinks that this is not history because it was only a trivial incident. But Dr Kitson Clark cited this triviality in his Ford Lectures in Oxford. That, Carr then tells us, makes it a candidate for history; if another historian takes up Kitson Clark's reference, Carr continues, then the gingerbread vendor will become history. This is an absurd argument. Everything that has happened or existed in the past is history, even if only a small part of it can be discovered by historians.[1]

My belief that everything is history at least has the advantage that I have saved a lot of time by not arguing about which bits qualify and which do not. It also means that I do not have to worry about the philosophical differences between history and archaeology, science, art and literature. All of these, possessing their past, are history, and all of them produce tools that historians may use, depending upon what they are studying and how they describe it.

Believing that everything is history also has a satisfactorily levelling effect on one's view of all its different aspects that historians choose to present. I recognize that some of those aspects may reasonably be described as being more important than others and that, biographically, some people are much more important than others. But even these distinctions beg the question of what is meant by 'important'. For example, is an aspect of history which seems more relevant to the present age necessarily more important than one which seems less relevant or irrelevant? Moreover, something which today seems irrelevant may tomorrow become relevant.

Worse than the distinction of relevance, however, is naming one aspect of it as fashionable and another as unfashionable. Fashion is a more controversial concept than importance, but not because its meaning is not clear: it is all too clear. It is because fashion can damage the long-term value of historical work. Many excellent writers are drawn or driven into writing about affairs and people more on account of their being fashionable than of there being scope for the discovery of new information. The numerous biographies of Edward VII that have appeared since Philip Magnus's study was published in 1964, provide a case in point. There is also the pernicious habit of regarding books that seem to be written in unfashionable terms as being out of date and therefore in need of replacement. Of course revisions of history have to be made by each succeeding generation, and such revisions will and should reflect the essence of the age in which they are made. That is not, however, the same thing as writing everything in fashionable, or politically correct, terms. Even Vernon Bogdanor in his important and interesting study, *The Monarchy and the Constitution*, falls into this trap, and it is irritating to find that he applies the 'he or she' rule to the point of absurdity. For example, Bogdanor, when discussing the constitutional conventions of modern Norway, writes that the sovereign has seldom been asked to exercise 'his or her discretion'. He must know that all three sovereigns of modern Norway have been kings and that a queen regnant is yet to come.[2]

My chief aim as an historian has been to discover and reveal new knowledge. Before the official history of the strategic air offensive was published, no significant literature on the subject existed. It could not have done, as the primary evidence was contained in files that were not then open to public inspection. Nor, which is stranger, have I seen any important addition to the body of knowledge contained in that history in works subsequently published. I had expected that there would be revisions of – and original additions to – what Webster and I produced. They have not appeared. The fundamentals of strategic air power, it seems, have not yet entered into the general field of historical research, either in Britain or in America. The reasons, I believe, are threefold.

In planning the structure of the official history of the strategic air offensive,

I evolved, and Webster approved, an original vocabulary. Generally agreed meanings, even for the most fundamental phrases such as 'air superiority', or 'strategic bombing', did not exist. The need for definitions arose from the newness of the subject. It did not arise in the case of naval and military history because over the centuries those subjects had yielded generally understood vocabularies. Between the student of history and the strategic air offensive there is a language barrier, unless he is content simply to accept Webster and Frankland's syntax. If he does that, he is well on the way to accepting their interpretations. Second, while Webster and I were at work on the official history, the bulk of the primary British material was still in the Cabinet Office and the Air Historical Branch of the Air Ministry. For the most part, the files were still in their working contexts and they were easy to find. Since those days, they have been transferred to the Public Record Office. Here the Cabinet files are still easy to find, but the Air files are not. The problems involved in carrying out systematic research into these Air files are immensely greater than they used to be.

The third reason lies in the United States. There the Air Force authorities kept a watchful and commanding eye on the work of the official historians. Their results were therefore nearer to what Sir Maurice Dean and Lord Portal wished should have been contained, or not contained, in the British air history. There was also an unfortunate difficulty arising from the creation of the independent United States Air Force after the Second World War. This meant that the records of the former Army Air Forces belonged to the Army and were by no means automatically made available to the air historians who were employed by the Air Force.

The consequences of all this have been disappointing for me. New knowledge needs revision, refinement and development. In the case of the strategic air offensive, the need has not been met. I am satisfied, however, that what I wrote in my thesis and the extension of it that Webster and I produced in the official history was new knowledge in the sense that the evidence adduced was to a great extent previously unknown and the conclusions reached were unexpected.

I cannot claim that my study of Nicholas II produced any new knowledge. All the evidence I made use of was contained in published, even if in some cases rather obscure, sources. *Crown of Tragedy*, as I have explained, was developed from a play. Although I did my best to make it historically valid, it was not a work of original research and, in that sense, it was the least historical of all the books I have written. Its only claim to be related to what I have chiefly aimed to achieve as an historian, is that it did introduce a more sympathetic view of Nicholas's life and, I believe, a fairer one, than had prevailed when the discussion seemed to be dominated by communists and royalists.

My studies of Prince Henry and of Prince Arthur, on the other hand, were wholly original works which, for that reason, were fully as exciting to write as was the history of the strategic air offensive. Neither was a fashionable subject and some would argue that neither was an important one. That does not matter to me. What does matter is that I found them both engagingly interesting subjects. Indeed, in both cases, as my work progressed, I found them to be more interesting than I had expected when I started. Interest, in my view, is the key factor which should govern a historian's selection of subjects. This is not the way to court popularity. Professional colleagues and critics will say, why choose that when such and such could have been done? But that too does not matter to me. The job-satisfaction of producing a book which answers one's own curiosity and which engages one's own active interest, is sufficient unto itself. It is, I believe, the best kind of motivation open to an historian, and it has been the dynamo without which I do not think I could have faced the long stints of exacting research that were involved.

I have found too that the choice of idiosyncratic subjects has the added value of broadening one's interest, knowledge and outlook in surprising ways. Before I wrote the life of Prince Arthur, I had, for example, thought of the history of Canada as a dull subject. This was a silly and prejudiced view deriving from ignorance. Prince Arthur freed me from it. I detected another example of the same thing, this time from the other end of the telescope, in Professor Margaret Gowing's official history of atomic energy. This was a subject of apparently specialized interest and, had I not been invited to comment on the draft, I might well not have read it. I am glad I did because, in the course of describing the development of atomic energy in Britain, Gowing revealed more about the working of the Government and Civil Service than I have read in any constitutional history.[3]

The differences between presenting history in the gallery, on the screen and on the site, as also between those media and the writing of history on the page, are substantial. But the principle in all these cases is the same. The apparently wide freedom of presentation which the historian has on the page is in actuality restricted. He cannot include three-dimensional evidence, he cannot show the moving picture of the screen and he cannot convey the quality of original works of art. All these things can be done in the gallery, on the screen and on the site; but freedom of presentation in these cases is also restricted. Unless the object shown is entirely self-explanatory in historical terms, which few are, additional explanation is needed. In the gallery and on the site, the extent of this explanation is limited by the consideration that the object, and not the caption, is the primary evidence. On the screen, the explanation must be quick enough to allow the moving image to keep on moving.

All these historical modes of expression are complementary: they are not alternatives. If the exhibition, the site or the film are in the mind's eye while the book is read, the product of each alone will be many times enhanced. The same applies to the many permutations available. That is why I argue that the principle in the production or presentation of any of these modes is the same. The practice is vastly different. The work I did in the gallery, on the screen and on the site was more akin to that of a general editor on the page than an author; but the motivation, standards and objective should all be much the same. I recognize that there are many museumists who are not much – if at all – concerned with history. I, however, have been primarily an historian and only secondarily a museumist, which obviously is what the appointing authorities, who chose me to run the Imperial War Museum, expected.

By no means all historians would reckon that these 'extramural' modes of historical work fall within the ambit of historians. Professor Vincent, for example, closes all but conventional avenues with the abrupt statement that 'History is not archaeology'. Each must judge for himself. I have declared my position.[4]

The exclusions and restrictions some historians like to impose on the practice, or even the existence, of history, find another curious reflection in the categories into which it is customary to place the practitioners. These are variously described as academic, professional, amateur, serious or popular. I have never quite understood what these terms mean. A popular historian is presumably one who sells a great number of copies of his works. But the inference that he therefore must be playing to the gallery, or that he is slipshod or repetitive, is not necessarily justified. Was G.M. Trevelyan any of these things? Was Gibbon? An amateur historian is presumably one who is unpaid or perhaps untrained, and the inference is that he is inferior to a professional. I admit that I was surprised to be told by Sir Charles Webster that one of the best books he had ever read on an aspect of his own special subject was by a Major John Hall. In December 1951, I bought the book, *England and the Orleans Monarchy*, which had been published in 1912. I soon saw why Webster had been so impressed. All the same, Major Hall was an amateur, or at least Webster said he was. All these considerations and my own dubious position with regard to them, have led me to distrust such categorizations.[5]

Historians, nevertheless, do fall into various categories. I prefer to label them with simpler definitions, such as good and bad. Between such extremes it is not difficult to use equally simple terms for works to define what is meant, such as scholarly and well written, scholarly but badly written, unscholarly but interesting, unscholarly and repetitive, and so on. By scholarly, I mean work that is based on an assemblage of the ascertainable evidence, a carefully balanced evaluation of it and an estimate of what may reasonably be concluded from it, with a display of the sources used. This is what I have sought to achieve since, when I was an undergraduate, R.B. Wernham filled me with belief in such ideas. No doubt I am harsher to other historians in the light of them than I am to myself.

So much for my conclusions about the nature of history and of the classification of historians, and how my own work seems to relate to them. It is only now, after these many years of endeavour, that I have begun the serious consideration of such things. My curiosity, my wish to delve into unknown or misunderstood aspects of history and the rush of the ensuing work have been sufficient to occupy my mind. For the same reasons, it is only recently that I have sought to define what, in the light of my own experience, the use of history is. I think that all historians should be concerned with this question, for it is natural for those of any calling to wonder what use their work is and the work of others in their profession.

The polarities for this question are conveniently illustrated by the conflicting views of Arnold Toynbee and H.A.L. Fisher. Toynbee believed that he had discerned rhythms and patterns in history which, having governed the past, indicated the future. As his work approached its end, he wrote that he had always kept one foot in the present and the other in the past. From this stance, he believed that he could peer into the future. H.A.L. Fisher, writing in 1936, when Toynbee's fame was rising towards its zenith, perhaps with a touch of sarcasm declared that only men wiser and more learned than he could discern in history 'a plot, a rhythm, a predetermined pattern'. All he could see, he wrote, was 'one emergency following upon another'. That was as nearly the opposite of Toynbee's view as it was possible to get. But it was not quite as opposite as might be supposed, or even as Fisher believed. He compared his succession of emergencies to a succession of waves; he did not pause to consider that the historical study of the behaviour of waves, tides and wind directions does in fact provide a sound basis for forecasting their future behaviour. Moreover, Fisher compromised his own conclusion by claiming that he could detect in history a measure of progress. Although he thought that the gains of one generation might be lost by the next, he could still see the 'fact' of progress 'written plain and large on the page of history'.[6]

By progress, Fisher meant advance towards liberal concepts of civil, political and religious freedom. And so, despite his protestations, he could see a direction in history or, to put the same thing in another way, he saw the future as a contest between the further advance of liberalism and the totalitarian threat. In principle, this was not greatly different from Toynbee's view of the use of history, which suggested that mankind's choice was between catastrophe and universal government and civilization. He even hoped that his own work as an historian might help to create the understanding which would avert the catastrophe and promote progress.[7]

My reservation about Toynbee's peering into the future and Fisher's claim that he could not do so is that both thought too big. Because their subjects were on the grand scale, Toynbee's being on the grandest scale imaginable, they could not bring data to bear on their conclusions that in its detail was of a consistent quality and accuracy. To finish their books within a lifespan, they had to rely on information supplied by a mass of much more specialized historians than they were. As these specialized historians were necessarily of varying quality, as they necessarily had a myriad of different view-points and as they worked on different scales, the aggregate of their output was incapable of producing sound evidence on which to base overall conclusions.

To be historically efficient, Toynbee would have had to know all the primary evidence about everything, and Fisher would have had the lesser but still unattainable task of knowing all the evidence about the history of Europe. I do not say that the work of these two titans and that of their predecessors and successors is valueless. On the contrary – particularly in the case of Toynbee – there is a stream of unusual historical insight and intellectual stimulus that goes beyond the bounds of what can be derived from ordinary historical research. There is also, again especially with Toynbee, a startling display of erudition. But as I understand it this is not history: it is theorizing about history, which is not the same thing.

If, as I believe, history is the assemblage and balancing of the best evidence available, it follows that it can only be undertaken on a relatively small scale, or, relative to Toynbee's, a very small scale. True history in this sense is not, alas, the truth because the surviving evidence of any event, however recent it may be, is only a small component of that event. Much of what happens disappears without trace as each hour of the day passes. The historian can only assemble and consider those bits of evidence which, for one reason or another, happen to survive. Thus, his conclusions, like those of Fisher and Toynbee, are likely to be wrong on many counts. But because his evidence is primary and is on a small enough scale to be considered in detail, they are likely to be less wrong than those of the titans. It is a question of providing sounder conclusions about smaller matters, or more unsound ones about larger matters. As a source of wisdom, in distinction from intellectual excitement, I think the smaller scale is the more effective.

The study of history from primary evidence is, in my view, a potent source of wisdom. The apparent truism that history does not repeat itself is not entirely true. In many respects, it often does. The reality is that people are often unable to perceive which parts of history have been repeated, and that historians can never predict with certainty which parts of it will be. Even so, although it may be overconfident to declare that there are lessons to be learnt in history, it is safe to say that history does offer indications. The history of reform, for example, indicates that the intentions of the benefactors are seldom reflected in the outcome of their measures. The liberation of the Russian serfs by Alexander II and the introduction of the British socialist economy by the Labour government of 1945 produced consequences which were not apparently expected by the Tsar and by Attlee's Labour cabinet. Over and over again, the outcome is similar: what the reformers expect does not happen. A sense of history would at least provide an early warning and at best might even conjoin reforming zeal with realistic appreciation. Had Hitler substituted the study of Napoleon's campaign of 1812 for his dream of Lebensraum, he might well have avoided the emasculation of the German army on the eastern front. Had Lord Trenchard read and digested Mahan's studies of the influence on history of sea power instead of indulging in the fantasy of a strategic revolution, Bomber Command would probably have been a much more effective weapon of war than it was.

It may not be reasonable to expect that such deductions should have been made without the guidance of hindsight. Whether it is reasonable or not, the fact remains that in these cases as in those of hosts of others the indications of history were available to those who had the wit to search for them. A sense of history is the first requirement for the attainment of that wit. Without a sense of history, people cannot know where they have come from or where they are, and so they can have no idea of where they are going.

Bibliography

ARTS COUNCIL AND IMPERIAL WAR MUSEUM, *The Rose of Death, Paintings and Drawings by Captain Albert Richards (1919–1945)*, 6th Airborne Division and Official War Artist

BARRACLOUGH, Geoffrey, *History in a Changing World*, Basil Blackwell, Oxford, 1955

BULLOCK, Alan, 'Has History Ceased to be Relevant?' *The Historian*, No.43, Autumn 1994

BOGDANOR, Vernon, *The Monarchy and the Constitution*, Clarendon Press, Oxford, 1995

CARR, E.H., *What is History?* 2nd ed, Penguin, London, 1990

COLLINGWOOD, R.G., *The Idea of History*, Clarendon Press, Oxford, 1946

CRAVEN, Wesley Frank and CATE, James Lea (ed), *The Army Air Forces in World War II*, 6 vols, University of Chicago Press, Chicago, 1948–55

DEAN, Sir Maurice, *The Royal Air Force and Two World Wars*, Cassell, London, 1979

ELLIS, L.F., *Victory in the West*, vol 1, HMSO, London, 1962

ELTON, G.R., *The Practice of History*, Fontana Press (re-issue), London, 1987

FISHER, H.A.L., *A History of Europe*, Arnold, London, 1936

FRANKLAND, Noble, *Documents on International Affairs 1955–1957*, 3 vols, OUP, Oxford, 1958–60

FRANKLAND, Noble, *Crown of Tragedy, Nicholas II*, Kimber, London, 1960

FRANKLAND, Noble, *The Bombing Offensive against Germany, Outlines and Perspectives*, Faber and Faber, London, 1965

FRANKLAND, Noble, *Bomber Offensive, The Devastation of Europe*, Macdonald, London, 1969, Ballantine, New York, 1970

FRANKLAND, Noble, *Prince Henry Duke of Gloucester*, Weidenfeld & Nicolson, London, 1980

FRANKLAND, Noble, *Witness of a Century, The Life and Times of Prince Arthur Duke of Connaught 1850–1942*, Shepheard-Walwyn, London, 1993

FRANKLAND, Noble, *The Planning of the Bomber Offensive and its Contribution to German Collapse*, unpublished thesis, 1951, PRO AIR 41/57

FRANKLAND, Noble, and WEBSTER Sir Charles, *The Strategic Air Offensive against Germany 1939–1945*, 4 vols, HMSO, London, 1961, cited as *SAO*

GARRETT, Stephen A., *Ethics and Air Power in World War II, The British Bombing of German Cities*, St Martin's Press, New York, 1993

GOWING, Margaret, *Britain and Atomic Energy 1939–1945*, Macmillan, London, 1964 (read in draft); *Independence and Deterrence*, 2 vols, Macmillan, London, 1974; Professor Gowing carried this history on from 1945 to 1952, thus producing the first peacetime British official history

HALL, Major John, *England and the Orleans Monarchy*, Smith Elder & Co, London, 1912

HAMPTON, James, *Selected for Aircrew, Bomber Command in the Second World War*, Air Research Publications, 1993

HARRIS, Sir Arthur, *Bomber Offensive*, Collins, London, 1947.

HARRIS, Sir Arthur, *Despatch on War Operations*, introduction by S. Cox, Frank Cass, Ilford, 1995

HASTINGS, Max, *Bomber Command*, first published 1979, Papermac re-issue, London, 1993

HAYCOCK, Ronald G., *Sam Hughes, The Public Career of a Controversial Canadian 1885–1916*, Wilfrid Laurier University Press in collaboration with the Canadian War Museum, the Canadian Museum of Civilization and the National Museums of Canada, 1986

JONES, H.A., and RALEIGH, Sir Walter, *The War in the Air*, 7 vols, Clarendon Press, Oxford, 1922–37

KEGAN, John, *The Battle for History*, Hutchinson, London, 1995

KIRBY, S.W., *The War against Japan*, vol 2, HMSO, London, 1958

LEE, David, '25 Years of Duxford' 2 parts, *Duxford Newsletter* September 1996 and January 1997

LLOYD, Sir John, *Owen Glendower*, first published 1931, Llanerch Publishers reprint, Felinfach, 1992

MAHAN, Captain A.T., *The Influence of Sea Power upon History 1660–1783*, Samson Low, Marston, Searl & Rivington, London, preface dated 1889

MORRIS, Richard, *Guy Gibson*, Viking, London, 1994

OVERY, R.J., *War Economy in the Third Reich*, OUP, Oxford, 1994

OVERY, R.J., *The Air War 1939–1945*, Europa Publications, London, 1980

POLAND, Rear-Admiral E.N., *The Torpedomen, the Story of HMS Vernon and her People 1872–1986*, privately published 1993 (ISBN 0859373967)

RALEIGH, Sir Walter, and JONES, H.A., *The War in the Air*, 7 vols, Clarendon Press, Oxford, 1922–37

RICHARDS, Denis, *Portal of Hungerford, The Life and Times of Marshal of the Royal Air Force Viscount Portal of Hungerford KG, GCB, OM, DSO, MC*, Heinemann, London, 1977

RICHARDS, Denis, *The Hardest Victory, RAF Bomber Command in the Second World War*, Hodder & Stoughton (John Curtiss Book), London, 1994

ROWSE, A.L., *Historians I have Known*, Duckworth, London, 1995

ROYAL AIR FORCE HISTORICAL SOCIETY, *Reaping the Whirlwind*, a symposium on the strategic bomber offensive 1939–45, Bracknell Paper No.4, 1993

SAWARD, Dudley, *'Bomber' Harris, The Story of Marshal of the Royal Air Force Sir Arthur Harris Bt., GCB, OBE, AFC, LLD*, Cassell, Buchan & Enright, London, 1984

TAYLOR, A.J.P., *Beaverbrook*, Hamish Hamilton, London, 1972

TOYNBEE, Arnold, *A Study of History*, OUP and Thames Hudson, Oxford and London, 1972

VERRIER, Anthony, *The Bomber Offensive*, Batsford, London, 1968

VINCENT, John, *An Intelligent Person's Guide to History*, Duckworth, London, 1995

WATT, D.C., *Survey of International Affairs 1963*, OUP, Oxford, 1977

WEBSTER, Sir Charles, *The Foreign Policy of Castlereagh* vol 1 1812–1815, vol 2 (2nd ed.) 1815–1822, G.Bell and Sons, London, 1931, 1934

WEBSTER, Sir Charles, *The Foreign Policy of Palmerston 1830–1841*, 2 vols, G. Bell and Sons, 1951.

WEBSTER, Sir Charles, and FRANKLAND, Noble, *The Strategic Air Offensive against Germany 1939–1945*, 4 vols, HMSO, London, 1961, cited as SAO

Source References

NOTE

Being distrustful of unsupported recollection, I have sought to document this book to the greatest possible extent, and I here supply the references to the sources I have used. My own archive (NF Arch) and the military archive of Sir Charles Webster (CW Arch) are not open to public inspection and, for the time-being, I have exclusive access to them. I have, however, shown where I have used these sources and in each case I have stated the nature of the item cited. In doing this, I have followed the method adopted by Sir Charles Webster and myself in our official history of the strategic air offensive. Though most of the documents we cited in that history were, at the time, closed to public inspection, we insisted upon the need to tell the reader what they were. So far as I can discover, we are unique among British official historians in that insistence. Even so, I maintain that we were right. Though at the time our readers could not look up the documents we had cited, they could at least see what types of evidence they furnished. The same, admittedly restricted, advantage applies in this case to the references to my own archive and that of Sir Charles Webster. Where more than one source is quoted in a single note, I have differentiated between them by using semicolons. I have used 'ibid' to show that the source in question is the same as the immediately preceding one, and 'ditto' to show that the correspondent, or writer of the memorandum, are the same as the immediately preceding ones.

ABBREVIATIONS

Adm	Admiralty
Arch	Archive
Air Min	Air Ministry
CAB	Cabinet document
COH	Committee for the Control of Official Histories
COS	Chiefs of Staff Committee
CRO	Commonwealth Relations Office
CW	Professor Sir Charles Webster
DST	Director of Staff Training, Air Ministry
DUS	Deputy Under Secretary of State, Air Ministry
encl	enclosure
FO	Foreign Office
IWM	Imperial War Museum
Min	Minute
MoW	Ministry of Works
NF	Noble Frankland
PM	Prime Minister
PRO	Public Record Office
PS	Private Secretary
RIIA	Royal Institute of International Affairs
S4	Air Ministry Secretariat 4
SAO	Webster and Frankland, *The Strategic Air Offensive against Germany*, 4 vols
telecon	telephone conversation
Treas Solic	Treasury Solicitor
WO	War Office

Introduction (pages 1 to 8)

1. Collingwood, *The Idea of History*; Elton, *The Practice of History*; Barraclough, *History in a Changing World*; Carr, *What is History?*; Bullock, 'Has History Ceased to be Relevant?' *The Historian*, Autumn 1994; Vincent, *An Intelligent Person's Guide to History*.
2. CW to Butler, 2nd November 1952, PRO CAB 140/103.
3. Raleigh and Jones, *The War in the Air*.

Chapter 1 (pages 9 to 34)

1. Collingwood, *The Idea of History*, p.8.
2. NF Diary, 23rd March 1941; 20th June 1941.
3. Ibid, 19th July 1942.
4. See below p.71 and *SAO* vol 2, pp.79–80.
5. Morris to NF, 14th July 1943; 4th October 1943, NF Arch.
6. NF Diary, 4th December 1942.
7. Ibid, 17th November 1942.
8. Ibid, *passim*; NF Flying Log Book.
9. N.F. Diary, 20th December 1942. My recollection of what Willis told me is confirmed in S.W. Kirby, *The War against Japan* vol 2, pp.117–18, though Willis is there given the initials A.V. In fact, they were A.U.
10. NF Flying Log Book, 28th February 1943; 10th April 1944.
11. NF Diary, 23rd April 1943; 29th April 1943; 25th April 1943.
12. Ibid, 29th April 1943.
13. Ibid, 6th May 1943; 8th May 1943; 9th May 1943.
14. Ibid, 5th–17th June 1943.
15. Ibid, 19th August 1943; 4th August 1943.
16. Ibid, 22nd August 1943.
17. NF Flying Log Book.
18. *SAO* vol IV, pp.4–6.
19. NF Flying Log Book.
20. Ibid; NF navigation chart (Munich), NF Arch.
21. NF Flying Log Book.
22. Ibid.
23. Ibid.
24. Ibid; for the history of *Goodwood*, see L.F. Ellis, *Victory in the West*, vol 1, pp.338ff.

Chapter 2 (pages 35 to 59)

1. NF Diary, 9th March 1948.
2. Illegibly signed letter, Air Min to N.F., 31st March 1948, NF Arch.
3. The bomber narratives, *The RAF in the Bombing Offensive against Germany*, were completed in six volumes and were issued anonymously. For Wernham's vol 1, part 1 and my vol 1, part 2, see PRO AIR 41/39.
4. Air Min correspondence, 31st October 1944–24th July 1945, PRO AIR 2/8372 encls 1A–37A.
5. Mins, NF to Nerney, 28th October 1948; Nerney to NF, 2nd November 1948; NF to Nerney, 8th November 1948; Nerney to NF, 9th November 1948, NF Arch.
6. Note of telecon with Wernham, 14th November 1948; Goodwin to NF, 30th November 1948; Wernham to NF, 20th December 1948; Faculty certificates, 31st January and 10th June 1949, ibid.

Chapter 2 (pages 35 to 59) continued

7. Nerney to NF, 2nd November 1948; ditto, 9th December 1948; Synopsis, ibid.

8. NF to Wernham, 24th May 1949, ibid.

9. Butler to Wernham, 12th November 1947; Wernham to Butler, 13th November 1947; Butler to Wernham, 3rd February 1949; Wernham to Butler, 11th February 1949, PRO CAB 140/55.

10. Butler to Wernham, 19th May 1949, PRO CAB 140/55; Wernham to NF, 12th January 1995, NF Arch.

11. COH 53 (revise), 8th October 1941, PRO CAB 103/307. Min Bridges to Winnifrith, 10th September 1943, PRO CAB 103/107.

12. Caines to Bridges, 20th November 1942, PRO CAB 103/307.

13. Note by H.A. Jones of interview with Trenchard, 11th April 1934, NF Arch; Caines to Bridges, 20th November 1942; Min Brook to Bridges, 28th November 1942; Bridges to Caines, 30th November 1942, PRO CAB 103/307.

14. Adam to Bridges, 11th December 1942, ibid.

15. Correspondence between Bridges and Clarke, 26th–27th July 1946, PRO CAB 103/303; Winnifrith to Crudas, 15th February ?1946, PRO CAB 103/307; Topham to Butler, 22nd October 1946, PRO CAB 103/535 encl 7.

16. NF, *Prince Henry*, pp.49–50.

17. Memo by Butler, 5th December 1946, PRO CAB 103/545 encl 23.

18. Note of meeting in Cabinet Office, 8th January 1947, PRO CAB 103/535 encl 28; Butler to Eastwood, 10th January 1947, PRO CAB 103/536 encl 16; ditto, 19th January 1947, PRO CAB 103/536 encl 22; revised memo by Butler, 19th January 1947, PRO CAB 103/537.

19. Evill to Bridges, 4th March 1947, PRO CAB 103/536 encl 42; Caines to Brook, 3rd April 1947, ibid; COS(47) 46th meeting, 28th March 1947, PRO AIR 2/10022 encl 6A.

20. Hubback to Luke, 8th April 1947, PRO CAB 103/536 encl 56.

21. Note for record by Hubback, 15th April 1947, PRO CAB 103/536 encl 58.

22. Note for record by Brook, 22nd April 1947, ibid encl 61.

23. Hubback to Luke, 24th April 1947, ibid encl 62.

24. Luke to Brook, 2nd May 1947, ibid encl 63.

25. Luke to Brook, 2nd May 1947, ibid encl 63; Butler to Luke, 7th May 1947, ibid encl 64; Evill to Murrie, 19th June 1947, ibid encl 81; Blake to Murrie, 5th July 1947, ibid Encl 95; Pownall to Murrie, 21st June 1947, ibid encl 84; Jacob to Murrie, 25th June 1947, ibid Encl 89.

26. Mins of Panel meeting, 17th September 1947, COH(M)(47) 1st meeting, PRO CAB 103/537 encl 5.

27. Mins of Panel meeting, 17th February 1949, PRO CAB 103/333 encl 1; Butler to Waldock, 24th February 1949, and Waldock to Butler, 27th February 1949, PRO CAB 140/55.

28. Butler to Benians, 3rd March 1949, PRO CAB 140/54; Mins of Panel meeting, 29th April 1949 (item 2), PRO CAB 103/333 Encl 1; Butler to Thistlethwaite, 29th March 1949, and Thistlethwaite to Butler, 7th April 1949, PRO CAB 140/55; Mins of Panel meeting on 29th April 1949 (cited above).

29. Butler to Garrod, 19th May 1949, PRO CAB 103/333 encl 2.

30. Jacob to Butler, 15th July 1949; Carrington to Butler, 24th October 1949; note by Butler, 25th October 1949; Carrington to Butler, 24th October 1949; Butler to Carrington, 28th October 1949, PRO CAB 140/54.

31. Min to Brook, 17th October 1949, PRO 103/333 encl 4; Butler to Acheson, 18th October 1949, ibid encl 5; Butler to Garrod, 21st October 1949, ibid encl 6; Mins of Panel meeting, 3rd November 1949, ibid encls 7 and 7G; Acheson to Luke to Brook, 11th November 1949, ibid encl 8; Luke to Plumbley, 25th November 1949, and Plumbley to Luke, 8th December 1949, ibid encls 10 and 11.

Chapter 2 (pages 35 to 59) continued

32. Acheson to Luke, 13th December 1949, PRO CAB 103/333 encl 12; Acheson to Luke to Brook, 8th February 1950, ibid encl 19.
33. e.g. NF to Nerney, 25th March 1950, NF Arch; Clark to Butler, 14th February 1950, PRO CAB 103/333 encl 20.
34. Nerney to NF, 31st October 1949; draft min NF to Nerney, 21st November 1949, NF Arch.
35. Butler to CW, 19th May 1950; CW to Butler, 21st May 1950, PRO CAB 140/103.
36. Butler to CW, 16th June 1950; Garrod to Butler, 10th July 1950; Butler to Garrod, 11th July 1950, ibid.
37. CW to Butler, 31st July 1950; Butler to CW, 4th August 1950, ibid.
38. Butler to CW, 8th August 1950, CW Arch; Butler to NF, 8th August 1950, NF Arch; NF Diary, 15th August 1950; 5th October 1950.
39. Note for record by Acheson, 31st August 1950, PRO CAB 103/333 encl 36
40. CW and NF Arch *passim*, e.g. NF to CW, 4th December 1950, CW Arch; NF Diary, 20th December 1950.
41. Agenda for meeting of military historians to be held on 19th January 1951, circulated by Acheson, 22nd December 1950, NF Arch; CW to Butler, 15th January 1951, CW Arch.
42. CW to NF, 15th January 1951, NF Arch; NF Diary, 11th February 1951; mins of meeting of military historians, 19th January 1951, NF Arch.
43. Butler to CW, 27th January 1951, CW Arch; NF to CW, 29th January 1951, ibid; NF Diary, 11th February 1951; CW to NF, 10th February 1951, NF Arch; NF to CW, 12th February 1951, ibid; ditto, 19th February 1951, ibid.
44. NF Diary, 11th February 1951.
45. Min Butler to Acheson, 22nd February 1951, PRO CAB 103/541; CW to NF, 18th March 1951, NF Arch.
46. CW to Brook, 23rd April 1951; Brook to CW, 9th May 1951; CW to Brook, 15th May 1951, CW Arch.
47. Anderson to NF, 2nd May 1951; NF to Anderson, 8th May 1951, NF Arch; NF Diary, 23rd May 1951.
48. Ibid; Anderson to NF, 26th June 1951, NF Arch.

Chapter 3 (pages 60 to 79)

1. Laperouse-Bonfils, *Histoire de la Marine Française* (quoted in Mahan, *The Influence of Sea Power upon History*, p.133).
2. NF thesis (final draft), Introduction, NF Arch.
3. Ibid, list of source material.
4. NF to Nerney (draft), 16th November 1949; ditto, 25th July 1949; Nerney to NF, 26th July 1949; NF to Nerney, 25th July 1949; and a more outspoken version which was not sent, NF Arch.
5. G.R. Elton, *The Practice of History*, p.43.
6. NF thesis (final draft), p.252, NF Arch.
7. NF Day Book, 10th February 1953.
8. NF thesis (final draft), for Trenchard, *passim*; for Tedder, p.248.
9. Ibid, p.249.
10. Ibid, p.247.
11. Ibid, p.248.
12. NF Day Book, 10th February 1953.
13. Ibid, 8th October 1954; 9 March 1955.
14. Zuckerman to Nerney, 9th February 1952, NF Arch.
15. Ditto; NF to Nerney and accompanying papers, 14th February 1952, ibid.
16. Ditto; NF Day Book, 24th March 1952.
17. Nerney to NF, 6th March 1951, NF Arch.

Chapter 4 (pages 80 to 113)

1. NF to CW (draft/copy), 12th July 1951, ibid; CW Diary, 18th August 1951; NF Diary, 30th August 1951.

2. Ibid; NF Day Book, 28th July 1952.

3. CW to NF, 22nd November 1951; e.g. Saundby's comments and correspondence, 19th September–15th November 1952, NF Arch.

4. CW (US) Diary, 9th September–22nd December 1952.

5. CW to NF, 18th November 1952, NF Arch; NF Day Book, 26th November 1952; NF to CW, 26th November 1952, NF Arch; Harris to Cochrane, 20th November 1952, Harris Papers RAF Mus Ac 85/5, Mixed Air Min and Official.

6. NF to CW, 26th November 1952; CW to NF, 30th November 1952, NF Arch.

7. CW (US) Diary, 3rd–4th December 1952; CW to NF, 5th December 1952, NF Arch; NF Day Book, 1st December 1952.

8. SAO, vol 3, pp.75–94.

9. Harris to Barnes, 25th November 1952; Harris to Dean, 25th November 1952; Barnes to Harris, 5th December 1952; Dean to Harris, 1st December 1952, Harris Papers RAF Mus Ac 85/5 Mixed Air Min and Official.

10. Harris to Cochrane, 11th December 1952; Harris to Barnes, 16th December 1952, ibid.

11. Harris to De L'Isle and Dudley, 27th February 1953, ibid.

12. Portal to CW, 20th January 1953; CW to Portal, 21st January 1953, CW Arch; CW to NF, 28th January 1953, NF Arch; see above pp.71–2.

13. CW Diary, 20th May 1954.

14. Portal to NF, 16th March 1953, NF Arch.

15. Note for record by Acheson, 12th March 1953, PRO CAB 103/333 encl 60.

16. CW to NF, 14th November 1953, NF Arch.

17. Professor Frank Craven, one of the general editors of the official history of the United States Army Air Forces, told me that the air historians were allowed to see secret material only if it belonged to the United States Air Force, NF Diary, 9th December 1953.

18. Ibid, 5th December 1953.

19. Ibid, 9th–15th December 1953.

20. CW to NF, 20th May 1953; NF to CW, 19th May 1953, NF Arch.

21. Jacob to NF, 2nd April 1956; NF to Jacob, 5th April 1956, ibid.

22. Trend to Brook, 9th March 1959, PRO CAB 103/553/206.

23. Butler to Hale, 28th April 1959, ibid.

24. Letters of invitation from CW or NF; Harris to CW, 24th December 1958; correspondence with Thurso, 18th November 1958–13th March 1959; Newall to CW, 15th December 1958, CW Arch.

25. Comments by Slessor (undated); Ludlow-Hewitt's comments and correspondence with Slessor, ibid; Slessor to NF, 30th April 1959, NF Arch; comments by Tizard (undated), CW Arch.

26. Tedder to CW, 4th May 1959, ibid.

27 Correspondence with Peirse, 20th November 1958–14th May 1959, ibid; SAO, vol 2, pp.254–7.

28. Comments by Saundby, CW Arch; Harris to Dean, 10th October 1959, Harris Papers RAF Mus Ac 85/5 Personal A–F; Portal to CW, 9th March 1959, CW Arch.

29. Butler to CW, 28th October 1958, PRO CAB 140/103; ditto, 8th November 1958, CW Arch; mins of Panel meeting, 21st January 1959; comments by Garrod, Jacob, Blake and Pownall, 12th January 1959, NF Arch.

30. Min Acheson to Trend, 24th August 1957, PRO CAB 103/601; Key (WO) to Hale, 12th June 1959, CW Arch; Snelling (CRO) to Butler, 9th June 1959; min CW to Butler, 15th June 1959; Snelling to Butler, 23rd June 1959; Fone (FO) to Butler, 24th June 1959; Lang

Chapter 4 (pages 80 to 113) continued
   (Adm) to Butler, 23rd June 1959; CW to Butler, 9th July 1959; Butler to Lang, 9th July
   1959, PRO CAB 140/104.
31. e.g. Butler to CW, 22nd July 1959, CW Arch; min Smith to Dean, 22nd April 1959; min
   Nerney to DST and DUS II, 29th April 1959, PRO AIR 20/10467.
32. Min Macdonald (PS to Dean) to Smith, 14th May 1959, ibid.
33. Min Nerney to Smith, 20th May 1959; min Jenkins (Head of S4) to Smith, 27th May
   1959, ibid.
34. Smith to Ware (Treas Solic), 27th May 1959; Ware to Smith, 29th May 1959; Smith to
   Dean, 4th June 1959, ibid; Dean to Hale, 10th June 1959, CW Arch; Dean to Brook,
   17th June 1959, PRO AIR 20/10467.
35. Portal to Boyle, 24th June 1959, PRO CAB 103/554 encl 237; Dean to Brook, 26th June
   1959, ibid encl 238.
36. Mins of meeting in Brook's office, 14th July 1959, ibid encl 242.
37. Smith to Brook, 14th August 1959, ibid encl 243; CW to NF, 20th August 1959, NF
   Arch.
38. NF's draft reply, amended by CW, 14th September 1959, CW Arch; CW to Butler, 16th
   September 1959, PRO CAB 140/104.
39. Note by Butler (not sent), 21st September 1959; min (?)Hale to Brook (undated), ibid;
   Brook to Smith, 26th August 1959, PRO CAB 103/554 encl 246.
40. Dean to Brook, 24th September 1959, ibid encl 250.
41. Portal to Smith, 30th September 1959, PRO CAB 103/554; Harris to Dean, 10th October
   1959; Dean to Harris, 26th October 1959, Harris Papers RAF Mus Ac 85/5 Personal A–F.
42. Dean to Brook, 26th October 1959, PRO CAB 103/554 encl 255; Butler to Brook, 28th
   October 1959, ibid encl 257; min Brook to Hale 21st November 1959, ibid encl 259;
   CW to Brook, 16th December 1959, ibid encl 263; Hale to Dean, 23rd December 1959,
   ibid encl 268; *SAO*, vol 3 pp.93–4.
43. Min of meeting of Brook, Dean and Hale, 21st December 1959, PRO CAB 103/554 encl
   267; Brook to Dean, 21st December 1959, ibid encl 264; Brook to CW, 21st December
   1959, CW Arch; min Hale to Theobald for Bishop, 29th December 1959, PRO CAB
   103/554 encl 270.
44. Dean to Brook, 14th January 1960 (2 letters), PRO CAB 103/554; Kent to Hale, 27th
   January 1960, ibid encl 281; min Stephen to Bishop, 29th January 1960, ibid encl 284.
45. Min Hale to Bishop, 20th January 1960, ibid encl 277; min Brook to PM (Pretoria), 27th
   January 1960, PRO CAB 103/554.
46. Min PM to Brook, 9th February 1960; min Brook to PM, 25th February 1960; PM's
   endorsement, 26th February 1960, ibid

Chapter 5 (pages 114 to 135)

1. See above p.113.
2. *Sunday Telegraph*, 17th September 1961; 24th September 1961; 1st October 1961.
3. *SAO*, vol 3, p.310; vol 2, p.169.
4. *Daily Express*, 3rd October 1961; 2nd October 1961.
5. *Evening Standard*, 3rd October 1961.
6. See above p.109.
7. *Evening Standard*, 13th October 1961 (syndicated).
8. *Observer*, 1st October 1961; *News of the World*, 1st October 1961; *The People*, 1st
   October 1961; *Irish Independent*, 20th October 1961; *Daily Mail*, 2nd October 1961.
9. New Zealand: *Southland Daily News*, 2nd October and 16th December 1961;
   Wellington Evening Post, 2nd, 3rd and 5th October 1961; *Christchurch Star*, 30th
   October 1961; *Christchurch Press*, 3rd October 1961; *Dominion, Wellington*, 30th

Chapter 5 (pages 114 to 135) continued

October 1961; *Otago Daily News*, 3rd October 1961; *New Zealand Herald*, 14th October 1961. <u>Australia</u>: *West Australian*, 2nd and 3rd October 1961; *Launceston Examiner*, 2nd October 1961; *Perth Daily News*, 2nd October 1961; *Melbourne Herald*, 2nd October 1961; *Sydney Morning Herald*, 3rd October 1961; *Adelaide Advertiser*, 3rd and 11th October and 11th November 1961; *Sun Herald*, 8th October 1961; *Newcastle Morning Herald*, 20th October 1961. <u>Canada</u>: *Montreal Gazette*, 3rd October 1961; *Toronto Globe*, 3rd and 5th October 1961; *Montreal Star*, 3rd and 14th October 1961; *Ottawa Journal*, 3rd October 1961; *Vancouver Sun*, 11th and 23rd October 1961; *Kitchener Waterloo Record*, 2nd October 1961. <u>South Africa</u>: *East London Despatch*, 2nd, 3rd and 10th October 1961; *Cape Argus*, 5th, 23rd October and 14th November 1961; *Natal Witness*, 9th October 1961; *Johannesburg Star*, 2nd and 30th October 1961; *Natal Daily News*, 2nd October 1961; *Pretoria News*, 2nd October 1961; *Friend*, 2nd October 1961. <u>Southern Rhodesia</u>: *Bulawayo Chronicle*, 2nd and 9th October 1961. <u>Northern Rhodesia</u>: *Northern News*, 11th November 1961. <u>Pakistan</u>: *Pakistan Times*, 4th October 1961. <u>Hong Kong</u>: *South China Morning Post*, 2nd October 1961; *South China Sunday Post*, 19th November 1961. <u>Trinidad</u>: *Trinidad Guardian*, 2nd October 1961. <u>Malta</u>: *Times of Malta*, 2nd October 1961. <u>Bermuda</u>: *Mid Ocean News*, 2nd October 1961. <u>Portugal</u>: *Diario Do Governo*, 1st October 1961. <u>France</u>: *Le Figaro* 2nd October 1961; *Le Nouveau Candide*, 12th–19th October 1961. <u>Italy</u>: *Epoca Milano*, 15th October 1961; *Il Nationale*, 22nd October 1961; *Il Messaggero de Roma*, 28th October 1961; *Il Giorno*, 1st November 1961; *L'Italiano*, December 1961; *Meridiano D'Italia*, 15th February 1962. <u>Ethiopia</u>: *Voice of Ethiopia*, 7th–8th December 1961. <u>U.S.A.</u>: *New York Herald Tribune* (Paris), 3rd October 1961; *Washington Post*, 5th and 8th October 1961; *Montgomery Advertiser*, 2nd October 1961. <u>Germany</u>: *Der Kurier*, 7th October 1961; *Deutsche Zeitung*, 29th October 1961.

10. (Dickson) *The Times*, 4th October 1961.
11. (Lynefield) *Daily Telegraph*, 4th October 1961; (Houghton) *The Times*, 5th October 1961; (Dudley Smith) ibid; (Seager) *Sunday Telegraph*, 8th October 1961; (Bader) *News of the World*, 8th October 1961; ('C.G.C.') *Manchester Evening News*, 9th October 1961; (Joubert) *Daily Telegraph*, 13th October 1961.
12. (NF) *Daily Telegraph*, 13th October 1961; (Defence Corresp) *The Times*, 2nd October 1961; (Special Corresp) *Glasgow Herald*, 2nd October 1961; (Boyle) *Yorkshire Post*, 2nd October 1961; (Beaton) *Guardian*, 2nd October 1961; (Hunter) *Scotsman*, 2nd October 1961; (Howard) *TLS*, 20th October 1961.
13. *The Times*, 7th October 1961; 10th October 1961.
14. (Saundby) *RAF Quarterly*, vol 1, no.4, Winter 1961.
15. (Wernham) *Oxford Magazine*, 17th May 1962; (Watt) *Quarterly Review*, October 1962.
16. (McFarland) *Military Affairs*, vol XXV, no 4, Winter 1961–2; (Taylor) *New Statesman*, 6th October 1961.
17. (Saundby) *International Affairs*, October 1965.
18. (Carver) *RUSI Journal*, anon, May 1965.
19. Verrier, *The Bombing Offensive*; (Taylor) *New Statesman*, 26th April 1968; (NF) *Daily Telegraph*, 11th April 1968.
20. Hastings, *Bomber Command*, p.113; chapter XIII; pp.183, 148, 102, 141, 164.
21. Saward, *Bomber Harris*, pp.328–30; pp.221–5; *SAO*, vol 2, p.193.
22. Richards, *The Hardest Victory*, pp.219–20; pp.178–9.
23. Richards, *Portal of Hungerford*.
24. Ibid, p.331; p.329; pp.330–1.
25. See above chapter 4; Baker to Margaret Kennedy, 27th November 1945, Kennedy Papers.
26. Wilson to NF, 7th March 1995, NF Arch; *SAO*, vol 3, p.302
27. *Reaping the Whirlwind*, p.5; ibid, p.27.

Chapter 5 (pages 114 to 135) continued

28. Overy, *War Economy in the Third Reich*, p.251.
29. Ibid, pp.288, 291, 302, 358, 360.
30. Overy, *The Air War 1939–1945*, pp.65, 74, 79–80.
31. Kegan, *The Battle for History*, p.39; Dean, *The Royal Air Force and Two World Wars*, p.297.

Chapter 6 (pages 136 to 159)

1. CW to NF, 2nd November 1951; ditto, 7th November 1951; Worsley to NF, 9th November 1951, NF Arch.
2. Noble to Butler, 19th May 1953; Butler to Williams, 10th June 1953; Williams to Butler, undated, PRO CAB 140/103.
3. Oxford RAF Courses, NF Arch; Gibbs to NF, 15 August 1956, ibid.
4. NF to Butler, 15th November 1955; Acheson to NF, 12th December 1955, PRO CAB 140/103.
5. *The Listener*, 4th October 1956; memo by NF, October 1956; NF to Gibbs, 13th October 1956; CW to Acheson, 15th October 1956, NF Arch.
6. CW to Butler, 14th November 1956, PRO CAB 140/103; ms draft by CW inserted into NF to Slessor, 15th October 1956, NF Arch.
7. Memo by Gibbs, 8th November 1956, ibid.
8. Memo by NF, circa 14th November 1956; aide memoire by NF, 14th November 1956, ibid.
9. Memo by Butler, 19th December 1956, PRO CAB 140/103, (original in CW Arch.)
10. CW to Butler, 20th December 1956; NF to Butler, 19th December 1956; Gibbs to Butler, 28th December 1956, PRO CAB 140/103.
11. Toynbee to NF, 8th March 1955, NF Arch.
12. *The Times*, 10th March 1955.
13. Toynbee to NF, 21st May 1955; NF to Toynbee, 23rd May 1955; Butler to NF, 25th May 1955; NF to Butler, 4th June 1955, NF Arch.
14. Henderson to NF, 29th June 1955; Toynbee to NF, 2nd July 1955, ibid.
15. Henderson to NF, 8th July 1955; Raven Frankland to NF, 24th July 1955; ditto, 23rd July 1955, ibid.
16. Henderson to NF, 20th February 1956; Woodhouse to NF, 16th January 1956; ditto, 20th June 1956, ibid.
17. Woodhouse to Barraclough, 18th June 1956; NF to Woodhouse, 18th June 1956, ibid.
18. *Documents on International Affairs* 1955 (1958); *1956* (1959); *1957* (1960); *Britain's Changing Strategic Position*, printed in *International Affairs*, vol 33, no.4, October 1957.
19. Mackay to NF, 1st November 1957; NF to Elliot, 9th December 1957, NF Arch.
20. e.g. memo on Chatham House research programme by NF, 21st January 1960; NF to Younger, 19th February 1960; memo on research programme by NF, 25th February 1960, ibid.
21. Younger to Bullock, 22nd December 1959, ibid.
22. NF to Younger, 21st December 1959 enclosing memo by NF, 20th December 1959; memo by Barraclough, 29th January 1960; Olver to Kitzinger, 5th May 1960; NF to Younger, 20th April 1960; e.g. Bullock to NF, 15th March 1960; NF to Younger, 25th July 1960, ibid.
23. Memo by NF on Chatham House research programme, 21st January 1960, ibid.
24. Olver to NF, 5th May 1960, ibid.
25. Bullock's views as reported by NF to Younger, 18th February 1960, ibid.
26. *Programme für den Besuch Britische Teilnehmer am Deutsch-Englischen Gespräch 1959 in Berlin*, ibid.

Chapter 6 (pages 136 to 159) continued

27. *Zehntes Deutsch-Englisches Gespräch, Königswinter, 12–15 März 1959*, ibid; NF Diary, 28th March 1959.
28. Ibid, 19th and 28th March 1959.
29. RIIA Reports of the Council for 1962–3; for 1961–2; *Survey of International Affairs 1963*, Preface.

Chapter 7 (pages 160 to 178)

1. *A Short Guide to the Imperial War Museum*, 2nd ed, 1956, section 41.
2. Ibid, section 82.
3. Jacob to NF, 3rd June 1960; Garrod to NF, 25th May 1960, NF Arch.
4. Maclagan to NF, 14th August 1960, ibid.
5. Memo by Bradley, undated, 1958 or 1959, IWM central file.
6. An illustrated account of the sinking of *Implacable* is in *The Illustrated London News*, 10th December 1949.
7. NF's draft of Willis's speech on 2nd November 1966, 10th October 1966, NF Arch.
8. Wheeler-Bennett to NF, 10th May 1966, IWM central file 30(a); Deakin to NF, 10th June 1966, ibid; Bullock to NF, 9th February 1965, ibid.
9. Richards to E.C. Gregory (War Artists Advisory Committee), 19th July 1944, *The Rose of Death*, p.37.

Chapter 8 (pages 179 to 195)

1. Harris to W.A. Whittaker (Association of British Picture Corporation), 30th January (1954), Harris Papers, RAF Museum Ac 85/5 Personal Letters G–M; Harris, *Bomber Offensive*, pp.157–8; SAO, vol 2, p.169.
2. Morris, *Guy Gibson*, pp.xxvi, 152, 314.
3. NF to F.H. Cheasley (District Surveyor, MoW), 22nd December 1961, NF Arch.
4. NF to C.H. Roads, 3rd July 1963; NF to Miss F.M. Loughnane (Treasury), 13th June 1963, ibid.
5. NF to Greene, 24th September 1964, ibid.
6. Greene to NF, 1st October 1964, IWM central file 23(a); memo by NF of discussion with Wyndham Goldie, 23rd October 1964, NF Arch.
7. NF to C.H. Roads, 29th October 1964; NF to Essex, 3rd November 1964; memos by NF, 11th and 16th November 1964, ibid; *Daily Telegraph*, 12th December 1964 and 21st January 1965.
8. Mountbatten to NF, 20th October 1965, IWM central file 23(a).
9. NF to Brabourne, 12th April 1966, NF Arch.
10. Notes of NF's speech at Mountbatten pre-view, ibid..
11. *The Listener*, 1st May 1969.
12. *The Times*, 1st and 8th April 1969.
13. *The Listener*, 1st May 1969.
14. NF to C.H. Roads, 13th May 1969; Isaacs to NF, 16th March 1971; NF to Isaacs, 23rd March 1971; N.T. Mustoe (Thames Television) to NF, 3rd May 1971, NF Arch.
15. Isaacs to NF, 23rd April 1971; memo by NF for Isaacs, undated (circa April–May 1971), ibid.
16. Isaacs to NF with second draft of outline, 21st May 1971, ibid.
17. *The World at War*, preview brochure.
18. R. Laughton (Deputy Editor Pebble Mill) to NF, 9th November 1976, NF Arch.
19. Isaacs to NF, 27th February 1985; N. Maslim to NF, 28th February 1985; NF to Maslim, 3rd March 1985, ibid.

Chapter 8 (pages 179 to 195) continued
20. Cheshire to NF 2nd September and 14th October 1983 (his doubts), ibid.
21. Correspondence, H. Bettinson and NF, January–April 1993; NF to *Daily Telegraph* 12th April 1993 (abridged version published on 15th April 1993), ibid.

Chapter 9 (pages 196 to 209)

1. *HMS Belfast*, Macmillan Press, London, 1973, p.29.
2. NF to Firth; NF to Holland-Martin, 17th April 1967, NF Arch.
3. *The Belfast Committee Report*, 18th June 1968, ibid; John Wingate, *HMS Belfast*, Profile Publications, Windsor, 1972.
4. NF to Dame Felicity Peake, 11th December 1967; *The Belfast Committee Report*, p.2, NF Arch.
5. *The Belfast Committee Report*; NF to Greenhill, 12th December 1967, ibid.
6. *The Belfast Committee Report*; NF to Cary, 15th December 1967; NF to Holland-Martin, 15th December 1967, ibid.
7. NF to Holland-Martin, 25th January 1968; aide memoire by NF re joint administration of *Belfast*, 17th May 1968; *The Belfast Committee Report*, ibid.
8. NF to Mountbatten, 15th and 19th February 1968; NF to Holland-Martin, 21st February and 19th March 1968, ibid.
9. NF to Morgan-Giles, 27th August 1968; NF to Holland-Martin, 7th February 1969, ibid.
10. NF to Holland-Martin, 21st August 1969, ibid.
11. NF to Morgan-Giles, 4th March 1970, ibid.
12. *Guardian*, 1st February 1971.
13. A good report on the arrival of *Belfast* in the Pool of London, and a photograph of her passing under Tower Bridge with the Swordfish overhead, appeared in *The Times*, 16th October 1971.
14. *The Belfast Committee Report*, p.5.
15. *Imperial War Museum Duxford Handbook*, 1977, p.11.
16. Ibid.
17. NF to Holland-Martin, 31st October 1975, NF Arch; Wright to NF, 3rd February 1976, IWM central file 27(a); David Lee, *25 Years of Duxford*, part 1, *Duxford Newsletter*, September 1996.
18. Ibid, parts 1 and 2 (*Newsletter January 1997*); *Imperial War Museum Duxford Handbook*.

Chapter 10 (pages 210 to 222)

1. *Radio Times*, 14th June 1957; *The Listener*, 27th June 1957.
2. *Daily Telegraph*, 11th November 1960 (Birkenhead); *Observer*, 13th November 1960 (Taylor).
3. Lewin to NF, 13th November and 5th December (twice) 1967; NF to Lewin, 22nd November 1967 and 7th January 1968, NF Arch.
4. NF, *Prince Henry*, p.132.
5. NF, *Witness of a Century*, pp.92–108 (Tel-el-Kebir), pp.205–6 (Buller).
6. Ibid, pp.137–60; ibid, pp.229–56.
7. Ibid, chapters 15–17.
8. Ibid, pp.271–3.
9. Haycock, *Sam Hughes*, p.154.
10. NF, *Witness of a Century*, pp.295–6.
11. Ibid, pp.346–7; Taylor, *Beaverbrook*, p.98.
12. Lloyd, *Owen Glendower*.

Conclusions and Comparisons (pages 223 to 230)

1. Barraclough, *History in a Changing World*; Vincent, *An Intelligent Person's Guide to History*, pp.2 and 4; Carr, *What is History?*, p.12.
2. Bogdanor, *The Monarchy and the Constitution*, p.169.
3. Gowing, *Britain and Atomic Energy 1939–1945*.
4. Vincent, *An Intelligent Person's Guide to History*, p.4.
5. Hall, *England and the Orleans Monarchy*.
6. Toynbee, *A Study of History* (1972), p.12; Fisher, *A History of Europe*, p.v.
7. Fisher, p.vi; Toynbee, p.11.

Index

Abbreviations

Air Cdre	Air Commodore
ACM	Air Chief Marshal
Adm	Admiral
A/F	Admiral of the Fleet
A/M	Air Marshal
AMC	Armed Merchant Cruiser
AVM	Air Vice-Marshal
BAOR	British Army of the Rhine
Cdr	Commander
Fl/Lt	Flight Lieutenant
F/M	Field-Marshal
F/O	Flying Officer
F/Sgt	Flight Sergeant
G/C	Group Captain
HMT	His Majesty's Troop Ship
Lt	Lieutenant
Lt Gen	Lieutenant-General
Maj Gen	Major-General
MRAF	Marshal of the Royal Air Force
NATO	North Atlantic Treaty Organisation
NF	Noble Frankland
OUAS	Oxford University Air Squadron
RFC	Royal Flying Corps
SAO	Official History of the Strategic Air Offensive
Sgt	Sergeant
S/L	Squadron Leader
V/A	Vice-Admiral
W/Cr	Wing Commander
W/O	Warrant Officer

1 (British) Corps, BAOR, 158–9
3 Advanced Flying Unit, Bobbington, 18
5 Group, Bomber Command, 23, 26
7 Elementary Flying Training School, Desford, 18
11 Operational Training Unit, Westcott and Oakley, 19, 118
12 Group, Fighter Command, 207
12 Infantry Brigade, BAOR, 159
41 Air School, Collondale, South Africa, 13
50 Group, Bomber Command, 23, 32
54 Group, Training Command, 12
90 Squadron, Bomber Command, 83

Aachen, 24
Aberystwyth, 52
Acheson, A.B. (Cabinet Office), 50, 52–5, 57, 59, 91,139–41
Adam, General Sir Ronald, 41–2
Adams, F/O (OUAS), 11
Addis Ababba, 215
Admiralty, comments on draft SAO, 102
Advanced Study, Institute for, Princeton, 91–2, 95
Air Historical Branch, 35–8, 50, 53, 56–7, 60, 64, 78, 88, 92, 103, 118, 225
Air Ministry, attempt to suppress or distort SAO, 102–12, 117
Air superiority and command of the air, 72–4, 84, 90, 127, 133–4

Air University, Montgomery, Alabama, 91–2
Air War 1939–1945 (Overy), 132–3
Alamein, Battle of, 216
Alanbrook, F/M Lord, 129, 210
'Albany' (*Sunday Telegraph*), 115
Albert, the Prince Consort, 216
Alcantara, AMC, 17
Aldershot Division, 216
Alexander II, Tsar, 230
Alexandra Feodrovna, Tsaritsa, 211–12
All Souls College, Oxford, 143
All-German Questions, Minister for, 156
Allied Military Mission to Greek Guerillas, 145
American Air Museum, Duxford, 207
Amos, A., 213, 215
Anastasia, Grand-Duchess, 210–11
Anderson, Anna, 211
Anne-Marie, Queen, of the Hellenes, 187
Anson aircraft, 15, 18, 21
Apamea, Syria, 208–9
Arctic convoys, 198
Ardennes offensive, 193
Army and Navy Club, Washington, 95
Army Council, 217
Arnhem, Battle of, 5
Arnold, General H.H. 63, 94–5
Area-bombing, 26, 33–4
Athenaeum, 75, 90, 143, 150
Athens, 145
Athlone Castle, HMT, 14
Atlantic, Battle of, 102
Attlee, Lord, 153, 155, 167, 230
Atomic bombing of Japan, 81
Auckland, New Zealand, 202
Australia, Governor-General of, 215
Aysgarth, 168

B17 Flying Fortress, 83
B52 bomber, 207
Bader, G/C Sir Douglas, 121, 123, 207
Bahia, 14–15
Baker, Harold, 131
Balfour, Lord (Harold), 128
Balliol College, Oxford, 56
Barnard Castle, 146
Barnes, George, 48–9
Barnes, Sir James, 88–9
Barnwell Manor, 213
Barraclough, Professor Geoffrey, 1, 147–55, 159, 223
Barron, S/L Fraser, RNZAF, 19
Battle of Britain, The (film), 179, 181, 207
Bayliss, Gwyn (IWM), 149
Beaton, Leonard (*Guardian*), 121
Beatty, A/F Lord, 185
Beaverbrook, Lord, 117–19, 219–20
Bedford College, London, 146
Belfast, 216
Belfast, HMS, 7, 179, 193, 197–206, 208–9
Belfast Board, 202–3
Belfast Committee, 199–201, 204
Belfast Trust, 202–4
Belgrade, 156
Beloff, Lord (Max), 153

Benham, Professor F., 151, 159
Benians, E.A. 47
Bennett, AVM Donald, 116–17, 123
Bergner, Elizabeth, 179
Berlin, 100, 133, 156, 192
Berlin, Battle of, 23, 67–8, 100, 117, 128–9, 134
Bettinson, Helen, 194–5
Bielefeld, 158
Bielefeld Viaduct, 159
Birkenhead, Lord, 212
Birmingham, 192
Birmingham University, 75
Bismarck, Otto von, 220
Blake, V/A Sir Geoffrey, 46, 101, 103
Blum, Léon, 156
Bobbington, *see* 3 Advanced Flying Unit
Bodleian Library, 56–7, 139, 218
Bogdanor, Vernon, 224
Bombay Army, 216
Bomber Command (Hastings), 128
Bomber Command, The Pre-War Evolution of (Wernham), 37, 82
Bomber Offensive (Harris), 180
Bomber Offensive, the Devastation of Europe (NF), 127
Bombers, the Battle of the (TV programme), 194–5
Bombing errors, estimates of, 76–7
Bombing Offensive against Germany, The, Outlines and Perspectives (NF), 126–7
Bombing Offensive in the Second World War, The Planning of the, and its Contribution to German Collapse (NF thesis), 39, 50, 53, 60–79, 85–6, 88–9, 139–43, 225
Bonham-Carter, Lady Violet, 156–7
Bonn, 156
Bootham School, York, 150
Boothby, Lord (Robert), 191
Borden, Sir Robert, 219–21
Borg, Dr Alan, 204
Bosson, W/O Paul, RNZAF (50 Squadron), 22, 25, 31
Bottlinger, Erich, 194
Bottomley, ACM Sir Norman, 99
Bournemouth, 26
Bowes Museum, 146
Boyle, MRAF Sir Dermot, 105
Boyle, Ronald (*Yorkshire Post*), 121
Brabourne, Lord, 185
Bradley, L.R., 163–5, 177, 182
Brandt, Willy, 155–6
Brentano, Dr von, 156
Brice, Martin (IWM), 197, 199
Bridges, Lord (Edward), 41–4
Britain, Battle of, 84, 93–4, 160, 181, 207
Britannic, HMT, 17
British Academy, 52, 81
British Army of the Rhine, 157–8
British Bombing Survey Unit, 65–6
British Library, 217
British Museum, 162, 169
Broad, W/Cr (later Air Cdre) Peter (OUAS), 10
Broadcasting Complaints Commission, 192
Broadlands, 186

Brook, Sir Norman (later Lord Normanbrook), 41, 44, 46, 49–50, 56–9, 98, 105–14, 131, 139
Brophy, John, 184
Brown, George (later Lord George-Brown), 156
Brunswick, 25
Bryant, Sir Arthur, 41
Buchan, Professor the Hon Alastair, 119
Buckingham Palace, 200
Buller, General Sir Redvers, 216
Bullock, Lord (Alan), 1, 146–7, 153–4, 172, 215
Butler, Professor Sir James, 3, 39–59, 80, 91, 97, 99, 101–2, 105–9, 111, 124–5, 136–7, 139–43, 145, 162–3
Butler, Lord (R.A.), 41–2
Butler, Sir Nevile, 42

Caen, 29
Caines, C.G. (Air Ministry), 41, 44–5
Calvocoressi, Peter, 144
Cambridge, 20, 38, 42, 45, 47–8, 51, 111, 126, 153
Cambridge, Prince George Duke of, 216
Cambridge University Library, 217–18
Cambridgeshire County Council, 206
Campbell, A.E., 153
Canada, Governor-General of, 217–21
Canadian Museum of Civilization, 218
Canadian War Museum, 218
Canberra, ACT, 202
Canberra aircraft, 83
Capetown, 16
Carline, Richard, 177,
Carline, Sydney, 177
Carr, Professor E.H., 1, 223
Carrington, Professor C.E., 48–9, 151, 159
Carteret, John, 35
Carver, F/M Lord, 126–7
Cary, Sir Michael, 198–9
Casablanca Conference, 73, 97, 134
Casey, G/C (later Air Cdre) B.A., 83
Castlereagh, the Foreign Policy of (Webster), 35, 52
Catherine the Great, 179
Cavendish Hotel, Eastbourne, 12
Chadwick, S/L W. (50 Squadron), 26
Chatham House, 10, 49, 90, 111, 138, 143–55, 157, 159, 161, 163–4
Chatham House, Adminstration and Finance, 151; Chair of Commonwealth Relations, 151; of International Economics, 151; of International History, 143, 151; Directorate of Studies, 144, 147, 159; Editorial Department, 151; Far Eastern Department, 151; Information Department, 151; Library, 151; Meetings Department, 151; Membership Secretary, 151; Press Library, 151; Research Committee, 147, 151, 153
Cherwell, Lord, 76–7, 86, 131
Cheshire, G/C Lord (Leonard), 25–6, 194
Chicago, 202
Christ Church, Oxford, 56–7
Churchill and the Prof (Wilson), 131
Churchill, Sir Winston, 10, 32, 42, 77, 86, 97–9, 102, 104, 119, 131, 222
Churchill Archive Centre, 217
Circus Operations, 133–4
Civil Service Commission, 163, 171
Clarendon, 3rd Earl of, 56, 59, 145–6
Clark, Professor Sir George (G.N.), 38, 42, 50
Clark, Dr Kitson, 223
Cleeve, Margaret, 144
Cobham, Sir Alan, 18

Cochrane, ACM Sir Ralph, 4, 23, 74, 85–6, 88
Cock, Cdr H.K.J., 199
Collingwood, R.G., 1, 9
Collondale, South Africa, 13
Collyer, A/M Sir Douglas, 47
Cologne, Thousand-bomber attack on, 19, 133
Colombo, 216
Colonial Office, 217
Combined Operations Command, 75
Command of the Air, see Air Superiority
Commonwealth Division, Korea, 158
Commonwealth Relations Office, comments on draft SAO, 102
Concorde 01 prototype, 206–7
Connaught, Prince Arthur Duke of, 212, 214, 216–22, 226
Constantine II, King, of the Hellenes, 187
Coultass, Clive (IWM), 171
Cox, Sir Trenchard, 163
Craig, Gordon, 96
Craven, Professor Frank, 96
Crawford, Robert (IWM), vii, 171
Crayford, 166
Creed, Pam, 192
'Crewing-up', 19
Critchley, Air Cdre A.C., 12
Cromwell, Oliver, 6
Crossman, R.H.S. 115
Crown of Tragedy, Nicholas II (NF) 211–12, 225
Crystal Palace, 170
Culley, Lt S.D., 160
Cunningham, A/F Lord, 93, 167

Dachau, 10
Daily Express, 116–19
Daily Mail, 119
Daily Telegraph, 120–1, 126, 184
D'Albiac, A/M Sir John, 116
Dam Busters, The (film), 179–81
Dams raid, 66, 117, 129, 180–1, see also Möhne and Eder
Darby, Sgt Dick (50 Squadron), 22, 31
Darmstadt, 128
Davis, Carl, 190
de la Mare, Giles, vii, viii
Deakin, Sir William, 172
Dean, Sir Maurice, 88, 103–5, 108–10, 112, 118, 153, 225
Defence, Ministry of, 205, see also Dockyard Department, Naval Construction Department and Navy Department
De L'Isle and Dudley, Lord, 89
Delmer, Sefton, 115
Desert Victory (film), 183
Desford, 18
Dickson, Brigadier, 159
Dickson, MRAF Sir William, 43–4, 120
Dieppe Raid, 5, 12, 71, 186
Dimbleby, Jonathan, 195
Dinison, T., 143
Diverse Reports (TV series), 193–4
Dockyard Department, Ministry of Defence, 199
Documents on International Affairs (NF), 148–9, 154, 159, 162
Donaldson, Lord, 204
Doolittle, General James, 90
Doubleday, W/Cr, 29
Douhet, Giulio, 63
Dowding, ACM Lord, 179–80
Dowling, Dr Christopher (IWM), 171
Dresden, 37, 97–8, 104, 119, 193, 195
Duguay-Trouin, see Implacable, HMS
Duncan, Sgt Mel, RCAF (50 Squadron), 20, 22
Durban, 13–14

Durham University Archive, 217
Düsseldorf, 157–8
Duxford, 7, 205–9
Duxford Aviation Society, 205–7

Eaker, General Ira, 68, 95
Earhart, Amelia, 18
Earle, Professor Edward Mead, 95
East Anglian Aviation Society, 205
Eastbourne, 12–13, 15, 24, 52
East London, South Africa, 13, 15
Eccles, Lord, 202, 204
Eden, Sir Anthony (later Lord Avon), 191
Eder Dam, 11, 63, 66, 107
Edinburgh, HMS, 198
Edinburgh, Prince Philip Duke of, 170, 187, 200
Education and Science, Department of, 200–2
Edward VII, King, 224
Edward VIII, King, 181, 214
Edward and Mrs Simpson (TV series), 179
Egyptian Expeditionary Force 1882, 216
Eisenhower, General Dwight, 6, 70, 84, 94, 97, 120
Ekaterinburg, 211
Elementary Air Navigation School, 12
Elizabeth, Queen, the Queen Mother, 187
Elizabeth II, Queen, 170, 187, 202, 214
Ellington, MRAF Sir Edward, 103
Elliot, ACM Sir William, 144
Elliott, P.J.V. (RAF Museum), vii
Elton, Professor G.R., 1, 66
England and the Orleans Monarchy (Hall), 277
Ephesus, 209
Epstein, Sir Jacob, 131, 177
Essen, 157, 195
Essex, Tony, 182–6, 188
Evening Standard, 117, 119
Evill, ACM Sir Douglas, 43–6
Extra Mural Studies, Department of, Oxford, 137

Fagg, Professor John, 96
Federal Record Center, Alexandria Va, 91–2
Feiling, Professor Sir Keith, 38
Filey, 21
Firth, Captain T.E.B., RN, 197–8
Fisher, A/F Lord, 123
Fisher, H.A.L., 228–9
Flensburg, 64
Flint, Fl/Lt Jimmy (50 Squadron), 28
Ford, Henry, 99
Ford, RAF, 28
Foreign Office, comments on draft SAO, 102
Fox, Edward, 179
Frankfurt-am-Main, 120
Frankland, Diana, viii
Frankland, Raven, 146–7
Frankland, Sarah, viii
Freeman, Ray (IWM), 197
Freemantle, 215
Freetown, 14, 17
Fulford, Sir Roger, 103
FW190 aircraft, 12

Gaitskell, Hugh, 59
Galileo, 195
Gambia, HMS, 197–8
Garrison Theatre, Rheindahlen, 158
Garrod, ACM Sir Guy, 42, 52, 56, 91, 101, 103, 162, 166
'Gee', 20–1
Gefaeler, Dr, 156
George V, King, 170, 213, 215, 218–20

George VI, King, 42, 213–15, 218
German Federal Republic, President of, 157
German war economy, expansion of and collapse of, 72–3
Gestapo, 116
Gibbon, 227
Gibbs, Professor Norman, 57, 79, 139–43
Gibbs-Smith, Charles, 163
Gibson, V/A Sir Donald, 203
Gibson, W/Cr Guy, 11, 19, 179–81
Gilbert, Sir Martin, 222
Givors, 30–1
Glasgow Herald, 121
Glendower, Owen, 222
Gloucester, Princess Alice Duchess of, 213, 215
Gloucester, Prince Henry Duke of, 42, 170, 212–17, 221–2, 226
Gloucester, Prince Richard Duke of, 215
Goldman, Martin R.R., 92
Gooch, G.P., 80
Goodwin, Professor Albert, 35, 38, 57, 139
Goodwood, Operation, 29
Goole, 21
Gowing, Professor Margaret, 226
Grand Hotel, Eastbourne, 12
Great War, The (TV series), 182–8, 190
Greene, Sir Hugh, 183, 185
Greenhill, Basil, 199, 201
Greenwich, 203
Grenville, Professor J.A.S., 188
Grey, Lord, 218
Grimble, Ian, 210
Guardian, 121, 201
Guards Brigade, 216
Guerlac, Professor Henry, 96
Guerre de course, 61–3, 71–3, 142

H^2S, 67
Habbaniya, 216
Haig, F/M Lord, 32
Haile Sellassie, Emperor, 215
Hale, Sir Edward (Cabinet Office), 98–9, 105–6, 110
Halifax aircraft, 22, 29, 174
Hall, Major John, 227
Hamburg, 64
Hamburg, Battle of, 67, 72, 133
Hamm, 157
Hancock, Professor Sir Keith, 56–7
Hardest Victory, The (Richards), 129
Harriman, Avrell, 191
Harris, MRAF Sir Arthur, vii, 5, 23, 32, 47–8, 63, 67, 69–71, 73, 85–91, 94, 99, 101, 103, 105, 108–10, 112–13, 115–17, 119, 121, 123, 128–30, 134–5, 180
Harris, Lady, 85
Harrogate, 18
Harvard, 59
Hastings, Max, 128
Haycock, Dr R.G., 218–19
Hays Wharf, 203
Head, Lord (Antony), 157
Healey, Lord (Denis), 155, 157
Heligoland, 83
Henry IV, King, 222
Hess, Rudolf, 10
Heuss, President Theodor, 157
Heward, ACM Sir Anthony (50 Squadron), 23, 25
High Wycombe, 83
Higham, R/A Philip, 204
Hillary, Richard, 13
Hinsley, Professor Sir Harry, 47
Historical Association, Film Committee of, 188
History, art exhibitions and, 176–8;

comprehensive nature of, 223; documentary films and, 182–92; dramatic films and, 177–81; eye-witness as source of 27, 34; fashions in, 7, 224; hindsight and, 76–7, 94; journalism and, 114–15, 123; lessons of, 4, 229–30; memory, unreliability of, 34, 99; misconceptions of, 2–6; morality of strategic bombing and, 33–4; museum exhibitions and, 172–6; official, of Second World War series, plans for, 40–59; reasons for studying, 8, 224, 226; royal biography and, 214–16, 220–2; scales of, 7–8, 223, 229; statistical methods and, 65–6, 76; *Study of* by Toynbee, 7–8; technical understanding, importance of, 21, 128; unique interest of the strategic air offensive in, 32, 122–3; various media of, 226–7
History in a Changing World (Barraclough), 147, 223
History of War, Chichele Chair of, Oxford, 137, 139
Hitler, 10, 67, 69, 116, 132, 195, 215, 230
Hoberge House, Bielefeld, 158
Holland-Martin, Adm Sir Deric, 168, 198, 201, 206
Home Office, 205
Houghton, G/C George, 120
Houlihan, Mike (IWM), 174, 213
House of Lords Record Office, 217
Hove Central Library, 217
Howard, Professor Sir Michael, 122–5, 136–7, 139–40
Hubback, D.F. (Cabinet Office), 45
Hughes, Sir Sam, 217–20
Hunter, George (*Scotsman*), 121
Hurricane aircraft, 160

Imperial War Museum, vii, 1, 7, 131, 160–6, 168–73, 175–8, 181–2, 184–5, 189–90, 192, 196, 198–9, 202, 204–6, 208, 213, 217, 227; Art Department, 165–6, 170, 172, 177–8; attendance figures increased, 173; Cinema, 170, 186; Data Retrieval, Department of, 172; Documents, Department of, 172; Education, Department of, 172; Exhibitions, Department of, 172, 213; exhibition galleries, enlarged, 170–1; exhibitions policy, 172–6; extension of 1966, 170–1; Film, Department of, 172, 181, 190; Library, 166, 170, 172; misconceptions of purpose, 171; Photographs, Department of, 161, 166, 172; Publications, Department of, 172; Records, Department of, 182; recruitment policy, 171–2; Research, Department of, 172; Sound Records, Department of, 172; staff numbers increased, 174; Trust, 202; Trustees, functioning of, 169
Imperial War Museum exhibitions, art, 176–8; *Blitz Experience*, 174–5; *Colditz*, 173; *Fifty Years After* displays, 173; *Fiftieth Anniversary of the founding of the RFC*, 173; *German Occupation of the Channel Islands*, 173; Mosquito sortie, 175; *Soldier Royal*, 213; *Victoria Cross and George Cross*, 202; virtual reality, 174–5; *War*, 174; *Women at War*, 173; *Zeebrugge*, 173
Implacable, HMS, 167–8
In Which We Serve (film), 181
India Office Library and Records, 218
India, Viceroy of, 42, 185, 187

Indian Army, 217
Inman, Edward (IWM), 171, 207
Inspector-General of the Forces, 217
International Affairs, 151
Irish Independent, 119
Ironbridge Gorge Museum, 197, 208
Isaacs, Sir Jeremy, 181, 189–90, 192, 194

Jack, Stephen, 211
Jackets, L.A., 103
Jacob, Lt Gen Sir Ian, 43, 46, 48, 97–8, 101, 162
James, T.C., 47, 49
Jellicoe, A/F Lord, 157
Jenkins, Lord (Hugh), 206
Jesus College, Oxford, 35, 38, 56
Johnson, Amy, 18
Johnson, G/C (later AVM) 'Johnnie', 138
Johnson, P., 47
Johnstone, Maj Gen R.F., 163
Jones, H.A., 4
Jorvic Museum, York, 174–5
Joubert, ACM Sir Philip, 121, 123
Ju88 aircraft, 25
Jutland, Battle of, 167, 176, 185
Juvissy rail yards, 24

Kamhüber Line, 192
Kay, Sgt, 11
Kegan, John, 134
Kelly, HMS, 181, 187
Kennedy, Maj Gen Sir John, 119
Kennedy, Margaret, 131
Kennington, Eric, 177
Kensington Palace, 213
Kent, Prince Edward Duke of 190
Kent, Sir Harold, 105, 110
Kenyatta, Jomo, 155
King's College, London, 136–7
Kipling, Rudyard, 49
Kirk, Sir Peter, 202–3
Kitzinger, U.W., 153
Knapp, W.F. 153
Knott, F/Sgt Frank (50 Squadron), 22, 31
Königswinter Conference, 156–7
Korean War, 56, 158, 198
Kuala Lumpur, 216

Laithwaite, Sir Gilbert, 222
Lancaster aircraft, 22–5, 27, 29–30, 83, 111, 160, 192–3
Lancaster Finishing School, 22
Langton, Jane, 216–17
Laughton, Roger, 192
Lavery, Sir John, 177
Law, Andrew Bonar, 219
Lee, Baroness (Jennie), 171
Lee Kuan Yew, 155
Lees Knowles Lectures, Cambridge, 126
Leigh-Mallory, ACM Sir Trafford, 179
Leverhulme Trust, 172
Lewin, Ronald, 212
Library of Congress, 92
Lightning aircraft, *see* P38
Lincoln, 20, 23
Listener, The, 141
Liverpool, 80
Liverpool University, 150
Lloyd, ACM Sir Hugh Pugh, 83–4
Lloyd, Professor, Sir J.E., 222
London School of Economics, 53, 81, 86, 89, 111, 136, 143
London University, 145
London University Military Studies Committee, 136
Long-range fighter operations, Spaatz's view of, 93–4
Los Angeles, 202
Louis XIV, King, 62

Lowe, the Very Rev Dr John, 57
Lowry, L.S., 159
Ludlow-Hewitt, ACM Sir Edgar, 99
Luke, S.E.V. (Cabinet Office), 45
Lynefield, C., 120
Lyons, 30

Macadam, Sir Ivison, 144
MacArthur, General Douglas, 123
McBey, James, 177
McCann, C.V. (IWM), 165
McCarthy, Denis, 211
McCarthyism, 91–2
McFarland, Professor Marvin, 92–4, 125
Mackenzie, Mr (PA to Evill), 45
Mackenzie, Professor W.J.M., 47
Mackesy, Maj Gen P.J., 119
MacLachlan, Donald, 114
Maclagan, Michael, 35, 162
Macmillan, Harold (later Lord Stockton), 81, 88, 110–14, 124, 131
Magdalen College, Oxford, 47
Maginot Line, 189
Magnus, Sir Philip, 224
Mahan, Adm A.T. 61–3, 230
Malim, Derek, 15
Mallaby, Sir George, 163
Malta, 167
Manchester aircraft, 128
Manchester Evening News, 121
Manchester University, 47
Mankind, Museum of, 163
Marham, RAF, 83–4
Mark V tank, 174
Marwick, Professor Arthur, 187–8
Mary, Queen, 192, 213, 218
Masefield, Sir Peter, 173
Maslim, Nigel, 193–4
Maxwell Air Force Base, see Air University
Maxwell, Sir Herbert, 56
Mayes, W.P. (IWM), 166, 172, 177
Mboya, Tom, 155
Me110 aircraft, 25
Medlicott, Professor W.N., 153
Middlesex Regiment, 163
Military Affairs, 125
Military Historian, Chief Official, selection of, 41–2
Military Historians, Official, selection of, 43–54; meeting of 19th January 1951, 55–6; restrictions upon, 54–6
Military Histories, Official, plans for series, 42–3; Panel of advisors for, 43–6, 79, 97, 101–2, 162; see also Official Histories
Militia and Defence, Canadian Ministry of, 217–18
Milne, Fl/Lt Murray, RNZAF (50 Squadron), 20, 23–4, 27, 31
Möhne Dam, 11, 63, 66, 107
Monarchy and the Constitution, The (Bogdanor), 224
Montgomery, Alabama, 92, 97; see also Air University, Maxwell AFB and Research Studies Institute
Montgomery, F/M Lord, 5–6, 29, 186, 193, 216
Moore, Henry, 177
Morality and bombing, 33–4
Morgan-Giles, R/A Sir Morgan, 200, 202–3
Morley, Peter, 185–8
Morris, F/O John, 13
Mosquito aircraft, 22, 25, 28, 175
Mountbatten, A/F Lord, 5–6, 13, 75, 185–7, 190–1
Mountbatten, The Life and Times of Lord (TV series), 185–8, 200, 202
Munich, 25–6, 34, 66
Munich Crisis (film), 188

Mustang aircraft, see P51

Nairobi, 216
Naish, G.P.B., 199
Nansen, 49
Napoleon, 230
Nash, John, 177
Nash, Paul, 177–8
National Army Museum, 217
National Gallery, 178
National Library of Scotland, 217
National Maritime Museum, 199, 202, 204
National Museums of Canada, 218
Naval Construction Department, Admiralty, 201
Navy Department, Ministry of Defence, 198–9, 202
New College, Oxford, 144
Nerney, J.C. 36–41, 50–3, 56, 58–61, 63, 66, 74–6, 78–9, 103–4
Nevinson, C.R.W., 169, 177
New Statesman, 125
New York, 85–6, 96, 202
Newall, MRAF Lord, 99
News of the World, 119, 121
Newsweek Building, Washington, 93
Nicholas II, Tsar, 185, 210–12, 221, 225
Nicolson, Sir Harold, 80
Noble, Peter, 136–7
Norman, Lady (Priscilla), 163
Normanbrook, Lord, see Brook, Sir Norman
Normandy, invasion of, in 1944, 27, 68, 73, 123, 178, 198
Northampton, 21
Northern Army Group, NATO, 158
Nottinghamshire Record Office, 217
Nuffield Foundation, 145
Nuremberg, 5, 117
Nye, Lt Gen Sir Archibald, 156

O'Farrell, Mary, 211
Oakley, RAF, 19–20, 32
Observer, 119, 126
Official Histories, Committee for the Control of, 40–1, 45; and Crown Privilege, 104, 106, 108; Butler's definition of, 124; intended restrictions upon, 54–6; suspicions of, 122, 124–5, 134; see also Military Histories
Oil bombing, 69–70, 77, 87, 123, 130
Olivier, Lord (Laurence), 190
Olver, Shane, 147, 151, 154
Oppenheimer, J.R., 95
Oriel College, Oxford, 50, 150
Orpen, Sir William, 177
Orr-Ewing, Lord (C.I.) 173
Osnabrück, 159
Overy, Professor R.J., 131–4
Overlord Operation, 97; see also Normandy, invasion of
Oxford, 9–11, 32, 35–6, 38, 40, 47, 50–1, 57, 59, 64, 79, 95, 122, 137–8, 141, 143, 145, 152–3, 161, 215, 220
Oxford aircraft, 20
Oxford Magazine, 125
Oxford Public library, viii
Oxford University Air Squadron, 9–10

P38 Lightning aircraft, 93
P51 Mustang aircraft, 13, 71–2, 92
Palmerston, The Foreign Policy of (Webster), 52, 56
Panel, see Military Histories, Panel of advisors for
Pares, Sir Bernard, 211
Paris, 24, 27, 29, 84
Park, ACM Sir Keith, 179
Parkinson, Sir Cosmo, 162

Passchendaele, Battle of, 115, 164
Peace, The Last Year of (NF), 37
Pebble Mill at One (TV series), 192–3
Pegasus aircraft engine, 21
Peirse, ACM Sir Richard, 98–100, 110
Penson, Professor Dame Lilian, 146
Pentagon, 90, 92
People, The, 119
Peterborough, 21
Pickering, 21
Pinsent, Dr John, 11
Plate, Battle of the River, 191
Playfair, Maj Gen I.S.O., 55
Pollitt, C.J. (Navy Department), 199
Pool of London, 203–4
Portal, MRAF Lord, 32, 63, 69, 71, 74, 78, 85, 87–91, 97, 99–101, 103–6, 108–10, 112–13, 116, 123, 125, 129–31, 134, 179, 185, 212, 225
Portland, 26
Portsmouth, 167, 196–7, 199, 201, 203
Postan, Professor Sir Michael, 51
Pownall, General Sir Henry, 46, 102, 104
Prater, W., 215
Precision selective bombing, 67–8, 94, 111, 129
Press Club, Washington, 93
Preston Capes, 21
Princeton University, 95
Public Archives of Canada, 217
Public Record Office, viii, 54, 57, 63, 78, 81, 217, 225
Pyle, Fl/Lt Gordon, RAAF (50 Squadron), 20, 29–32

Quarry Bank Mill, Styal, 197, 208
Queen Mary, RMS, 91

Raleigh, Professor Sir Walter, 4
Reach for the Sky (film), 181
Reading, 24, 29
Redoute, Bonn, 156
Research Studies Institute, see Air University
Revigny, 28
Reynolds, Professor P.A., 52
Rheindahlen, 157–9
Richards, Albert, 177–8
Richards, Denis, 49, 125, 129–31
Rifle Brigade, 216
Roads, Dr Christopher (IWM), 171, 182–4, 202–3, 205, 207
Robertson, F/M Sir William, 32
Rockefeller Fellowship, 91
Rooney, Micky, 181
Roosevelt, President Franklin D., 96
Roskill, Captain S.W., RN, 124
Ross Rifle, 219
Rostow, Professor W.W., 47
Rouen, 29
Rowe, John, 187
Royal Air Force, The, and Two World Wars (Dean), 134–5
Royal Air Force College, Cranwell, 47
Royal Air Force Historical Society, 132
Royal Air Force Staff College, Bracknell, 132, 137–9
Royal Archives, 213, 216–18
Royal Bethlehem Hospital, 166
Royal Commonwealth Society Library, 217
Royal Institute of International Affairs, see Chatham House
Royal Librarian, 218
Royal Opera House, 190

St Cyr, 29
St John's College, Cambridge, 47
St Leu D'Esserent, 27–8, 34
St Pierre du Mont, 26

San Francisco Conference, 81
SAO, comments on draft, 97–113;
  Dean's final verdict on,134–5;
  Harris's attitude to, 85–91, 99,
  108–9, 112–13; lack of significant
  revision of, 224–5; originality of,
  225; Portal's attitude to, 91, 101,
  103–5, 108–10, 112, 212;
  publication of, 114; reviews of and
  public reaction to, 115–26; revisions
  of, 127–34; selection of authors of,
  43–59; scheme of writing, 82–3;
  Tedder's attitude to, 90–1, 100, 112
Saundby, A/M Sir Robert, 48, 74–5,
  78, 85, 88, 99–101, 124–6, 138
Saunders, Hilary St George, 49–50,
  65–6, 125
Saward, G/C Dudley, 128–9
Scharnhorst, 198
School of Oriental and African Studies,
  217
Scientific Advisor to the Secretary of
  State for Defence, 75
Schlesinger, Arthur, Jr, 96
Schweinfurt, 25–6, 34, 68, 70, 129,
  134
Scott, Lady William (Rachel), 215
Scotsman, The, 121
Scrivener, S/L, 19
Seager, G.E. 120–1
Shannon, Ann, 181
SHAPE (Supreme Headquarters Allied
  Powers Europe), 84
Shawcross, Lord (Hartley), 59
Sheffield, HMS, 198
Shepheard, Sir Victor, 201
Sherriff, R.C., 181
Shinwell, Lord (Emanuel), 155
Shonfield, Sir Andrew, 159
Short, F/Sgt 'Shortie' (50 Squadron), 31
Shuttleworth Collection, 205
Simkins, Peter (IWM), 171, 174, 197,
  199
Sinclair, Sir Archibald, see Thurso,
  Lord
Skellingthorpe, RAF, 23–4
Slessor, MRAF Sir John, 43, 49, 84,
  99, 129, 138, 140, 144
Slessor, G/C John, 138, 140
Smith, Dudley, MP, 120
Smith, Gill (IWM), viii
Smith, Sir H.T. (Air Ministry), 104,
  106, 108
Smith, Sir John, 203
Smither, Roger (IWM), 171
Smuts, F/M J.C., 81
Smyth, (Maj Gen) Brigadier Sir John,
  119
Sneddon, F/Sgt (later F/O) Keith,
  RAAF (50 Squadron), 22, 25, 31–2,
  34
Snow, Lord (C.P.), 78, 96
Sokolov, Nicholas, 211
Somme, Battle of the, 32
Somme, The Battle of the (film), 183
Sopwith Camel aircraft, 160
South African War, 219
South East Asia, Supreme Commander,
  185, 187
Spaatz, General Carl, 6, 63, 90, 92–5,
  130
Speer, Albert, 63–5, 67–8, 133
Spencer, Sir Stanley, 177
Spitfire aircraft, 29
Stalin, 215
Stalingrad, Battle of, 192
Stationery Office, 50
Stirling aircraft, 13, 22
Stirling Castle, HMT, 13–14, 16–17
Stolypin, Peter, 222
Stonehouse, John, 187
Strachey, John, 157

Strang, Lord, 150, 155
Stratheden, HMT, 16–17
Suddaby, Roderick (IWM), viii, 171
Sudwestfunk, 194
Sunday Telegraph, 114–15, 121
Sunday Times, 126
Survey of International Affairs, 144,
  146–9, 154, 159
Sutherland, Graham, 177
Swan, Michael, 210
Swordfish aircraft, 203
Syerston, RAF, 22

Talavera House, Osnabrück, 159
Tangmere, RAF, 25, 34
Taranto, 189
Target for Tonight (film), 183
Tate Gallery, 177–8
Taylor, A.J.P., 119, 125, 127, 150–1,
  212, 219–20
Tedder, MRAF Lord, 45–6, 65, 70, 72,
  75, 90–1, 99, 112, 134
Teheran, 145
Tel-el-Kebir, Battle of, 216
Templer, F/M Sir Gerald, 158
Terraine, John, 186–8
Thames Television, 188–90
Thornycroft, Sir William, 6
Thesiger, Wilfred, 215
Thetford, 20
Thistlethwaite, Frank, 47
Thompson, Keith (Daily Express), 116
Thurso, Lord, 44, 99, 103
Tiger Moth aircraft, 11, 13, 18
Tilbury, 203–4
Times, The, 120–1, 124, 126, 144–5,
  161, 188
Times Literary Supplement, 122–3,
  126
Tizard, Sir Henry, 2, 6, 75, 77, 94, 99
Todd, Richard, 179–81
Tokyo, 215
Toomer, AVM S.E., 55
Tours, 23
Tower Bridge, 203
Toynbee, Arnold, 7–8, 10, 80, 123,
  143–6, 152, 228–9
Toynbee, Paget, 8
Toynbee, Veronica, 143, 146
Trafalgar, Battle of, 168, 196
Transport bombing, 65, 70, 75
Treasury, 164, 166, 168, 170, 172,
  182, 201–2
Treasury Solicitor, 104–5, 110
Trenchard, MRAF Lord, 41–2, 50, 63,
  72, 74, 93, 123, 125, 230
Trenchard doctrine, 4, 63, 127
Trend, Sir Burke (later Lord), 3, 98–9,
  187
Trevelyan, G.M., 227
Trevor-Roper, Hugh (later Lord
  Dacre), 65–6
Trinity College, Cambridge, 38, 42, 45
Trinity College, Oxford, 9, 11, 32, 38
Trinity Hall, Cambridge, 145
Tweedsmuir, Lord, 119

United States Air Force Academy,
  Colorado, 95
United States Strategic Bombing
  Survey, 65
University Historians, Film Committee
  of, 188
University of Sussex Library, 217
Uppingham School, 158

VI flying bomb, 27, 160
V2 rocket, 176, 193
Vanguard, HMS, 196
Verrier, Anthony, 127
Versailles Conference, 81, 152
Victoria, Queen, 216, 222

Victoria and Albert Museum, 7,
  162–3, 171
Victory, HMS, 167–8, 196, 204
Vietnamese War, 174
Vincent, Professor John, 1, 223

Waddington, RAF, 29
Wade-Gery, Robert, 143
Waldock, Professor C.H.M., 47
Wallis, Sir Barnes, 180
War Economy in the Third Reich
  (Overy), 131–3
War Office comments on draft SAO,
  102
War Studies, Department of, King's
  College, London, 136–7
Ward, General Sir Dudley, 157–8
Warpsgrove bombing range, 20
Warrior, HMS, 200
Warspite, HMS, 16–18
Wash, The, 24
Washington DC, 91–2, 95
Washington (B29) aircraft, 80, 83
Watt, Professor D.C., 125
Wavell, Maj Gen A.G., 42
Wavell, F/M Lord, 41–2
Weaver, J.R.H., 35
Webster, Professor Sir Charles, vii,
  3–4, 35–7, 40, 42, 51–60, 64, 78,
  80–91, 93, 96–100, 102–16,
  119–25, 127, 130, 132, 135–44,
  148, 162, 225, 227
Webster, Lady (Nora), 81, 96
Weldon, T.D., 47
Wellington, Duke of, 216
Wellington, New Zealand, 202
Wellington IC aircraft, 19–22
Wells, 21
Wernham, Professor R.B., viii, 9, 35,
  37–40, 46–7, 50, 125–6, 137, 139,
  144, 228
West, General Sir Michael, 158–9
West, Lady (Christine), 158–9
West Kent Archives Office, 218
Westcott, RAF, 19, 32
What is History? (Carr), 223
Wheeler-Bennett, Sir John, 172
Wilfrid Laurier University Press, 218
Williams, Professor C.H., 137
Willis, A/F Sir Algernon, 16, 18,
  162–4, 167–9
Willis, Lady (Olive), 167
Wilmot, Chester, 36
Wilson, Lord (Harold), 187
Wilson, Professor Thomas, 131, 134
Wiltshire Record Office, 217
Winchester, 42, 131, 144, 200
Window, 67
Windsor Castle, 213
Winnifrith, A.J.D. (Treasury), 42
Wolseley, F/M Lord (Garnet), 216,
  222
Woodham-Smith, Cecil, 222
Woodhouse, the Hon C.M., 144–8,
  150, 152–3
Woodward, Professor Sir Llewellyn, 38
Works, Ministry of, 170, 200–2
World at War, The (TV series), 181,
  189–92
World Today, The, 151
Worsley, Colonel S.J. 136
Wright, C.W. (Ministry for Arts), 206
Wyndham-Goldie, Grace, 183–5

Yorkshire Post, 121
Young, S/L H.M., 11
Younger, Sir Kenneth, 152–5, 159,
  161

Zeebrugge Raid, 173
Zuckerman, Professor Lord (Solly), 65,
  70, 75–8, 82